D1601264

A WEBERIAN THEORY OF HUMAN SOCIETY

THE ARNOLD AND CAROLINE ROSE MONOGRAPH SERIES
OF THE AMERICAN SOCIOLOGICAL ASSOCIATION

A WEBERIAN THEORY OF HUMAN SOCIETY

Structure and Evolution

WALTER L. WALLACE

RUTGERS UNIVERSITY PRESS
New Brunswick, New Jersey

Library of Congress Cataloging-in-Publication Data

Wallace, Walter L.
    A Weberian theory of human society : structure and evolution /
Walter L. Wallace.
        p.   cm. — (The Arnold and Caroline Rose monograph series of
the American Sociological Association)
    Includes bibliographical references and index.
    ISBN 0-8135-2069-X
    1. Weber, Max, 1864–1920.   2. Social structure.   3. Sociology—
Philosophy.   I. Title.   II. Series.
HM22.G3W466   1994
301'.01—dc20   93-37868
                                                                                                CIP

British Cataloging-Publication information available

Manufactured in the United States of America

To
Beatrice Warrington, Marty Morand, and Pete Rossi:
Lifesavers

CONTENTS

LIST OF FIGURES

ACKNOWLEDGMENTS

MY THANKS TO Sarane Boocock, absolute sine qua non—and also to Alfred Cook and his many accomplices—for keeping me more or less in my supposedly right mind and body. I am grateful, too, for Sarane's comments on various parts of this book and, especially, for inviting me to go with her to Japan eight years ago, where I started work on it in such perfect circumstances. I also appreciate the expert and unstinting technical assistance of Valery Mamedaliev (including his production of camera-ready figures); the secretarial help of Donna DeFrancisco, Cindy Gibson, and Blanche Anderson; the substantive comments of Signithia Fordham, Samir Khalaf, Ludwig Glaeser, George Ritzer, Judith Blau, and Edith Kurzweil; and the comments of several anonymous reviewers of early drafts—more than one of whom expressed very dim views of what they read. Regarding the latter comments, I hope it has turned out that "what doesn't kill me makes me stronger." If so, as Jomo Kenyatta once wrote, "I owe thanks also to my enemies, for the stimulating discouragement which has kept up my spirits to persist in the task. Long life and health to them to go on with the good work!"—although at the time I certainly thought Kenyatta went too far in that last wish.

A WEBERIAN THEORY OF HUMAN SOCIETY

1

INTRODUCTION

THIS BOOK SETS forth a general theory of human society—a theory whose primary inspiration is the work of Max Weber (1864–1920).

The sense in which the word *theory* is used here is easy to state: The book will propose a description of human society, a causal explanation of human society so described, and some speculations about where human society might be headed in the long run.[1]

It is also not difficult to state the sense in which the theory is "general": It examines human society as if from a great distance in time and space—enough to make the swirling particulars of daily news dwindle down and give way to a truly Big Picture. From this distance, the basic psychological and physiological characteristics of the individuals making up human society have been exactly the same at all times and places on Earth since *Homo sapiens sapiens* first evolved some 150 thousand—give or take 50 thousand—years ago (see Klein 1989:344). As Darling says, "Anything a contemporary child can do a child 100,000 years ago could do equally well if nurtured in the same way. Our brains have not evolved in all that time" (1993:29). From this distance, too, all the territorially separate societies (subdivisions of human society as a whole) that such individuals have formed appear the same—insofar as they all exist on the same small planet's small land surface in the same short epoch of that planet's long life course, they are all structured internally into the same basic complement of institutions, and they all explore the same set of evolutionary paths under impulse from the same set of basic forces (or so it will be argued here).

But why "Weberian"? My answer calls for some immediate elaboration—especially for those to whom Weber's work is not well known.

Max Weber's Work

The belief that Weber's work contains extraordinary insights into many persistently central concerns of late twentieth-century social science—and, indeed, of late twentieth-century human society—seems very nearly unanimous among sociologists, and widespread among other social scientists as well. I strongly share this consensus, but it is more important for present purposes that the consensus itself serves as prima facie assurance that a Weber-inspired theory is likely to address issues of continuing importance. Consequently, it seems fair to say that although this book may turn out to be wrong, it will at least be (as we used to say twenty-five years ago) "relevant."

Consider: the role of culture—especially various kinds of rationality and nonrationality—in social life; the nature and impact of charisma and its routinization; the nature of society's economic, political, and religious institutions and their evolving interrelations; the role of science and technology in these institutions; the impact of religious beliefs on economic behavior, and vice versa; the comparative sociology of religion; relations among economic classes, status groups, and political parties; relations among religious prophets, priests, and laypersons, and among bureaucrats, their political directors, and their clients; conceptualizations of sociocultural ethnicity and race, and relations among different ethnic groups and races; bureaucratic structure and functioning; types of education; the sociocultural functions of erotic and esthetic pleasure; and the roles of values, empathic understanding, and the "ideal type" in social science method. Fertile ideas about all these issues, and more besides, seem universally recognized as Weber's singularly illustrious legacy.

Eulogies to that legacy, therefore, are plentiful: for example, Ralf Dahrendorf wonders, "Is there any modern social science without Max Weber?" (1987:574); Edward Shils calls Weber's work "the most fundamental and most learned achievement of sociology" (1987:547); Martin Albrow observes that "the reputation of Max Weber has grown until he is now recognized as the major social theorist of the twentieth century" (1990:1); Julien Freund says Weber had a "fundamental influence . . . upon sociologists the world over, as well as upon many economists, historians, and philosophers, including these who opposed him" (1978:164, 165); Vatro Murvar says, "Max Weber's opus is a source of an apparently unending intellectual excitement, argumentations, and conflicting interpretations from Japan to continental Europe, England, the United States, Canada, and slowly but surely [in] the developing world" (1985:xi); Thomas W. Segady says, "Weber has been quoted more often, and used as a fundamental source, than either Marx or Freud" (1987:1); Dennis Wrong says, "Max Weber deserves to be called the last universal genius of the social sciences. . . . the only truly great man we sociologists have a clear right to claim as one of our own" (1970:1, 8); and Dirk Käsler says, "Weber has become regarded throughout the world as an undisputed 'classic' of sociology. Every lexicon or 'history' of this discipline mentions his name as central and emphasizes his authoritative influence on its development" (1988:211).[2]

But there is also nearly universal agreement that Weber's work is deeply puzzling when one tries to grasp it as a totality. Reinhard Bendix tells us, "The plain fact is that Weber's work is difficult to understand" (1960:18). Randall Collins agrees: "Weber's sociology is one of the least well understood" (1986a:1). And Ralph Schroeder explains: "There is no one place where [Weber] systematically spells out his methodological or theoretical standpoint" (1992:1). So Alan Sica sternly warns that "the task [of comprehending Weber's work] is overwhelmingly complex and demands inordinate pains" (1985:71). And Wilhelm Hennis, too: "Becoming involved with the work of Max Weber is a hazardous enterprise" (1988:21). Indeed, Weber himself is reported to have said, "I am a scholar who arranges knowledge so that it can be used. My instruments are to be found in bookcases, but they make no sound. No living melody can be made out of them" (quoted in Hennis 1988:165)—although Weber's claim that he "arranges" rather than scrambles knowledge seems to imply that some "melody" did, after all, inform his work.

Instead of any overall integration of Weber's work, then, previous interpreters have found only a loose assemblage of vignettes. Collins labels the work "schizophrenic" and concludes that "discovering [Weber's] theories is like peeling an onion, except that we cannot be sure which part is the core" (1986b:11, 61). Jonathan H. Turner believes Weber's work is "filled with unreconciled dimensions" (1986:8). Dahrendorf finds "extraordinary ambiguities, not to say . . . explosive contradictions [in Weber's] work," concluding that "the whole of Weber's work can be described as a quarry. It is . . . not a system in any sense of the term" (1987:576). Neil J. Smelser and R. Stephen Warner say that "although [Weber's] work has profound depths and brilliant facets, he never achieved closure on a single theory of society" (1976:95). Käsler claims Weber "does not present [his] specific sociological viewpoint in a self-contained theory. . . . [and employs] completely different perspectives and aspects" (1988:215).[3]

Although I appreciate much of the justification for these opinions, and I have learned a great deal from those who propound them, my own long wrestle with Weber's work has brought me to a very different conclusion. This book presents that conclusion in the form of a theory that I hope will in one stroke integrate Weber's work, connect it to the works of many others, and cast a broad and researchable new light on human society. I believe this theory will be found neither schizophrenic, nor overwhelmingly complex, nor filled with unreconciled dimensions, nor employing completely different perspectives and aspects, nor composed of extraordinary ambiguities and explosive contradictions, nor hazardous to become involved with—and it will not demand inordinate pains to understand, even for readers with no previous contact with Weber's work.

At the same time, however, my view of Weber's work is so sharply and consistently at variance with the established commentaries on it that in order to be at all persuasive to the authors of that large literature, and to their many followers, it must be well grounded in Weber's own words. I therefore rely heavily here on direct quotations and, at almost every turn, I shall ask the reader to examine the textual evidence, and to reconsider others' opinions—which are also sampled here—in its light.[4]

Having said all that, however, let me emphasize that the integration of Weber's work I shall offer is (of course) not to be found in

Weber's published work itself. I have more than half-invented this integration—piecing it together from often scattered passages in what Weber did publish, and with much help from many others' publications. But the reader may well wonder what justification there can be for even attempting such an integration when, in addition to denying the presence of "melody" in his work, Weber pointedly described himself as "like a tree-stump, which is able to put out buds, again and again—without playing the part of being a whole tree" (quoted in Green 1974:114, italics removed). Paul Honigsheim, in his memoir and commentary on Weber, adds that

> some persons remember [Max Weber] as an unbalanced, self-contradictory, charming figure, or at least refer to the abundance of interests without apparent interconnection that he harbored. And indeed, for the person who did not know him in depth, it must have been tempting to judge him in this way. . . . seldom has a man segmented himself in his external relations with the world as much as this one and on every occasion presented himself not as a whole, but as belonging [to many different spheres separately]. (1968:125; see also Hennis 1988:187)

In my judgment, however, we need not feel compelled to take Weber's word for the absence of "melody" or "whole tree" in his work. Indeed, one wonders—as Honigsheim himself may wonder (see below)—whether Weber may not have been deliberately throwing his trackers off the scent. Short of that mischievous possibility, however, Weber may have been so urgently creating his ideas that he had neither time nor patience to stop and spell out for us their internal connections. Indeed, Marianne Weber (his wife and first biographer) says, "Weber did not care about the systematic presentation of his thinking. . . . And he attached no importance whatever to the form in which he presented his wealth of ideas. Once he got going, so much material flowed from the storehouse of his mind that it was hard to force it into a lucid sentence structure" (1975:309; see also Andreski 1984:145).[5]

It should be emphasized that despite some popular stereotypes, unreflective outpourings of this kind are far from unknown even among the "hard" sciences. Burtt, musing about the founders of modern physics, tells us that "one of the most curious and exasperating features of this whole magnificent movement is that none of its great representatives appears to have known with satisfying clarity just what he was doing or how he was doing it" (Barrow 1988:58). And even those who do claim to know what they are doing may change their minds. McConnell, writing about chemistry, says, "A man's own account of the route by which he has arrived at his ideas may be inaccurate. Dalton is known to have given several contradictory accounts of the origin of his atomic theory" (1971:60). At the same time, however, it is hard to believe that such profoundly innovative scientists (all of whom, it should be noted, systematically took into account their predecessors' achievements) could have been quasi-automatons, nearly idiot savants, with never any structure in mind that made sense, to them, of their work as a whole—even though that structure may have been under constant revision, and even though it may not have made much sense to anyone else.[6]

So it is not at all surprising that Honigsheim says of Weber's work that "the question must arise whether behind all these compartments, behind these separated spheres . . . a totality is not concealed" (1968:125; see also Hennis 1988:187).

Constructing the Present Theory

Now I certainly do not claim the theory to be proposed here expresses *that* totality, *Weber's own* totality, nor do I claim it expresses the *only* totality that could be legitimately constructed from the written work Weber (and the others discussed here) left us. Therefore, it should be clearly understood that I do not claim to have discovered "the one true essence of Weber." In fact, I do not believe a "one true essence" of any speech-act can exist; language, no matter how rigorous, is too inescapably ambiguous (and usefully so) for that (see Wallace 1988:61–62). Moreover, my real goal has not been to understand Weber's work; it is human society I would understand—although almost every page of this book will testify that Max Weber's insights have pointed the way for the particular understanding I shall try to present here.

These insights, however, have only pointed the way; they have not, by themselves, unambiguously marked it out in all respects.

Indeed, I believe there are several major shortfalls in Weber's work. By far the most important of these is the fact that Weber proposes no theory—no conceptualization, even—of human *society* (see also Schroeder 1992:7). He has much to say about micro-level social phenomena among individuals ("social action" and "social relationships"); and especially about meso-level social phenomena within and among the several institutions of a society (e.g., the church, the polity, and the economy—and within them, prophets, priests, and laypersons; parties, administrative bureaucrats, and clients; and entrepreneurial and working classes), and within and among ethnic, racial, and nationality groupings. But he never explicitly concerns himself with the macro-level: global human society and its various territorial subdivisions. The reader should clearly understand, then, that I have deliberately imposed the latter concern on Weber's work. It will turn out that that imposition is the crucial step in my attempt to tie Weber's work together, tie it more securely to the works of others, and render it still more useful than it already is to modern social science.[7]

Two Further Questions

There remain two still more fundamental (and more formidable) preliminary questions. The first question is, Why rely on someone else's theoretical work when trying to formulate a theory of human society; why not rely on empirical findings and create one's own theory from scratch? After all, empirical findings are the main products of our discipline (see Davis 1990), and as for relying on quotations from other people's theories, Ralph Waldo Emerson is as astringent as one could want: "I hate quotations. Tell me what you know" (quoted in Barrow 1991:279).

Now it would be easy for me to fend off Emerson by noting that no single person's direct knowledge could possibly ground a theory of the scope that I shall propose here. But one can hardly doubt that the power of this (or any other) theory would be greatly increased if it could be shown to synthesize all the existing empirical findings pertinent to its chosen subject matter.[8] Because this book will not try to demonstrate this synthesis in detail, I must admit to having aimed less high here than I would have liked. Bowing to constraints of time and space, I have chosen a predominantly heuristic goal rather than a properly balanced synthetic-heuristic goal. Another way of saying this is to repeat the comment made earlier with a different emphasis: although it will almost certainly be "relevant," the theory set forth here may be judged *wrong* in one or more of its aspects by virtue of not reflecting all the relevant empirical findings of behavioral and social science to date.

Still, a predominantly heuristic theory can be useful—as Vilfredo Pareto implies ("Give me a fruitful error any time, full of seeds, bursting with its own corrections"), and Abraham Kaplan agrees: "The value of a theory lies not only in the answers it gives but also in the new questions it raises. . . . New questions often arise, not only out of turning to new subject-matters, but also out of viewing old subject-matters in a new light" (1964:320, 303). Moreover, it should be emphasized that this book is only "predominantly" heuristic; I have not forgotten that it must have some grounding in empirical research—otherwise it would run itself right out of town, out beyond the limits of imagination, into the wilds of fantasy where anything goes. Much recent empirical literature will, therefore, be cited here, but the book will rely heavily on the inference, mentioned above, that the frequency and variety of contexts in which Weber's work is still so approvingly cited by late twentieth-century social scientists justifies treating that work as at least not flagrantly contradicted by empirical findings made since his time.

With that expedient (though not altogether satisfactory) sweatband tied around my head, I have tried to climb up onto the shoulders of Max Weber, and many other investigators, in the hope that I might see a little further—to a researchable pattern that would integrate and subsume the patterns they saw.[9]

The second preliminary question is, Inasmuch as it is patently impossible for anyone born, raised, and living in human society—and, moreover, trained in a social science—to start out with a totally open mind when constructing a theory of human society, what preconceptions do I bring to the present construction?[10] As Weber himself puts it, when a theory "appears for the first time . . . it is customary to ask about its 'line'" (1949:50). Although I am in complete agreement with this custom and shall try to comply with it forthrightly, I am also aware that some readers may prefer coming to grips immediately with the theory itself, leaving its underlying preconceptions until later. For such readers, the section that follows brings this introduction quickly to a close by scanning the entire book, and chapter 2 then raises the curtain on the theory itself. Readers interested in the preconceptions on which I think the theory rests may detour, at any time, to appendix A.

Overview

It seems obvious that every theory claiming human society as its subject matter must rest (whether explicitly or implicitly) on some selective notion of what the typical human individual is like. I say "obvious" because the term *human society* always means a society composed mainly of human individuals—exactly as ant or bee or termite societies are defined as societies composed mainly of ant or bee or termite individuals.[11] Chapter 2, therefore, sets forth an explicit, largely (but not entirely) Weberian, conceptualization of certain selected psychological, and physiological, behavior capabilities that seem entailed in human nature. Central to the discussion of psychological capabilities here are generic definitions of human "rationality" (a concept that appears frequently in Weber's work, but one he never quite defines), and nonrationality. Conceptual relations among the eight types of rationality and the two types of nonrationality that Weber discusses are also systematized. Then, after considering several types of physiological behavior capabilities of human individuals (capabilities that Weber, unfortunately, almost entirely overlooks—thereby constituting another shortcoming of his work), chapter 2 employs both sets of behavior capabilities (and their limitations) as grounds for an essentially Darwinian explanation of the universality of societies among such individuals.

At that point, the theory shifts its focus from the human individual to the societies such individuals form. Chapter 3 takes a cross-sectional view of society (the title of the book calls it, loosely, structural), and chapters 4, 5, and 6 take longitudinal (evolutionary and processual) views.[12]

Chapter 3 looks upon a society as a relatively stable and long-lasting system. But this system is unlike, say, the solar system or the interstate highway system or the human circulatory system or a telecommunications system. In the latter cases, the systems' constituent elements may be treated as fixed when compared to the speed with which matter, energy, or information passes through them. In the typical society, however, it is the constituents of the system (i.e., the living individual participants) that pass quickly through, whereas the system's characteristic configurations of matter, energy, and information generally change much more slowly.

It follows that three processes go forward together in almost every human society: (1) new participants are taken in (through biological reproduction and immigration) and trained (through socialization and schooling) to play roles in the configurations of matter, energy, and information that characterize the society—that is, its social structure and cultural structure; (2) trained participants are organized into the four interdependent institutions that constitute what might be called the metabolic core of the society; and finally, (3) unwanted and disabled participants are temporarily or permanently expelled from the society, disaffected participants temporarily or permanently emigrate, and dead participants are disposed of.[13] All the chapters that focus on human society (chapters 3–6) pay most attention to the four participant-organizing institutions (economic, political, religious, and scientific) mentioned under number 2, but the participant-intake and participant-outlet institutions are not ignored.

Chapter 4 describes human society as having evolved—over its entire prehistory and history—through irregular phases of long continuous (ramp), and short discontinuous (step) change. Both sorts of change have driven human society in four interconnected directions: toward greater institutional specialization, toward greater cultural rationality, toward higher levels of organizational scale, and toward greater spatial extension and consolidation (the absence of any analysis of this latter direction is another shortcoming of Weber's work). Chapter 5 offers a Weberian explanatory model of societal evolution so described. In this model, culture is the primary source of impetus, but the nonrational culture called *charisma* (a concept here developed beyond Weber's treatment), augmented by *psychic contagion*, plays the key role in the step phase, whereas rational culture is key in the ramp phase.

Chapter 6 presents a Weberian view of how the evolution of human society has manifested itself inside the economic, political, scientific, and religious institutions, respectively. Chapter 6 also offers a new perspective on Weber's best-known analysis—that of how the Western European "Protestant ethic" in the religious institution contributed to forming the "capitalist spirit" in the economic institution. The same chapter proposes an unconventionally Weberian image of how the political, and the religious, institutions of complex societies function internally (including processes that link together classes, status groups, and parties; legislators, bureaucrats, and the public; and prophets, priests, and laypersons).

Chapter 7 summarizes the foregoing chapters and then launches from that base some more optimistic (and definitely more far-out) speculations about the future of human species survival and individual freedom than Weber's own baleful forecast of a "new serfdom." These speculations are offered, not necessarily in rejection of Weber's forecast, but as a possible (and, I believe, reasonably probable) alternative to it.

Finally, although the main focus of this book is on theory (that is, specifications of the types of phenomena and causal relationships on which observations have been made in past researches, and that are projected to be made in future researches), theory is inextricably linked to method (specifications of the types of procedures to be followed in making and analyzing the observations called for by the theory). Consequently, appendix B offers a new approach to integrating certain methodological issues associated with Weber's work and pertaining to the systematic study (and the systematic modification) of human society.

2

STRUCTURE OF THE INDIVIDUAL

WEBER TELLS US that "collectivities must be treated as solely the resultants and modes of organization of the particular acts of individual persons," and "when reference is made in a sociological context to a state, a nation, a corporation, a family, or an army corps, or to similar collectivities, what is meant is . . . only a certain kind of development of actual or possible social actions of individual persons" (1978a:14, italics removed; see Popper 1950:291).[1] It follows that the theory of human society to be set forth here chiefly on Weber's inspiration (and, indeed, all other theories of human society as well) must depend first and foremost on some image of the phylogenetically "human" individual—of course, together with an image, which both Weber and I allow to remain largely implicit, of an ecosystem or "natural environment" that is the ultimate source of life for such individuals.[2]

Note that insofar as any exhaustive listing of human behavior capabilities would be, to say the least, unmanageably large, the most important differences among theories of human society very often derive from the fact that they employ different selections of these capabilities. The following discussion, then, is in no way intended to cover all the human behavior capabilities; it selects only a few to be used as foundation for the theory of human society that will be set forth in succeeding chapters.

Material and Ideal Interests

The structure of the human individual as seen in this chapter is founded on Weber's claim, in which he acknowledges that both "material and ideal interests directly govern man's conduct" (1946:280). But to the question, Exactly what constitutes an "interest," and how do its "material" and "ideal" varieties differ? Weber, unfortunately, gives no explicit answer. The following definitions, then, are proposed as remedy for that omission: (1) an *interest* is here regarded as a conceptualization, consciously or unconsciously held by a human individual, of events to which that individual attaches some degree of preference or value; (2) a *material* interest is a conceptualization of a valued state (event) of the individual's own body—in general, and speaking broadly, physiological comfort; and (3) an *ideal* interest is a conceptualization of a valued state of the individual's own mind and emotional feelings—in general, and again speaking broadly, psychological understanding and appreciation of the world (including the individual him/herself). As we shall see below, Weber implies these interests are universal because they are part of our phylogenetic heritage—that is to say, they are features of human nature (compare Marx 1977:67–69; Marx and Engels 1947:16–20).

It is also important to emphasize that both material and ideal interests, as Weber conceives them, are *self*-interests. That is to say, it is the individual's *own* material and ideal interests which are at stake. Thus, regarding the material interest, Weber claims that a "market economy" depends on "action oriented to advantages in exchange on the basis of *self-interest*" (1978a:109, italics added), and although acknowledging that "economic action which is oriented on purely ideological grounds to the interests of others does exist," he insists that "it is even more certain that the mass of men do not act in this way, and it is an induction from experience that they cannot do so and never will" (Weber 1978a:203). Similarly, regarding the ideal interest, he refers to it as "an *inner* [that is, the individual's *own*] compulsion to understand the world as a meaningful cosmos and to take up a position toward it" (Weber 1978a:499, italics added).

No less important, the two interests—material and ideal—have equal causal weight in Weber's image of human nature,[3] although one may be more important than the other in determining a particular behavior of a particular actor. Thus, Weber tells us, "It is . . . not my aim to substitute for a one-sided materialistic an equally one-sided spiritualistic causal interpretation of culture and of history. Each is equally possible, but each, if it does not serve as the preparation, but as the conclusion of an investigation, accomplishes equally little in the interest of historical truth" (1958a:183).

Now the human individual not only possesses material and ideal interests or *ends*, but also certain material and ideal *means* of pursuing those ends. The latter are represented by phylogenetically inherent physiological (skeletalmuscular and visceral) and psychological (neuroendocrine) behavior capabilities.[4]

Let us, therefore, consider the following conceptualizations of human psychological behavior capabilities and then, after that, human physiological behavior capabilities.

Psychological Behavior Capabilities

In what he clearly intends to be a major premise of all his work, Weber claims, "The transcendental presupposition of every cultural science . . . [is] that we are cultural beings, endowed with the capacity and the will to take a deliberate attitude towards the world and to lend it significance. Whatever this significance may be, it will lead us to judge certain phenomena of human existence in its light and to respond to them as being (positively or negatively) meaningful" (1949:81). But in order to understand this premise we must know what is meant by "significance," or "meaning."

Meaning

Weber defines "meaning" both anthropocentrically and psychologically: The "meaning" of a thing, he says, is "its relation to human action in the role either of means or of end; a relation of which the actor or actors can be said to have been aware and to which their action has been oriented. . . . That is to say [objects] are devoid of meaning if they cannot be related to action in the role of means or ends but constitute only the stimulus, the favoring or hindering circumstances" (1978a:7).

Thus, for Weber, the meaning of the world is not fixed and inherent in the world; it is a variable and changeable construct—a labeling of some features of the world as means, and other features as ends, of given actions.[5] Of course, Weber is concerned here with the meaning that *humans* give to the world, but this does not rule out the likelihood that other life forms give the world other meanings. The point is that, to Weber, without some such means-end labeling by some such life forms the world would have no meaning at all.

Two Objects of Meaning

Now in addition to this emphasis on meaning as something that is mentally, and variably, assigned to objects (rather than inherent in them), it also seems essential to emphasize Weber's view of meaning as attributable to objects (including, of course, imagined objects) as means as well as ends (that is to say, the meaning of an object lies in "its relation to human action in the role *either* of means or of end"). This is a key point for the present chapter, but it must be noted that other interpreters of Weber think otherwise. Wuthnow claims that in Weber's view, "[as] rationalization increased, life was gradually being stripped of meaning. . . . Rather than living in relation to ultimate values that provided meaning . . . the individual was caught within a mechanical system of rationally calculated means" (1987:25)—thereby implying that, to Weber, meaning resides only in "ultimate values" and not in "rationally calculated means." The same view is held by Sayer, who claims "value . . . [is] exactly that which gives all human life and action their meaning" (1991:150), and who also attributes a modern loss of meaning to rationality (especially the scientific variety).[6] Bologh holds a similar position, pointing to what she believes to be Weber's acceptance of "the ultimate irrationality of modernity, the replacement of human values (ends) with technical bureaucratic means" (1990:93).

It is an absolutely essential view of the present argument, however, that life loses as much meaning when we fail to identify *means* that can serve our chosen ends as when we fail to identify *ends* that our available (or imaginable) means can serve. Putting this in more Durkheimian terms (although Durkheim himself does not address the question), two distinct kinds of anomie are implied here—one of which may be called *means-anomie* and the other *end-anomie*. In the first case, culture offers no guidance on *how* to live; in the second case, it offers no guidance on *why* to live (see Merton 1957:131–60). These two separate and equally life-threatening kinds of meaninglessness will be recalled in chapter 3 when we examine the universally human-societal ways of defending against them.

Meaning, Motive, and Conduct

The individual's mental labeling of objects as means or ends, when-ever and wherever that labeling occurs, is a principal determinant of that individual's physiological behavior toward the world: "We un-derstand in terms of motive the meaning an actor attaches to [a physiological behavior] in that we understand what makes him do this at precisely this moment and in these circumstances" (Weber 1978a:8, italics removed). (Appendix B discusses Weber's method of configuring inferred meanings into inferred motives for an action.) For this reason, "All serious reflection about the ultimate elements of meaningful human conduct is oriented primarily in terms of the categories 'means' and 'end'" (Weber 1949:52).

It follows that, in Weber's view, if we want to answer the most fundamental explanatory question of social science (see Wallace 1983, 1988)—namely, Why does a given individual participate with one or more other individuals in a given social phenomenon and, therefore, why do they all participate in it? (that is to say, why does it exist?)—we must, in principle, discover each separate participating actor's own motive for so doing. To do this, we must find out the manner and extent to which each actor conceives of the behavior in question as being a means toward some end s/he has in mind. Thus: "A correct causal interpretation of a concrete course of action is ar-rived at when the overt [physiological] action and the [psychologi-cal] motives have both been correctly apprehended and at the same

17

time their relation has become meaningfully comprehensible" (Weber 1978a:12).

But how does the individual go about constructing such motives—that is to say, how does the individual identify a given phenomenon as being a means appropriate to a given end?

Rationality

The answer proposed here rests on imagining two possibilities: either the individual believes a given end has only *one* means appropriate to it or s/he believes the end in question has two or more *alternative* means appropriate to it. In the only-one-means case, the individual cannot make comparisons and cannot make choices; the individual automatically applies the one and only appropriate means when pursuing the end in question. Weber gives this orientation no categorical name, but divides it into two types that will be grouped together later in this chapter as *nonrational*—namely, "affectual," and "traditional." In the two-or-more-alternative-means case, however, the individual must choose, and must somehow compare the available alternatives in order to do so. Weber calls all mental processes in which alternative possibilities are compared, in which choices are made on the basis of such comparisons, and in which rules—of whatever content—govern the making of these comparisons and choices, "rational."[7]

Accordingly, the theory being set forth here takes *consciously rule-guided comparison and choice among alternative means to a given end* as its generic definition of rationality.[8]

It is important to emphasize that this definition is not written out in Weber's work. I infer it, however, from many remarks that he does write out. For a first example, Weber tells us "rational action [is] integrated as to meaning, end, and means, and governed by principles and rules" (1978a:549; see also 1949:165, quoted below). He stops short, however, of telling us what he means by "integrated"— and that is what the generic definition given above tries to do.

Before going into more complicated remarks on rationality from Weber, several aspects of the generic definition offered above deserve special attention because they will set the stage for examining these complications. First, note the centrality of subjectively held rules. This accounts for the importance Weber gives to the analysis of law (see chapter 3)—insofar as law is the communicable expression of such rules—so that when Weber refers to the "transition from empirical to rational technology" (1951b:151), the generic definition allows us to infer that he means this is a transition from hit-and-miss, trial-and-error, methods to consciously rule-guided deductions from theory as guides to technological invention and use (see also Weber 1981:179).

Second, the definition requires that rational comparison and choice among means be not only regulated, but consciously so. The line between consciousness and unconsciousness is admittedly fuzzy, and the definition specifies consciousness primarily in order to exclude such rule-guided comparison and choice as occurs among honeybees when they instinctively decode the waggle dance of a nestmate and then take off in the direction indicated by that dance, or when people who have formed the habit of shaking hands as a sign of greeting do so "automatically"—without considering alternative signs of the same greeting (see the discussion below of affectual and traditional nonrationality).[9]

Third, note that the substantive content of the rules is not relevant to the definition. Such content may be expected to vary from society to society and to change over time (viz., the fifteenth-century shift from the rules of alchemy to those of chemistry, and the twentieth-century shift from the rules of classical physics to the distinctly non-commonsensical rules of relativity and quantum mechanics), and it may direct attention to things divine and sacred or to things mundane and secular. For the latter reason, one can be no less rational in discharging a duty, or pursuing beauty, a religious call, or some impersonal "cause," as in pursuing one's personal health, wealth, knowledge, power, and prestige; no less rational in service to omniscient gods as to one's own stupid self. Therefore what counts in a generic definition of all rationalities—past, present, and future—is reliance on conscious comparison-and-choice rules of *any* kind.[10]

Finally, whether the rules are collectively shared or not is also irrelevant to the generic definition of rationality—although, as we shall see, it is the key to Weber's distinction between the special types of rationality he calls subjective and objective.

In order to satisfy the definition of rationality set forth above as generic, then, the only thing required is that there be *some* consciously rule-guided comparison and choice among *some* alternative means to *some* given end.

Different Expressions of the Definition

To appreciate the consistency of Weber's adherence to the generic definition as explicated above, we must see its presence in the different expressions he uses in connection with rationality—terms such as *methodical* (1946:281), *generalization, systematization,* and *controlled by the intellect* (1978a:655, 656). But in order to see this, it is important to underscore two points: First, the root meaning of "rational" (and Weber's original *rational,* and *Rationalität*) pertains to counting and calculation (see Partridge 1959:553, who cites *rate, ratio,* and *ration* as cognates; see also *Ration, rational,* etc. in *New Muret-Sanders Encyclopedic Dictionary of the English and German Languages*). Second, all such counting and calculating operations—involving, as they must, distinction and classification (such as between the categories "one," "two," and "three," or, for that matter, "high" and "low," "red" and "green," or "good" and "evil")—require systematic comparison between two or more elements and choice of which element to place here or there, first or last, above or below, etc., in the final schema.

With this in mind, it is not difficult to see the generic definition proposed above in such of Weber's remarks as that "'rational' technique is a choice of means which is consciously and systematically oriented to the experience and reflection of the actor, which consists, at the highest level of rationality, in scientific knowledge"; that "bureaucracy has a 'rational' character, with rules, means-end calculus, and matter-of-factness predominating" (Weber 1978a:65, 1002); that

> so far as [capitalist] transactions are rational, calculation [of the costs and benefits of alternative transactions] underlies every single action of the

partners. That a really accurate calculation or estimate may not exist, that the procedure is pure guess-work, or simply traditional and conventional, happens even to-day in every form of capitalistic enterprise where the circumstances do not demand strict accuracy. But these are points affecting only the degree of rationality of capitalistic acquisition. (Weber 1958a:19, italics removed)

Finally, one notes Weber's claim that

the acting person weighs, insofar as he acts rationally . . . the "conditions" of the future development which interests him, which conditions are "external" to him and are objectively given as far as his knowledge of reality goes. He mentally rearranges into a causal complex the various "possible modes" of his own conduct and the consequences which these could be expected to have in connection with the "external" conditions. He does this in order to decide . . . in favor of one or another mode of action as the one appropriate to his "goal." (1949:165, italics removed)

And this is very close indeed to the generic definition proposed above.

It is true that Weber says, "We have to remind ourselves . . . that 'rationalism' may mean very different things . . . in spite of the fact that they belong inseparably together"; and "rationalism is an historical concept which covers a whole world of distinct things" (1946:293; 1958a:78; see also 1978a:655–58, 998). But these statements, too, are consistent with the generic definition of rationality set forth above—as becomes apparent when Weber proposes four ways rationality may vary—or, to use his phrase, four "different things" it can "cover"—as follows:

First, there is variation among the substantively different domains of social life within which rationality can be pursued. In each such domain, individuals may be expected to generate rules, ends, and means that are specific to that domain. Thus, "rationalizations of the most varied character have existed in various departments of life and in all areas of culture. . . . There is, for example, rationalization of mystical contemplation . . . just as much as there are rationalizations of economic life, of technique, of scientific research, of military training, of law and administration" (Weber 1958a:26; see also 1978a:815); and "the following methods are rational: methods of mortificatory or of magical asceticism, of contemplation in its most consistent forms. . . . In general, all kinds of practical ethics that are systematically and unambiguously oriented to fixed goals of salvation are 'rational'" (Weber 1946:293–94).

Second, there is variation among the ends which, within a given domain, one holds constant when comparing the contributions to it of alternative means: "Each [domain] may be rationalized in terms of very different values and ends, and what is rational from one point of view may well be irrational from another. . . . [T]he idea of a calling and the devotion to labour in the calling . . . [is] irrational from the standpoint of purely eudaemonistic self-interest. . . . For the unbeliever every religious way of life is irrational, for the hedonist every ascetic standard [is irrational]" (Weber 1958a:26, 78 194). This variability in "values and ends," then, is the meaning here attached to Weber's claim that "one may . . . rationalize life from fundamentally different points of view and in very different directions" (1958a:77–78).

Third, there is variation among the alternative means to a chosen end which, within a given domain, are available for comparison and choice. Thus, Weber argues (as chapter 6 will try to show) that the set of alternative means considered by Protestant business entrepreneurs, and the set of alternative means considered by Protestant wage workers—as they both, with equal rationality, pursue the same end, namely, divine salvation—differ sharply but complement each other.

Finally, as indicated above, there is variation in the content of the rules governing the above comparisons and choices, in all domains. Thus, one rule may call upon the rational individual to choose the alternative that comes out highest, another may call for choosing the median alternative—or whatever—on some given scale of comparison. And most important (as we shall see in the next section), one rule may call for choosing the most efficient or cost-effective means toward a given end, whereas another may call for choosing the most effective means regardless of cost.

Rationality, then, is indeed "a whole world of distinct things," but these things "belong inseparably together"—that is to say, they are the same *generic* thing.

Different Types of Rationality

Now let us see how the generic definition of rationality makes sense of conceptual relations among the eight different types of orientations that Weber calls rational (but does not say why he calls them so)—namely, *Zweckrationalität, Wertrationalität,* substantive rationality, subjective rationality, objective rationality, formal rationality, theoretical rationality, and practical rationality.

Zweckrationalität

At first glance, Weber's definition of this type of rationality dissolves into an endless regress of comparisons of both means and ends: "Action is instrumentally rational (*zweckrational*) when the end, the means, and the secondary results are all rationally taken into account and weighed. This involves rational consideration of alternative means to the end, of the relations of the end to the secondary consequences, and finally of the relative importance of different possible ends" (Weber 1978a:26). However, closer examination reveals that only means, not ends, are being compared here.

By pointing out that *Zweckrationalität* involves "the relative importance of different possible ends" (see also 1978a:65), Weber invites us to ask: According to what criterion is the assignment of such "relative importance" made?[11] This is a pivotal question because whatever that criterion turns out to be, it will express the *ultimate* end toward which all the other so-called different possible ends must be treated not as ultimate ends but as intermediate means—that is, as anticipated links (no matter how remote) in the causal chain that the individual expects will produce the desired ultimate end.

Weber seems very clearly to identify personal aggrandizement (that is, gratification of the acting individual's own material and/or ideal interests) as the criterion in question and, therefore, as the ultimate end in this type of rationality. Thus, "a uniformity of orientation may be said to be 'determined by self-interest' if and insofar as the actors' conduct is instrumentally (*zweckrational*) oriented toward identical expectations" (Weber 1978a:29).[12] Such uniformities result, Weber says, when

> the dealers in a market . . . treat their own actions as means for obtaining the satisfaction of the ends defined by what they realize to be their own typical economic interests. . . . The more strictly rational (*zweckrational*) their action is, the more will they tend to react similarly to the same situation. . . . [Thus,] orientation to the situation in terms of the pure self-interest of the individual and of the others to whom he is related can bring about results comparable to those which imposed norms prescribe. (1978a:30; see also 331)

It seems fair to conclude from this that Weber regards the desire for personal aggrandizement as phylogenetically innate among humans—a point he nearly makes explicit when he says that "the 'true' economic interest . . . is among the most fundamental and universal components of the actual course of interpersonal behavior" (1978a:601). Therefore, if one asks why "orientation to the situation in terms of . . . pure self-interest" has the power to "bring about results comparable to those which imposed norms prescribe," the present theory—interpreting and explicating Weber—replies that self-interest is already fixed in the human individual by the genetic inheritance of the species and requires no further fixing there by learned normative imposition. This presumption of an inherited fixity of self-interest (sometimes called "the instinct of self-preservation"), I argue, is why Weber says the "belief in 'freedom of his will' is of precious little value to the manufacturer in the competitive struggle or to the broker on the stock exchange" (Weber 1975a:193) and "decisive are the need for competitive survival and the conditions of the labor, money, and commodity markets; hence matter-of-fact considerations that are simply non-ethical determine individual behavior [in business]" (Weber 1978a:1186).[13]

Now let us contrast these strong implications of instinctual self-interest in Weber's treatment of *Zweckrationalität* with the equally strong implications of socially learned nonself-interest in his treatment of *Wertrationalität*.

Wertrationalität

Weber indicates (by the examples he selects, rather than explicitly) that this type of rational orientation is not instinctual, not universal, and not fixed—but learned, variable, and changeable: "Examples of pure value-rational [*wertrational*] orientation would be the actions of persons who, regardless of possible cost to themselves, act to put into practice their convictions of what seems to them to be required by duty, honor, the pursuit of beauty, a religious call, 'personal loyalty,' or the importance of some 'cause' no matter in what it consists" (1978a:25).[14] And in sharp contrast with his treatment of *Zweckrationalität*, Weber's phrase "regardless of possible cost to themselves" here makes it very clear that the individual's interest in *Wertrationalität* is not limited to self-interest.

In short, we have the conceptual situation shown in figure 1, which partitions the "end" to be served by the alternative means that are being rationally compared into two dimensions: an end-object specifying the object that is to be served, and an end-effect specifying what is to be done to that object.[15] Thus, *Zweckrationalität* (cell A) stipulates the acting individual's self (mind and/or body) is the end-object, and assumes the end-effect is defined by some phylogenetically innate mechanism. We may, accordingly, paraphrase *Zweckrationalität* as "innate self-interest rationality." Indeed, I propose this paraphrase as more accurate than the orthodox translation "instrumental rationality" because the latter misleads us into thinking *Wertrationalität* is not instrumental, when *Wertrationalität* most definitely is instrumental and purposive—but to a different sort of end from *Zweckrationalität*. Specifically, the end of *Wertrationalität* (cell D) contrasts in two ways with that of *Zweckrationalität* insofar as it stipulates a nonself end-object and a learned end-effect. For this reason, I also propose to paraphrase *Wertrationalität* as "learned nonself-interest rationality." This paraphrase also seems preferable to the orthodox "value-rationality," because the latter misleads us into thinking that *Zweckrationalität* does not pertain to a value, when it definitely does pertain to a value—albeit innate personal self-interest, a different type of value from that in *Wertrationalität*.[16]

Now it is in cell D of figure 1, *Wertrationalität*, that we reach the

End-Effect

End-Object	Phylogenetically Innate	Socioculturally Learned
Self	(a) *Zweckrationalität*	(b)
Nonself	(c)	(d) *Wertrationalität*

Figure 1. Types of Rational Psychological Psychological Orientations

first point at which the present theory claims a powerfully explana-tory species-survival utility for society. The theory asserts that what lone individuals cannot do for the survival of their species, societies of two or more individuals can do. Thus, it may be hypothesized that the universal presence of society among humankind is to be ex-plained in just the same way that the universally human facts of, say, large brains, opposable thumbs, and stereoscopic color vision are to be explained—and in just the same way that sociality as manifested by virtually every form of terrestrial life, from the lowest to the highest, is to be explained (see Wilson 1975; Dawkins 1987)—namely, by its species-survival advantages.[17]

Thus it seems to be only in some sort of social phenomenon, espe-cially the long-lived one we call society, that individuals can learn definitions of nonself end-objects (especially, definitions of other per-sons as such end-objects) and valued end-effects for them. Once learned, such end-objects and end-effects coexist and interact, in the individual social participant's psyche, with the phylogenetically designated end-object and end-effects of innate and purely self-interested *Zweckrationalität*.

Accordingly, it seems essential to note the great weight Weber seems to assign to the distinction between *Zweckrationalität* and

Wertrationalität when he says,[18] "The broad masses are occupied in the fight to secure their daily needs. . . . But in great moments, in [times] of war, their souls too become conscious of the significance of national power. Then it emerges that the national state rests on deep and elemental psychological foundations . . . that it is by no means a mere 'superstructure,' the organization of the economically dominant classes" (1989b:202, italics removed). Once we recognize that "the fight to secure [one's] daily needs" to which Weber refers here represents a manifestation of the innate self-interest implicit in *Zweckrationalität* and that "the significance of national power" represents a learned nonself-interest (i.e., *Wertrationalität*), it becomes clear that Weber not only distinguishes between these two types of rationality but also sees the possibility of an epic struggle between them— both within and between individuals—and that sometimes one, sometimes the other, most often a mix, is victorious.[19]

On this struggle, needless to say, much has been written. But let us pause to focus only on an important relationship between Freud and Weber on this subject. As implied above, Weber anticipates Freud's opinion that "the development of the individual seems to us to be a product of the interaction between two urges, the urge towards happiness, which we usually call 'egoistic,' and the urge towards union with others in the community, which we call 'altruistic'" (1961:98). Freud goes on to argue that neither of these urges can be eliminated, so the best we can do is deflect egoistic aggressiveness to people that do not belong to one's own community: "It is always possible to bind together a considerable number of people in love, so long as there are other people left over to receive the manifestations of their aggressiveness (1961:68). And Weber calls upon exactly this possibility when he refers to wars between nations as "great moments" when the masses of each nation "become conscious of the significance of [their own] national power" (see above). After that agreement, however, Weber and Freud part company. Freud refuses to offer any justification for favoring learned altruism over innate egoism ("For a wide variety of reasons, it is very far from my intention to express an opinion upon the value of human civilization" [1961:103]). Weber, however, does offer a justification—of what nature and persuasiveness, we shall see in chapter 4.

Rules Governing Choice among Means

In accordance with figure 1, then, let us assume the individual wishes to pursue some end (that is to say, some end-effect for some end-object), and let us assume the individual has consciously applied some rule for comparing two or more means to achieve that end. At that point, some rule for choosing among these compared means must come into play, and this introduces a further complexity in Weber's concept of rationality.

Here, Weber's discussions of "ethics" are central—insofar as an ethic may be regarded as a socially valued rule for choosing among alternative means of pursuing a given end (which is to say, as a collectively approved behavior strategy):[20] "From a sociological point of view an 'ethical' standard is one to which men attribute a certain type of value and which, by virtue of this belief, they treat as a valid norm governing their action" (Weber 1978a:36). Weber classifies such strategies into two types: "Conduct that follows the maxim of an ethic of ultimate ends—that is, in religious terms, 'The Christian does rightly and leaves the results with the Lord'—and conduct that follows the maxim of an ethic of responsibility, in which case one has to give an account of the foreseeable results of one's action" (1946:120, italics removed).

An "ethic of ultimate ends," then, is a behavioral strategy that applies *effectiveness* as its criterion in choosing among alternative means to a given end. This strategy says: never mind the cost (damn the torpedoes); choose the means that promises best to secure the benefit. An "ethic of responsibility," however, applies *efficiency* as its criterion (i.e., choose the means that promises the most effect for the least cost—and this includes choosing the first adequate means that is discovered because early choice removes the cost of further search among possible means—see March and Simon 1957:140–141). Note that conscious, rule-guided calculation is implied in both ethics— hence, they are both rational, and they may both serve the two types of rationality discussed above.[21]

Thus, the learned nonself-interest pursuit represented by *Wertrationalität* may be guided by an "ethic of responsibility" (in which the obligation to carry out a given duty is tempered by the obligation to carry out other duties as well) *or* by an "ethic of ultimate ends" (in which a given duty is carried out no matter what its cost to other duties). Similarly, the innate self-interest pursuit represented by *Zweckrationalität* may be guided by an "ethic of ultimate ends" (in which, for example, one uses the natural environment in such a way as to despoil and pollute it, leaving its regeneration to luck and one's heirs) or by an "ethic of responsibility" (where constant conservationism dominates). It would seem that this double applicability at least partly accounts for Weber's agnostic opinion that "one cannot prescribe to anyone whether he should follow an ethic of absolute ends or an ethic of responsibility, or when the one and when the other" (Weber 1946:127).[22]

In summary so far, it seems fair to say that at least three distinct problems (and their projected solutions) are implicit in Weber's conceptualization of *Zweckrationalität* and *Wertrationalität*. These are: (1) the nature of the end-object, (2) the nature of the end-effect, and (3) the nature of the means-choosing strategy or ethic to be followed in bringing about the end-effect in the end-object.

Substantive Rationality

It is also clear, however, that both *Wertrationalität* and *Zweckrationalität* consist of before-the-act, predictive, assessment of possible means—which is to say, planning. Substantive rationality therefore complements them in its reference to after-the-act assessment of actual results of the employment of given means—which is to say, evaluation (compare Mommsen 1974:68; see Wallace 1983:452–54): "The concept of 'substantive rationality' conveys only one element common to all 'substantive' analyses: namely, that they . . . apply certain criteria of ultimate ends, whether they be ethical, political, utilitarian, hedonistic, feudal, egalitarian, or whatever, and measure the results of the economic action . . . against these scales of 'value rationality' or 'substantive goal rationality'" (Weber 1978a:85–86; see also 844). Note how Weber here indicates that the evaluation "scales," or criteria, employed in substantive rationality are variable,[23] but that they covary with the planning scales employed in *Zweckrationalität* (suggested by the terms *utilitarian* and *hedonistic*), and *Wertrationalität* (suggested by the terms *ethical, political, feudal,* and *egalitarian*).

Such constancy of before-and-after assessment criteria is required, of course, if the observed success or failure of a particular action is to be taken into account when planning the next action. This, of course, is why the constant criterion called "money"—with its higher formal rationality than barter (see below)—is so indispensable to capitalist economic action. On this point, Weber is explicit:

> [An] enterprise is always faced with the question as to whether any of its parts is operating . . . unprofitably, and if so, why. It is a question of determining which components of its real physical expenditures . . . could be saved and, above all, could more rationally be used elsewhere. This can be determined with relative ease in an ex-post calculation of the relation between accounting "costs" and "receipts" in money terms. . . . But it is exceedingly difficult to do this entirely in terms of an in-kind calculation and indeed it can be accomplished at all only in very simple cases. (1978a:102)

In the plan-act-evaluate iterations thus implied, then, not only should the criterion scales for planning and evaluation be the same, the technical procedures for applying them should also be the same—in order to ensure their comparability. But the question arises: Same in what respects?

Weber conceptualizes one such respect that nowadays we would call *reliability*, and a second respect that we would call *precision*. In reliability, "subjective" and "objective" rationalities designate the poles; in precision, low and high "formal" rationality designate the poles—as follows.

Subjective Rationality and Objective Rationality

Weber tells us that "without 'empirical' generalizations about the course of events . . . 'rational' conduct is impossible" and "without the belief in the reliability of empirical generalizations, there could be no action based upon an estimation of the means required for an intended result" (1975a:132, italics removed; 187). This seems so because the individual's present judgment of what *will* be an efficient (or an effective) means at the time and place of its future application depends on the conditions s/he believes will exist at that future time and place, and the latter prediction (when rule-guided) is very likely to be some sort of extrapolation from what s/he believes has existed in the past and now exists in the present.

Further (and although Weber does not say this—perhaps because it is more obvious), the same general argument holds for what is required in order to evaluate the extent to which the operation of a given means has actually realized the goal to which it was directed. That is, such an evaluation always rests on beliefs in the reliability of empirical generalizations based on some sample of results of employing the means in question, and then, of course, on procedures for comparing these generalizations to the generalizations ("intended result") one wanted to achieve in the first place.

Weber argues that all such beliefs may be classified as being constructed according to (1) "subjective" rationality, or (2) "objective," "correct," or "scientific" rationality: "A subjectively 'rational' action is not identical with a rationally 'correct' action (the latter defined as one which uses the objectively correct means in accord with scientific knowledge). Rather, it means only that the subjective intention of the individual is planfully directed to the means which [the individual him/herself regards] as correct for a given end" (Weber 1949:34, italics removed; see also 1981:156). And then, most significantly, Weber adds:

> Magic, for example, has been just as systematically "rationalized" as physics. The earliest intentionally rational therapy involved the almost complete rejection of the cure of empirical symptoms by empirically tested herbs and potions in favor of the exorcism of (what was thought to be) the "real" (magical, daemonic) cause of the ailment. Formally, it had exactly the same highly rational structure as many of the most important developments in modern therapy. (1949:34, see also 1978a:400)[24]

In these remarks, Weber implies two orthogonal dimensions of the reliability of empirical generalizations. One dimension contrasts the reliability conferred by a single individual with that conferred by a collectivity of individuals (first quotation above); the other contrasts the reliability conferred by sensory observation with that conferred by simple assertion in the absence of sensory observation (second quotation).

Weber implicitly identifies subjective rationality with nonempirical, as well as with single-person, reliability and he quite explicitly identifies objective rationality (which generates "correct" or "scientific" statements) with reliability that is both collectively agreed-upon and empirical. Thus: "Scientific truth is precisely what is valid for all who seek the truth" (Weber 1949:84, italics removed); "it is one of the essential features of [a scientific] account that it aims at inter-subjectively valid 'objective truth'"; and the "'motives' [underlying a given human action] are in principle always subject to verification on the ground of observational experience" (Weber 1975a:148, 198; italics removed).[25] Consequently, Weber argues, "only an empirical discipline [presumably, he means by this a collectivity of persons who follow a given set of rules for empirically investigating a given class of phenomena] . . . can determine whether 'technical progress' exists" (1949:35).

Surely it is because of this double (intersubjective-plus-empirical) reliability of empirical generalizations constructed according to scientific methods that Weber can assert so uncompromisingly that "those for whom scientific truth is of no value will seek in vain for some other truth to take the place of science . . . in the provision of concepts and judgments which . . . facilitate [the] analytical ordering [of empirical reality] in a valid manner" (1949:110–11). From all this, a further principle may be inferred: the lone individual is, by definition, incapable of formulating reliable empirical generalizations (and therefore incapable of formulating reliable assessments of the anticipated impact of given means, and reliable evaluations of their observed results) without the help of other individuals in identifying, interpreting, and testing the relevant observations. Here, then, is a second crucial point at which a powerful species-survival utility for society may be claimed—insofar as, again, what the individual cannot do, society can do.

Formal Rationality

Weber says that "the term 'formal rationality of economic action' [designates] the extent of quantitative calculation or accounting which is technically possible and which is actually applied," and "a system of economic activity will be called 'formally' rational according to the degree in which the provision of needs . . . is capable of being expressed in numerical, calculable terms, and is so expressed" (1978a:85).[26]

When one notices Weber's reference here to formal rationality having a variable "extent," and a variable "degree," Stevens's (1946) effort to systematize variability in unidimensional scales of all kinds comes to our assistance. Stevens posits four types of measurement scales (nominal, ordinal, interval, and ratio), and apparently orders them according to whether they contain a natural origin (zero-point), and whether the distances between scale points have meaning.[27] Nominal scales permit only the lowest degree of precision in measurement operations, whereas ratio scales permit the highest degree of precision.

A dim presentiment of such a scale of scales as Stevens proposes seems sure to underlie Weber's claims that "both calculation in kind and in money are rational techniques" (1978a:107) but that "expression in money terms" (which employs a ratio scale) "yields the highest degree of formal calculability" (1978a:85), whereas "calculation in kind" yields a much lower degree (see 1978a:100–107, and 1975a:121)—presumably because it employs only an ordinal, or even a nominal, scale. "Formal rationality," then, seems clearly the name Weber gives, not to some unique measurement process, but to a systematically variable range of measurement processes (compare Marcuse 1971:136).

I believe this variability enables us to understand Weber's otherwise misleading assertion that "formal rationality and substantive rationality [may be] in conflict" (1946:331; see also Mommsen 1974:69; and Albrow 1990:133). In establishing a context for this assertion, Weber says:

> The more the world of the modern capitalist economy [relies on money], the less accessible it is to any imaginable relationship with a religious ethic of brotherliness. . . . [That ethic cannot regulate] the relations between the shifting holders of mortgages and the shifting debtors of the banks that issue these mortgages: for in this case, no personal bonds of any sort exist. If one nevertheless tried to do so. . . . formal rationality and substantive rationality [would come into] conflict. (1946:331)

Thus it becomes apparent that Weber is claiming not that *all* levels of formal rationality must conflict with substantive rationality, but that the *low* level of formal rationality (characterized by nominal or ordinal scales) necessitated by a substantive rationality whose criterion is "brotherliness" conflicts with the *high* level of formal rationality implicit in an economy based on "money."[28]

As Weber finally puts the substantive-formal question, "Substantive and formal (in the sense of exact calculation) rationality are . . . largely distinct problems" (1978a:111, italics removed) Note: not conflicting problems, merely "distinct" problems; and not even entirely distinct problems. Weber strengthens this point with the claim that law making and law finding "are formally irrational when one applies . . . means which cannot be controlled [in this case, measured] by the intellect, for instance when recourse is had to oracles or substitutes therefor. Lawmaking and lawfinding are substantively irrational . . . to the extent that decision is influenced by concrete factors of the particular case . . . rather than by general norms." Weber concludes from this that " 'rational' lawmaking and lawfinding may be rational in a formal *or* a substantive way" (1978a:656, italics added)— and one infers they may be rational in *both* ways if they apply means that can be controlled by the intellect and if they also decide on the basis of general norms.

Theoretical Rationality and Practical Rationality

The passage in which Weber sets forth his final pair of rationalities (here called *rationalisms*) reads as follows: "We have to remind ourselves that 'rationalism.' . . . means one thing if we think of . . . an increasing theoretical mastery of reality by means of increasingly precise and abstract concepts. Rationalism means another thing if we think of the methodical attainment of a definitely given and practical end by means of an increasingly precise calculation of adequate means" (1946:293). The first thing to emphasize, of course, is that these are indeed types of rationality insofar as they both consist of rule-guided mental comparisons and choices among alternative means to a given end. Secondarily, however, the types differ in the following way: In theoretical rationality, the means in question are mental "concepts" and the end is the "theoretical mastery," or *mental understanding*, of the world. In practical rationality, the means are both mental and physical (i.e., both conceptual know-how and physical do-how, a combination that accounts for Weber's calling them broadly "means"), and the end is human *physical control* of the world. Weber proposes, then, one type of rationality directly (but of course not exclusively) serving the human ideal interest, and another serving the human material interest.

Integrating the Eight Types of Rationality

Now let us try to integrate, within a single dynamic frame of reference, all eight types of subjective orientations that, as we have just seen, Weber terms *rational*.

First, let us review the types. Two types (*Zweckrationalität* and *Wertrationalität*) serve to plan the use of means, before they are put into operation. One type (substantive rationality) evaluates the results achieved after the chosen means have been put into operation. Two types (subjective rationality and objective rationality) represent polarities in a range of measurement techniques that achieve various degrees of reliability in the planning and evaluation procedures specified by the preceding rationalities. One type (formal rationality) represents the range of techniques that achieve various degrees of precision in those procedures. Finally, two types (theoretical and practical) represent different but interdependent summary applications of all the preceding six types. That is to say (and although Weber himself does not make the claim more explicit than the quotation above), in principle, there exist theoretical sides and practical sides of all the above rationalities—that is, of *Zweckrationalität*, of *Wertrationalität*, and so on—and each side is "inseparately" linked to the other.

For the sake of simplicity let us consider only the practical side of the rationalities (one does science, Weber says, "first, for purely practical purposes" [1946:138]). The process of rational human action adopted here, then, occurs in four phases: mental planning of a physiological act; the physiological act itself; mental evaluation of the physiological act's observed consequences; and finally, feedback of

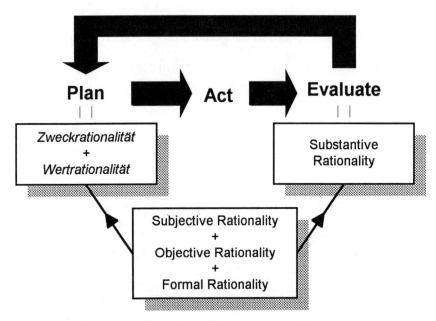

Figure 2. The Process of Rational Human Action

that evaluation into mental planning of the next physiological act (compare Miller et al. 1960; Wallace 1983:97–101).[29] These phases—and the relation of subjective rationality, objective rationality, and formal rationality to them—are depicted in figure 2.

The planning and evaluation phases call for mentally assessing the empirical conditions under which some physiological act is to take place or has already taken place (knowledge or cognition), and mentally designating a desired end toward which that act is to be or was aimed (affect or cathexis). The planning phase also calls for mentally selecting from the individual's behavior repertoire the particular physiological act that is to be actually manifested (conation). The desired end, Weber argues, may be phylogenetically innate self-interest, or socially learned nonself-interest, or some combination of both. The conditions are assessed by applying some variety of subjective-objective rationality, and of formal rationality, to observation.

Comparing and Choosing Ultimate Ends

Having reached this point of systematizing what Weber calls the "complexity of the only superficially simple concept of the rational" and the "whole world of distinct things [covered by] rationalism," it must not be overlooked that my discussion so far is incomplete in two crucial ways. First, I have focused entirely on means *assessment*—that is to say, on how the individual chooses among, and then evaluates the effects of, alternative means to some end—without asking how conceptualizations of such means originate. Second, I have focused entirely on *means* assessment, without asking about ends assessment—that is, without asking how the individual chooses among alternative ends given some fixed means.

That Weber is aware of the logical complementarity of ends-assessment and means-assessment seems quite clear from his remark that "economic action is primarily oriented to the problem of choosing the end to which a thing shall be applied; technology, to the problem, given the end, of choosing the appropriate means" (1978a:66–67, italics removed).[30] This, however, is as far as his examination of the problem goes. In other words, Weber does not generalize "the problem of choosing the end to which a thing shall be applied" beyond the economic domains. Unfortunately, he is even less explicit about how conceptualizations of alternative means to a given end originate. Chapter 3 will tackle these problems.

The rest of the present chapter is devoted to rounding out our conceptualization of the human individual by bringing in (1) the nonrational psychological behaviors Weber says humans also use to construct meanings and motivations; and (2) the physiological behaviors (the acts) Weber almost overlooks—or rather, quietly takes for granted—in human action.

Nonrationality

Having identified rationality with calculation ("both calculation in kind and in money are rational techniques"), Weber says that "there also exist types of action which . . . do not know calculation. [Such] action may be traditionally oriented or may be affectually determined" (1978a:107; see also 1172). So whereas the rational orientations involve the individual's conscious, rule-guided, comparison and choice among alternative means, the nonrational orientations prohibit such comparison and choice.[31] In them, a given end is *intrinsically and indissolubly linked to one and only one means* as far as the acting individual is concerned.

Here, Weber is far too brief—saying only that "traditional" orientation is "very often a matter of almost automatic reaction to habitual stimuli which guide behavior in a course which has been repeatedly followed," whereas "affectual" orientation is "determined by the actor's specific affects and feeling states. . . . [and] may, for instance, consist in an uncontrolled reaction to some exceptional stimulus" (1978a:25). Nevertheless, it seems beyond doubt that the terms *automatic* (*ablaufendes*) and *uncontrolled* (*hummungsloses*) point to the absence of consciously regulated comparison and choice in both orientations. What, however, is the difference between them?

The terms *habitual* (*gewohnte*) and *exceptional* (*ausseralltaglichen* [Weber 1956:12]), seem to be the key differentia, and they imply that these two nonrational orientations differ in just the same way that the two rational orientations do. That is, Weber's reference to traditional orientation as a reaction to habitual stimuli indicates that the reaction has been learned over multiple trials, whereas his reference to affectual orientation as a reaction to an exceptional stimulus indicates that the reaction has not been learned (the very exceptionality of the stimulus rules out such learning) but is, rather, innate to the individual and latent there until called out by some stimulus innately recognized as appropriate (see Lorenz 1970:vol. 1, 103–5 for discussion of "innate releasing mechanisms").[32] Thus, Weber claims, "In its more primitive aspects, the [affectual] search for food on the part of human beings is closely related to that of animals, dominated as the latter is by instinct. Economically oriented action dominated by a [traditional] religious faith, by war-like passions, or by attitudes of personal loyalty and similar modes of orientations, is likely to have a very low level of rational calculation" (1978a:107).

In a word, then, we may look upon both traditional and affectual orientations as involuntary, noncomparing, nonchoosing, mental reflexes—the former being an act-motivating conditioned reflex, and the latter being an act-motivating unconditioned reflex.[33]

Two final points about the nonrationalities. First, insofar as (by definition) a tradition can only be established by two or more individuals in different age-cohorts, and insofar as collaboration between individuals can intensify their affect (via a mechanism Weber calls "psychic contagion"—see chapter 5), these too become points at which society crucially augments the lone individual's psychological behavior. Once again, what the individual cannot do for species survival, society can do.

Second, the nonrationalities are not impermeably walled-off from the rationalities either in their structure or in their function. Structurally, the nonrationalities shade into rationality according to the degree to which conscious rules governing the comparison and choice of alternatives are operative in them (see Weber 1978a:25). Moreover, as we saw above, the rationalities (*Zweckrationalität* and *Wertrationalität*) can only come into play after some ultimate end has been selected. Insofar as the selection of that ultimate end is, for Weber, always a nonrational process that relies, in one way or another, on some combination of phylogenetically innate affect and socially learned tradition, rationality is always dependent on nonrationality to set its direction.[34]

Integrating the Rational and Nonrational Psychological Behavior Capabilities

It now seems reasonable to ask whether any overall schema may incorporate all the human individual's psychological behavior capabilities as set forth above. One answer lies in bringing together the claims that means are chosen in the rationalities but not in the nonrationalities and that one rationality and one nonrationality have phylogenetically inherited (hardwired) origins, whereas their complements have socially learned (software) origins—as summarized in figure 3.

Thus, the human individual's psychological behavior capabilities

Source of End

Choice of Means	Phylogenetically Innate	Socioculturally Learned
Present	Innate Self-Interest Rationality (*Zweckrationalität*)	Learned Nonself-Interest Rationality (*Wertrationalität*)
Absent	Affectual Nonrationality	Traditional Nonrationality

Figure 3. Types of Rational and Nonrational Psychological Orientations

are portrayed as a variable mix of rational and nonrational qualities, including innate and learned aspects of each. Such a mix seems in full accord with Weber's repeated observations that "it would be very unusual to find concrete cases of action . . . which were oriented *only* in one or another of these ways"; that "when a civil servant appears in his office daily at a fixed time . . . his action is . . . determined by the validity of an order . . . which he fulfills partly because disobedience would be disadvantageous to him [*Zweckrationalität*] but also because its violation would be abhorrent to his sense of duty [*Wertrationalität*]"; that "it is even possible for the same individual to orient his actions to contradictory systems of order. . . . A person who fights a duel follows the code of [*wertrational*] honor, but at the same time . . . he takes [*zweckrational*] account of the criminal law"; that "submission to an order is almost always determined by a variety of interests and by a mixture of adherence to tradition and belief in legality" (1978a:26, 31, 32, 37–38); and that "the action of men is *not* interpretable in . . . purely rational terms, that not only irrational 'prejudices,' errors in thinking and factual errors but also 'temperament,' 'moods,' and 'affects' disturb his freedom [i.e., his rationality]" (1975a:125).

40

Physiological Behavior Capabilities

So far, we have considered only aspects of the individual's psychological, neuroendocrine, behavior. However, Weber also alludes to the individual's physiological, skeletalmuscular and visceral, behavior—despite the fact that these allusions are secondary, scattered, and unsystematic. Indeed, Weber becomes logically compelled to offer some image of physiological behaviors once he has asserted that "it is obviously not the conventional *rule* of greeting that tips my hat when I meet an acquaintance. On the contrary, my *hand* does it" (1977:108, italics added). Weber clearly and repeatedly asserts the distinction in question, saying "no competent scholar would deny . . . that there is an absolutely strict distinction between all 'physiological' and all 'psychological' being" (1975a:130); claiming behavior may be "overt or covert" (1978a:4), " 'external' or 'internal' " (1981:151), and derogating "everyday speech [as] always a cloak for confusion of thought and action" (1975b:110).

His image of the physiological, overt, external, or action side of that distinction, however, suffers dramatically from two shortcomings. First, he makes this image almost completely dependent on the analyst's inferral of motivating psychological behaviors. That is to say, Weber's descriptions of a given physiological act as "rational" refers to the individual's (inferred) psychological orientation for that act and not to the (observed) physiological act itself. We have already seen an important instance of this in Weber's remark that "examples of pure value-rational *orientation* would be the *actions* of persons who . . . [etc.]."

Second, whereas Weber distinguishes between *Zweckrationalität* and *Wertrationalität* partly on the basis of whether the conceptualizations of the end-effects it seeks to bring about in the end-object are phylogenetically innate or socially learned, he draws no such distinction in the realm of physiological behavior—such as one might draw, for example, between the innately human capacity to make utterances of any kind and the learned capacity to make the particular kind of utterances called, say, "English."

The result, in Weber's work, of these two shortcomings is a far less comprehensive and less systematic conceptualization of the individual's physiological acts than of the individual's psychological orientations. Thus, Weber's definitions of action ("We shall speak of 'action' insofar as the acting individual attaches a subjective meaning to his behavior") and social action ("Action is 'social' insofar as its subjective meaning takes account of the behavior of others" [1978a:4]) too narrowly rule out of consideration physiological acts that are not already known by the investigator to be guided by the actor's subjective meaning. Still more unfortunately, Weber persists in adopting these definitions even though he admits "there is no guarantee at all that . . . feelings [attributed to the acting individual by an observer] will correspond in any way to the feelings of the historical persons with whom the writer and the reader empathize" (1975a:180); and even though, by asking "did [the participants in a given social process] consciously ascribe any 'meaning' at all to the process?" (1977:112), he implies that social processes can occur *without* any such meaning.[35]

Nevertheless, a number of terms remain identifiable in Weber's work that elaborate on the simple but fundamental notion that, as he puts it, one's physical "hand," not the rules in one's mind, tips one's hat (see above). Such terms introduce into the image of the individual favored in this essay purely physiological behavior capabilities (that is to say, capabilities whose description depends not on the subjective meaning imputed by the analyst to the individual, but solely on effects directly observable by the analyst). Although Weber himself does not categorize these terms, they appear to fall into three general classes—each of which may be thought of as having, like psychological behavior capabilities, a phylogenetically innate component and a socially learned component—as follows:

First is constructive behavior (physiological behavior that, regardless of its motivation, has some analytically specified building-up, technically negentropic, effect)—including what Weber refers to as *labor, work, production, function, performance* ("A mere glance at the facts of economic action reveals that different persons perform different types of work and that these are combined . . . with each other and with the non-human means of production, in the most varied ways" [Weber 1978a:114]), and *the sexual act* (see Weber 1978a:603).

Second is destructive or tearing-down, entropic, behavior—

including what Weber refers to as *physiological violence, physiological force,* and *force of arms.* Thus, "organized domination requires the control of those material goods which in a given case are necessary for the use of physiological violence" (Weber 1946:80, see also 82), and "participants in a 'political community' [have a] readiness to resort to physiological force, including normally force of arms" (Weber 1978a:901, see also 54).

Third is transportative-transmissive (carrying and/or sending) behavior—encompassing human going and coming, putting and taking, pushing and pulling, as well as physiological message sending of various kinds. The former is implicit in Weber's mention of *migrations* (1978a:7) and, by implication, in his references to *labor, work,* and the like (see above), and the latter is implicit in his remark that "the pre-exilic prophets from Amos to Jeremiah and Ezekiel. . . . were primarily speakers. . . . [who] addressed their audiences in public" (1952: 267–68, italics removed), and in his definition of *obedience* as physiological behavior brought about by a *command* (see chapter 6).

In addition (and although Weber does not suggest such a breakdown), all three of the above classes of physiological behavior may be said to share the same general types of potential objects. That is, each human individual is apt to be physiologically capable of constructing him/herself (through breathing, drinking, eating, exercising), other people (through helping to reproduce them, feed them, exercise them), and nonhuman things (for example, through combining wood, stone, metal, and the like, into axes, plows, books, buildings and other implements, and through domesticating, cultivating, and breeding plants and animals). Similarly, we are only too obviously capable of physiologically destroying ourselves, other people, and nonhuman things; and we are also capable of spatially transporting these same objects, and of transmitting messages through and/or to them.

The nine broad categories of physiological behaviors,[36] summarized in figure 4, are included in the present image of the individual as representations (in all their various combinations) of what the individual's motivation motivates. It follows that they, fully as much as the individual's psychological behaviors, make society possible. But of equal importance, they also help make it necessary—as becomes clear once we realize how tiny is the energy potential of any single individual's physiological behavior compared to the energy requirements of many of the tasks s/he can become motivated to accomplish (e.g., building the Great Wall of China). Weber puts this idea as follows: "Our most ideal needs are everywhere confronted with the quantitative limits and the qualitative inadequacy of the necessary means, so that their satisfaction requires planful provision and work, struggle with nature and the association of human beings" (1949:63–64).

Here, then, is yet another crucial point at which we may claim that what lone individuals cannot do for the survival of their species, society can do.

Finally in this connection, it is important to note Weber's consideration of different psychological motivations as alternative possible causal explanations for the same physiological behavior (see the discussion of equifinality in appendix A). Thus, after noting that "it is obviously . . . [my hand] that tips my hat when I meet an acquaintance" (see above), Weber goes on to ask, "But what is causally responsible for this [i.e., my hand moving up to tip my hat]?" and then implicitly invokes traditional nonrationality, *Zweckrationalität*, and *Wertrationalität*, respectively, as alternative explanatory motivations: "I may merely be in the 'habit' of following such a 'rule.' . . . [or] the action [may be] a consequence of an 'utilitarian' calculation [designed to avoid an unpleasant reaction from the acquaintance]. Or, finally, I may act on the belief that it is 'not proper' for me to disregard a harmless 'conventional rule' that is universally observed (1977:108).

Natality, Mortality, Metabolism, Motility, and Mutability

Now, after considering all the above psychological and physiological human behavior capabilities, a final set of features to which Weber alludes when he says that "human mortality, indeed the organic life cycle . . . is naturally of the very greatest sociological importance" (1987a:7) must be added: So far, every human individual that has

Effect of Behavior

Object of Behavior	Constructive	Destructive	Transportative-Transmissive
Self	Labor, Work, Production, Function, Performance	Violence, Force	Motility, Transportation, Gestures
Other people			
Nonhuman things			

Figure 4. Types of Physiological Behavior Capabilities

ever lived came into existence in only one way—by being born of woman and man; sooner or later, we all die; between birth and death we breathe, ingest, digest, assimilate, and excrete; we move ourselves and other things from place to place; and we are constantly changing under the influence of internal as well as external factors. Human individuals, in short, are natal, mortal, metabolic, motile, and mutable.

Although the next chapter will implicate all aspects of the human individual that have been discussed in this chapter, it will begin with these latter aspects.

Summary

This chapter has conceptualized every human individual's actions as comprising psychological behavior and physiological behavior. Psychological behavior comprises phylogenetically innate and socially learned rationalities and nonrationalities. The rationalities consciously carry out planning and evaluation strategies with reference to different kinds of ends; the nonrationalities are conditioned and unconditioned mental reflexes. Physiological behavior is very seriously underdeveloped in Weber's work, and to flesh that work out in this respect, constructive, destructive, and transportative-communicative types have been posited here.

The most important general conclusions to be drawn from this chapter, however, are that human individuals, at all times and places, are (1) *able* to conceptualize alternative means to a given end but *unable* reliably and precisely to compare and choose among these alternatives—and therefore unable reliably and precisely to plan the future operation of means, or to evaluate their past operation—without help from other humans; (2) *able* to conceptualize alternative ends which a given means might serve but *unable* to compare and choose among those ends without help from other humans; and finally, (3) *able* physiologically to bring about small physical changes in the world but *unable* to bring about large physical changes in the world without help from other humans. And here one especially remembers Spencer: "Cooperation . . . is at once that which cannot exist without a society, and that for which a society exists. It may be a joining of many strengths to affect something which the strength of no single man can effect; or it may be an apportioning of different activities to different persons, who severally participate in the benefits of one another's activities" (1898:vol. 2, 244).

It is to the structure of this survival-serving cooperation that we turn next.

3

STRUCTURE OF SOCIETY

THIS CHAPTER RESTS on the idea that certain exigencies are imposed on all human societies (the latter defined as the most nearly self-sufficient and self-reproducing collectivities of human individuals) by the prior nature of those individuals as naturally evolved living organisms, and of the world in which we live. After introducing what appears to be the universal institutional adaptation to these exigencies, I concentrate on the economic, political, religious, and scientific institutions, their typical products and their interrelations, and close by suggesting a set of basic causal relations between the human individual (as conceptualized in chapter 2) and his/her society.

A Society as a Nearly Self-Sufficient and Self-Reproducing Throughput System

If we take seriously the claim with which chapter 2 opened—namely, that "when reference is made in a sociological context to a state, a nation, a corporation, a family, or an army corps, or to similar collectivities, what is meant is . . . only a certain kind of development of actual or possible social actions of individual persons" (Weber 1978a:14), then any theory of human society must begin by taking into account the facts (derived from the natality, mortality, metabolism, motility, and mutability of the human individual discussed in chapter 2) that we are all born into some ongoing society; that we typically grow and are socialized into full participation in that (or some other) society; that we may exit it and enter some other society; and that in the end we must exit all societies.

Every human society, then, is here regarded as a *throughput system*—that is, an open system that exists in continuous, overlapping, iterations of (1) taking-in participants; (2) organizing the behavior of these participants while they last; and eventually, (3) allowing (or forcing) these participants to leave it.[1] Ryder clearly implies such a view of society when he says, "Any [social] organization experiences social metabolism: since its individual components are exposed to 'mortality,' the survival of the organization requires a process of 'fertility.' The problem of replacement is posed not only for the total organization but also for every one of its differentiated components" (1964:461).

Conceptualizing every human society as a throughput system, then, leads to the hypothesis that it always consists, at minimum, of three sets of institutions. The first set is comprised of what I shall call participant-intake institutions. Through them, society manages the biological production of new individual participants; the immigration—including both voluntary enticement and involuntary conquest and incorporation by purchase—of participants biologically produced elsewhere; and the physiological and psychological nurture, education, and training of both kinds of recruits so that they may perform roles in the set next in line, namely, that of the participant-organizing institutions.[2] The latter institutions coordinate certain activities of the individuals provided by the participant-intake institutions for as long as these individuals are members of the society. The third set comprises participant-outlet institutions. Through them, the society manages the disposal of its dead participants and the temporary and/or permanent emigration (including voluntary and involuntary hospitalization, incarceration, exile, and tourism) of its disaffected, disabled, unwanted, or adventure-seeking participants.

Regrettably, Weber overlooks the participant-outlet institutions almost entirely—although he does discuss "migration" in general (see 1989a:174; 1989b:193; 1989c:217; and 1978a:70). His treatment of the participant-intake institutions, however, is somewhat more extensive. For example, he mentions the role of sexual relations in recruiting new social participants: "Sexual relationships and the relationships between children based on the fact of their common parent or parents can engender social action" (Weber 1978a:358; see also 1950:30–37);[3] and he stresses the control that "ethnic consciousness" exerts over intermarriage and, to that extent, over biological reproduction: "In all groups with a developed 'ethnic' consciousness the existence or absence of intermarriage. . . . means the fact that the offspring from a permanent sexual relationship can share in the activities and advantages of the father's political, economic or status group" (Weber 1978a:385–86).

Also relevant to the participant-intake set of institutions, Weber briefly identifies three types of education and training institutions: the type that seeks "to awaken and to test a capacity which was considered a purely personal gift of grace," the type that seeks "to train the pupil for practical usefulness for administrative purposes," and the type that seeks "to educate a cultivated type of man, whose nature depends on the decisive stratum's respective ideal of cultivation" (1951b:119–20; see also 1946:351). Weber does not say—but one should add—that such institutions generally incorporate some sequence of experience (e.g., primary, secondary, and higher education), and some specialization of that experience (e.g., modern vocational and academic secondary educations, undergraduate majors, and graduate and professional school departments), with the result that those who enter the awakening, education, and training institutions to which Weber refers are likely to become more or less disciplined and skilled participants in their society. Indeed, when they leave such participant-intake institutions, at whatever level, and with whatever specialization, trainees are normally allocated to various roles and statuses in all the institutions to be discussed next, namely, the economic, political, religious, and scientific.

It is overwhelmingly on the latter set of participant-organizing institutions that Weber's attention, and the present chapter's attention, are focused.

Participant-Organizing Institutions and the Ultimate Ends of Life

Chapter 1 ended by referring to certain intrinsic "abilities" and "inabilities" of human individuals, and by claiming that human society should be thought of as the way such individuals organize themselves so that their inabilities are compensated for and their abilities are augmented. Clearly, however, what is an ability from the standpoint of one end may very well be an inability from the standpoint of another end. It follows that when we consider the participant-organizing set of institutions, the first question to be considered is, Organizing *to what end*? And in its answer to this question, Weber's work is unique in the corpus of classical sociological theory.

Weber repeatedly espouses what Hennis calls "ethical agnosticism" (1988:187) and what Weber himself seems to refer to as "a morally skeptical type of rationality, at the expense of any belief in absolute values" (1978a:30). (It is worth emphasizing, however, that to adopt value agnosticism is not to claim that sociological researches should, or can, be "value-free"—see appendix B.)[4] Thus, Weber tells us, repeatedly, that "there is an infinite number of possible value scales" (1978a:86); "life with its irrational reality and its store of possible meanings is inexhaustible. The concrete form in which value-relevance occurs remains perpetually in flux, ever subject to change in the dimly seen future of human culture" (1949:111, italics removed); "the various value spheres of the world stand in irreconcilable conflict with each other"; "different gods struggle with one another, now and for all time to come"; "the ultimately possible attitudes toward life are irreconcilable, and hence their struggle can never be brought to a final conclusion" (1946:147, 148, 152); and "the fruit of the Tree of Knowledge, so disturbing to human complacency yet so inescapable, is nothing but the recognition of these [valuational] oppositions" (1978b:84). Moreover, at the start of his most famous work, Weber warns us that "whoever wants a sermon should go to a conventicle. The question of the relative value of the cultures which are compared here will not receive a single word" (1958a:29).

But once we accept such a perspective, there arises a problem of the utmost analytical importance: If the number of logically possible ultimate ends of human life is indeed "infinite" and if they are all in principle "irreconcilable," why have we not observed anything even remotely suggesting that limitlessness? Why have billions of different individuals, in different circumstances, in different parts of the world and across the entire span of human history so far, adopted what amounts to a mere handful of "ultimately possible attitudes toward life"? *Where have all the possible attitudes toward life gone?*

Let us pause briefly here to note that this type of problem is not unique to Weber's theory. Marx claims the individual is capable of producing without limit: "Man produces even when he is free from physical need and only truly produces in freedom therefrom. . . . man reproduces the whole of nature. . . . man knows how to produce in accordance with the standard of every species" (1977:68). Durkheim claims the individual is capable of consuming without limit: "How determine the quantity of well-being, comfort or luxury legitimately to be craved by a human? Nothing appears in man's organic nor in his psychological constitution which sets a limit to such tendencies. . . . the more one has, the more one wants" (1951:247, 248). And as implied above, Weber claims the individual is capable of philosophizing (i.e., imagining possible value scales for human life, and also possible means to achieve the ends these scales stipulate) without limit.

But any theorist who posits a limitless human potential of some kind must face the problem of accounting for the self-evidently limited number of actual manifestations of this potential—and Marx, Durkheim, and Weber all name society as the limiting agency. Marx argues that the individual's qualitatively limitless productive potentials are narrowed down to only a few manifestations by a social division of labor: "As soon as the distribution of labor comes into being, each man has a particular, exclusive sphere of activity, which is forced upon him and from which he cannot escape" (Marx and Engels 1969–70:vol. 1, 35). Durkheim says the individual's consumption manifestations are limited by a socially generated morality: "At every moment of history there is a dim perception . . . of the respective value of different social services, the relative reward due to each, and the consequent degree of comfort appropriate on the average to workers in each occupation" (1951:249).

Weber, in his turn, claims that both the variety of ultimate ends the individual can actually adopt, and the variety of means s/he can actually employ, are specified by society—in particular, by the participant-organizing institutions of society. Indeed, it is precisely this specification that justifies thinking of these institutions as participant-organizing.

Before examining these institutions in detail, however, it should be emphasized that the above remarks depart radically from the view that Weber "was firmly convinced that there was no other foundation for values than the spontaneous decision of the personality" (Mommsen 1974:7, see also 106, 110), that Weber believed "each person must ultimately find [the good] for himself and make . . . a personal decision" (Burger 1977:173; see also Loewith 1970:108), and that Weber took an individualistically "'decisionistic' view of the value choices one must make in life" (Turner and Factor 1984:2). Now *of course* the individual makes his/her own value choices, but the point Weber (and virtually every other sociologist) emphasizes is that these choices are never made spontaneously by the lone individual, never made independently of the choices other individuals in his/her neighborhood are making and have already made.

Thus, although he says that "according to our ultimate standpoint . . . the *individual* has to decide which is God for him and which is the devil" (1946:148, italics added), Weber does not mean that according to his, *Weber's*, own "ultimate standpoint" the individual must decide.[5] He means the individual must decide, according to what might be better translated as "the *generally accepted* standpoint of ultimacy"—that is to say, the standpoint that claims such ultimate ends exist objectively—a standpoint that, though dominant in his culture, Weber himself, as an ethical agnostic, explicitly and repeatedly rejects (see above). From the standpoint Weber regards as valid, every individual's decision regarding "which [value] is God . . . and which [value] is the devil" is always determined by the society into which the individual is born. Thus "from a certain standpoint, 'cultural values' are 'obligatory'—even when they are in inevitable and irreconcilable conflict with every other [personal] sort of ethics" (Weber 1949:15).[6]

Indeed, although Weber does not say so, the very concepts "God" and "devil" seem indisputably cultural inventions rather than either innate to, or inventions by, human individuals in isolation (Mannheim says the individual "speaks the language of his group; he thinks in the manner in which his group thinks. He finds at his disposal only certain words and their meanings" [1955:3; see also Durkheim 1965]). It seems clearly for this reason that Weber says so vehemently, "It is a tremendous misunderstanding to think that an 'individualistic' method should involve what is in any conceivable sense an individualistic system of values" (1978a:18, italics removed), and asserts (in the same way we ourselves often refer vaguely to "the powers-that-be"—meaning especially the political and economic institutional powers) that "forces other than university chairs have their say" (1946:148) in deciding which ultimate ends the individual adopts as his/her own.

Let us try to see, then, how Weber analyses these "forces other than university chairs."

Institutions

"The term 'social relationship,'" Weber says, "will be used to denote the behavior of a plurality of actors insofar as, in its meaningful content, the action of each takes account of that of the others and is oriented in these terms" (1978a:27). He then notes that "a social relationship can be of very fleeting character or of varying degrees of permanence. In the latter case there is a probability of the repeated recurrence of the behavior" (Weber 1978a:28).

Now although Weber himself does not do so, let us cross-classify probability of occurrence with duration of occurrence, thereby deriving four polar types of social relationships: (1) low probability and short duration, (2) high probability and short duration, (3) low probability and long duration, and (4) high probability and long duration. Weber seems to illustrate the first three types in his discussions of (1) a "collision of two cyclists," (2) people who "put up their umbrellas at the same time" at the start of a shower, and (3) "action conditioned by crowds" (1978a:23), respectively—although the point he himself wishes to make with these illustrations bears more directly on the place of "meaningful orientation" in defining "social action" (see appendix A).

With the fourth type of social relationship—high probability and long duration—we come to a type of social relationship that, following current custom, I shall call an *institution*. Weber sometimes calls this type of social relationship a *life order* (1946:323), or *sphere*—as in "The Economic Sphere," "The Political Sphere," etc. (see 1946:331, 333, 340, 343, 350), but he also refers to *institutions*, and cites the political and religious as examples. Thus:

> Individuals . . . are empirically "obligated" to participate in the social action constituting the community. . . . We want to designate such communities [of social action] as *"institutions"* or compulsory associations . . . [wherein,] in contrast to the voluntary association, participation is ascribed on the basis of purely objective facts independent of declarations by those persons ascribed. . . . Valid examples are the structural form of the political community designated as "state" and that of the religious community designated in the rigorous technical sense as "church." (Weber 1981:174)

Thus, in the term *institution*, Weber not only has in mind social relationships of high probability and long duration, but he also intends to claim (in the terms *obligatory, compulsory,* and *ascribed*) that *all* members of a given society participate in *every* such institution.[7] The present theory makes this view explicit—claiming that all human societies include the same basic complement of participant-organizing institutions, and that every human participant in such societies possesses one or more statuses and plays one or more roles in each of these institutions.

That is to say, every member of a given society participates in its economic institution—whether in the role of employer, employed, nonemployed, or unemployed, professional, skilled, or unskilled, working in one or another sector of the economy, and so on. In the same way, every member participates in the political institution— whether in the role of active or passive supporter of this party or that, officeholder or not, etc. Each participates in the religious institution—whether in the role of believer, nonbeliever, or disbeliever, cleric or layperson, in this faith or that faith or no faith. And each participates in the scientific institution—whether in the role of credentialed professional, trainee, or layperson, in this discipline or that, in pure science or applied science.

Parenthetically, it should be emphasized that Weber's analysis of the impact of the Protestant (religious) ethic on the spirit of (economic) capitalism rests squarely on the assumption that because the same individuals play roles in at least these two institutions, the influence of one institution is readily transmitted to the other. The generality of his remark that "we are placed into different life-spheres, each of which is governed by different laws" (Weber 1946:123), together with his reference to the "state" (quoted above), strongly suggests that he intends the individual's institutional participations to include religious, economic, and political ones. To these three, however, we should add a fourth.

Economic, Political, Religious, and Scientific Institutions

Vague and open-ended complements of institutions (rarely named such, however) have been attributed to Weber. For example, Parsons says Weber develops "a system of ideal types of social relationship. . . . culminating in such concepts as church and state" (1937:653); Gerth and Mills say that in Weber's view, "all spheres—intellectual, psychic, economic, religious—to some extent follow developments of their own" (1946:62); Andreski says Weber refers to "the economic, political and religious realms" (1984:51); Lachmann refers to "the whole range of institutions, religious, political, economic, legal, and educational which [Weber's] powerful mind encompassed," but he also claims that "no general theory of institutions is to be found anywhere in Weber's work. . . . [although fragments] of such a theory can be found" (1971:52). Schroeder comes close to my own view when he says, "Weber distinguishes between several spheres of social life—the most important being the political, economic, religious and intellectual spheres," and then adds that the latter is "dominated by science" (1992:10, 23), but he does not tell us what the metaphor "sphere of life" denotes, nor does he attempt to formulate the substantive meanings of the names given to these "spheres." Collins says, "Weber's threefold scheme—class, status, and party (or economics, culture, and politics)—echoes throughout his works" (1986b:7; see also 1990:71, 74), but he does not say what this is a scheme of.[8]

The present chapter holds that what really echoes throughout Weber's works is a *fourfold* scheme; that this is a scheme of the participant-organizing *institutions;* and that these include a *scientific* institution along with an economic institution, a political institution, and a religious institution (see Weber's 1949:64–65 mention of all four institutions in the same context; and see Topitsch 1971:9–10). Now it will be at once noted that although there is little agreement among the interpreters cited above regarding which institutions Weber does include, there seems to be near-unanimity that he does not include a scientific institution. Such an institution, however, is essential to the present theory, so let us concentrate first on the analytical problems it presents before examining the participant-organizing institutions as an integrated set.

Weber's Neglect of the Scientific Institution

Although this book takes a very different view of the matter, interpretations that omit a scientific institution from Weber's basic image of society are not groundless. Weber does grossly neglect the analysis of science as an institution—when compared with the attention he lavishes on the economy, the polity, and the church as institutions.[9] This neglect is expressed in at least three major ways: First, Weber's own title for the work translated as *Economy and Society* is "The Economy and the Normative and De Facto Powers" (see Roth 1978:lxv), and this title signals his overlooking the scientific institution—assuming that by "Normative and De Facto Powers" he means the religious, and the political, institutions (see Roth 1978:lxv for a radically different interpretation). Second, Weber does not analyze the premodern stages of science as thoroughly as he does the premodern stages of the economy, the polity, and the religious institution. And third, when he does refer to such stages in science, Weber implies that a sharp separation of what we would call pure science (aimed at theoretical understanding of the world) from applied science (aimed at practical control over the world) characterized them—such that "the inventors of the pre-capitalistic age worked empirically; their inventions had more or less the character of accidents" (1950:312)—but he never applies the term *scientist* to such "inventors" (see chapter 6).

At the same time, however, Weber expresses his evaluation of science in uniquely superlative terms. "Scientific progress," he declares, "is . . . the most important fraction of the process of intellectualization which we have been undergoing for thousands of years"; and "science today. . . . is the inescapable condition of our historical situation. We cannot evade it so long as we remain true to ourselves" (1946:138, 152). Nowhere does Weber make such claims for the economy, the polity, or the church—and it would seem perverse to exclude from their ranks the one institution for which he does make them.

In order to open the way to raising the analysis of the scientific institution to the level of that of the economy, the polity, and the church, consider the following two propositions: (1) the scientific institution, like all the others, follows a life course in which growth eventually gives way to decline, but throughout which it remains an analytically identifiable institution—though successively incipient, mature, and finally moribund; and (2) at all these stages, pure science and applied science are inseparably interdependent components of the scientific institution and of every discipline in it.

The first proposition (institutional life-course) follows out the implications of Barber's observation that "not only has some form of science existed in all societies, but the several forms have been built each upon its historical antecedents. For at least the last three or four thousand years, and even beyond that, the record of the evolution of science runs fairly continuously, without unbridgeable gaps" (1952:26; for similar views, see Neugebauer 1952:1; Sarton 1962:1; Palter 1962:viii–ix; Parsons 1967a:147). The second proposition (pure-applied interdependence) accords with Bernal's claim that "the interaction of the theoretical and practical activities of man furnishes a key to the understanding of the history of science" (1939:13; see also Barber 1952:55–56, 100).

So let us suppose these two propositions do indeed open the way to identifying the scientific institution as being no less intrinsic to human society than the economic, political, and religious institutions.[10] One may then ask what that institution does for the society of which it is a part.

General Functions of the Scientific Institution

Weber argues that the principal function of science is to provide an empirical basis for choosing among alternative conceivable means to a given end—which is to say, for the *Zweckrationalität* and *Wertrationalität* comparisons and choices (see chapter 2) that are implicit in carrying out roles in all the institutions. "The question of the appropriateness of the means for achieving a given end," Weber says, "is undoubtedly accessible to scientific analysis" (1949:52), and in "appropriateness" he implicitly includes the likely costs and benefits of using a given means not only in terms of its main-effects but its side-effects and long-run effects: "On scientific grounds it is possible . . . to inquire, what would be the probable results of any specific proposal, and thus what consequences would have to be accepted if the attempt were made" (Weber 1978a:112).

Therefore, Weber says, "One does [science] first, for purely practical, in the broader sense of the word, for technical purposes: in order to be able to orient our practical activities to the expectations that scientific experience places at our disposal" (1946:138); and "science contributes to the technology of controlling life by calculating external objects as well as man's activities" (1946:150).[11] Scientists, Weber says,

> are in a position to help you gain clarity. . . . [We] can make clear to you the following:. . . . If you take such and such a stand, then, according to scientific experience, you have to use such and such a means. . . . Does the end 'justify' the means? Or does it not? The teacher can confront you with the necessity of this choice. . . . He can, of course, also tell you that if you want such and such an end, then you must take into the bargain the subsidiary consequences which according to all experience will occur. (1946:151, italics removed)

And if the answer is no, the end does not justify using this particular means with all its subsidiary consequences (although Weber does not make this point explicitly), the scientist can frequently propose one or more alternative means to which the answer *may* be yes.[12]

But if such practical concerns are one reason for doing science, the other (probably evolutionarily coeval and certainly no less important) reason is cognitive—which is to say, intellectual curiosity. The academic scientist "maintains that he engages in 'science for its own sake' and not merely because others, by exploiting science . . . can better feed, dress, illuminate and govern" (Weber 1946:138).[13] And how does such pure science occur? Weber answers as follows: "The really great advances in knowledge. . . . all arise intuitively in the intuitive flashes of imagination as hypotheses which are then 'verified' vis-à-vis the facts, i.e., their validity is tested in procedures involving the use of already available empirical knowledge and they are 'formulated' in a logically correct way" (1949:176).[14]

On all the above grounds, then, the present theory includes a participant-organizing institution called *natural science* (including social science) as equal partner of the economic, political, and religious institutions. This institution is specialized for the pursuit of (1) empirical bases for choosing satisfactorily effective or efficient practical steps toward achieving whatever empirical ends the participants in a given society adopt, and (2) satisfaction of the universally human intellectual curiosity about the nature of the world at large.[15] Such an institution, however—no matter how highly developed—has two inescapable limitations.

General Limitations of the Scientific Institution

"In science, each of us knows that what he has accomplished will be antiquated in ten, twenty, fifty years. That is the fate to which science is subjected; it is the very meaning of scientific work. . . . We cannot work without hoping that others will advance further than we have. In principle, this progress goes on *ad infinitum*" (Weber 1946:138, italics removed).[16] The first intrinsic limitation of science, then, is that its conclusions are always incomplete and imperfect; they can satisfy our practicality demands and our curiosity only partially and temporarily.

The second limitation resides in the fact that although science is unexcelled in identifying, comparing, and choosing among the *means* that we employ in our lives, it is forever unable to identify, compare, choose, or justify any *ends* to which those means, and our lives, should be devoted (but see chapter 2, note 30).[17] Indeed, science cannot even defend the value of its own existence: "No science can prove its fundamental value to the man who rejects [its] presuppositions" (Weber 1946:153). Weber's views are unmistakable regarding this limitation of science: "What we must vigorously oppose is the view that one may be 'scientifically' contented with the conventional self-evidentness of very widely accepted value-judgments"; "an empirical science cannot tell anyone what he *should* do"; "[it is only a] confused opinion that economics does and should derive value-judgments from a specifically 'economic point of view'"; "the creation of . . . generally valid ultimate value-judgments cannot be . . . the task of any empirical science"; "we cannot discover . . . what is meaningful to us by means of a 'presuppositionless' investigation of empirical data"; "empirical data . . . can never become the foundation for the empirically impossible proof of the validity of evaluative ideas" (1949:13, 52, 54, 57, 76, 111); "no branch of science and no scientific knowledge . . . results in any 'world view'" (1978b:387, italics removed; see also Marianne Weber 1975:380). And once more: "[It cannot] be proved that the existence of the world which [the] sciences describe is worth while, that it has any 'meaning,' or that it makes sense to live in such a world. . . . Natural science gives us an answer to the question of what we must do if we wish to master life technically. It leaves quite aside, or assumes for its purposes, whether we should . . . master life technically and whether it ultimately makes sense to do so" (Weber 1946:144). It follows that "we know of no scientifically ascertainable ideals. . . . [We] must not and cannot promise a fool's paradise and an easy road to it, neither in thought nor in action. It is the stigma of our human dignity that the peace of our souls cannot be as great as the peace of one who dreams of such a paradise" (quoted in Roth 1978:xxxiii).[18] And in what is undoubtedly his most eloquent and best-known statement of this position, Weber tells us:

The fate of an epoch which has eaten of the tree of knowledge is that it must know that we cannot learn the meaning of the world from the results of its analysis, be it ever so perfect; it must rather be in a position to create this meaning itself. It must recognize that general views of life and the universe can never be the products of increasing empirical knowledge, and that the highest ideals, which move us most forcefully, are always formed only in the struggle with other ideals which are just as sacred to others as ours are to us. (1949:57, italics removed)

Now we come to a key question for the present theory: What difference does it make to our understanding of human society if we conceptualize its basic participant-organizing institutions as four-fold rather than threefold or fivefold or whatever? What difference does it make if we include a scientific institution along with the economic, political, and religious institutions—and stop there, including no others?

The answers proposed here are as follows: (1) the inclusion of a scientific institution is the key to accounting for two types of technical inventions that play central roles in Weber's work—namely, machinery and bureaucracy; and (2) that inclusion makes possible a more systematic and parsimonious analysis of the participant-organizing institutional structure of human societies. Let us consider these two points in turn.

Explaining Machinery and Bureaucracy

Weber uncharacteristically resorts to the passive voice when he says, "In the 15th century . . . was invented the iron drill for the preparation of cannon barrels. At the same time appeared the large heavy trip hammer" (1950:304) and "the bureaucratic structure is everywhere a late product of historical development" (1978a: 1002)—as though these inventions had no identifiable institutional source.

That these failures to account for machinery and bureaucracy should not be regarded as trivial seems clear from the magnitude of the consequences Weber attributes to these two phenomena. Regarding machinery, he says, "Iron became the most important factor in the development of capitalism; what would have happened to this system or to Europe in the absence of this development we do not know"; "the mechanization of the production process through the steam engine liberated production from the organic limitations of human labor"; "the railway is the most revolutionary instrumentality known to history" (Weber 1950:305–6, 297); and the modern economic order "is now bound to the technical and economic conditions of machine production (Weber 1958a:181). Regarding bureaucracy, he tells us "it would be sheer illusion to think for a moment that continuous administrative work can be carried out in any field except by means of officials working in offices" and "the future belongs to bureaucratization" (Weber 1978a:223, 1401; see also Beetham 1985:71). And regarding both together: "Bureaucracy . . . [and] the factory . . . determine the character of the present age and of the foreseeable future" (Weber 1978a:1400–1401).

But perhaps most memorable of all his references to machinery and bureaucracy is this gloomy (but not deterministic) prediction: "Together with the inanimate machine. . . . that animated machine, the bureaucratic organization, with its specialization of trained skills, its division of jurisdiction, its rules and hierarchical relations of authority. . . . is busy fabricating the shell of bondage which men will perhaps be forced to inhabit some day as powerless as the fellahs of ancient Egypt" (Weber 1978a:1402).[19] The origins of phenomena claimed to have such far-reaching consequences cry out for identification, but unfortunately Weber does not volunteer any. What follows here, then, is an effort to fill this gap.

Weber notes that "the development of modern forms of organization in all fields is nothing less than identical with the development and continual spread of bureaucratic administration" (1978a:223), and he stresses the near-finality of this development: "Where administration has been completely bureaucratized, the resulting system of domination is practically indestructible. The individual bureaucrat cannot squirm out of the apparatus into which he has been harnessed. . . . [and the] ruled, for their part, cannot dispense with or replace the bureaucratic apparatus once it exists" (1978a:987–88). But why should this be so? Why is bureaucracy so "indestructible"? Why cannot the bureaucrat "squirm out of the apparatus," and why cannot the ruled "dispense with or replace the bureaucratic apparatus"?

Weber answers, first, that bureaucracy is "capable of attaining the highest degree of efficiency and is in this sense formally the most rational known means of exercising authority over human beings. It is superior to any other form in precision, in stability, in the stringency of its discipline, and in its reliability. It thus makes possible a particularly high degree of calculability of results" (1978a:223). Second, and no less important, bureaucracy is "capable of application to all kinds of tasks. . . . This is true of church and state, of armies, political parties, economic enterprises, interest groups, endowments, clubs, and many others" (Weber 1978a:223).

But, again, *why* is bureaucracy so efficient, precise, stable, disciplined, reliable, calculable, and widely applicable? Weber's answer, ultimately, is that bureaucracy is founded on technically oriented, systematic, empirical knowledge: "The primary source of the superiority of bureaucratic administration lies in the role of technical knowledge which, through the development of modern technology and business methods in the production of goods, has become completely indispensable. . . . Bureaucratic administration means fundamentally domination through knowledge" (1978a:223, 225; see also 1417–18). Such knowledge, as we have seen in chapter 2, Weber regards as "objective" and "scientific." As a result, it seems fair to say that his explanation of bureaucracy indirectly but eventually refers back to a specifically scientific institution—at first only an incipient one, but one that evolves (as do the other institutions) over the course of human history.

The impact of scientific knowledge on the development of machinery, he says, is very similar to that of bureaucracy: "Through the union [of technological invention] with science, the production of goods was emancipated from all the bonds of inherited tradition and came under the dominance of the freely roving intelligence. . . . The connection of industry with modern science, especially the systematic work of the laboratories . . . enabled industry to become what it is today and so brought capitalism to its full development" (1950:306). So it comes as no surprise that when Weber considers bureaucracy and machinery together, he defends this coupling by claiming they share characteristics he elsewhere (see 1975a:148, 187, 198; 1949:34, 35, 110–11; 1978a:85) regards as specialized products of natural science: "The fully developed bureaucratic apparatus compares with other organizations exactly as does the machine with the non-mechanical modes of production. Precision, speed, unambiguity, knowledge of the files, continuity, discretion, unity, strict subordination, reduction of friction and of material and personal costs—these are raised to the optimum point in the strictly bureaucratic administration" (Weber 1978a:973).

The theory being developed here, then, explicitly locates the causal origins of machinery and bureaucracy in natural science (physical, and social, respectively), that is, in science as an institution. Indeed, Weber himself almost makes precisely this attribution when he observes that "today capital has enlisted science in its service and uses it to develop large units of production with internal division of labour [i.e., bureaucracy] and concomitant technology [i.e., machinery]" (Weber 1976:208).

Conceptual Relations among the Participant-Organizing Institutions of Human Societies

Now let us examine the conceptual systematization of the participant-organizing system of institutions that the inclusion of a scientific institution makes possible. Consider figure 5 and the different pairings among the four participant-organizing institutions (and their specialized products) that it suggests.

The Economic-Scientific Pair and the Political-Religious Pair

One pair of institutions (economic, and scientific) pursues ends already given in the phylogenetically innate human nature of their individual participants (see chapter 2), and constrains only the means such participants employ in seeking these ends. Thus, in the economic institution, social participants pursue the single, fixed and universal, end of enhancing their own self-interest: "The market and the competitive economy resting on it form the most important type

Object of Constraint

Type of Constraint	Only Means	Means and Ends
Material	Economic (Wealth)	Political (Power)
Ideal	Scientific (Knowledge)	Religious (Honor)

Figure 5. Types of Participant-Organizing Institutions and Their Typical Products

of the reciprocal determination of action in terms of pure self-interest" (Weber 1978a:43, see also 109, 111).[20] However, the alternative means among which individuals choose (via *Zweckrationalität*, discussed in chapter 2) in pursuing this interest are heavily constrained by the social institution in which they pursue it, for "the mode of [economic] distribution monopolizes the opportunities for profitable deals for all those who, provided with goods, do not necessarily have to exchange them" (Weber 1978a:927), and "the unequal distribution of wealth, and particularly of capital goods, forces the non-owning group to comply with the authority of others in order to obtain any return at all for the utilities they can offer on the market. . . . In a purely capitalistic organization of production, this is the fate of the entire working class" (Weber 1978a:110).[21]

In the scientific institution, social participants also pursue the single, fixed and universal, end of enhancing their own self-interest—but whereas the economic institution emphasizes material interests in goods and services, here the emphasis is on ideal interests in empirical knowledge of the world (including the predictions on which rational efforts to control the world for economic or other reasons are based—see Wallace 1988:24–26). Thus "science today is a 'vocation' organized in special disciplines in the service of self-clarification and knowledge of interrelated facts" (Weber 1946:152).

In sharp contrast with the economic and scientific institutions, the political and religious institutions—because they are not bound to serve any set ends—are free to choose the ends, as well as the means, they require their participants to adopt. Thus, Weber says that "the political association is particularly capable of arrogating to itself all the possible values toward which associational conduct might be oriented" (1978a:902) and that "sociologically, the state cannot be defined in terms of its ends. There is scarcely any task that some political association has not taken in hand, and there is no task that one could say has always been exclusive and peculiar to those associations which are designated as political ones" (1946:77). (Weber makes an exception to this claim when he says the state does seek an end—namely, "the glory of power over other communities" [1978a:911]—and chapter 4 will return to this point.) The same freedom to choose the ends as well as the means that it imposes on its participants, Weber says, holds for the religious institution: "In formulating the concept of a hierocratic organization, it is not possible to use the character of the religious benefits it offers, whether worldly or other-worldly, material or spiritual, as the decisive criterion. What is important is rather the fact that its control over these values can form the basis of a system of spiritual domination over human beings" (1978a:56).

Thus, it seems reasonable to conclude that although there may be in principle "an infinite number of possible value scales," although "life with its . . . store of possible meanings is inexhaustible," and although "the ultimately possible attitudes toward life are irreconcilable, and hence their struggle can never be brought to a final conclusion" (Weber 1978a:86; 1949:111; 1946:152), these possibilities are drastically reduced, and the struggle among them is mitigated, in practice, by the political and religious institutions of society. These two, in short, are the institutions whose ongoing, everyday, taken-for-granted accomplishment is what science and the economy can never accomplish—namely, the actual specification and mass adoption of some few values out of all the infinite number of possible, and humanly indiscriminable, values. That is to say, "Only positive religions . . . are able to confer on the content of cultural values the status of unconditionally valid ethical imperatives" (Weber 1949:57, italics removed), and only positive political organizations—

governments—are able physically to enforce the content of such cultural values.

The Economic-Political Pair and the Religious-Scientific Pair

In addition to the above two pairings, the economic and political institutions may also be paired together—on the ground that they both organize social participants primarily through the use of material means. That is to say, the economic institution produces and then distributes physical goods and services, and the political institution monopolizes and then distributes physical force and violence, among their participants. Regarding the economic institution, Weber says, "We shall apply the term economic order to the distribution of the actual control over goods and services . . . moreover, the term shall apply to the manner in which goods and services are indeed used by virtue of these powers of disposition" (1978a:312, italics removed). And regarding the political institution, he says categorically that "the decisive means for politics is violence" (Weber 1946:121), and that "it is absolutely essential for every political association to appeal to the naked violence of coercive means in the face of outsiders as well as in the face of internal enemies. It is only this very appeal to violence that constitutes a political association in our terminology" (Weber 1946:334; see also 1978a:54).[22]

In contrast with this economic-political pairing, the religious and scientific institutions may be paired on the ground that they employ ideal (ideational) means in achieving their participant-organizing constraints—by generating ideas about the existence of various supernatural and natural phenomena, and ideas about the capability of these phenomena to affect the distribution of significant benefits and injuries among participants in the institution. Thus, regarding the religious institution, Weber says, "A 'hierocratic organization' is an organization which enforces its order through psychic coercion by distributing or denying religious benefits ('hierocratic coercion'). A compulsory hierocratic organization will be called a 'church' insofar as its administrative staff claims a monopoly of the legitimate use of hierocratic coercion" (1978a:54). And regarding the scientific institution, he says (as seen above) science is "in a position to help you gain clarity [of mind]" (Weber 1946:151), and "on scientific grounds it is possible . . . to [generate mental images] of the probable results of any specific proposal, and thus what consequences would have to be accepted if the attempt were made" (Weber 1978a:112).

Typical Products of the Four Institutions

Note also the suggestion of figure 5 that each participant-organizing institution has its own typical product that it distributes among its participants and among the other institutions in which the latter participate. These products are *wealth* (consumer, and producer, goods and services), in the economic institution; decision-making *power* (i.e., the ability to make and implement decisions regarding the behaviors that participants either engage in or refrain from engaging in), in the political institution;[23] beliefs in the *honor* (both positive and negative) that participating individuals accord to themselves and others, in the religious institution; and systematic empirical *knowledge* of the world (human and nonhuman, animate and inanimate, social and nonsocial) as humanly experienced, in the scientific institution.[24] And it is essential to add that the production of a given product is not held to be limited to the indicated specialized institution. It seems more in accord with Weber's view to say that production is partly diffuse among all the institutions (e.g., the political, religious, and scientific institutions, as well as the economic institution, may produce wealth) but nevertheless largely specialized within a given institution—as indicated.

Before going any further, it will be useful to pause for a moment and say a little more to justify calling "honor" (or "prestige") the specialized product of the religious institution. Weber defines "status situation" as "social estimation of honor" (1978a:932, italics removed), and it is important to note that the primary status distinction drawn by the religious institution is always between believers and nonbelievers—which is to say, between those who are believed to have the honor of being acceptable to the god and those who are believed not to have this honor. Thus, "when fully developed, [the god] was altogether exclusive with respect to outsiders, and in principle he accepted offerings and prayers only from the members of his group, or at least he was expected to act in this fashion" (1978a:413). In addition, of course, finer honorific distinctions are almost always drawn within the group of believers (Weber refers to "the inequality of religious charisma" [1946:338] and to differences among prophets, priests, and laypersons [see chapter 6])[25] and among nonbelievers— for example, between believers in gods of other groups presently allied with the god's group, believers in the gods of present non-allies (including enemies) of the god's group, and disbelievers in all gods.

Honor, of course, "may be connected with any quality shared by a plurality" (Weber 1978a:932)—which is to say, its origins are institutionally diffuse (see above)—but the linkage to the specifically religious institution is uniquely close: "Where the consequences [of status situations] have been realized to their full extent, the status group evolves into a closed caste. Status distinctions are then guaranteed not merely by conventions and laws, but also by religious sanctions" (Weber 1978a:933). Accordingly, "mystical salvation definitely means aristocracy; it is an aristocratic religiosity of redemption" (Weber 1946:357), and "behind all ethnic diversities is somehow naturally the notion of the [divinely] 'chosen people'" (Weber 1978a:391).

Now (as will be detailed in chapter 6) it is the analytical problem of how one historical instance of such religiously sanctified honor came to generate high personal morale in the pursuit of economic wealth is the central concern of Weber's most famous work, *The Protestant Ethic and the Spirit of Capitalism*. In his words, "We are interested . . . [in] the influence of those psychological sanctions which, originating in religious belief and the practice of religion, gave a direction to practical conduct and held the individual to it" (Weber 1958:97). Basically, Weber's conclusion rests on the following two points of general theoretical relevance. First, if it is true that behind ethnic distinctions among groups of people there lies the honor-laden notion of the "chosen *people*," it is also true that behind at least some cultural distinctions among individuals within such groups there lies the honor-laden notion of chosen *persons*. Second, just as the notion of being a chosen people can engender a high level of *group morale*— and this can have important consequences for the group's competition with other groups—so the notion of being a chosen person can engender a high level of *personal self-confidence* and can have important consequences for that individual's competition with other individuals.

Applying these claims to the particular case at hand, Weber argues that within the predominantly Protestant societies of Western Europe, any individual Protestant who came to be honored by his/her peers as having been individually chosen by the omniscient and omnipotent kingly Deity to eternal membership in His most favored Inner Court was apt to experience "above all an amazingly good, we may even say a pharisaically good, conscience in the acquisition of money, so long as it took place legally." When to this was added "the comforting assurance that the unequal distribution of the goods of this world was a special dispensation of Divine Providence," a person could "follow his pecuniary interests as he would" and feel not the least bit conscience-stricken for unbridled selfishness but, rather, transcendently self-righteous for "fulfilling a [God-given] duty" (Weber 1958:176–77).

To conclude: From the standpoint of the present theory, wealth, decision-making power, honor, and empirical knowledge are the four basic, societally generated, resources of individual human life, human society, and the human species. These four, in other words, are the principal payoffs of multiple individuals' having organized their collective abilities toward overcoming each separate individual's inabilities (as discussed at the end of chapter 2). These are the ends in pursuit of which the many individuals, and many subgroups, of human society cooperate, and these are also the most fundamental spoils for which they compete.

It should be noted, of course, that such spoils can be more or less easily transmuted into one another: Wealth can buy power, honor, and knowledge; power can direct the production and distribution of wealth, honor, and knowledge; honor can set the levels of group morale and personal self-confidence with which participants compete for wealth, power, and knowledge; and knowledge can help participants choose among alternative strategies in all these competitions. A major consequence of this mutual fungibility is that spoils won or lost in one institutional arena can strengthen or weaken a participant's competition in all the other arenas, thereby exacerbating what Merton calls the "Matthew effect" (see 1973:446; see also Michels 1958:105–6). This point will contribute in an important way to the discussion, in chapter 6, of Weber's view of relations between classes, status groups, and political parties.

Summary

This chapter has set forth an image of human society viewed cross-sectionally or "structurally." In this image, every society is at all times composed of three systems of institutions (in various stages of development, of course). These systems are here called participant-intake, participant-organizing, and participant-outlet. The participant-organizing institutions are the main focus of this book, and they are viewed as comprising functionally differentiated but interdependent economic, political, religious, and scientific components, whose distinctive products are specified as wealth, power, honor, and knowledge, respectively. The chapter made a special point of arguing that the scientific institution (unduly slighted by Weber himself and by all previous interpreters of his work) performs indispensable cognitive and conative functions in every human society but is incapable of performing cathectic (valuational) functions. The typical individual participant in human society genetically inherits some ultimate ends (values) of life (e.g., self-preservation) and is socialized, from infancy, to accept other such ends (e.g., duty). Then, insofar as s/he behaves rationally, the individual systematically compares, chooses among, and evaluates the anticipated and the actual success of alternative means to such ends by relying upon various combinations of eight types of rationality. On the other hand, insofar as s/he behaves nonrationally, the individual evokes an automatic or habitual—but in either case, singular and indissoluble—means-end pair. Typically, the acting individual employs some combination of rationalities and nonrationalities.

In this general manner, a motive is constructed within the individual's mind that then directs the individual's physiological body to act. The psychological motive plus the subsequent physiological act comprise "action" as Weber conceptualizes it.

Action has two main effects (in addition to its immediate back-effects on the mind and body that motivated and carried it out). One of these impacts directly on other human individuals (i.e., the actor's society) and the other impacts directly on "things" (the nonsocial universe—ecosystemic and artifactual) with which the subject is in contact. Both society and things act back on the subject's body, and also enter into his/her mental perception and evaluation of the results of his/her act.

Society is affected by the individual's several roles in the participant-intake, participant-organizing, and participant-outlet sets of institutions—especially the economic, political, religious, and scientific institutions. In turn, events in these institutions influence the individual's next mental assessment of means and ends, and also influence the individual's body by nurturing or impoverishing, restraining or facilitating, its next act.

And so it goes, through each individual's lifetime of such iterations, performed in complex interlockings and superimpositions, as the individual interacts with his/her fellows and with the nonsocial world in ways broadly ordered by a structure of society that could not exist without its individual constituents—who, in turn, could not exist without it.

4

EVOLUTION OF SOCIETY: DESCRIPTIVE MODEL

THE PRECEDING CHAPTER proposed a cross-sectional view of human society. This chapter and the two following chapters will propose longitudinal perspectives that permit the descriptive and explanatory analysis of change. The present chapter describes only nonrepetitive change that moves human society in a particular direction (i.e., "evolution"). Before introducing the main features of this image, however, some preliminary justification for using the term *evolution* in a theory called Weberian is appropriate.

First, consider Weber's own confusing remarks on this issue. On the one hand, he tells us that "sociology seeks to formulate . . . generalized uniformities of empirical process" (Weber 1978a:19) and "developmental sequences . . . can be constructed into ideal types" (Weber 1949:101, italics removed), and these comments seem to imply at least the possibility of such "generalized uniformities" and "developmental sequences" as they apply to human society as a whole. On the other hand, Weber never tells us what they might be. Instead, he claims that "the scheme of three uniformly distinct stages of hunting economy, pastoral economy, and agriculture, current in scientific discussion, is untenable" (Weber 1950:37); that the "three basic types of domination" whose conceptualization he himself originated—namely, traditional, charismatic, and rational legal—"cannot be placed into a simple evolutionary line: they in fact appear together in the most diverse combinations" (1978a:1133; see also 1949:51).[1]

Yet, in addition to making the explicit claim that "the monopolization of legitimate violence by the political-territorial association and its rational consociation into an institutional order is nothing primordial, but a product of evolution" (1978a:904–5), Weber also implies that an evolutionary line (though not a "simple" one) did characterize ancient societies, at least: "One thing is clear," he says, "there are certain stages of organization, and these were recapitulated by all the peoples of Antiquity from the Seine to the Euphrates among whom urban centres developed" (1976:69, italics removed).

What are we to make of these statements? Can Weber really want us to believe societal evolution ended with the emergence of a specialized political institution, or with the end of "antiquity," and that there has been no further evolution since then?

Consider, also, what some of his leading interpreters say about the applicability of the term evolutionary to Weber's work. Collins believes that "Weber's position might well be characterized as historicist, in the sense of seeing history as a concatenation of unique events and unrepeatable complexities" (1986a:35) and calls Weber's theory "nonevolutionary" (1988:20). Roth argues that "the main point about [Weber's] interpretive sociology was that we should try to understand the ideas and intentions of historical actors rather than search for 'scientific' laws of social evolution" (1979d:205). Turner et al. claim "Weber argued that there are no laws of historical development" (1989:175). Gross expresses a similarly categoric judgment: "Weber was clear that there [is] . . . no direction, no unfolding of temporal 'stages' on the way to some supposed end of history. . . . For Weber, reality was simply 'a vast chaotic stream of events, which flows away through time'" (1988:114). At first, Mommsen seems to agree: "It . . . appears impossible to view the essence of Max Weber's sociological theory as an evolutionistic reconstruction of past history" (1989:143), but then he says "it will have to be admitted that Weber's early writings on the social history of antiquity, on the origins of modern capitalism and on the city in ancient and medieval history broadly follow, if not always explicitly, an evolutionist scheme of some sort" (1989:158; for similar ambivalence, see Tenbruck 1980:333). Mommsen does not say of what sort.

Other interpreters, somewhat ambivalently, do allow for evolutionism in Weber's theory, but none of them specify its details. Parsons claims that although Weber "leaned" toward a "mosaic" theory of history rather than a "rigid evolutionary scheme," there is an "evolutionary element present in his process of rationalization" (1937:621), and later, "Weber's theoretical scheme is inherently evolutionary" (1971:43, see also 44). Andreski claims that "many of [Weber's] views imply the assumption of evolutionary sequences. . . . [Weber] guardedly postulated the existence of a universal trend in the history of human culture" (1984:54, 55, see also 115). Schluchter says, "Weber's sociology of religion contains . . . a rudimentary historical theory of the stages of rationalization" (1979a:21, but see 1979:148), and, later, "indeed [Weber's] sociology as a whole. . . . is a theory of cultural stages and directions" (1989:204).

Schluchter, however, makes two other assertions that provide illuminating contrasts with the view I shall take here. Schluchter says (1) "whoever speaks of development . . . has to think of change in terms of a final condition, in terms of which sub-phenomena realize stages or for whose realization they are conditions. In this sense, every developmental theory proceeds teleologically" (1980:40; see also Mommsen 1989:157, 159; Hennis 1988:171); and (2) Weber only "contrasts [the West's developmental history] with others for the sake of identifying its distinctiveness and its specific historical course" (1981:5, 175; also see Wrong 1970:47; and Andreski 1984:56).

Schluchter's first assertion is categorically rejected here. In my judgment, no image of any "final condition" is required in order to speak of development or evolution. One of Darwin's leading modern "bulldogs," Richard Dawkins, for example, devotes an entire monograph to the proposition that "natural selection, the blind, unconscious, automatic process which Darwin discovered . . . has no purpose in mind. . . . It has no vision, no foresight, no sight at all" (1987:5; see also Barrow 1991:222; Darling 1993:xiv). It is enough, when one refers to evolution, to perceive a persistent *direction* (e.g., toward species survival from one generation to the next, indefinitely)—and incidentally, it is not necessary to impute any moral value to such a direction (compare Schluchter 1989:43; and Hennis 1988:173). Schluchter's second assertion is belied by Weber's own remark that "in Western civilization, and in Western civilization only, cultural phenomena have appeared which . . . lie in a line of development having universal significance and value" (1958a:13, italics removed). Reading this, it would seem quite clear that Weber focuses on Western civilization because (rightly or wrongly) he believes it reveals something not merely about that civilization's own "specific historical course" but about the general historical course of human society (see also Habermas 1984:178–80).

In varying contrast with the views just cited, then, the present chapter will propose mainly a Weberian description of the path taken by human societal evolution. The chapter will claim this path is a universal one (although it is essential to note that the path has been trod at widely different speeds by different societies at different times and places)—because the essential constituents (individual humans) of all human societies are universal, and because their environment (the Earth) is for them, so far, also universal (see Tenbruck 1980:342). The chapter following this one will try to specify a Weberian explanation for this path.[2]

Societal evolution is here divided into four components that develop more or less simultaneously. The first component refers to the increasing institutional specialization of society, the second refers to the increasingly rational culture of society, the third refers to its increasing level of organizational scale, and the fourth refers to its increasing spatial extension and consolidation.

The Evolution of Institutional Specialization

As figure 5 and its accompanying discussion have suggested, the economic institution is here regarded as specialized for producing and distributing wealth (goods and services) among the individuals who participate in a society; the political institution is specialized for producing and distributing power among these individuals; the scientific institution is specialized for producing and distributing knowledge among them; and the religious institution is specialized for producing and distributing honor among them—although, once again, each production and distribution is spread more diffusely than its specialized institution.

Clearly, however, these institutional specializations have not existed at their present high levels from the beginning of human social history and prehistory. Indeed, their starting point seems almost certain to have been in a small institutionally undifferentiated society: "The free community of nomads, tenting, wandering, and herding together, which arose out of the need for security, lacked any special organs" (Weber 1978a:909; see also 905, 358–59, 411).[3] From this point of origin in what we may think of as a functionally symmetrical participant-organizing superinstitution, the internal differentiation of this superinstitution seems to have proceeded in two discrete breaks in its symmetry—driven mainly by population increase (see Marx and Engels 1947:20; Durkheim 1984:201; for a cosmological analog, see Gribbin 1986:337). The first, prehistoric, break occurred when the political and religious institutions of some societies jointly split off from the economic and scientific institutions. The second, early modern, break occurred when the political institution of some of those societies split off from the religious institution, and, more or less at the same time, the scientific institution separated from the economic institution. In these two steps, the participant-organizing institutions seem to have evolved toward increasingly differentiated (but persistently interdependent) functions.[4]

The following discussion traces the evolving differentiation in all six pairs of institutions: political-religious, political-economic, religious-economic, political-scientific, religious-scientific, and economic-scientific.

Political-Religious

Weber describes the political institution and the religious institution in almost identical terms when he calls the state "a compulsory organization with a territorial basis" and the church "a compulsory association" for which it is "normal . . . to strive for complete control on a territorial basis" (1978a:56). Similarly, if "a 'ruling organization' will be called 'political' insofar as its existence and order is continuously safeguarded . . . by the threat and application of physical force on the part of the administrative staff" (Weber 1978a:54), the same holds for religious organizations: "Every organization of salvation by a compulsory and universalist institution of grace feels responsible before God for the souls of everyone, or at least of all the men entrusted to it. Such an institution will therefore feel entitled, and in duty bound, to oppose with ruthless force any danger through misguidance in faith" (Weber 1946:336, italics removed).

This near-identity between the political and religious institutions, then, serves as basis for Weber's claiming that the political and religious institutions were very intimate in the earliest, prehistoric, times: "Originally there must have been a union of political and religious authority everywhere" (1976:78); and, again,

> every permanent political association had a special god who guaranteed the success of the political action of the group. When fully developed, this god was altogether exclusive with respect to outsiders, and in principle he accepted offering and prayers only from the members of his group, or at least he was expected to act in this fashion. . . . In general, political and military conquest also entailed the victory of the stronger god over the weaker god of the vanquished group. (Weber 1978a:413; see also 1951b:143–45)[5]

Relations between the political and religious institutions, however, evolved toward increasing autonomy on both sides (the separation of church and state) as the church grew more universalistic in its goals while the state remained particularistic:

> The consistent brotherly ethic of salvation religions has come into . . . sharp tension with the political orders of the world. . . . The gods of locality, tribe, and polity were only concerned with the interests of their respective associations. . . . The problem only arose when these barriers of locality, tribe, and polity were shattered by universalist religions, by a religion with a unified God of the entire world. And the problem arose in full strength only when this God was a God of "love." (Weber 1946:333)

And although "the subordination of the state in all ecclesiastically regulated spheres of life remains the real will of God . . . in a democracy where power is vested in the hands of elected deputies, the hierocracy can tolerate the 'separation of church and state.' . . . the resulting flexibility and freedom from state control may provide the hierocracy with so much power that it can overcome the loss of its formal privileges" (Weber 1978a:1195; see also Burns 1990).

Political-Economic

Regarding the change in the economic-political relation, Weber argues that in ancient times the latter institution dominated the former:
"Political . . . considerations determined ancient ideas on the subject
[of commerce]. Reasons of state, equality of citizens and autarky of
the *polis* were at the centre of these ideas" (1976:67). In general, then,
"ancient capitalism was based on politics, on the exploitation for
private profit of the political conquests of the imperialist city-state,
and when this source of profit disappeared capital formation ceased"
(Weber 1976:364). Proceeding to make the ancient-modern contrast
explicit, however, Weber adds that "whereas in Antiquity the policies of the polis necessarily set the pace for capitalism, today capitalism itself sets the pace for bureaucratization of the economy"
(1976:365).[6]
Weber also draws another "fundamental distinction in the lines of
development as between antiquity and medieval and modern times"
(1950:335) in the West—a distinction that centers on the city as the
primary arena in which the struggle of the political institution to
retain its control over the economic institution was manifested.[7]
Here, Weber argues that "in antiquity the freedom of the cities was
swept away by a bureaucratically organized world empire within
which there was no longer a place for political capitalism" (1950:335).
"Quite different," however, "was the fate of the city in the modern
era" (Weber 1950:336). The early modern cities, Weber says, "came
under the power of competing national states in a condition of perpetual struggle for power in peace or war. This competitive struggle
created the largest opportunities for modern western capitalism"
(1950:337)—a case, it would seem, of *tertius gaudens* (see Simmel
1950:154–62), wherein the independence of Western economic
capitalism was enhanced by the political competitions that raged
around it.

In a similar way, although "the powers-that-be in a polity are
politically and economically interested in the existence of large home
factories for war engines," Weber immediately points out that "this
interest compels them to allow these factories to provide the whole
world with their products, political opponents included"
(1978a:918). Thus, even in those industries on which the state is most

dependent for its dearest activity, the modern economy manifests increasing autonomy from the state.[8]

Religious-Economic

Weber characterizes the religious-economy relation as having evolved from religious domination of the economy toward increasing autonomy for the latter. Thus, noting that "every one of the great religious systems . . . has placed, or has seemed to place [particular difficulties] in the way of the modern economy," Weber directs his study of the religion of India toward discovering "the manner in which Indian religion, as one factor among many, may have prevented capitalistic development (in the occidental sense)." Weber concludes that the long-established, religion-based Indian caste system blocked "technological change and occupational mobility, which from the point of view of caste were objectionable and ritually dangerous" (1958b:112, 4, 104).

In the West, however, Weber claims the religious institution exerted a liberating rather than a restricting influence on the economic institution, for "when ethical prophecies have broken through the stereotyped magical or ritual norms, a sudden or a gradual revolution may take place, even in the daily order of human living, and particularly in the realm of economics" (1978a:577). As already noted, chapter 6 will examine Weber's special study of this "revolution" (*The Protestant Ethic and the Spirit of Capitalism*) more closely, but meantime here is Weber's summary remark on the economic institution's modern tendencies toward autonomy from religious restrictions: "The more the world of the modern capitalist economy follows its own immanent laws, the less accessible it is to any imaginable relationship with a religious ethic of brotherliness" (1946:331).

Political-Scientific

Weber sees the science-politics relation as having shifted from the dominance of politics over science toward increasing autonomy for science. Social science, for example, "first arose in connection with practical considerations. Its most immediate and often sole purpose was the attainment of value-judgments concerning measures of State economic policy. . . . [but it] has now become known how this situation was gradually modified" (Weber 1949:51, italics removed), such that the modern scientific institution has become greatly distanced from the modern Western political institution. Weber epitomizes this distancing as follows:

> To take a practical political stand is one thing, and to analyze political structures and party positions is another. When speaking in a political meeting about democracy, one does not hide one's personal standpoint; indeed, to come out clearly and take a stand is one's damned duty. The words one uses in such a meeting are not means of scientific analysis but means of canvassing votes and winning over others. . . . It would be an outrage, however, to use words in this fashion in a lecture or in the lecture-room. (1946:145)

Religious-Scientific

In Weber's view, the science-religion relation has moved from the dominance of religion over science toward increasing autonomy for science ("Ethical religiosity has appealed to rational knowledge [but the latter] has followed its own autonomous and innerworldly norms" [1946:355]). The early stage is indicated when Weber says of the feudal era that "the priesthood and strict adherence to ritual prescriptions serve as means of magical control over nature, especially as a defense against demons" (1978a:1179) and a later, transitional, stage is indicated when he says that "useful and naturalist knowledge, especially empirical knowledge of natural sciences, geographical orientation as well as the sober clarity of a realist mind and specialized expert knowledge were first cultivated as planned educational needs by Puritans. . . . Such knowledge was the only avenue to knowledge of God's glory and the providence embodied in His creation" (1951b:246–47; see also 1946:142).

But Weber is most emphatic, and repeatedly so, when asserting the recently emerging separation of church and science: "Who— aside from certain big children who are indeed to be found in the natural sciences—still believes that the findings of [natural science] could teach us anything about the meaning of the world? . . . If these natural sciences lead to anything in this way, they are apt to make the belief that there is such a thing as the 'meaning' of the universe die out at its very roots" (1946:142, italics removed; see also 350–51). "The tension between the value-spheres of 'science' and the sphere of 'the holy' is unbridgeable," Weber says, for "science . . . does not know of the 'miracle' and the 'revelation,'" and "there is absolutely no 'unbroken' religion working as a vital force which is not compelled at some point to demand . . . the 'sacrifice of the intellect.'" Thus "the cosmos of natural causality and the postulated cosmos of ethical, compensatory causality have stood in irreconcilable opposition" (Weber 1946:154, italics removed; 147, 352, 355; see also Wuthnow 1993b:296–97).

Economic-Scientific

Weber argues that the economy-science relation has evolved from early dominance by the economy toward a later dependence of the economy on science, and recently an increasing autonomy of science.

Thus, whereas "economic premiums . . . were necessary for the transitions from empirical to rational [scientific] technology," and "economic and technological interests of the Northern European economy . . . assisted intellectual forces in transferring the [practice of the controlled] experiment [from the arts] to the natural sciences" (1951b:151), once this transfer was made, Western capitalism became "dependent on the peculiarities of modern science"—although it is also true that "the development of these sciences and of the techniques resting upon them [still] receives important stimulation from these capitalistic interests in its practical economic application" (1958a:24). More characteristically, however, nowadays, "in the field of science only he who is devoted solely to the work at hand has 'personality'. . . . an inner devotion to the task, and that alone, should lift the scientist to the height and dignity of the subject he pretends to serve" (Weber 1946:137, italics removed).

In summary on the evolution of institutional specialization, then, it seems fair to say that to the more commonplace notion of the "separation of church and state" (the rendering "unto Caesar the things that are Caesar's; and unto God the things which are God's") the present Weberian theory adds the claim that this is but one of six such evolving institutional separations.[9] The latter include the separations of market and state, market and church, science and state, science and church, and market and science—as well as church and state. Nowadays (as already noted here) "we are placed," Weber says, "into various life-spheres, each of which is governed by different laws" (1946:123), whereas in the prehistoric, functionally symmetrical and control-integrated, superinstitution, all these life-spheres were but one sphere, governed by only one law.[10]

Interinstitutional Integration

Now obviously, centrifugal interinstitutional specialization within a given society can only be sustained if it is counterbalanced by some centripetal interinstitutional integration.

Marx and Engels propose that such integration can be accomplished in only one way—namely, by the domination of the economic institution over all others. Thus, "The sum total of [the] relations of production constitutes the economic structure of society, the real foundation, on which rises a legal and political superstructure and to which correspond definite forms of social consciousness" (1969:vol. 1, 503; see also 1969:vol. 3, 133). The present Weberian theory, as noted in chapter 3, allows for the dominance of any one, and any combination, of the four participant-organizing institutions (also see the discussion of equifinality in appendix A). Perhaps needless to add, the theory also allows for variation in that dominance from society to society and from time to time within each society. On this, Weber tells us "The explanation of everything by economic causes alone is never exhaustive in any sense whatsoever in any sphere of cultural phenomena, not even in the 'economic' sphere itself" (1949:71, italics removed), and "groups that are not somehow economically determined are extremely rare. However, the degree of this influence varies widely and, above all, the economic determination of social action is ambiguous—contrary to the assumption of so-called historical materialism. . . . conversely, the economy is usually also influenced by the autonomous structure of social action within which it exists" (1978a:341; see also 1949:65–66).

As a result of his allowing such wide variability in interinstitutional causal dominance, Weber compels us to look elsewhere for a consistent source of interinstitutional integration. Of course, he recognizes such integration as an important problem—noting that "there is a growing demand that the world and the total pattern of life be subject to an order that is significant and meaningful" and adding that "the conflict of this requirement of meaningfulness with the empirical realities of the world and its institutions and with the possibilities of conducting one's life in the empirical world are responsible for the intellectual's characteristic flight from the world" (Weber 1978a:506)—but he does not seem to offer an explicit solution to the problem of interinstitutional integration. I argue that such a solution is, nevertheless, close at hand in his work.

Common Organizational Ways and Means

In the first place, of course, there is the continuous exchange of each institution's specialty product for all the other institutions' specialty products (i.e., the "exchange of services" to which Durkheim refers [1984:21]—for example, the economic institution's provision of wealth as input to all the other institutions, and their provision to it of decision-making power, empirical knowledge, and honor). In addition, however, there is the convergence of all four participant-organizing institutions of a given society on the same organizational ways, and the same organizational means.

I have in mind bureaucracy and machinery (see chapter 3). The bureaucratic way of systematizing rights and responsibilities in each institution increasingly renders all subjects/clients of all the bureaucracies in a society roughly equal, all low-ranking officials there roughly equal, all middle-ranking officials there roughly equal, and all high-ranking officials there roughly equal. This implies the emergence of a single metric for appraising, and comparing, one's status in all the participant-organizing institutions—economic, political, religious, and scientific (see Broom 1959).[11]

Machine technology, too (including its general operating principles and very often the specific machines themselves—from paper and pencils to automobiles and highways, airplanes, telephones, television, and computers—and all their shared energy-producing and waste-removing infrastructures), grows increasingly uniform across all the participant-organizing institutions of all human societies. Such uniformity establishes a single means for carrying out individuals' rights, duties, and options in all the participant-organizing institutions.

The result is that an individual participant in any highly bureaucratized and highly mechanized society can think and act as though carrying out a single (four-dimensional) role, and pursuing a single (four-dimensional) career, within a single (four-dimensional) institutional setting. The participant-organizing institutions in such a society, therefore, seem likely to be held together not only by the exchanges mentioned earlier but also by the fact that they all share the same individual participants employing the same bureaucratic status metric and the same machine technology.

But if one asks what beliefs, values, and behavior predispositions such participants must have in order to do this, the answer brings us to another powerfully integrative factor—namely, culture, or rather the cultural structure (see Wallace 1986; 1988:35–37) shared at a given moment across all four participant-organizing institutions of a given society.

The Evolution of Societal Culture

Recalling, once again, Weber's bedrock presupposition that "we are *cultural beings*, endowed with the capacity and the will to take a deliberate attitude toward the world and to lend it significance" (1949:81), one is not surprised to see him emphasize the relative independence of such attitudes from physical conditions: "Religious ideas . . . simply cannot be deduced from economic circumstances. They . . . contain a law of development and a compelling force all their own" (1958a:277–78).[12] To this we may add two points. First, not only religious ideas but also economic, political, and scientific ideas seem to have such force and development. Second, although the specific content of these institutionally specific ideas will vary greatly ("The cultural problems which move men form themselves ever anew and in different colors, and the boundaries of that area in the infinite stream of concrete events which acquires meaning and significance for us . . . are constantly subject to change" [Weber 1949:84]), at any given moment they are likely to be integrated, within a given society, in a particular way (see also Berger and Luckmann 1967:92).

In the theory being set forth here, these ways of integrating institutional subcultures are viewed as having themselves evolved (at widely different speeds from one society to another and from one time period to another), and that evolution has been toward greater freedom of conscious choice. By specifying this direction, I intend to capture the simple but vastly significant fact that virtually all participants in modern societies—whether industrialized or not—can make all the choices prehistoric humans could make, plus some usually large number of choices they could not make.

The first stage in this evolution is dominated by what Weber calls *natural norms;* here nonrational instinct prevails and choice is therefore at an absolute minimum. The second stage is dominated by socially generated *tradition;* here nonrational habit prevails but choice is incipient by virtue of that habit being socially learned and transmitted—and variable from one society to the next. The third stage is dominated by *rational legality,* in which (according to the definition of rationality set forth in chapter 2) the prevalence of consciously rule-guided comparison and choice reaches high levels, for both societies and their individual participants.[13]

Natural Norms

Although he argues that "the beginnings of actual regularity and 'usage' are shrouded in darkness everywhere" and that "we have no access . . . to the 'subjective' experiences of the first *Homo sapiens*" (1978a:333, 321), Weber nevertheless speculates that "it is not due to the assumed binding force of some rule or norm that the conduct of primitive man manifests certain external factual regularities, especially in his relation to his fellows. On the contrary, those organically conditioned regularities which we have to accept as psychophysical reality, are primary" (1978a:321) and that human sociation first arose from "the instinctive habituation of a pattern of conduct which was 'adapted' to given necessities. At least initially, this pattern of conduct was neither conditioned nor changed by an enacted norm" (1978a:333). Obviously, the key concept here is "instinct," and the implicit dominance of *Zweckrationalität* and affectual nonrationality (see chapter 2) seems clear.

Once these inborn definitions and motivations of the individual are fully engaged, Weber says, "It is from them that the concept of 'natural norms' arises" (1978a:321).

Tradition

The present model of societal evolution, because it is probabilistic (see appendix A), does not require that natural norms ever be transcended. Conceivably, a society may remain permanently in the natural norms stage, or, indeed, permanently in any other stage. And it is also essential to emphasize that the transition from one stage to another is an addition rather than a substitution (for example, households continue to exist after modern nations have been formed, and natural norms still function even after modern rational legality has been established). Thus, "the inner orientation toward [natural norms] . . . can be observed even today by everyone in his daily experiences" (Weber 1978a:321; see also 25).

But if and when the transition to the dominance of tradition culture does occur (under impulse from forces discussed in the next chapter), the general characteristics of the latter are everywhere the same—although its phenotypes have wide variability: "The psychological 'adjustment' arising from habituation to an action causes conduct that in the beginning constituted plain habit later to be experienced as binding; then, with the awareness of the diffusion of such conduct among a plurality of individuals, it comes to be incorporated as 'consensus' into people's semi- or wholly conscious 'expectations' as to the meaningfully corresponding conduct of others" (Weber 1978a:754). Therefore, "authority will be called traditional if legitimacy is claimed for it and believed in by virtue of the sanctity of age-old rules and powers. . . . Rules which in fact are innovations can be legitimized only by the claim that they have been 'valid of yore,' but have only now been recognized by means of 'Wisdom'" (Weber 1978a:226, 227). And tradition culture always has the effect of placing "serious obstacles in the way of formally rational regulations, which can be depended upon to remain . . . calculable in their economic implications and exploitability" (Weber 1978a:239). If and when these obstacles are overcome, the next stage is typically that of rational legality (see Goody's discussion of the role of alphabetic writing in accomplishing this transition; especially 1977:36–51).

Rational Legality

In defining *legal,* Weber says that "so far as the agreement underlying the [legal] order is not unanimous . . . the order is actually imposed upon the minority" (1978a:37)—that is, imposed through the threat and application of physical force (see chapter 3)—but he also argues that the cultural perception of that imposition as "legitimate" and therefore deserving voluntary obedience is also involved. In this way, Weber implicates both the positive motivation of *Wertrationalität* (i.e., adherence to "duty, honor, [etc.]"), and the negative motivation of *Zweckrationalität* (i.e., "expediency" [Weber 1978a:37] in avoiding the physical pain and deprivation that constitutes enforcement).

As a result, we have "the ever-increasing integration of all individuals and all fact-situations . . . [under the principle of] formal 'legal equality'" (Weber 1978a:698; see Huff 1989:52–53). The essence of that "formal 'legal equality'" is a shared rational orientation toward a "consistent system of abstract rules" governing comparison and choice among alternative means—and the consistency is such that "the typical person in authority, the 'superior,' is himself subject to [that] impersonal order" (Weber 1978a:217; see Denny 1991:75–76).

Now in every such society there seems bound to be a competition of some kind among different groups of individuals striving to install and maintain different systems of abstract rules (laws) as dominant. Such groups of individuals Weber calls political "parties" (see

1978a:284–85). One outstanding feature of the stage of rational legality, then, is the emergence of parties that compete with each other for the power to determine and enforce the rules governing rational comparisons and choices (and also rules establishing the purview of traditional and affectual nonrationality) by individuals in their society. Such parties, Weber says, "may represent interests determined through class situation or status situation. . . . But they need be neither purely class nor purely status parties; in fact they are most likely to be mixed types" (Weber 1978a:938). (More on this in chapter 6.)

Two other key features of rational legality have already been introduced in chapter 3. First, the "continued exercise of . . . domination" by any such party rests on "modern bureaucratic administration," which "is fully developed . . . only in the modern state, and in the private economy only in the most advanced institutions of capitalism" (Weber 1978a:954, 956). And second, such administration is "bound to the technical and economic conditions of machine production" (Weber 1958a:181). Now in extreme cases, bureaucratic administration and machine technology are likely to produce what chapter 2 called *end-anomie*—loss of effective ideas about why to live: "The Puritan wanted to work in a calling; we are forced to do so. . . . the modern economic order. . . . is now bound to the technical and economic conditions of machine production which to-day determine the lives of all the individuals who are born into this mechanism, not only those directly concerned with economic acquisition, with irresistible force" (1958a:181).

But if end-anomie can afflict the modern economic institution by "forcing" us to work in what was once a calling, it seems reasonable to think that it can afflict all the other participant-organizing institutions as well. Indeed, Weber warns of a society dominated by bureaucrats "who need 'order' and nothing but order, who are so totally adjusted to it that they become nervous and cowardly if this order falters for a moment" (quoted in Beetham 1985:65).

Thus, just as in the economic institution the individual may become forced to work in what was once a calling, in the political institution the individual may become forced to profess allegiance to a particular party or leader or ideology. Similarly, in the religious institution the individual may become forced to confess a particular faith, prophet, or god; and in the scientific institution the individual may become forced to adopt a particular theory or methodology. In short, the modern economic institution need not be regarded as having a monopoly on end-anomie or "iron cages." The condition seems potentially general among all the participant-organizing institutions in the rational legality stage of cultural evolution. Chapter 7 will consider some possible countermeasures.

We turn next to the third component of societal evolution—namely, organizational scale—and then to the evolution of spatial extension and consolidation.

The Evolution of Organizational Scale

Weber suggests that the evolution of organizational scale has proceeded in more or less discrete steps. Thus (as noted at the beginning of this chapter), "one thing is clear: there are certain stages of organization, and these were recapitulated by all the peoples in Antiquity from the Seine to the Euphrates among whom urban centers developed"; in the first stage, "household and village [were] the centres of economic life," but "later ties based upon blood developed," and "once a king emerged. . . . the formation of larger realms became possible. . . . This was the origin of nearly all ancient 'states'" (Weber 1976:69, 70, italics removed; 71).

We may therefore hypothesize that, during the evolution of a society's organizational scale, a relatively sudden transition (a *punctuation, pulse,* or *step,* often preceded by a *crisis*—see Tilly 1975b:608–611) marks the aggregation of previously separated households and neighborhoods ("the neighborhood of households settled close to one another") into communities ("the neighborhood is the natural basis of the local community . . . by virtue of political action comprising a multitude of neighborhoods"). In a later transition, the "kin group" (which cuts across neighborhoods and sometimes also households) emerges ("the kin group presupposes the existence of others within a larger community" and "with the kin group begins inheritance outside the household" [Weber 1978a:361, italics removed; 363, 365]). Later still, kin groups become aggregated into an "ethnic group"—and eventually "the concept of the 'ethnic group' . . . [corresponds to] the nation" (Weber 1978a:395, italics removed).

Despite Weber's declaration that "the ultimate goal of our science must remain that of co-operating in the political education of our nation" (1989b:207), he hints at higher levels of organizational scale than the nation when he claims that "the international division of labour is a normal corollary of expanding capitalism," that "the rising significance of fixed capital will gradually bring about a situation in leading nations whereby interest in stabilization of mutual trade relations will gain a constantly increasing force" (1989c:214, 213), and that "barriers of locality, tribe, and polity were shattered by universalist religions, by a religion with a unified God of the entire world" [1946:333]). Now although Weber rejects the full implications of these hints (as we shall see), nevertheless, to Eisenstadt's claim that Weber's "most general concern . . . was with what may be called . . . the processes of institution building, social transformation, and cultural creativity" (1968:xvi) it seems clear that we must add at least one other process—namely, that of building organizational scale.

But it also seems clear that the organizational scale of a society is closely related to its spatial extension and consolidation (the fourth and final component of societal evolution to be discussed here). This is so because (1) the higher the organizational scale of a society the larger its population must be, and the larger its population, the more spatially extensive it must be; and (2) given that the Earth is a closed sphere—less than 30 percent of whose surface is more or less readily habitable by humans—continued increase of population size and organizational scale in territorially separate societies must eventually lead to the consolidation of such societies. Unfortunately, Weber has very little to say about these issues, crucial though they are for the future of our species, and so it will be necessary in what follows to attempt to strengthen his work on this score.

The Evolution of Spatial Extension and Consolidation

Weber, of course, is not completely blind to the spatial extension and consolidation of human society, but he died before the crucial discoveries were made regarding the African origin of Homo sapiens and its dispersion to the rest of the world (see below) and he also seems to have been unwilling to develop systematically a level of organizational scale beyond that of nations.

Thus, completely ignoring the problem of human origins, Weber argues as follows: Inasmuch as the amount of humanly habitable land is presently fixed, and inasmuch as the nation level is the ultimate achievable level, the ongoing increase in world population necessitates an ongoing struggle among such nations to conquer and defend territory for their populations:

> The deadly seriousness of the population problem . . . prevents us from imagining that peace and happiness lie hidden in the lap of the future, it prevents us from believing that elbowroom in this earthly existence can be won in any other way than through the hard struggle of human beings with each other. . . . Our successors will not hold us responsible before history for the kind of economic organization we hand over to them, but rather for the amount of elbow-room we conquer for them in the world. . . . [Thus, the] first positive political task [that] began to come on the nation's horizon, after the wars of unification [was] . . . overseas expansion. (1989b:198, 205)

It may therefore be said that where Malthus proposes universal checks (preventive and positive) on worldwide population growth, Weber proposes localized insulation against such growth— somewhat in the way the inert walls of a thermos bottle provide (temporary) insulation against a rising outside temperature.[14]

Weber considers, and rejects, the possibility of a level of organizational scale that is more inclusive than nations: "Has [the] situation perhaps changed since economic development began to create an all-embracing economic community of nations, going beyond national boundaries? We know that this is not the case: the struggle has taken on other forms" (1989b:198, italics removed). In these new forms, he says, the struggle penetrates and divides each nation and can divide the will of each individual citizen: "The world-wide economic community . . . aggravates rather than mitigates the struggle for the maintenance of one's own culture, because it calls forth in the very bosom of the nation material interests opposed to the nation's future, and throws them into the ring in allegiance with the nation's enemies." Weber fully expects this situation to continue, without essential change, indefinitely. "We do not have peace and human happiness to bequeath to our posterity," he says, "but rather the eternal struggle for the maintenance and improvement by careful cultivation of our national character" (1989b:198, italics removed).

At this point, the present theory unequivocally parts company with Weber. One important basis for this parting lies in our different views of population growth. Weber regards such growth as a major influence on societal evolution in the present and future, but a minor one in the past. Thus, whereas he claims "it is . . . the increase of population. . . . which will in the future intensify the struggle for existence," he asserts that "it is a widespread error that the increase of population is to be included as a really crucial agent in the [past] evolution of western capitalism"—although he immediately admits that "the growth of population in Europe did indeed favor the development of capitalism, to the extent that in a small population the system would have been unable to secure the necessary labor force, but in itself it never called forth that development" (Weber 1950:352).

By contrast, the present theory regards population growth as a persistently major objective influence (i.e., an influence acting independently of how various actors subjectively perceive and value, or devalue, it) on the evolution of human society. The influence of this factor seems especially strong in driving the spatial extension and consolidation of human society. This evolution will be conceptualized here as having taken place (and as still taking place) in three broad stages: (1) population dispersion followed by the differentiation of local societies from each other, (2) proliferating contacts among these different societies, and (3) their eventual consolidation into a single global society.

Population Dispersion

Virtually all modern paleoanthropologists agree that the taxonomic family called Hominids originated in a relatively small locale— somewhere in a narrow strip of east Africa that ranges from the Afar Depression bordering the southwestern end of the Red Sea, down through the Great Rift Valley, into southern Africa—and that the genus called *Homo* (and at least the first two if not all three of its successively emergent species—*habilis, erectus, and sapiens*), originated there too.[15]

There seems to be general agreement on an answer to *why*, from this single locus of origin, the human species extended its habitat beyond Africa: the ecosystem changed. Roberts, for example, argues that

> the global climate for [the last 1.7 million years] indicates intensified glacial-interglacial cycles after 0.8–0.9 Mya. . . . This cyclic alternation between savanna, forest and desert presented early hominids with a number of choices. . . . [one of which was] the possibility of moving beyond the limits of the tropics altogether, into habitats previously unoccupied by human populations. . . . The Sahara would have acted in this regard as a pump, sucking in population during wetter savanna phases and forcing it out towards the Mediterranean as dessication subsequently set in. . . . In these extra-tropical environments *Homo erectus* . . . had to cope with the continual and extreme environmental fluctuations which characterized the European Middle and Upper Pleistocene. . . . Consequently, new economic strategies had to be devised every time mixed deciduous woodland replaced steppe-tundra or vice-versa. Such environmental pressures must have . . . helped speed the pace of cultural development. (1984:45–46; see also Fagan 1990:66–73)

Turner supplements Roberts's specification of nonliving ecosystem variables (i.e., climate) with one that emphasizes the role of living components of that ecosystem:

> Man . . . dispersed into temperate Eurasia at a time when other large predators [in particular, the lion, leopard, and spotted hyaena], originating in a similar area of the world, were also finding conditions there to their advantage. . . . man as a facultative carnivore clearly became a member of the Middle Pleistocene large-predator community in temperate Eurasia and part of the predator-prey system. . . . The total food requirement of these carnivores was such that man . . . competed for a selection from an already exploited range of species. (1984:199; see also Fagan 1990:18–19)

There is less agreement on *how* this extension of habitat occurred. Indeed, there are currently two contending hypotheses on this question.[16] Both hypotheses agree, however, that slow population migrations out of east Africa progressively established more or less permanent human habitations in one land basin after another—spreading into northern, western, and southern Africa, and, via the northern extension of the Great Rift (across the Sinai peninsula and up through the Jordan River valley), into the Near East and Eurasia, then into Japan and Australia, and finally into the Americas (see Finney and Jones 1985:15–21; Tanner 1985:222–26; Schwartz 1985; Klein 1989:406, 388, 395, 391; Marshall 1990; Fagan 1990:90, 141, 201–3). Eventually in one way or another, then, *Homo sapiens* colonized all the major (and most of the minor) landmasses of the Earth except Antarctica—at first in the form of relatively small, scattered, bands.

This vast human diaspora seems to have resulted in two achievements of cardinal importance for the survival of the species as a whole: first, it reduced the species' physical liability to extinction from localized causes such as floods, droughts, earthquakes, volcanic eruptions, plagues, pestilences, and the like; and second, by exposing the species to a wider habitat containing a variety of life conditions, it resulted in drastically increasing the species' store of sociocultural and biogenetic adaptations to different environmental demands (see Diamond 1992:218; Dawkins 1987:267; Leakey and Lewin 1992:57, 85, 213).

These achievements were not without cost, however, for they also resulted in dividing the species into many relatively isolated subpopulations that could, and often did, become murderously hostile whenever they met in conditions in which some scarce life resource could be monopolized. It is, of course, impossible to know much about such early human subpopulations, but Diamond offers some insight into how isolated they might have been when he quotes a New Guinea highlander as saying that before 1930 "we had not seen far places. We knew only this side of the mountains. And we thought we were the only living people" (1992:229). Diamond also offers some insight into how many they might have been prior to their neolithic consolidations: "New Guinea, with less than one-tenth of Europe's area and less than one-hundredth of its population, has about a thousand languages, many of them unrelated to any other known language in New Guinea or elsewhere" (1992:232).[17]

How did such massive differentiation come about? The answer

seems to be that isolation of any kind normally produces differentiation among human groups (see Leakey and Lewin 1992:57, 84–85).
Moreover, the differentiation seems to occur not all at once, but in
three broad steps. General *sociocultural* differentiation among the
groups emerges first—including differences in status systems and
symbol systems (see Sherif and Sherif 1953:238–89; Smith and
Layton 1987)—as each group responds, more or less independently
of the others, to its own internal dynamics and to its own external
conditions. With the passing of centuries of continued relative isolation, a particular kind of sociocultural differentiation among the
subpopulations—called *ethnic* differentiation—is apt to develop.
Then, as millennia of further isolation pass, various biogenetic
differentiations—some of which are called *racial*, are apt to be added
to the two preceding differentiations.[18] The result is that at any given
moment in the later history of our species, we can find many sociocultural groups within each ethnic group, and many ethnic groups
within each racial group—although none of these differences is ever
sharp and clear when examined closely (see Kottack 1987:43–50;
Molnar 1992:25).[19]

Consolidation Begins

But driven by that almost explosive growth in technological and
organizational capacity called the Neolithic revolution, and its powerful boosts to population size, mobility, and adaptability, large-scale
contact and competition among human subpopulations did start up
some ten thousand years ago: "With the domestication of plants and
animals. . . . [there began] a radically new phase of human history. . . . [in which the] grain-centered agriculture of the Middle East
provided the basis for the first civilized societies" (McNeill 1963:10,
11).[20] As McNeill implies here, however, the growth in technological
and organizational capacity mentioned above did not take place
everywhere at the same moment, to the same extent, or with the
same speed; some human subpopulations drew significantly ahead
of others in these respects.

Why was this the case? "Why was the ancient rate of technological
and political development fastest in Eurasia, slower in the Americas

(and in Africa south of the Sahara), and slowest in Australia?" (Diamond 1992:235). To this question, Diamond's own answer seems especially persuasive: The differences, he says, stemmed "ultimately from continental differences in *geography*" (1992:237, italics added). That is to say, the differences went with the territories on which different groups happened to settle. The differences were, in this sense, the luck of the draw—in the same way that the current differences between countries that do produce oil and countries that do not produce oil is a matter of geographical luck. Diamond continues: "Continental differences in level of civilization arose from geography's effect on the development of our cultural hallmarks, not from human genetics. Continents differed in the resources of which civilization depended—especially in the wild animal and plant species that proved useful for domestication. Continents also differed in the ease with which domesticated species could spread from one area to another." In addition, "Dense populations [resulting from the agriculture that depended on such domestications] were prerequisite to the rise of centralized states. Dense populations also promoted the evolution of infectious diseases, to which exposed populations then evolved some resistance but other populations didn't." "All these factors," Diamond concludes, "determined who colonized and conquered whom" (1992:236, 237).

Thus, war and conquest—initially based on such fortuitous differences in geographical resources—came to play pivotal roles in the first Neolithic stirrings, in the Middle East, of human consolidation (and note that "there is no evidence of frequent violence or warfare in human prehistory until after about ten thousand years ago, when humans began to practice food production—the leading edge of agriculture" [Leakey and Lewin 1992:xviii, see also 233]). This was so, it seems, largely because for the first time there were significantly large stores of collected food, as well as large expanses of arable land and large aggregates of laborers, to be conquered, and the domestication of the horse made such war and conquest feasible at some distance from home (see Diamond 1992:240; Leakey and Lewin 1992:234). Accordingly, "Sumerian and Egyptian civilizations, the earliest on record, both began with conquest" (McNeill 1985:7–8; see also Childe 1942:88, 141–43, 154–55), and "unprecedented patterns of extended territorial control were to be found in Mesopotamia as a result of the Akkadian conquests and in the Aztec realm on the eve of its rapid destruction by the Spaniards" (Adams 1966:153; see also Mann 1986:174).[21]

Ethnicity, Political Action, Inbreeding, and Race

Under such conditions of growing contact among what had long been relatively isolated human societies, subjective conceptions generally referred to as 'ethnicity' began to play an increasingly important role. As Weber puts it, "When groups of people that had previously lived in complete or partial isolation from each other . . . came to live side by side. . . . the obvious contrast usually involves, on both sides, the idea of blood disaffinity, regardless of the objective state of affairs" (1978a:392). And note Weber's claim here that the contrast lies in the "idea" of blood disaffinity, not in objective blood disaffinity. Thus, he says, "We shall call 'ethnic groups' those human groups that entertain a subjective belief in their common descent because of similarities of physical type or of customs or both, or because of memories of colonization and migration. . . . it does not matter whether or not an objective blood relationship exists. Ethnic membership differs from the kinship group precisely by being a *presumed* identity" (Weber 1978a:389, italics added).

Weber is making a characteristic ("we are cultural beings, endowed with the capacity and the will to take a deliberate attitude towards the world") point here: it does not matter whether an objective blood relationship exists; what matters is whether such a relationship is subjectively "presumed" to exist. *Ethnicity* ("ethnic membership"), therefore, is here defined as a shared subjective presumption of common ancestry. Note that *any* shared subjective presumption of common ancestry can qualify, regardless of the observable (and often easily counterfeitable) markers that may be used in support of that presumption.[22] At a minimum, one or more *behavioral* features (including language, dress, religion, dietary and other esthetic preferences, general social deportment, etc.) are used in determining ethnicity in sociocultural relations.[23] But other markers may also be used. Sociocultural *race* may be defined, then, as a particular kind of ethnicity (that is, a particular kind of shared subjective presumption of common ancestry)—one that usually relies on *anatomical* markers (including skin color, hair texture, eye, nose and mouth shape, etc.).

This definition of sociocultural race, resting on subjective presumptions made by the participating individuals (usually collectively, of course) is to be distinguished from definitions of race that rest on objective criteria—that is, criteria observable through genetic analyses—and the distinction is an important one. According to objective criteria, such as Molnar implies when he says that "the term race [means] a group . . . of breeding populations sharing a number of traits" (1992:31), any and all living things (not only humans) may be divided into races—so there can be objective races (sometimes also called *types, strains,* or *breeds*) of wheat, corn, dogs, cats, and so on, as well as of humans.

By contrast, the concept of *sociocultural* race pertains only to humans because its criteria are entirely subjective rather than objective. That is to say, a person's sociocultural race is what people (including the person him/herself) think it is—and that subjective judgment may have little or nothing to do with the person's objective race. The fact that it is the former and not the latter that determines how people react to the person and how s/he reacts to them justifies calling this sense of the term *race* sociocultural rather than biogenetic.[24]

Now different individuals' shared presumptions of their distinctive "common descent" (whether ethnic, or racial, or both) typically entails a collective attribution of special honor or charisma (see chapter 5) to themselves and their group—an attribution that is usually supported and enhanced by their religious faith. Thus Weber tells us that "the belief in ethnic affinity. . . . [concerns] one's conception of what is correct and proper and, above all, of what affects the individual's sense of honor and dignity. . . . The conviction of the excellence of one's own customs and the inferiority of alien ones [is] a conviction which sustains the sense of ethnic honor," and, most important, "behind all ethnic diversities there is somehow naturally the notion of the 'chosen people'" (1978:391).[25] From a group's belief in its being "chosen" and thus specially honored, Weber says, both joint political action, and joint religious beliefs are apt to follow. Thus, (1) "in practice . . . tribal consciousness usually has a political meaning: in case of military danger or opportunity it easily provides the basis for joint political action" (1978a:394) and (2) we recall that "every permanent political association had a special god who guaranteed the success of the political action of the group. When fully developed, this god . . . accepted offerings and prayers only from the members of his group" (1978a:413).

To this, however, it is essential to add that the reverse causal direction is no less important: "All history shows how easily political action can give rise to the belief in blood relationship," and "the ritual regulation of life, as determined by shared religious feelings, everywhere are conducive to feelings of ethnic affinity" (Weber 1978a:393, 390). Belief in common descent, then, can generate joint political and religious behavior; and also joint political and religious behavior can generate belief in common descent. The result is that each side of the relationship enhances the other, and both together strongly enhance in-group marriage and the restriction of social inheritance to lines of presumed "blood" relationship.[26]

In this way, a powerfully self-perpetuating circle is closed: ethnic consciousness leads to joint political and religious behavior; joint political and religious behavior leads to ethnic consciousness; and both lead to endogamy and other closure of the group to outsiders—which then leads to more ethnic consciousness and more joint political and religious behavior. One expects societies characterized by such a self-enhancing, positive feedback, circle to draw increasingly apart from other societies.

But the crucially significant fact is that things have simply not worked out this way. Far from drawing apart, every day a larger and larger proportion of the total world population of humans comes in some sort of contact (including media as well as direct contact) with individuals whose immediate ethnic and/or racial ancestry differs from their own. The question is: What has brought about this accelerating consolidation, rather than the separation that the relationships described above would lead us to expect?

Consolidation of Local Societies

The answer proposed here may be stated in a crude analogy: A number of soap bubbles (local societies) is expanding separately and at widely different rates, but within the same confined space (the

Earth). All other things being equal, their eventual contact and consolidation into a diminishing number of larger and larger bubbles (and finally into one single bubble—but that is a matter we shall leave for chapter 7) would seem to be a virtual certainty.

The analogy is, indeed, crude because it glosses over a huge question: Why should these bubbles, these local societies, expand? Why shouldn't they shrink instead, or stabilize at some point? The answer proposed here focuses on the internal dynamics of the societies— specifically, on their political, religious, economic, and scientific institutions—for here we may expect to find the most important of all forces leading to societal consolidation.[27]

The Political Institution as Consolidator

As an earlier discussion in this chapter has argued, in premodern times politics and religion always made excellent bedfellows ("it is a universal phenomenon that the formation of a political association entails subordination to its corresponding god" [Weber 1978a:413]). It may now be added that close mutual support between such normally threat-and-force-wielding, empire-building, institutions in ethnically (including racially) different but spatially proximal societies is apt to lead to wars, wars to conquest (see Weber 1976:394–95 on the Roman wars of conquest), and conquest has "perennially resulted in mixing one sort of people with others" (McNeill 1985:6).[28]

As a result, "marginality and pluralism were and are the norm of civilized existence. . . . [insofar as] civilized societies have nearly always subordinated some human groups to others of a different ethnic background, thereby creating a laminated polyethnic structure" (McNeill 1985:6–7).[29] And although Weber himself does not say so, the present theory regards such polyethnic structure as a product, in large part, of the joint political action called a *nation* and its cultural counterparts, *nationality* and *nationalism*—in the following sense.

Nations and Nationalities

Although Weber claims that "the concept of 'nationality' shares with that of the 'people'—in the 'ethnic' sense—the vague connotation that whatever is felt to be distinctively common must derive from common descent" (1978a:395), he immediately adds that "in reality, of course, persons who consider themselves members of the same nationality are often much less related by common descent than are persons belonging to different and hostile nationalities" (1978a:395), and that "it goes without saying that 'national' affiliation need not be based upon common blood. Indeed, especially radical 'nationalists' are often of foreign descent. Furthermore, although a specific common anthropological type is not irrelevant to nationality, it is neither sufficient nor prerequisite to nation founding" (1978a:923).[30]

A crucial question then arises: What is it that enables nationality to bind together different—even hostile—ethnic groups into a single "powerful political community of people"? One part of the answer seems to rest on the reliance by the political institution of the nation-state on physical force and the threat thereof (see chapter 3; for summaries of other answers as well see Tilly 1975a, 1975b). That is, expanding nation-states often incorporate ethnic groups through military action (see Finer 1975), and then secure that incorporation with police power. (In Weberian terms, this means the nation-state overwhelms the learned *wertrational* loyalty appeals of ethnic groups with threats to the innate *zweckrational* self-interest of their individual members in avoiding physical pain.) While claiming that "An army uses force to defend a community from threats outside itself; a police force protects against threats from within" (1975:329), Bayley specifies that the threat of *crime* from within has not been sufficient to account for police forces in European nation-states (see 1975:353). "[P]olice," Bayley says, "will be utilized in politics if [the] process of penetration [of a given territory by a coherent set of governmental institutions] . . . is resisted by violence" (1975:362)—although he does not mention specifically ethnic violence (but see Enloe 1981, on this). Braudel elaborates by pointing out that French troops of the *ancien régime* "were only rarely used to put down civil disorder. . . . [but] their mere presence tended to calm a town or province, even if the intendants hesitated to use them to the full" (1988:374, italics removed).

In addition, however, there seems to be another feature of the nation-state that produces its own *wertrational* "convictions of . . . duty, honor [etc]"[31] with their own power to consolidate the competing convictions that spring from ethnicity. I have in mind what Weber calls the nation-state's "very intimate relation to . . . the legend of a providential 'mission'" and to a "common political destiny" (1978a:925, 923).

Whereas ethnicity is backward-looking (i.e., ethnic groups characteristically venerate their past ancestry or descent), nationalism is forward-looking (i.e., nations venerate their future "mission" or "destiny"). So if one can say that "behind all ethnic diversities there is somehow naturally the notion of the 'chosen people'"—i.e., the people chosen in the past—it may also be claimed that behind all national diversities there is somehow naturally the notion of the predestined people—i.e., the people who will triumph in the future. Now Weber calls the particular destiny that nationalism venerates "the glory of power over other communities" (1978a:911).[32] And, most importantly, it is an essential part of pursuing that destiny that

> The individual is expected ultimately to face death in the group interest. This gives to the political community its particular pathos and raises its enduring emotional foundations. The community of political destiny, i.e., above all, of common political struggle of life and death, has given rise to groups with joint memories which often have had a deeper impact than the ties of merely cultural, linguistic, or ethnic community. It is this "community of memories" which . . . constitutes the ultimately decisive element of "national consciousness." (Weber 1978a:903)

Accordingly, the following hypotheses seem reasonable: Every external (i.e., military, rather than police) application of the political institution's legitimized deadly force has two major effects. First, of course, some individuals on both sides are likely to be physically killed or wounded, and thereby removed from their customary roles in their respective societies. No matter which side 'wins' the war, some consequences of this cohort-depletion (see Waring 1976) are independent of whatever subjective meaning the surviving participants may assign to it. But second, survivors are very likely to remember their dead long after they have buried them, and painfully seek some justifying meaning for these deaths—that "these honored dead . . . shall not have died in vain." In sorrow and guilt (that they survived though their comrades did not), the living are apt to reduce cognitive dissonance by concluding that the nation on whose behalf their comrades gave "the last full measure of devotion" *must* be morally superior to all other groups to which dead and survivors alike might belong—otherwise that "last full measure" should never have been given.[33] In this way, citizens' estimations of the honor (including the specifically God-granted honor) of the nation are greatly enhanced relative to its component ethnic groups.

In such shared death-related attitudinal unifications, then, would seem to reside important keys to the ability of new national loyalties to incorporate and otherwise manipulate even the oldest ethnic loyalties—melding (as every American coin reads), from many, one. Weber is persuasively explicit here:

> War creates a pathos and a sentiment of community. War thereby makes for an unconditionally devoted and sacrificial community among the combatants. . . . And, as a mass phenomenon, these feelings break down all the naturally given barriers of association. . . . Moreover, war does something to the warrior which . . . is unique: it makes him experience a consecrated meaning of death which is characteristic only of death in war. . . . Death on the field of battle differs from death that is only man's common lot. . . . [for] in war, and in this massiveness only in war, the individual can believe that he knows he is dying "for" something. . . . This location of death within a series of meaningful and consecrated events ultimately lies at the base of all endeavors to support the autonomous dignity of the polity resting on force. (1946:335, italics removed)

Under pressure from such shared and mutually supportive inferences, sooner or later, nearly all survivors of wars won or lost become patriots—firmly convinced that "who for his country dies has lived greatly"; that "for our country, 'tis a bliss to die"; and ready, even eager, to experience that bliss no matter what the country's cause may be. "Our country! In her intercourse with foreign nations may she always be in the right; but our country, right or wrong." (Finer may be alluding to such convictions when he refers to "a new set of beliefs which made populations actually *anxious* to go to the battlefield and sacrifice their material wealth" [1975:162, see also 163].) So when Tilly lists, among six "general conditions which appear, in the European experience, to predict . . . state-making," both "success in war" and "homogeneity (and homogenization) of the subject population" (1975a:40), the present argument—though admittedly more relevant to nation building than to state building—suggests the independent power of deaths in war (whether the war is successful or not) and a causal connection between these deaths and the homogenization of the surviving population. Braudel may have such an argument in mind when he tells us "the strenuous effort on both land and sea [of defending and pushing outward the frontiers of France] was in itself an instrument of unity: in some sense, it penetrated and mobilized the whole country, not merely the frontier regions" (1988:373). To this, however, Braudel makes the important additional point that

> Under the *ancien régime*, there was no province, however remote from the frontier, which did not contribute its share of [army] recruits. . . . recruitment to the army mingled Frenchmen of different origins, creating a melting pot, obliging men who did not speak the same language to live together and sever their provincial ties. Alongside the crown administration then, the army became the most active instrument in the unification of France" (1988:373–375).

And this makes it possible to bring in McNeill's comment on the impact of "learning to move in unison and keep formation": "All modern armies depend upon being able to generate an entirely subrational comradeship among new recruits simply by marching about on a parade ground . . . Drill, and the psychological residue it left behind, was indeed the principal secret of [the Greek, Macedonian, and Roman armies'] imperial success" (1985:47–48).[34]

Gellner's summary of the many consolidation effects of nationalism may seem an overstatement—considering Braudel's claim that inside its borders modern "France's name is diversity," and his allowing that modern "England, Germany, Italy or Spain, examined in detail have a perfect claim to be named diversity too" (1988:38). Nevertheless, his summary supports the view taken here:

> [C]onsider two ethnographic maps, one drawn up before the age of nationalism, and the other after the principle of nationalism had done much of its work. . . . the minute social groups [on the first map] have complex and ambiguous and multiple relations to many cultures; some through speech, others through their dominant faith, [etc.]. . . . Look now instead at the ethnographic and political map of an area of the modern world. . . . There is very little shading; neat flat surfaces are clearly separated from

each other. . . . [and] we see that an overwhelming part of political authority has been concentrated in the hands of one kind of institution, a reasonably large and well-centralized state. In general, each such state presides
over, maintains, and is identified with, one kind of culture . . . which
prevails within its borders. (Gellner 1983:139–40; see also Tilly 1975a:42–
43; Finer 1975:109–10, 124–34; Watkins 1991)

It therefore seems no accident that the directors and administrators
of nation-states are always careful to nurture their subjects' readiness
to die in such causes by dedicating to them war commemorations in
almost every town and city, perpetually tended tombs, cemeteries,
and glass-walled ossuaries, state citations for personal bravery on
the field of battle and for sacrifice at home, fireworks, parades, sol-
emn song, public eulogy, and the blood red in almost every nation's
flag. This seems no accident, that is, given Weber's description of
these directors' and administrators' *zweckrational* (self-interest) motivation: "Feudal lords, like modern officers or bureaucrats, are the
natural and primary exponents of this desire for power-oriented
prestige for one's own political structure. Power for their political
community means power for themselves, as well as the prestige
based on this power. For the bureaucrat and the officer, an expansion
of power means more office positions, more sinecures, and better
opportunities for promotion" (Weber 1978a:911).

So it seems fair to suggest, somewhat paradoxically, that the
peaceful consolidation of ethnically heterogeneous members of
modern nation-states has hitherto depended crucially on sustaining
military casualties in conflicts with other nation-states or would-be
nation-states. In Tilly's felicitous phrase, "War made the state, and
the state made war" (1975a:42; see also 73–76; 1975b:623), and, as
already quoted here, Freud summarizes: "It is always possible to
bind together a considerable number of people in love, so long as
there are other people left over to receive the manifestations of their
aggressiveness" (1961:68; see also Mearsheimer 1990).

At the same time, however, it must be emphasized that when a
polyethnic nation's universalistic patriotism and/or its secession-
inhibiting police force either breaks down or is seized by ethno-
centrics, the latter typically seek to add an orientation toward nationalistic destiny to the descent orientations of their ethnic group or

groups. The result is that one or more of these groups may choose war in pursuit of their own political unification and segregation from other ethnic groups. The process of consolidation must then begin again, following a different route—as a mountain stream eventually finds a new course to the sea when it encounters an obstacle to continuing its old course.[35]

The Religious Institution as Consolidator

In at least one case, Weber argues, consolidation (ecumenical-universalistic) tendencies in the religious institution were related to—indeed, sponsored by, similar tendencies in the political institution. Thus:

> Where the development was in the direction of a religiously buttressed confederation, there developed a special god of the political organization as such, as was the case with Yahweh. . . . In this case, universalism was a product of international politics, of which the pragmatic interpreters were the [prophets]. As a consequence of their preaching, the deeds of other nations that were profoundly affecting Israel's vital interests also came to be regarded as wrought by Yahweh. . . . Thus, the ancient warrior god of the confederacy . . . took on the prophetic and universalistic traits of transcendently sacred omnipotence and inscrutability. (Weber 1978a:412, 418–19)

But with the increasing separation of church and state, the religious institution began to play an independent role in the eventual global consolidation of human society—such that (as quoted earlier) "barriers of locality, tribe, and polity were shattered by universalist religions, by a religion with a unified God of the entire world" (Weber 1946:333)—see also chapter 6.

The Economic Institution as Consolidator

The economies of different societies, too, have operated to increase the chances for global consolidation. Weber looks upon the market itself as one of the earliest consolidation mechanisms (war, as discussed above, being the other earliest mechanism of this sort): "The market is a relationship which transcends the boundaries of neighborhood, kinship group, or tribe. Originally, it is indeed the only peaceful relationship of such kind" (1978a:637). To this, McNeill adds the following consolidation consequences of the market-centered cities' constant recruitment of fresh labor forces—a recruitment driven by the prevalence of high disease and death rates in those cities: "In many instances, when spontaneous immigration from the nearby countryside proved insufficient, resort to enslavement supplied the shortfall, moving across cultural boundaries and greater distances to bring an unfree labor force into action. The result . . . was ethnic mixture and pluralism on a grand scale in major centers of imperial government" (1985:14–15). This same recruitment of fresh labor forces, through both "spontaneous immigration" and "enslavement," has characterized the ethnic and racial mixing and pluralization of the New World (see Daniels 1990; Steinberg 1989; Lieberson and Waters 1988; Reich 1992:32; Kennedy 1993:41–46).

And Marx and Engels make the claim, especially penetrating in our own age of economic globalization, that "big industry . . . produced world-history for the first time, in so far as it made all civilized nations and every individual member of them dependent for the satisfaction of their wants on the whole world, thus destroying the former natural exclusiveness of separated nations. . . . [In addition,] big industry created a class, which in all nations has the same interest and with which nationality is already dead" (1947:56–57).

The Scientific Institution as Consolidator

Here, we must begin by acknowledging the incomparably important prehistoric and early historic contributions to societal consolidation that were made by the nascent scientific institutions of different local societies. These include the invention of such crucially important technological artifacts (and their associated sociocultural know-how) as controlled fire, stone hand axes, wheels, looms, kilns, and forges, the plough, the spear, spear thrower, bow and arrow, the domesticated horse and metal chariot, and perhaps most important of all, writing, map making, and computation (see, for example, Gouldner 1976)—as well as bureaucratically regimented work- and war-forces. The list of further contributions of this sort that have been made by the scientific institutions of many societies over the past five hundred years of modern history is enormous and still growing. Thus, writing in 1853, Marx says, "Steam has brought India into regular and rapid communication with Europe. . . . The day is not far distant when, by a combination of railways and steam vessels, the distance between England and India, measured by time, will be shortened to eight days" (in Marx and Engels 1978:660). Of course, the "eight days" Marx mentions here are today not much more than eight hours for commercial airlines and only a matter of minutes for orbiting astronauts.

The Continuous and Discontinuous, Progressive and Retrogressive, Fourfold Path of Societal Evolution

Figure 6 suggests that all the above-mentioned evolutions (of institutional specialization, culture, organizational scale, and spatial extension and consolidation) experience both continuous and discontinuous change,[36] and they do so more or less in step with each other. The several vertical arrows upward from one level to the next in this figure are meant to suggest that different societies may make the "progressive" transitions at different times.

It is important to add, however, that the indicated transitions are not likely to be taken (or not taken) by different societies independently of one another. In particular, intersocial modeling and queuing effects may be identified—as Tilly points out with reference to the scale-related transition to nation-statehood. First, the modeling effect: "The European state-building experiences will not repeat themselves in new states. . . . The statesmen of the contemporary world find themselves faced with alternative models of state-building, not to mention eager promoters of these models. . . . In Europe of the fifteenth or sixteenth century the available models were fewer, different, [and] less well-defined." And then the queuing effect: "As the nineteenth and twentieth centuries have worn on, the newcomers to the system have had less choice of the positions they

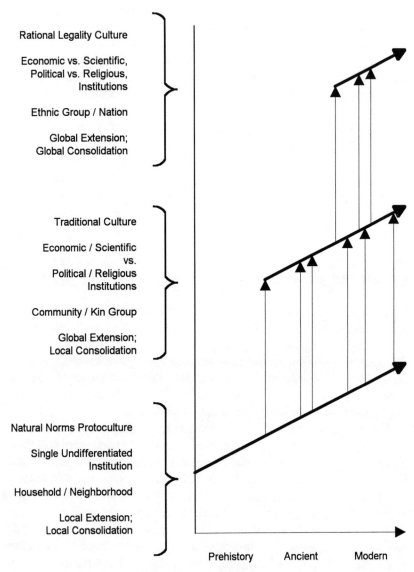

Figure 6. Descriptive Model of Societal Evolution

would occupy in it, even down to the exact territories they would control" (Tilly 1975a:81).

It is also important to say the directions of continuous and discontinuous change may be negative rather than positive—that is, they may be devolutionary and catastrophic, rather than evolutionary and revolutionary (see Wallace 1983:43–51). Overlaying all the positive and negative directions would produce the comprehensive diagram that is really called for here. I have chosen to omit the negative direction in Figure 6 not only because the overlay would be nearly unreadable but also because not only human life and human society, but all life and all society seem to display a main tendency to move toward expansion into new niches and toward increasing adaptation in these new niches until uprooted by some catastrophe or other.[37]

Seen from the standpoint of the present theory, then, human societal evolution proceeds like someone traversing branching flights of Escher-like ramps and steps—and doing so with some increasing (but never perfect) understanding of the person's own nature as well as that of the environment, and some increasing (but never perfect) control over which branches are open and which open branches are actually taken. In this process, the attainment of a given equilibrium state (a "landing") constitutes a necessary condition for the typically sudden transition (analogous to taking a tall step from a landing onto a new ramp) to a climb, or a descent, toward one or more other states. No given state nor any subsequent state is inevitable in this model, but achieving one state does affect the probability that some specifiable next state will be achieved; and achieving that state affects the probability that some given next state will be achieved—and so on.[38]

To sum up, then, the present theory sees human societal evolution as a fourfold (institutional specialization, culture, organizational scale, and spatial extension and consolidation), continuous-discontinuous, and progressive-retrogressive historical process. It is this described evolution that the next chapter will try to explain.[39]

In closing the present chapter, however, it seems important to emphasize that the main features of human societal evolution as shown in figure 6 are shared with current models of evolution in several other scientific disciplines—thereby suggesting deeply unifying isomorphisms between those disciplines and our own.

Punctuational Models in Other Disciplines

The models I have in mind include those referring to quantitative accumulation and "qualitative leaps" (Engels 1939:52); "stages of economic growth" in which a brief stage of rapid change—called "the take-off"—intervenes between two much longer stages of slower and steadier change (see Rostow 1960:4–11); "the [step-wise and ramp-wise] course of the Urban Revolution" in late archaeological prehistory and early history (Adams 1966:170); Kondratieff cycles of economic growth and stagnation (see Taylor 1993:13–17); "punctuated equilibria" (Eldredge and Gould 1972) and "quantum speciation" (Stanley 1981:115; see also Kerr 1992:1622; compare Wolpoff et al. 1984:449ff) in biological evolution;[40] periods of "crisis" science and "normal science" in the history of physical science (see Kuhn 1962); "periods of institutional creation and periods of institutional stasis" (Krasner 1984:240) in state-building; the difference between first-order and second-order phase transitions in physical phenomena (see Weinberg 1993:160), the succession of symmetry-maintenance and "symmetry-breakings" in the very early physical universe (see Weinberg 1984; Trefil 1983:22–36); and the "onset of turbulence" in normally smooth physical systems (see Gleick 1987:122–25).[41]

The characteristic that punctuational models in all disciplines have in common seems well summarized by the theoretical physicist Davies:

> Many physical systems behave in the conventional manner under a range of conditions, but may arrive at a threshold at which predictability suddenly breaks down. There is no longer any unique course, and the system may "choose" from a range of alternatives. This usually signals an abrupt transition to a new state which may have very different properties. In many cases the system makes a sudden leap to a much more elaborate and complex state. (1988:72; see also Woodcock and Davis 1978)

Stanley, a paleontologist, draws a general conclusion at some variance with the one reached here when he claims that "the punctuational view accentuates the unpredictability of large-scale evolution. . . . Because of its haphazard quality, speciation represents a kind of experimentation, but experimentation without a plan.

It is very much a trial and error process. By speciation, orders and families of animals and plants continually, but unknowingly, probe the environment" (1981:181). Against this, I prefer to argue (especially in chapter 7) that because the participants in human societal evolution are so big-brained and so social that they are not so inherently "unknowing" (or so physically powerless) as other organisms, the broad outlines of evolution in human society are neither entirely unpredictable nor entirely haphazard—nor are they doomed to remain as largely outside human control as they are at present.[42]

In any case, it seems reasonable to claim that the punctuational, ramp-and-step, progressive-and-retrogressive model of human societal evolution shown in figure 7 (see chapter 5) is comfortably similar to models of evolution in several other disciplines. And, in this connection, although the view expressed in 1908 by the astrophysicist George Ellery Hale was premature, it may also be prophetic: "We are now in a position to regard the study of evolution as that of a great single problem, beginning with the origin of stars in the nebulae and culminating in those difficult and complex sciences that endeavor to account, not merely for the phenomena of life, but for the laws which control a society composed of human beings" (quoted in Ferris 1983:95–96; see also Gribben 1993:213, 254).

Summary

This chapter has offered a view of the way both human society as a global whole, and also particular human societies, have typically evolved. This evolution has proceeded simultaneously, but at different rates from society to society, in the specialization of each society's participant-organizing institutions, in the degree of choice (i.e., rationality) provided by the society's dominant culture; in the society's organizational scale; and in the society's spatial extension and consolidation.

And now, for some ideas about what may explain this fourfold societal evolution, let us turn to chapter 5.

5

EVOLUTION OF SOCIETY: EXPLANATORY MODEL

CHAPTER 4 HAS CLAIMED that since prehistoric times the typical human individual's social world has grown (1) more role-diverse, as a result of increasing institutional specialization (coupled with new modes of institutional integration); (2) richer in choices, as a result of increasing cultural rationality; (3) more interdependent with other people, as a result of increasing organizational scale; and (4) bigger, as a result of increasing spatial extension and consolidation.

The question to which the present chapter is devoted is, What can explain this many-sided evolution?

Cultural Evolution as the Pilot Evolution

The first Weberian answer to this question is that although the four evolutionary components interact at all times, that interaction is not symmetrical; cultural evolution is what orients, sustains, and en-trains the other three. Ultimately, this view rests on the premise (already quoted in Chapter 2) that all humans are given, in the very nature of things, as "cultural beings, endowed with the capacity and the will to take a deliberate attitude towards the world and to lend it significance. Whatever this significance may be, it will lead us to judge certain phenomena of human existence in its light and to respond to them as being (positively or negatively) meaningful" (Weber 1949:81, italics removed). But let us see how this premise works itself out in each of the three other components of societal evolution.

First, regarding the evolution of institutional specialization, the premise implies that the prehistoric all-purpose superinstitution was dependent on natural norms; the subsequent splitting-off of polity-religion from economy-science was dependent on the emergence of tradition culture; and the later splitting-off of polity from religion, and science from economy, were dependent on the emergence of rational legal culture. But it is in the bureaucracy-and-machinery integration of these increasingly specialized institutions (see chapter 4), that the pilot role of culture (as defined in chapter 3) may be clearest.

Note that neither bureaucracy nor machines can be regarded as a modern invention; each is at least ancient, if not prehistoric, in origin. Indeed, "The historical model of all later bureaucracies [was] the New Kingdom in Egypt" (Weber 1978a:964) and the horse and cart-chariot, and the Great Wall, canals, and military fortifications of China (see Weber 1978a:1178; 1946:255; 1978a:1047; 1951b:26)—among many other machines—were all invented and adopted in antiquity.

What is fundamentally new about modern bureaucracy and machinery, however, is the cultural context in which their developments occur—that is to say, the particular constraints to which they and all other aspects of social life become subjected when a culture of rational legality permeates all the participant-organizing institutions. Thus, characterizing the ancient bureaucracies as "highly irrational forms of bureaucracy," Weber notes that "in contrast with these older forms, modern bureaucracy has one characteristic which makes its 'escape-proof' nature much more definite: rational specialization and training" (1978a:1401; see also 956, 964). For this and other reasons, Weber concludes that "legal authority with a bureaucratic staff" (note: not bureaucracy in general but a bureaucracy that administers legal authority) is the "specifically modern type of administration" (1978a:217). And almost needless to add, "the railway"—which Weber enthusiastically calls "the most revolutionary instrumentality known to history" (1950:297)—is also a specifically modern machine technology.

Thus, in what seems to be his most explicit statement of the dependence of rational bureaucracy and rational machine technology on a culture of rational legality, Weber tells us that "the specific features of modern capitalism . . . the strictly rational organization of work [i.e., bureaucracy] embedded in rational technology [i.e., machines], nowhere developed in . . . irrationally constructed states . . . [and] could arise only [where there is a legal and judicial] apparatus . . . whose function is by and large calculable or predictable" (1978a:1395, italics removed).

And here let us pause to note that a culture (and administrative apparatus) of rational legality also makes possible what Weber terms the "all-important economic fact: the 'separation' of the worker from the material means of production, destruction, administration, academic research, and finance"—a legal, and therefore violently enforced, separation that is "the common basis of the modern state, in its political, cultural and military sphere, and of the private capitalist economy" (1978a:1394) and that renders these "material means" preeminently rational—which is to say, controllable and calculable. Gerth and Mills rightly follow by pointing out that "Marx's emphasis upon the wage worker being 'separated' from the means of production becomes, in Weber's perspective, merely one special case of a universal trend. The modern soldier is equally 'separated' from the means of violence; the scientist from the means of enquiry, and the civil servant from the means of administration" (1946:50)

—although Gerth and Mills do not mention the no less equal separation of the religious laity from the means of worship, which chiefly rest in the hands of clergy.

It therefore seems fair to conclude that a culture of rational legality (Weber actually says "a developed money economy," but the very notion of "money" is predicated on a high degree of legally enforced formal rationality—see chapters 2 and 3) "is the normal precondition at least for the unchanged survival, if not for the initiation, of pure bureaucratic administration" (1978a:964), and also for the fullest development and application of machine technology. A theory taking its main inspiration from Weber, then, should regard the emergence of a society-wide culture of rational legality as ultimately responsible for holding the increasingly specialized institutions together. It is this culture that stands behind the institution-integrating status metric (bureaucracy) and role instrumentality (machinery) discussed in chapter 4.

Second, Weber implies that the evolution of organizational scale depends on cultural evolution when he says that "the great achievement of the ethical religions . . . was to shatter the fetters of the sib. These religions established the superior community of faith and a common ethical way of life in opposition to the community of blood, even to a large extent in opposition to the family" (Weber 1951b:237). Similarly, he attributes the "national" level of organizational scale to a combination of tradition culture and rational legality culture when he says that "the concept [nation] seems to refer . . . to a specific kind of pathos which is linked to the idea of a powerful political community of people who share a common language, or religion, or common customs, or political memories. . . . The more power is emphasized, the closer appears to be the link between nation and state" (Weber 1978a:398).

Third (and here I go beyond Weber again—inasmuch as his perspective on the matter is, as chapter 4 has indicated, severely truncated), it would seem that the evolution of spatial extension and consolidation is also piloted by the evolution of culture. A "natural norms" culture seems likely to have led to the first spatial expansion of the first human society. Traditional culture seems likely to have inhibited further change in the space occupied by any separate society that resulted from that first expansion. Then, however, the breakthrough to rational legality culture entailed powerfully expansionistic and inclusionistic tendencies (see Huff 1989:54–55). These tendencies include all the institutional mechanisms of societal consolidation (i.e., nations and supranational organizations, markets and cities, religious universalism, and technological inventions) discussed in chapter 4.

We now arrive at a key question: If the evolutions of institutional specialization, organizational scale, and spatial extension and consolidation depend on cultural evolution, *on what does cultural evolution depend?* In constructing a Weberian answer to this question, it is first useful to recall the idea (put forward in chapter 4) that all four components of societal evolution manifest a ramp phase and a step phase—and to suggest that each type of phase may require its own distinctive explanation.[1] Let us consider the ramp phase first because it is simpler and because it occupies more of human history.

Here Weber aids us with the opinion that "law, convention, and custom belong to the same continuum with imperceptible transitions leading from to another." He defines the second two as follows:

> We shall define custom to mean a typically uniform activity which is kept on the beaten track simply because men are "accustomed" to it and persist in it by unreflective imitation. It is a collective way of acting, the perpetuation of which by the individual is not "required" in any sense by anyone. Convention, on the other hand, shall be said to exist whenever a certain conduct is sought to be induced . . . [by] the expression of approval or disapproval on the part of those persons who constitute the environment of the actor. (Weber 1978a:319, italics removed)

Of "law" he says, "Whenever we shall use the term 'law' without qualification, we shall mean norms which are directly guaranteed by legal coercion," and "as long as there is a chance that a coercive apparatus will enforce, in a given situation, compliance with . . . norms, we . . . must consider them as 'law'" (1978a:313, 312).

On the basis of these remarks, it seems fair to say Weber explains the relatively continuous ramp phase of cultural evolution as the consequence of gradual enhancements of shared traditional (i.e., custom, and some convention) orientation plus *wertrational* and *zweckrational* orientations (i.e., some convention, and law—including, as noted in chapter 4, expediency in avoiding the pains of enforcement).

The step phase, however, is very different from this, and it seems differently explained. Here is Weber's explanation of the prehistoric step from the natural norms protoculture to the culture of tradition: "We must ask how anything new can ever arise in this world [of natural norms], oriented as it is toward the regular as the empirically valid. . . . The most important source of innovation [here] has been the influence of individuals, who have experienced certain "abnormal" states . . . and hence have been capable of exercising a special influence on others" (1978a:321).

In a word, then, Weber identifies *charisma* (in this quotation, "the influence of individuals who have experienced certain 'abnormal' states" but, as we shall see below, charisma is not limited to such influence) as the force that instigates the change from natural norms to tradition culture. But then we also read that "in traditionalist periods, charisma is the great revolutionary force";[2] that "charisma, in its most potent forms disrupts rational rule as well as tradition altogether"; that "in a revolutionary and sovereign manner, charismatic domination transforms all values and breaks all traditional and rational norms"; and, most sweepingly of all, "charisma is indeed the specifically creative revolutionary force of history" (Weber 1978a:245, 1115, 1117).[3]

In short, we seem compelled to conclude that charisma plays the pivotal role in Weber's explanation of *all* stepwise change in culture—and therefore (to the extent that the latter draws change in institutional specialization, organizational scale, and spatial extension and consolidation in its wake) in societal evolution as a whole.[4] So let us now give full attention to the concept of charisma itself.

The following discussion addresses four questions. First, What is charisma? Here we want to consider whether charisma should be thought of as a quality of the object said to possess it; whether charisma should be thought of as involving a special relationship to divinity or other transcendence; and what roles should be assigned to cognitive beliefs and emotional feelings in charisma. Second, What are the dimensions of variability in charisma, regardless of its object, as manifested in a given society? Here we want to consider something about the intensity of charisma in a given locus, and something about the breadth of that locus. Third, What is the full range of phenomena that may be objects of charisma? Here we want to consider whether charisma should be thought of as attributable to phenomena other than "individuals, who have experienced certain 'abnormal' states" (see above). And finally, How does charisma achieve its effects? Here we want to consider how the individual social participant's psychological behavior (especially expressions of the rational and nonrational capabilities discussed in chapter 2) is affected by charisma.

Charisma: What Is It?

Although Weber appears to define charisma as a characteristic objectively belonging to the person who is regarded as charismatic when he says that "the term 'charisma' will be applied to a certain quality of an individual personality by virtue of which he is considered extraordinary and treated as endowed with supernatural, superhuman, or at least specifically exceptional powers or qualities" (1978a:241), this appearance is misleading.

Subjective Attribution, Not Objective Possession

Weber argues more often and more forcefully that charisma requires a shared cognitive attribution—an attribution that lies only in the eyes of beholders, independently of its "objective" possession—followed by a shared emotional response, among those beholders, to that attribution: "What is alone important is how the individual is actually regarded by [others]. . . . It is the recognition on the part of those [others] which is decisive for the validity of the charisma. . . . if the people withdraw their recognition, the master becomes a private person" (1978a:242, 266, 1115).[5] And more generally, "there is nothing in . . . things themselves to set some of them apart as alone meriting attention," Weber says. "A chaos of 'existential judgments' about countless individual events would be the only result of a serious attempt to analyze reality 'without presuppositions'" (1949:78, italics added). Remember: "We are cultural beings, endowed with the capacity and the will to take a deliberate attitude towards the world and to lend it significance" (see chapter 2).

All these statements clearly imply that even when the object in question does not objectively possess any extraordinary qualities at all, if actors subjectively attribute such qualities to it, that object becomes charismatic ("If men define situations as real, they are real in their consequences" [Thomas and Thomas 1928:572]). The present conceptualization of charisma, then, hinges entirely on attribution—whether that attribution is a response to qualities actually possessed by the recipient of the attribution is not a relevant consideration. In the hallucinatory case, absolutely nothing (nothing external to the perceiver) need be perceived, and still charisma may be attributed (see Turner 1981:146; Coleman 1990:75).

Thus, in a word, "charismatic appeals" (Eisenstadt 1968:xxix) are not accepted because they are charismatic; they are charismatic because they are accepted. But why are some accepted and others not?

Connotations of Transcendence Not Necessary

In Weber's view, the attribution of charisma does not necessarily entail a prior imputation of the supernatural, the divine, the sacred, or any putatively transcendent feature of cosmic, or human, existence or nonexistence. Cognitively, charisma only requires a judgment that the object in question is "exceptional" or "extraordinary" (see above; see also Simmel 1950:30). This claim stands in sharp contrast with Parsons's view that "charisma. . . . is the quality which attaches to men and things by virtue of their relations with the 'supernatural'" (1937:668; compare 1947:75–76); with Marcuse's claim that charisma "contains the pre-judgment that endows every form of successful personal leadership with a religious aura" (1971:145); with Shils's claim that "charisma . . . is the quality which is imputed to persons, actions, roles, institutions, symbols, and material objects because of their presumed connection with 'ultimate,' 'fundamental,' 'vital,' order-determining powers" (1968:386, see also 387); and with Bradley's claim that Weber held "recognition and legitimation of [the charismatic] leader's authority [must be] based on 'sign' or proof of divine grace" (1987:33). Against all such claims, Weber himself tells us charisma "derives from the surrender of the faithful to the extraordinary and unheard-of, to what is alien to all regulation and tradition and *therefore* is viewed as divine. . . . [Charisma] enforces the inner subjection to the unprecedented and absolutely unique and *therefore* Divine" (1978a:1115, 1117, both italics added; in both cases, the German original is *deshalb* [Weber 1956:vol. 2, 665, 666]).

Weber thus unmistakably designates the "extraordinary and unheard-of," the "unprecedented and absolutely unique," as fundamental to charisma and the "divine" as derivative from it, rather than the other way around.[6] He also indicates that the "extraordinary and unheard-of" need not be revered; it may be despised: "Persons who are externally different are simply despised irrespective of what they accomplish or what they are, or they are venerated superstitiously if they are too powerful in the long run" (Weber 1978a:385). In this way, room is made for an avoidance response as well as an attraction response to the cognitive attribution of exceptionality.

Weber also denies, therefore, the linkage and causal direction implicit both in Shils's claim that "the disposition to attribute charisma is intimately related to the need for order. The attribution of charismatic qualities occurs in the presence of order-creating, order-disclosing, order-discovering power as such; it is a response to great ordering power" (1965:204), and in Eisenstadt's claim that the "charismatic fervor is rooted in the attempt to come into contact with the very essence of being, to go to the very roots of existence, of cosmic, social, and cultural order, to what is seen as sacred and fundamental" (1968:xix). Weber, in other words, permits charismatic fervor to be no less deeply rooted in what actors think is thoroughly frivolous or disorder-creating, than in what they think is essential or order-creating—so long as that fervor attributes exceptionality to its object: "For present purposes it will be necessary to treat a variety of different types as being endowed with charisma in [my] sense. . . . Value-free sociological analysis will treat all these on the same level as it does the charisma of men who are the 'greatest' heroes, prophets, and saviors according to conventional judgements. . . . In our value-free sense of the term, an ingenious pirate may be a charismatic ruler" (Weber 1978a:242, 1113). One imagines, then, that in his "value-free" sense, Weber would say an urban graffiti artist, a rock or rap star, a stand-up comic, the inventor of a computer virus, a drug dealer, a leader of organized crime, a terrorist, a satanist, an atheist, can be no less charismatic in their realms than the saintliest prophet and priest, or the most imperial regent and hero, can be in theirs (see Gerth and Mills 1946:52; Giddens 1972:57; Lindholm 1990).

Learned Cognitive Attribution Plus Innate Emotional Affectuality

As suggested above, Weber implicitly but very clearly regards charisma as having two components: a variable (because socially learned) cognitive attribution of exceptionality and a fixed (because phylogenetically innate) emotional response of awe, adoration, enthusiasm (or their opposites) to that attribution.

Conceptualizing the cognitive attribution component of charisma as socially learned rather than innate carries two important implications: (1) at any given time in human history, individuals who have acquired cognitive familiarity with a given field are apt to make very different charisma attributions from those who have not acquired such familiarity—such that Jelly Roll Morton, John Archibald Wheeler, Maria João Pires, and Pat Robertson seem likely to be regarded as charismatic by at least somewhat different audiences; and (2) persons and things that were widely regarded as surpassingly charismatic thousands of years ago in the Middle East, would be very unlikely to be so regarded if they occurred in our own scientifically skeptical and Houdini-sophisticated culture.

Conceptualizing the emotional response to a charisma attribution as innate, however, acknowledges that Weber calls the charisma response "turbulently emotional," and says it arises "out of enthusiasm, or of despair and hope" and expresses "acutely emotional faith" (Weber 1978a:1120, 242, 1122). And as we have seen in chapter 2, Weber holds that every instance of such "affectual behavior" consists in "an uncontrolled reaction to some exceptional stimulus." The conceptualization implies that the reflex itself is unconditioned, although its object is learned—like the attraction experienced in the presence of something one has learned enhances life (say, goat cheese, raw fish, dry martinis), or the repulsion experienced in the presence of something one has learned threatens life and limb (say, a loaded pistol, a faulty electrical connection, a published declaration of war).

Finally, consider Weber's specification of the mechanism (which he calls "psychic contagion"—"Some types of reaction are only made possible by the mere fact that the individual acts as part of a crowd" [1978a:23, see also 1377]) whereby a given charisma emotional response can become diffused among a large number of individuals who, though not present when and where a given event occurred, respond in exceptional ways, not to the event itself, but to the exceptional responses of those who were present and who deemed the event exceptional at that time and place.[7] "Psychic contagion" is, in short, a self-amplifying interaction among the affectual responses of different individuals—an interaction that does not require these individuals to make any cognitive attribution of exceptionality to whatever might have been its initial object. Participants in such contagion are reacting emotionally to *one another's* expressions of emotion (sometimes, across many generations and many thousands of miles) and not to the original stimulus. As Simmel so neatly puts it, "The individual, by being carried away, carries away" (1950:35).[8]

When one considers all these factors relating to charisma and to psychic contagion, the conclusion that Weber claims "emotional action. . . . [does] not operate to change the world" (Collins 1986a:43) seems quite remarkable. Indeed, one feels forced to conclude the exact opposite—namely, that insofar as he claims charisma is "the specifically creative revolutionary force of history" and believes charisma to be founded on "acutely emotional faith" (see above), Weber looks upon emotional action as having been the *most* world-changing force of all (see also Lyman 1984:194; Wuthnow 1987:31; Schroeder 1992:9).[9]

Charisma: Variable Intensity and Variable Dispersion

Now let us consider the further possibilities that charisma emotional response—no matter what its cognitive object—may vary in its intensity, and may also vary in the extent to which it is dispersed (i.e., experienced in common) among members of a given society. Along these lines, Shils claims that "some societies are characterized by a greater frequency of intense and concentrated charisma; others by a greater frequency of attenuated and dispersed charisma" (1968:386). But it seems useful to go beyond this claim by decoupling intensity and dispersion—as follows.

Intensity

Let us think of low-intensity charisma (Shils calls it "attenuated" charisma) as the normal permeation of every individual social participant's life by the moment-to-moment flicker of weak emotional ties to (and repulsions from) other people, social institutions, ideas, and animate and inanimate nonhuman things—including what Weber refers to as the ordinary, everyday, "social estimation of [our own and others'] honor" (1978a:932, italics removed).[10] In this extension of Weber's view, the overwhelming majority of charisma attributions and the emotional responses to them either do not deviate significantly from tradition or, if they do, are so weak as to be absorbed by tradition's massive inertia. The net result is a bumpy stability: "In prerationalistic periods, tradition and charisma between them have almost exhausted the whole of the orientation of action" (Weber 1978a:245).[11]

Charisma responses at their highest levels of intensity, however, are altogether abnormal (exceptional) and not easily regulated. They are violently disruptive, breathtaking, away-carrying, knee-jerk emotional responses that summarily override all other feelings (see Lyman 1984:196). As Freud says concerning the charisma of sexual love (discussed below), "When a love-relationship is at its height there is no room left for any interest in the environment" (1961:61).

Dispersion

High-intensity charisma response, however, does not seem likely to occur in all participants in a given society equally and at the same time (see Glassman 1984:231). This, in turn, leads to the strong probability that the combination of high intensity and low dispersion (high concentration) of charisma responses to given objects will engender contention between different groups in the society—as one group cheers while other groups Bronx-cheer. Hence wars, revolutions, crusades, and the often genocidal suppression of minority (or majority) charisma responses.

Charisma: What Can "Possess" It?

Weber does not limit "exceptional" or "extraordinary" objects to individual human persons but includes "charismatically endowed natural objects, artifacts, [and] animals"; "the charisma of office—the belief in the specific state of grace of a social institution"; and "the charismatic glorification of [an idea, for example,] 'Reason'" (1978a:401, 1140, 1209; see also 1946:149).

Accordingly, the present theory holds that literally anything perceivable or conceivable by the human mind can become a charismatic object and can, in this sense, change human society.[12] The discussion that follows selects for consideration the following types of potentially charismatic objects: (1) an entire human society; (2) the several participant-organizing, participant-intake, and participant-outlet institutions of that society; (3) the ordinary human individual participant in those institutions; and (4) the natural ecosystem and human technological artifacts—both animate (e.g., domesticated animals and plants) and inanimate (e.g., machines)—that both environ and empower the society, its institutions, and their participants.

A Society as a Whole

The charisma of one's own society has been called *patriotism, love of one's country,* and *ethnocentrism.* Although Weber uses none of these terms, their sense seems clearly present in his claim (already cited more than once here) that "behind all ethnic diversities there is somehow naturally the notion of the 'chosen people'." The implication seems undeniable that members are likely to respond with emotional enthusiasm to their own ethnic group and the society it comprises. Moreover, chapter 4 has argued that the nation-state manifests its special charisma in consolidating different descent-based ethnic groups, and their societies, under the banner of "a [single] providential mission" and a "common political destiny" of domination over other societies.[13]

Charismatic Features of the Participant-Organizing Institutions

Marx and Engels see conflict over the rulership of society as occurring chiefly among groups of individuals holding different statuses in the economic institution ("the history of all hitherto existing society is the history of class struggle").[14] Weber, however, argues that both charismatic and traditional authority "are found in all areas of life" (1978a:1117), thereby implying that charisma-induced revolutionary changes in society may originate in the scientific institution, the religious institution, and the political institution—as well as in the economic institution. Thus, "the power of charisma rests upon the belief in revelation and heroes, upon the conviction that certain manifestations—whether they be of a religious, ethical, artistic, scientific, political or other kind—are important and valuable; it rests upon 'heroism' of an ascetic, military, judicial, magical or whichever kind" (1978a:1116). And lest any scientist think otherwise, Weber points specifically to the vulnerability of the scientific institution to charisma: "The values to which the scientific genius relates the object of his inquiry may determine, i.e., decide the 'conception' of a whole epoch, not only concerning what is regarded as 'valuable' but also concerning what is significant or insignificant, 'important' or 'unimportant' in the phenomena" (1949:82).

Now in addition to all these potentially charismatic features of the participant-organizing institutions, let us consider that there may be other such features in the participant-intake institutions, and in the participant-outlet institutions as well.

In the participant-intake institutions we find erotic love and esthetic pleasure. I refer to these as features of institutions insofar as they satisfy the definition set forth in chapter 3 of an institution as "a type of social relationship . . . [having] long historical duration and high historical probability," and I refer to them as features of the participant-intake institutions insofar as they satisfy the definition, also set forth in chapter 3, of such institutions as managing "biological reproduction. . . . [and] the physical and psychical nurture, education, and training of . . . recruits.")

Charismatic Features of the Participant-Intake Institutions: Erotic Love and Esthetic Pleasure

By way of indicating the charismatic nature of erotic love and esthetics pleasure (and, under certain public circumstances, their liability to psychic contagion—see Wilson 1975:41), Weber says that "the erotic frenzy stands in unison . . . with the orgiastic and charismatic form of religiosity" and "the creative artist [may experience] his work as resulting either from a charisma of 'ability' (originally magic) or from spontaneous play" (1946:349, 341)—and, obviously, the artist's audience may experience that work in this way too.

In suggesting that erotic love manifests an innate and nonrational capability (as defined in chapter 2), Weber calls sexuality "the drive that most firmly binds man to the animal level" and refers to "the peculiar irrationality of the sexual act, which is ultimately and uniquely unsusceptible to rational organization" (1978a:603–604). It therefore seems fair (indeed, almost self-evident) to say Weber regards erotic love as affectual in its orientation (see figure 3) and as involving a charismatic attribution of exceptionality and an intense emotional response to its object.

Weber does not so clearly state his view of the nature of esthetic pleasure. Thus, although he says the "constitutive values" of art "are quite different from those obtaining in the religious and ethical domain" (1978a:608), he does not say what these values are—nor, unfortunately, does he consider how they might relate to erotic values.[15] Despite this, Weber's overall discussion seems ample justification for classifying both erotic and esthetic experiences as charismatic in nature—as follows.

Weber tells us, "The tension of religion and sex has been augmented by evolutionary factors on both sides" (1946:344), and claims that an "evolutionary sequence" characterizes relations between "sexual relations" and "religious or economic regulations" (1978a: 607). The same kind of evolution applies, Weber says, to art: "The sublimation of the religious ethic and the quest for salvation, on the one hand, and the evolution of the inherent logic of art, on the other, have tended to form an increasingly tense relation" (1946:341).

When we examine the nature of the evolutions Weber has in mind, they both seem to follow the same path of increasing specialization and autonomy that chapter 4 claimed for the four participant-organizing institutions. Thus, "Originally the relation of sex and religion was very intimate. Sexual intercourse was very frequently part of magic orgiasticism or was an unintended result of orgiastic excitement"—and in "magical orgiasticism . . . every ecstacy was considered 'holy'" (Weber 1946:343). Similarly, "Religion and art are intimately related in the beginning" (Weber 1978a:607), and "magical religiosity stands in a most intimate relation to the esthetic sphere. Since its beginnings, religion has been an inexhaustible fountain of opportunities for artistic creation" (Weber 1946:341).

In time, however, conflicts with religion emerged in both cases. First, the erotic: "A certain tension between religion and sex came to the fore . . . with the temporary cultic chastity of priests. . . . [and] subsequently the prophetic religions, as well as the priest-controlled life orders, have . . . regulated sexual intercourse in favor of marriage. The contrast of all rational regulation of life with magical orgiasticism and all sorts of irrational frenzies is expressed in this fact" (Weber 1946:344, italics removed; see also 1978a:603). Nowadays, "the euphoria of the happy lover. . . . always meets with the cool mockery of the genuinely religiously founded and the radical ethic of brotherhood" (Weber 1946:348).

The esthetic experience, too, came into conflict with religion: "The sublimation of the religious ethic and the quest for salvation, on the one hand, and the evolution of the inherent logic of art, on the other, have tended to form an increasingly tense relation" (1946:341).

Throughout the time that these two conflicts with religion were evolving, the parties to them (erotic, and esthetic, experiences) were also evolving. Thus, Weber says, "On the side of sexuality, the tension has led through sublimation into 'eroticism'. . . . The extraordinary quality of eroticism has consisted precisely in a gradual turning away from the naive naturalism of sex" (note the parallel with the evolution from "natural norms" to "convention," as discussed in chapter 4), and, he continues, "the reason and significance of this evolution. . . involve the universal rationalization and intellectualization of culture" (1946:344). "The decisive development," Weber says, "is the sublimation of sexual expression into an eroticism that becomes the basis of idiosyncratic sensations, hence generates its own unique values and transcends everyday life" (1978a:607)—and Simmel also stresses charismatic exceptionality "the lovers think that there has never been a love like theirs; that nothing can be compared either to the person loved or to the feelings for that person" (1950:406). With the development of eroticism, Weber says, "specifically extramarital sexual life, which had been removed from everyday affairs, could appear as the only tie which still linked man with the natural fountain for all life. . . . [The lover] knows himself to be freed from the cold skeleton hands of rational orders. . . . this inner, earthly sensation of salvation by mature love competes in the sharpest possible way with the devotion of a supra-mundane God, with the devotion of an ethically rational order of God" (1946:346, 347–348; see Goode 1959).

Esthetics has also evolved—toward greater internal differentiation ("Orgiastic religion leads most readily to song and music; ritualistic religion inclines toward the pictorial arts; religions enjoining love favor the development of poetry and music" [Weber 1978a:609]) and toward greater independence from religion:

> The development of intellectualism and the rationalization of life. . . . [transform art into] a cosmos of more and more consciously grasped independent values which exist in their own right. Art takes over the function of a this-worldly salvation. . . . It provides a salvation from the routines of everyday life, and especially from the increasing pressures of theoretical and practical rationalism. With this claim to a redemptory function, art begins to compete directly with salvation religion. (Weber 1946:342, italics removed; see also 1978a:608–610)

In short, it seems reasonable to look upon the erotic and the esthetic as two related features of the participant-intake institutions that provide steady access for nonrational charisma responses into an increasingly rationalized everyday life (see also Shils 1987:569). Note, however, that the erotic and esthetics are not the only possible participant-intake channels for infusions of charisma; one could also examine birth (e.g., Zeus and Athena, Adam and Eve, Amma and the Nommo, Mary and Jesus), and immigration (Simmel says the stranger "is freer, practically and theoretically . . . he is not tied down in his action by habit, piety, and precedent" [1950:405]), as equally prominent in this respect—even though Weber leaves them unexamined in his work and they will not be discussed further here either.

Charismatic Features of the Participant-Outlet Institutions: The Dead

Given the preceding argument, largely based on Weber, that the participant-organizing and participant-intake institutions of society have potentially charismatic features, one suspects such features may also be found among the participant-outlet institutions. Here one thinks not only of the charisma sometimes associated with imprisonment, hospitalization, exile, and emigration, but especially of dead-disposal institutions such as funeral, burial, cremation, or ex-

posure to the elements—with burial dating back at least to the Nean-
derthals (see Klein 1989:285, 327). Weber does not mention dead-
disposal institutions at all, but let us look briefly elsewhere for insights on them.

Habenstein and Lamers raise the key question here: "Assume that
we are confronted with the dead body of a man. . . . What do men
generally think this body is?" (1955:4). A Weberian answer would be
that men generally think such a body is charismatic, precisely in the
sense stated here—as evidenced by the awe, reverence, fear, and
horror in which the dead and ghosts of the dead are almost universally held, and the particular care with which corpses are generally
treated (see Gordon 1984; especially 9–10, 151). Spencer's argument
focuses on this charisma (although he does not use the word): "The
shade of an enemy becomes a devil, and a friendly shade becomes a
divinity. . . . Even in our own day the kinship is traceable. The statement that God is a spirit, shows the application of a term which,
otherwise applied, signifies a human soul. . . . A divine being is still
denoted by words that originally mean the breath which, deserting a
man's body at death, was supposed to constitute the surviving part"
(1898:vol. 1, 303, 304).

The Human Individual as Charismatic Object

Now given that all human individuals can become objects of erotic
love and esthetic pleasure (both to others and to themselves), and all
eventually become potential objects of dead-charisma, it seems but a
short generalizing step to claim that every living human
individual—each in his/her own undoubted exceptionality—is a
potential object of charisma attribution and response. Indeed, Weber's concept of psychic contagion (see above) clearly implies that
any human individual can become intensely charismatic for his/her
neighbors—and insofar as communications technology extends the
spatiotemporal dimensions of one's neighborhood, that charisma
can be diffused to all human individuals—and not only for the fif-
teen minutes Andy Warhol had in mind. Shils puts it this way: "One
of the greatest dispersions [of charisma] in history is that which has
taken place in modern states, in which an attenuated charisma, more

dispersed than in traditional aristocracies (where it was already more dispersed than in primitive tribes or absolute monarchies), is shared by the total adult citizenry" (1968:390). Chapter 7 will return to this general point.

The Natural Environment as Charismatic Object

Regarding the charismatic potential of geographical, geological, climatic, floral, and faunal features of the natural ecosystem, Weber argues that

> Jahweh . . . was originally a god of the great catastrophes of nature. His appearance is accompanied by phenomena such as earthquakes . . . volcanic phenomena . . . subterraneous . . . and heavenly fire, the desert wind from the South and South East . . . and thunderstorms. . . . flashes of lightning are his arrows. . . . For Palestine the orbit of nature catastrophes comprised also the insect, above all, the locust plague, which the South Eastern wind brought into the country. Hence the god punishes the enemies of his people with locusts and he sends swarms of locusts to confound them. He sends snakes *en masse* to punish his own people. (1952:128–129)

And then, by way of underscoring the exceptionality of such phenomena (meanwhile implicitly distinguishing between step and ramp evolution as set forth in chapter 4), Weber tells us Jahweh was "a god of frightful natural catastrophes, not of the eternal order of nature" (1952:129).

Technological Artifacts as Charismatic Objects

We have seen Weber's claim that "charisma is indeed *the* specifically creative revolutionary force of history" (see above). But Weber also argues that

> bureaucratic rationalization, too, often has been a major revolutionary force with regard to tradition. But it revolutionizes with technical means, in principle . . . "from without": It first changes the material and social orders, and through them the people, by changing the conditions of adap-

tation, and perhaps the opportunities for adaptation, through a rational determination of means and ends [sic]. By contrast, the power of charisma rests . . . upon [internal] conviction. . . . Charismatic belief revolutionizes men "from within" and shapes material and social conditions according to its revolutionary will. (1978a:1116, italics removed)

Thus, we have a second "specifically creative revolutionary force of history"—namely, "technical means."

The differences between these forces, however, form a powerful complementarity during the step phase of societal evolution—such that charisma initiates the break, and technical means maintains the new level once it has been achieved (see also Durkheim 1982:119–125). Thus, although Weber holds that the charismatic individuals and ethical precepts of Protestantism initiated the break with feudal economic relations, he argues that "this support has long since ceased to be necessary for modern capitalism. . . . on the whole, modern capitalism is . . . exceptionally emancipated from the importance of such ethical factors" (1978c:1124, 1125). What is now required to maintain modern capitalism are not ethics but machines: "The mechanization of technology . . . [is] decisive for capitalism in its contemporary form" (Weber 1978c:1128). The upshot (as already noted in chapter 4) is that "the Puritan wanted to work in a calling; we are forced to do so. . . . [The modern economic order] is now bound to the technical and economic conditions of machine production."

Of course, Weber was not the first theorist to lay special emphasis on "technical means" as causal influences in human society. Comte had already argued that "it is the formation of capital that is the true source of the great moral and mental results [often attributed] to the distribution of industrial tasks" (1975:406), and Marx and Engels had already claimed that the "social relations of production change, are transformed, with the change and development of the material means of production" (1969, I:160).

But Weber makes a distinctive contribution to these claims when he includes technological artifacts among the objects that may be "charismatically endowed" (see above). The unspoken implication of this inclusion is to recognize that Marx and Engels's "change and development of the material means of production" is a greatly simplifying gloss for the following process: (1) Some new "material means of production" is cognitively perceived as exceptional (which is to say, some exceptionally improved outcome—relative to the outcome which the old means generated—is, at least tentatively, attributed to this new means). (2) That perception of exceptionality then elicits sufficient emotional enthusiasm to invest the time and energy necessary to try out the new means, evaluate its preliminary production outcomes, and, if these are satisfactory, integrate the new means into the regular production process. Without such shared cognitive attribution of exceptionality, and without a similarly shared emotional enthusiasm, no new means of production is at all likely to become a regular part of the production process, and without that, none can bring about the changes in the social relations of production that are the centerpieces of Marxian theory. This cognitive attribution and emotional enthusiasm (as we have seen above) is exactly what Weber means by charisma, when the concept is applied, as he says it should be, to technological artifacts. (It also seems to be what McLuhan means by "the medium is the message" [1964:23–35].)[16] Nor should we forget, in this context, the charisma response one experiences from works (artifacts) of art—insofar as we are impressed with their exceptionality (originality, authenticity) and regard them as marvelous, sublime, awesome.[17]

Thus, the theory being proposed here applies everything said earlier in this chapter concerning the cognitive-and-emotional nature of charisma, its lack of intrinsic transcendence, and its variability in intensity and dispersion, to the full range of humanly perceivable (and imaginable) phenomena—including nonhuman as well as human objects.

Now, against the background of this explication of charisma, let us come back to its role in driving the step phase of cultural evolution (and all that the latter entrains). The thing to be emphasized again here is that high-intensity charisma, no matter what its object, is to be regarded as a solvent, not a crystallizer. It is an extraordinary, exceptional, unpredicted shock that breaks the old stable ties but does not form any new stable ties to take their place.[18] For this reason, Weber says, "charismatic authority is naturally unstable" (1978a:1114), and, given that natural instability, an outburst of high-intensity charisma is typically soon followed by a new crystallization, a new routinization: "When the tide that lifted a charismatically led group out of everyday life flows back into the channels of workaday routines, at least the 'pure' form of charismatic domination will wane and turn into an 'institution'" (Weber 1978a:1121).[19]

Charisma: How Does It Achieve Its Effects?

Phillips, despite the fact that he does not mention charisma, or Weber, is especially useful in outlining the manner in which charisma achieves its effects when he asks or implies the following questions: Why does an individual, in a given complex situation, give salience to one of his/her many status identifications rather than another (see also Wallace 1983:104–109)? Phillips himself does not put the question this way, but the question seems clearly implied when he points out that "the reference group 'persons with troubles' may be chosen over others [under certain conditions]. On the other hand, the reference group 'Christians' may become salient [under other conditions]" (1979:1169). Similarly, "Out of the enormous range of problems plaguing an individual, what makes him single out one for attention rather than another?" (Phillips 1979:1168)—and let me add: Out of the enormous range of gratifications that an individual may seek among the ordinarily many solutions to a given problem, what makes him/her single out one of these for attention? Additionally, "Why does an individual sometimes approach a problem in a deliberate, reasoning, and logical mode, while at other times he may approach the same problem in an impulsive, unreasoned, and illogical mode?" (Phillips 1979:1169). Finally, "What makes an individual respond to anomie with one type of behavior rather than another? Why do some individuals respond . . . by committing suicide, while others turn to alcohol and still others join anomie-reducing social movements?" (Phillips 1979:1170).

Phillips's own answer to all these questions centers on "suggestion, imitation, and modeling" (1979:1168, 1169), and this seems only another way of putting what this chapter has been discussing as "charisma" and "psychical contagion."

In this way, Phillips helps point toward the hypothesis that charisma (regardless of the nature of the object which is said to possess it) achieves its "revolutionary" effects by focusing the attention of all the individuals directly exposed to it in the same way—cognitively, cathectically, and conatively. Once these powerful psychological alignments among individuals who are directly exposed have occurred, psychic contagion (greatly augmented in our own time, as Phillips points out, by the mass media) can then spread the same foci of attention far beyond—to individuals who were never exposed to the original stimulus at all.

The Routinization of Charisma

Charisma becomes routinized because it is the metabolic nature of the individual human participant in charisma attribution and response (and psychic contagion) to require oxygen, water, food, and shelter on a regular basis, and when the charismatic object is a living organism, it is also routine for that object eventually to die (nonliving objects, of course, also change). Thus, "the problem of succession . . . is crucial because through it occurs the routinization of the charismatic focus of the structure. . . . [but] the most fundamental problem is that of making a transition from a charismatic administrative staff, and the corresponding principles of administration, to one which is adapted to everyday conditions. . . . [rather than living] on gifts, booty, or sporadic acquisition" (Weber 1978a:253, 249).[20]

Now when that routinization takes place, it may develop in one of two directions. It may result in "traditionalization *or* . . . legalization, according to whether rational legislation is involved or not"; "the tendency [may be] to traditionalization *or* legalization"; "charismatic authority. . . . cannot remain stable, but becomes *either* traditionalized *or* rationalized, or a combination of both"; "the transformation of the charismatic mission into an office may have more of a patrimonial *or* more of a bureaucratic character" (Weber 1978a:249, 250, 246, 251, all italics added; see also 1951b:113; compare Schluchter 1989:403).[21]

Therefore the general question arises: What determines whether a culture, once driven to a turning-point in its history by charisma, turns backward to the preceding stage, or turns forward to some next stage?

Pushing and Steering Around the Turning-Point

Weber provides the basis for answering this question in his remark (already partly cited in chapter 2) that "not ideas, but material and ideal interests, directly govern man's conduct. Yet very frequently the 'world images' that have been created by 'ideas' have, like switchmen, determined the tracks along which action has been pushed by the dynamic of interest" (1946:280). One therefore expects Weber's answer to the track-switching question mentioned above to implicate interests as the pushing motivations and ideas as the switching or steering devices—and that is indeed the case.

Weber claims that in Western civilization, the routinized and culturally shared Calvinist idea that at least some of the faithful Protestant laity have already been honored with salvation in the next world and for that reason deserve the highest honor in this world, performed the crucial steering function.[22] In this routinization, "the individual could only be sure of his state of grace [i.e., his predestined salvation] if he felt reason to believe that, by adhering to a principle of methodical conduct, he pursued the sole correct path in all his action" (Weber 1978a:1200).

Note, however, not only the importance of learned ideas here, but the importance of the individual's innate self-interest (see chapter 2) as manifested in the individual's striving for certainty about "his [*own*] state of grace." Weber emphasizes this motivating self-interest as follows: "One of the decisive motives underlying all cases of the routinization of charisma is naturally the striving for security. This means legitimization, on the one hand, of positions of authority and social prestige, on the other hand, of the economic advantages enjoyed by the followers and sympathizers of the leader" (1978a:252). Consequently, in order to accommodate the routinization process, Weber inserts a stage between traditional and rational legality that he calls *expediency*, wherein "substitution for the unthinking acceptance

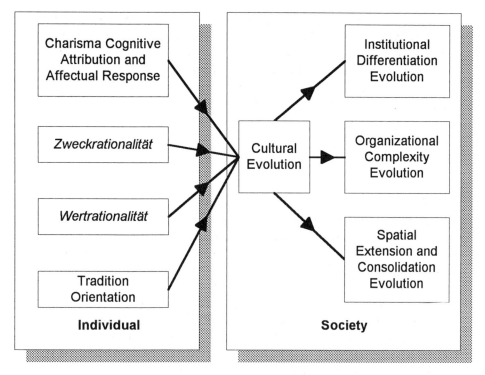

Figure 7. Explanatory Model of Societal Evolution

of ancient custom, of deliberate adaptation to situations in terms of self-interest" (Weber 1978a:30)—that is, self-interest in avoiding insecurity—takes place.[23]

We have, then, both the *pushing* "dynamic of interest" and the *steering* "switchmen" of "ideas" (see above) as jointly determining the direction taken by the routinization of charisma, and thereby determining which new (or old) "track" is taken by cultural evolution.

So if one asks, once again, On what does human societal evolution depend?, the Weberian theory proposed here answers that that evolution moves in two kinds of phases, both of which are driven by culture—but different kinds of culture. One phase is relatively continuous and ramplike; the other is discontinuous and steplike. The continuous phase is driven by a culture that incorporates traditional, *wertrational,* and *zweckrational* orientations; the discontinuous phase is driven by a culture that combines affectual and *zweckrational* orientations (see also Gerth and Mills 1946:54, and Deutsch 1971:121).[24]

This conclusion is diagrammed in figure 7 as a Weberian hypothetical model of the mechanism that causally explains the path taken by human societal evolution shown in figure 6.

Summary

The preceding chapter set forth a four-component descriptive model of societal evolution—comprising evolution in institutional specialization, in culture, in organizational scale, and in spatial extension and consolidation. The present chapter has proposed that although these components are interdependent, the evolution of culture is their pilot and integrator, not only because of the distinctly Weberian priority of psychological behavior over physiological behavior but also because culture responds most directly to the revolutionary impact of charisma (whether human or nonhuman phenomena are its objects) and the routinization of that charisma.

The simplest extrapolation of this explanatory model suggests the possibility of an irregularly repeated process that predicts that *any* established stage of human societal culture is likely, sooner or later, to succumb to outbursts of high-intensity charisma (having any of a variety of possible objects) that, together with their subsequent routinization, may then force a relatively sudden transition to a new and different stage—or back to a previous one.

6

INSTITUTIONAL EVOLUTIONS AND PROCESSES

ALTHOUGH CHAPTERS 4 AND 5 have set forth a view of how and why the specializations of the participant-organizing institutions evolved (and have also put forward some inferences concerning the bureaucratic and machine technology, and the rational legal culture, that integrates and sustains them), we have not yet examined how each of these institutions has evolved internally in response to the overall driving force of that culture and its predecessors. That is the principal aim of the present chapter.

The order in which the institutions will be examined here is determined by the position taken in chapter 3 that the economic and scientific institutions only exert influence over their individual participants' choice of means, whereas the political and religious institutions exert influence over these individuals' choice of ends as well as means. We therefore take up first the evolutions of the economic and scientific institutions, and then go on to the more complicated (and in the sense just mentioned, more important) evolutions of the political and religious institutions. In the latter discussions we also examine certain recurrent processes inside the political institution and inside the religious institution. Finally, we analyze Weber's well-known study of the connection between recent evolution in the religious institution and in the economic institution of Western European societies.

The Evolution of the Economic Institution

Weber suggests three stages in the evolution of the economic institution that parallel the three stages of cultural evolution in general (see chapter 4).[1] In the first, "natural norms," stage individuals engage in an "instinctively reactive search for food" (Weber 1978a:70).

In the second stage, "traditional acceptance of inherited techniques and customary social relationships" (Weber 1978a:70) becomes dominant. The latter relationships include "sacred taboos [and] monopolistic consociations of status groups which render exchange with outsiders impossible" and "the right to share in the commons, [which] may have become vested definitively and hereditarily" (1978a:638).

The third stage has two phases. In the first (called the "development of rational economic action" [Weber 1978a:70]), economic activity is freed of constraint by the above-mentioned traditional values and consociations ("The 'free' market . . . is an abomination to every system of fraternal ethics" [1978a:637]), because it is dominated by individually self-interested *Zweckrationalität* (see chapter 2). Thus, in "an emerging capitalist economy, the stronger it becomes, the greater will be its efforts to obtain the means of production and labor services in the market without limitations by status or sacred bonds, and to emancipate the opportunities to sell its products from the restrictions imposed by the sales monopolies of status groups" (Weber 1978a:638).

In the second phase of the third stage, *Zweckrationalität* comes under the protection of market norms prohibiting encroachment by traditional or *wertrational* values, and permitting only those economic monopolies that are organized solely for the maximization of personal profit (see figure 8). Thus, "Capitalistic interests . . . favor the continuous extension of the free market, but only up to the point at which some of them succeed . . . in obtaining for themselves a monopoly for the sale of their products or the acquisition of their means of production" (Weber 1978a:638, 639). After this, "no further modes of association develop," Weber says, "except in cases where certain participants enter into agreements in order to better their competitive situations, or where they all agree on rules for the purpose of

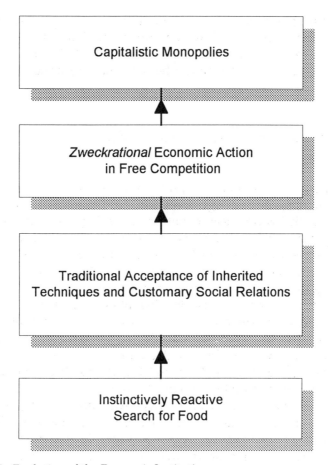

Figure 8. Evolution of the Economic Institution

regulating transactions and of securing favorable general conditions for all" (1978a:43).

Note also the great emphasis Weber gives to the role of tools, instruments, machines, and other physical artifacts (produced by the scientific institution, as discussed in chapter 3) in developing the economic institution: "The building of the turnpikes wrought a revolution in commercial life comparable to no other before the appearance of the railways"; "coal and iron released technology and

productive possibilities from the limitations of the qualities inherent
in organic materials. . . . [The consequent] mechanization of the production process through the steam engine liberated production from
the organic limitations of human labor" (Weber 1950:296, 297, 305–6).

The Evolution of the Scientific Institution

In figure 9, two lines of development, interacting only weakly at first
but with increasing strength over time, lead to modern science. The
dominant line is practical invention (including that of the economically pivotal artifacts just mentioned), driven mainly by human material interests in controlling the world, and the other, subsidiary, line
is abstract theory, driven mainly by human ideal interests in understanding the world (see chapters 2 and 3).

Weber holds that the practical invention line developed largely
independently of the abstract theoretical line until recently. Thus,
"the inventors of the pre-capitalistic age worked empirically; their
inventions had more or less the character of accidents," and "all the
inventors of [the seventeenth century] are dominated by the object of
cheapening [economic] production" (Weber 1950:312, 311). Even in
the case of "the greatest inventor of pre-capitalistic times, Leonardo
da Vinci," his goal was still the "mastery of technical problems as
such" (Weber 1950:311–12). Abstract theory, however, has been influenced by practical concerns from the beginning. Thus, as far back
as Plato's *Republic*, "the concept. . . . seemed to open the way for
knowing and for teaching how to act rightly in life and, above all,
how to act as a citizen of the state. . . . And for these reasons one
engaged in science" (Weber 1946:141).

But with the invention of the rational experiment (and it is worth
noting that such experiments depended heavily on practical inventions such as the weight balance, pendulum, clock, test tube, retort,
furnace, telescope, microscope, and spectroscope), there began an
increasingly intimate interaction between practical invention and
abstract theory—at least in Western Europe: "Through the union

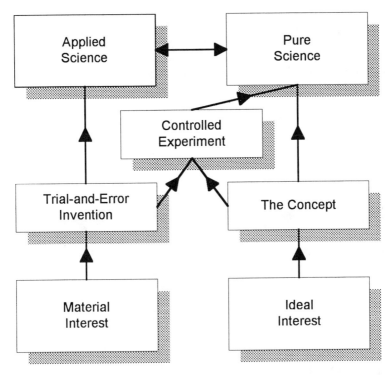

Figure 9. Evolution of the Scientific Institution

with science, the production of goods was emancipated from all the bonds of inherited tradition, and came under the dominance of the freely roving intellect. . . . only the occident possesses science in the present-day sense of the word. . . . a rational science and in connection with it a rational technology remained unknown to [other] civilizations" (Weber 1950:305, 313).

Finally, in this connection, special attention should be paid to Weber's punctuational view of the overall evolution of social science:[2]

All research in the cultural sciences in an age of specialization . . . [eventually comes to] consider the analysis of the data as an end in itself. . . . Indeed, it will lose its awareness of its ultimate rootedness in the value-ideas in general. And it is well that should be so. But there comes a moment when the atmosphere changes. The significance of the unreflectively utilized viewpoints becomes uncertain and the road is lost in the twilight. . . . Then science too prepares to change its standpoint and its analytical apparatus and to view the streams of events from the heights of thought. (Weber 1949:112)[3]

The Evolution of the Political Institution

We come now to the first participant-organizing institution for which Weber proposes not only an overall evolutionary path but also certain recurrent internal processes. Let us consider the evolutionary path first.

Weber tells us that "violent social action is obviously something absolutely primordial. . . . However, the monopolization of legitimate violence by the political-territorial association and its rational consociation into an institutional order is nothing primordial but a product of evolution" (1978a:904–5).[4] A more detailed analysis of this evolution may be divided into the four stages shown in figure 10.

In the first stage, violence "was not bound by norms" (Weber 1978a:905), but in the second stage, violence "acquires legitimacy . . . [initially in cases where] it is directed against members of the fraternity who have acted treasonably or who have harmed it by disobedience or cowardice." This stage, Weber says, is then "transcended gradually, as this *ad hoc* consociation develops into a permanent structure. Through the cultivation of military prowess and war as a vocation such a structure develops into a coercive apparatus able to lay effective and comprehensive claims to obedience. These claims will [also] be directed against the inhabitants of conquered territories" (1978a:906).[5] In the fourth and most recent stage, "the prosecution of an ever widening sphere of injuries to persons and property is . . . placed under the guaranty of the political coercive apparatus. Thus the political community monopolizes the legitimate application of violence for its coercive apparatus" (Weber 1978a:908).

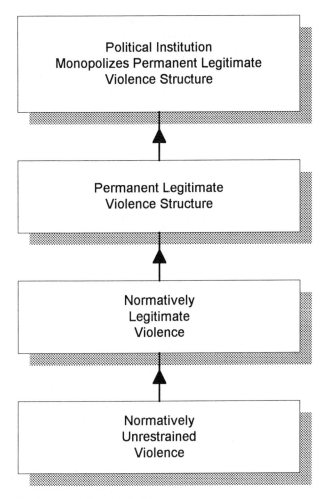

Figure 10. Evolution of the Political Institution

Processes in the Political Institution

Now, against the above background of nonrecurrent political evolution, let us focus on models of three cyclical political processes that Weber regards as peculiar to the most recent evolutionary period—

the period of legal rationality (see chapter 4), during which the political institution has become "transformed into an institution for the protection of rights" (see above). The models in question refer to (1) how political decision makers are produced, (2) how political decisions are produced, and (3) how political decisions are administered.

How Political Decision Makers Are Produced

The first thing to be said here is that Weber somewhat misleadingly presents his discussion of classes, status groups, and parties as though these phenomena belonged only to a static, nonprocessual, typology. Thus, he tells us "'classes,' 'status groups,' and 'parties' are [all] phenomena of the distribution of power in a community" (1978a:927). More specifically, "We may speak of a 'class' when . . . a number of people have in common a specific causal component of their life chances, insofar as . . . this component is represented exclusively by economic interests in the possession of goods and opportunities for income" (Weber 1978a:927); "'Parties' reside in the sphere of power. . . . a party always struggles for political control" (Weber 1978a:938, 939); and status groups are "determined by a specific, positive or negative, social estimation of honor" (Weber 1978a:932, italics removed).

That classes, status groups, and parties also bear a processual relation to each other, however, starts to become clear when we note Weber's further claims that "'classes' are *not* communities"; "in contrast to classes, status groups *are* normally [communities]";[6] and "party-oriented social action always involves *association*" (1978a:927, 932, 938, all italics added). And, obviously, the keys to understanding these claims are the definitions Weber assigns to the terms *community* (and *communal*), and *association* (and *associative*). On this, he says,

A social relationship will be called "communal" if and so far as the orientation of social action . . . is based on a subjective feeling of the parties, whether affectual or traditional, that they belong together. A social relationship will be called "associative" if and insofar as the orientation of social action within it rests on a rationally motivated adjustment of interests or a similarly motivated agreement, whether the basis of rational judgment be absolute values or reasons of expediency. (Weber 1978a:40–41)

So classes are not communities because classes do not take "social action" (as do communities and associations): "'Classes' . . . merely represent possible . . . bases for social action" (Weber 1978a:927; see also 929). A class, then, exists for Weber to the extent that different individuals objectively occupy the same categorical position in the commodity or labor markets (as, say, primarily sellers in the former and buyers in the latter, or vice versa)—even though each may be totally unaware of occupying it and/or unaware of others who also occupy it.

Next, consider a status group. Weber says it is a socially acting community whose social action rests on a shared (consensual) subjective awareness and expectation of others: "Status honor is normally expressed by the fact that above all else a specific style of life is expected from all those who wish to belong to the circle. Linked with this expectation are restrictions on social intercourse. . . . Whenever [there exists] consensual action of this closing character, the status development is under way" (Weber 1978a:932, italics removed).

Finally, consider a party. It, Weber says, is a socially acting associative social relationship—which is, in turn, a status group (community) of a special kind. That is to say, the action of a party, like a status group, is "based on a [nonrational] subjective feeling of the [participants] that they belong together" but in addition, that action also "rests on a *rationally* motivated adjustment of interests" and it strives for "the acquisition of social power. . . . in a [rationally] planned manner" (see above).

Now let us generalize, in a way that Weber does not, on the concepts class, status, and party. First, it seems clear the concept of objective "class situation" is, in principle, applicable not only to the economic institution but to all the other participant-organizing institutions as well. That is to say, religious laity, scientific students/laity, and political subjects/clients all occupy the same objectively subordinate rank in their respective institutions—just as religious prophets and priests, scientific directors, and political leaders all occupy the same objectively superordinate rank—whether they are subjectively aware of each other or not (see chapter 4). This implies that any and all these objective rank situations may become bases for status-group formation if and when there develops a "subjective feeling of the parties [i.e., the individual members], whether affectual or traditional, that they belong together." Such status groups, in turn, may become bases for party formation if and when there also develops a "rationally motivated adjustment of interests or a similarly motivated agreement" to seek political power.

In addition, when the mutual fungibility of the four main spoils of social competition—namely, wealth, power, honor, and knowledge (discussed in chapter 3)—is recalled, one can hypothesize that the paths between status situations in different institutions are all two-way streets. Thus, not only may individuals who share an objective situation in, say, the economy, come to think of themselves as a status group and then go on to seek power in the polity, but individuals who share an objective political situation may come to think of themselves as a status group and then go on to seek economic wealth. Similar two-way streets would be found among all four spoils of social competition.[7]

Accordingly, the present theory allows not only for bourgeois, proletarian, peasant, and other economically based (Marx says "class") struggles and revolutions, but also for more purely political coups and uprisings, as well as revolutions on the part of a given religious faith, church, or sect, and revolutions by adherents of a given scientific paradigm (whether in pure or applied science), and, of course, any combination thereof.

With that, we turn to figure 11 and its summary of the general process implicit in the class-status-party relations, as follows. First, a Weberian class is defined as a category of individuals who occupy an "objective" position in *any* participant-organizing institution. A class may or may not add to this objective position a shared affectual orientation to that position—thereby becoming a "status [honor] group"—but if it does make this addition, it is then apt to make the still further addition of shared rational orientation toward attaining political power ("It has always been the case that, when a class has achieved economic power, it begins to think of its expectations of political leadership" [Weber 1978b:263, italics removed; see also 1989b:202]).

Second, a Weberian status group is characterized by a shared affectual orientation, although the status which is the object of that orientation need not be lodged in the economic institution (but it often is, for although "property as such is not always recognized as a

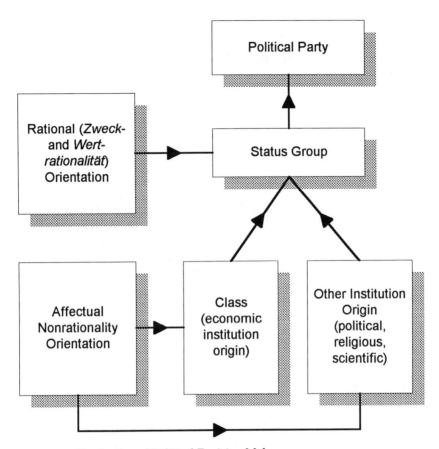

Figure 11. Production of Political Decision Makers

status qualification . . . in the long run it is, and with extraordinary regularity" [Weber 1978a:932]). A status group may or may not add to its shared affectual orientation a shared rational (i.e., combined *Zweckrationalität* and *Wertrationalität*) orientation toward achieving political power over other groups of its kind—thereby becoming, or giving rise to, a political party.

Finally, if, in the course of interparty competition, a given political party achieves dominance in the political institution, it thereby achieves the power to influence its own and others' class, status group, and party situations.[8] The cycle may begin again as another class becomes transformed into a status group and gives rise to its own political party (compare Pareto 1935:1430–32).[9]

How Political Decisions Are Produced

Weber (1) says "'power' is the probability that one actor within a social relationship will be in a position to carry out his own will despite resistance, regardless of the basis on which this probability rests"; (2) names one such basis "domination"—that is, "the probability that a command with a specific content will be obeyed by a given group of persons"; and (3) adds that "every genuine form of domination implies a minimum of voluntary compliance" and that the primary basis for that voluntary compliance is "the belief in [the] legitimacy" of the command (1978a:53, 212, 213). On this foundation, Weber then proposes "three pure types of legitimate domination," which he calls *rational, traditional,* and *charismatic* (1978a:215).

The topic on which the following discussion focuses is how the modern type of legitimate domination produces actual decisions—bearing in mind that "'ruling organizations which belong only to one or another of [the] pure types are very exceptional" (Weber 1978a:262). The general outlines of this process are shown in figure 12.

Weber says, "All inequalities of political rights [i.e., legitimized power to make decisions] in the past stemmed ultimately from the economically related inequalities of military qualification, which no longer have any place in the bureaucratised state and army" (quoted in Beetham 1985:105, italics removed; see also Bologh 1990:55), for "historically, the bureaucratization of the army has everywhere occurred along with the shifting of army services from the shoulders of the propertied to those of the propertyless. Until this transfer occurs, military service is an honorific privilege of propertied men" (Weber 1978a:981). Consequently, with bureaucratization, comes the leveling of the citizenry via bureaucracy's "characteristic principle"—namely, "the abstract regularity of the exercise of [decision-making] authority, which is a result of the demand for 'equality before the

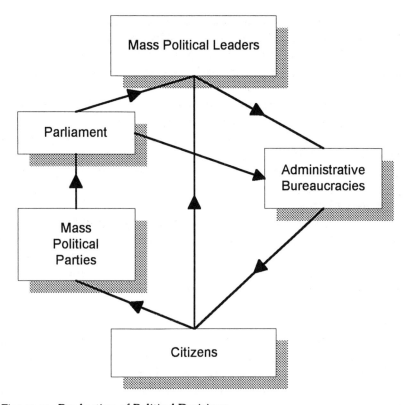

Figure 12. Production of Political Decisions

law' in the personal and functional sense—hence, of the horror of 'privilege'" (Weber 1978a:983).

This demand for "equality before the law," when successful, re-sults in universal suffrage: "It is no accident that the demand for universal suffrage is with us. This equality corresponds in its me-chanical character with the nature of the modern state" (Weber, quoted in Beetham 1985:105). From universal suffrage, in turn, there derives the pivotal decision-making roles of mass political parties, for inside such parties, Weber says, we find "active party members [who] have for the most part merely the function of acclaiming their leaders" (1978a:285); here, too, we find the mass leaders themselves, for "it is not a matter of the politically passive 'mass' throwing up a leader of itself, but rather of the political leader recruiting a following and winning the mass by demagogic appeal. This is true even in the most democratic constitutions" (Weber, quoted in Beetham 1985:106).

It is the political parties, then, that are central to the decision-making process in the political institutions of modern societies, for "present candidates and programs to the politically passive citizens. . . . They also create the norms which govern the administrative process. They subject the administration to control, support it by their confidence, or overthrow it by withdrawal of confidence" (Weber 1978a:294).

But in political institutions characterized by universal suffrage, it is in the elected parliaments that the various parties strive most openly, peacefully, and competitively for "the acquisition of social power in a planned manner"—parliaments being a kind of political party-of-the-whole in which the contending parties are as factions. More specifically, in Weber's view, parliaments serve three main functions: they exercise control over the administrative bureaucracy,[10] they serve as the medium through which the consent of the governed is registered,[11] and they serve as recruitment-and-training ground for popular political leaders.[12] Finally, Weber's view that "the President of the Reich could become the safety-valve of the demand for leadership if he were elected in a plebiscitarian way and not by Parliament" (1946:114; see also Beetham 1985:226–40) should also be noted because it justifies representing, in figure 12, both the indirect and direct election of popular political leaders.

How Political Decisions Are Administered

In the model to be examined next, we trace the application of decisions to the subject/clients of the decision makers, and the feedback from the former to the latter of information regarding the extent to which such decisions have been successfully implemented (for an analogous process, see figure 2). That is to say, we trace here the administration of decisions.

Weber says, "Rationally regulated association within a structure of domination finds its typical expression in bureaucracy" (1978a:954, italics removed).[13] In such a bureaucracy, "the person who obeys authority does so . . . only in his capacity as a 'member' of the organization and what he obeys is only 'the law' [not the person, per se, who holds the superior office]." Moreover, "the typical person in authority, the 'superior,' is himself subject to an impersonal order by orienting his actions to it in his own dispositions and commands" (Weber 1978a:217). Thus, "there is an obligation to obedience [and to command] only within the sphere of the rationally delimited jurisdiction which, in terms of the order, has been given to [each participant]" (Weber 1978a:218). The bureaucratic process, then, cycles from the superior's formally rule-defined right to issue commands, to his/her physically issuing such a command, to the subordinate's also formally rule-defined obligation to obey that command—which may entail a right to issue a command or dispensation to a subject/client—to the subordinate's physical obedience in this respect, to the subject/client's obligation to obey that command or accept that dispensation, to the latter's physical obedience in this respect. At that point, information regarding all these obediences, their consequences, and related conditions is reported back up the line—such that both the subordinate's and the superordinate's believed right to issue a further command are reinforced or modified (see Weber, 1978a:215–26).[14] This process is summarized in figure 13.

Thus, we have not only static typologies but interrelated processual models of political decision makers, decision making, and decision-administration.

The Evolution of the Religious Institution

We turn now to the second participant-organizing institution for which Weber proposes both an overall evolutionary path and recurrent internal processes, and again we consider the evolutionary path first. This path involves the evolution of monotheism and religious universalism and the evolution of divine rational legality (i.e., religious ethicality).

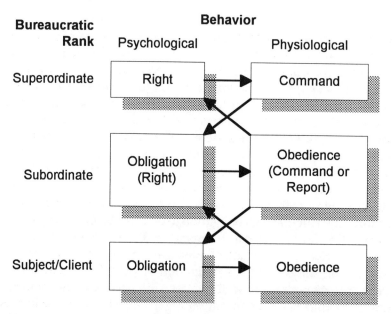

Figure 13. Production of Political Administration

Monotheism and Religious Universalism

Regarding the charisma of features of the natural ecosystem and technological artifacts as underlying evolution in the religious institution, Weber notes that

> the product of the potter, weaver, turner and carpenter is much less affected by unpredictable natural events, especially by organic reproduction that involves the mystery of "creation" for which only phantasy can provide an explanation. . . . the work is done largely within the *house* and is removed from the organically determined quest for food. . . . The forces of nature become an intellectual problem as soon as they are no longer part of the immediate environment. This provokes the rationalist quest for the transcendental meaning of existence, a search that always leads to religious speculation. (1978a:1178)[15]

And regarding the charisma of "persons" in religious evolution, he notes that belief in spirits . . . is most advanced in those societies within which certain persons possess charismatic magical powers. . . . Indeed it is this circumstance that lays the foundation for the oldest of all "vocations," that of the professional necromancer. In contrast to the ordinary person, the "layman" in the magical sense, the magician is permanently endowed with charisma. (Weber 1978a:401)

"The result of this process," Weber says, "is the rise on the one hand of the idea of the 'soul,' and on the other of ideas of 'gods,' 'demons,' hence of 'supernatural' powers, the ordering of whose relations to men constitutes the realm of religious behavior" (1978a: 403). This belief in spirits, however, "becomes really secure only through the continuing activity of a 'cult' dedicated to one and the same god—through the god's connection with an enduring association of men, for which he has special significance as the enduring god. . . . Once this preservation of the forms of the gods has been secured, the intellectual activity of those concerned in a professional way with such problems may be devoted to the systematization of these ideas" (Weber 1978a:407).

Now inasmuch as the "enduring association" that Weber calls the "cult" here has two dimensions of belief—magical and religious ("the cults we have just termed 'religious' practically everywhere contain numerous magical components" [1978a:424]), Weber contrasts "those professional functionaries who influence the gods by means of worship with those magicians who coerce demons by magical means" (1978a:425) and applies the term *priest* to the former. The main line of evolution in the religious institution follows (1) worship rather than coercion, and (2) the permanent priestly enterprise rather than the occasional magical enterprise—as shown in figure 14.

The main line of evolution also tends toward monotheism, Weber argues, insofar as "there is a tendency for a pantheon to evolve" (1978a:407) such that eventually one of the deities in this pantheon becomes thought of as superior to the others in the same pantheon. That deity may then become thought of as superior to others in other pantheons—thereby augmenting monotheism with universalism: "A god may dominate a pantheon without being an international or 'universal' deity. But his dominance of a pantheon usually suggests that he is on the way to becoming that" (Weber 1978a:418).

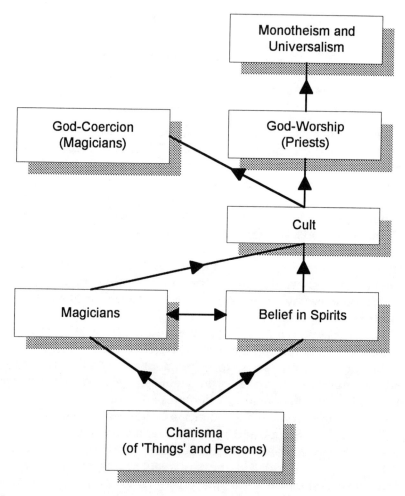

Figure 14. Evolution of the Religious Institution

Monotheism and religious universalism, then, develop together—their development nurturing, and nurtured by, that of the political and economic institutions: "The growth of empire . . . favored the rise of both universalism and monotheism. . . . [although it] has by no means been the sole or indispensable lever for the accomplishment of this development" (Weber 1978a:418).

Divine Rational Legality

The process (shown in figure 15) whereby obedience to a divinely sanctioned rational legality evolved, begins with the divergence of worship and the permanent priesthood from coercion and the occasional magician (as mentioned above). On the one hand, "magic involves a stereotyping of technology and economic relations. . . . [For example, it demands] that in the location of structures on certain mountains, forests, rivers, and cemetery hills, foresight should be exercised in order not to disturb the rest of the spirits" (Weber 1950:361), and on the other, "the full development of both a metaphysical rationalization and a religious ethic requires an independent and professionally trained priesthood, permanently occupied with the cult and with the practical problems involved in the cure of souls" (1978a:426).

The great significance of the priesthood's emergence is the impetus it gave to belief in a divine rational authority, which is to say, not an impulsively affectual, extemporaneous deity, but one consciously bound by rules of comparison and choice (see chapter 2). As a result, whereas "in the event of failure, the magician possibly paid with his life," priests "have enjoyed the contrasting advantage of being able to deflect the blame for failure away from themselves and onto their god." Furthermore, "priests may find ways of interpreting failures in such a manner that the responsibility falls . . . upon the behavior of the god's worshippers. . . . The problem of why the god has not hearkened to his devotees might then be explained by stating that they had not honored their god sufficiently" (Weber 1978a:428).

At this point, Weber says, "there might develop within the pantheon gods of a distinctly ethical character. . . . A specialized functional god of legislation and a god who controls the oracle will naturally be found very frequently among the ethical divinities" (1978a:429), and in this case, "honoring" the god would involve honoring the laws falling under that god's protection. In addition, there may be influences toward "increased ethical demands . . . made upon the gods" emanating from the other (economic, political, and scientific) participant-organizing institutions of society (see Weber 1978a:430). Then, of course, there is the role of the ideal interest itself (see chapter 2): "Intellectualism as such, more particularly the meta-

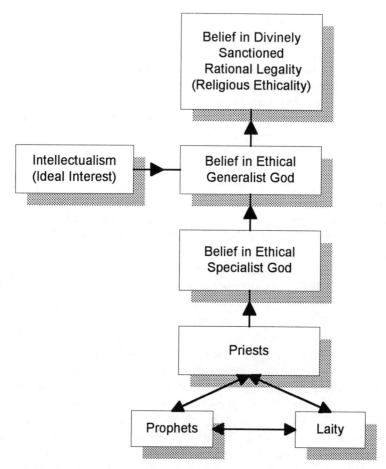

Figure 15. Evolution of Divinely Sanctioned Rational Legality

physical needs of the human mind as it is driven to reflect on ethical and religious questions, [is] driven not by material need but by an inner compulsion to understand the world as a meaningful cosmos and to take up a position toward it" (Weber 1978a:499, see also 506).

As a result of all these considerations, "Even the gods to whom one turns for protection are henceforth regarded as either subject to some moral order or—like the great kings—as the creators of such an order,"[16] and "it is naturally postulated that god will protect against injury the order he has created. The intellectual implementation of this postulate. . . . stimulated the development of a religious ethic" (Weber 1978a: 431). In summary, Weber says, "Hitherto, there had been two primordial methods of influencing supernatural powers. One was to subject them to human purposes by means of magic. The other was to win them over by making oneself agreeable to them . . . by gratifying their egotistical wishes. To these methods was now added obedience to the religious law as the distinctive way to win the god's favor" (1978a:431–32). But Weber cautions that "not every priesthood developed . . . a rational metaphysic and a religious ethic. Such developments generally presupposed the operation of one or both of two forces outside the priesthood: prophets, the bearers of metaphysical or religious-ethical revelation, and the laity, the non-priestly devotees of the cult" (1978a:427, italics removed).

Let us turn, therefore, to consider relationships among these three substructures of the religious institution (i.e., priests, prophets, and laity). It is here that Weber seems to suggest a rough parallel, in the religious institution, of the political decision maker, decision making, and decision-administration processes examined in the preceding section of this chapter.

Processes in the Religious Institution

In clear implication of process, Weber says that "in all times there has been but one means of breaking down the power of magic and establishing a rational conduct of life; this means is great rational prophecy" (1950:362), and locates the primary site of prophets in the prehistoric and early historic interaction between the religious institution and the political and economic institutions: "Perhaps prophecy in all its forms arose, especially in the Near East, in connection with the reconstitution of the great world empires in Asia, and the resumption and intensification of international commerce after a long interruption" (1978a:441). The prophet, arising from "the thinking laymen" (Weber 1946:351), is the object of a charismatic attribution and response that "usually means that he has the power to raise the dead, and possibly that he himself may rise from the grave. . . . If he is to continue to live on in some manner among large numbers of the laity, he must himself become the object of a cult, which means he must become the incarnation of a god" (Weber 1978a:467).

It is striking, however, that although Weber regards the popular response to the prophet as emotional and therefore nonrational, he looks upon the prophet him/herself as distinctly rational (specifically, *wertrational*): "To the prophet, both the life of man and the world, both social and cosmic events, have a certain systematic and coherent meaning, to which man's conduct must be oriented if it is to bring salvation and after which it must be patterned in an integrally meaningful manner" (Weber 1978a:450).

Like any other charisma, however, the charisma attributed to the prophet must eventually be routinized if it is to have lasting impact on the religious institution and thence on society as a whole. Thus, the "transformation of a personal following into a permanent congregation is the normal process by which the doctrine of the prophets enters into everyday life, as the function of a permanent institution. The disciples or apostles of the prophets thereupon become the mystagogues, teachers, priests or pastors (or a combination of them all), serving an association dedicated to exclusively religious purposes, namely the congregation of laymen" (Weber 1978a:454, italics removed). The priesthood, like the bureaucracy in the political institution, then, functions as prime routinizer of the prophet's charisma in the eyes of the laity, for the priesthood "had to assume the obligations of codifying either the victorious new doctrine or the old doctrine which had maintained itself despite an attack by the prophets. The priesthood had to delimit what must and must not be regarded as sacred and had to infuse its views into the religion of the laity, if it was to secure its own position" (Weber 1978a:457; see also 1976:78).

In summary, then, we may think of prophets as instigators of charisma—that is, as urging their audiences to make the cognitive judgment that certain events are (or were, or will be) exceptional, and to respond with intense emotionality to those events—thereby enabling the prophets' proposed *Wertrationalität* to be introduced into a religious institution hitherto dominated by traditional nonrationality. We may also think of priests as orchestrators of charisma— that is, as determining whether the religious institution then turns forward to that new *Wertrationalität*, or backward to traditional nonrationality. We have, in short, another pusher-steerer model ("very frequently the 'world images' that have been created by 'ideas' have, like switchmen, determined the tracks along which action has been pushed by the dynamics of interest" [Weber 1946:280; see chapter 5]—one in which the charismatic prophet is pusher and the routinizing priest is steerer.

But who or what determines the direction of this steering? Weber answers this question by referring to another, nonprophetic and nonpriestly, force: "The rationalism of lay circles is another social force with which the priesthood must take issue. Different social strata may be the bearers of this lay rationalism" (Weber 1978a:467, italics removed). Accordingly, Weber examines the extent to which "different social strata" (for example, the peasantry, the nobility, the political bureaucracy, and business entrepreneurs—all members of the laity) are apt to become such bearers (see 1978a:468–80). The likeliest of all possible "bearers of . . . lay rationalism," he concludes, are business entrepreneurs, for "the tendency toward affiliation with an ethical, rational, and congregational religion is more apt to be found the closer one gets to those strata which have been the carriers of the modern rational [business] enterprise" (Weber 1978a:479, italics removed; 480).

It seems clear, then, that when we look closely at that routinization of the Protestant ethic that Weber regards as crucial to the Occidental escape from tradition culture, what we find is that the key factor is not the priesthood alone but the priesthood in interaction (let us say, more exactly, in negotiation) with the laity—most particularly, with the business entrepreneurial laity. It was the latter's long-established "lay rationalism" that set the conditions under which the routinization in question could be accomplished by the priesthood, for "religion nowhere creates certain economic conditions unless there are also present in the existing relationships and constellations of interests certain possibilities of, or even powerful drives toward, such an economic transformation" (Weber 1978a:577).

Note that (although Weber does not tell us this) it seems fair to say that all three of the recurrent processes noted above in connection with the political institution—namely, the class-status-party process that produces decision makers, the citizen-party-parliament-leader-bureaucracy process that produces decisions, and the superordinate-subordinate-subject/client process that produces decision-administration—are all also incorporable, in principle, as components of the recurrent prophet-priest-laity process in the religious institution.

Finally in this chapter, we turn full attention to what is surely the single most famous of Max Weber's works—namely, *The Protestant Ethic and The Spirit of Capitalism*.[17] I shall view this work as Weber's explication of how a particular set of prophet-priest-laity relations in the religious institution impinged first on entrepreneur-worker relations in the economic institution, and eventually instigated a societywide transition from a tradition culture to a rational legality culture in Western Europe.

A Case-Study in Prophetic Decision-Maker Charisma, and Its Diffusion to the Economic Institution

In the opening pages of *The Protestant Ethic*, Weber sets forth the great breadth of the problem it is meant to address: "A product of modern European civilization, studying any problem of universal history, is bound to ask himself to what combination of circumstances the fact should be attributed that in Western civilization, and in Western civilization only, cultural phenomena have appeared which (as we like to think) lie in a line of development having universal significance and value" (1958a:13, italics removed). Weber then goes on to enumerate, among these "universal" phenomena, not only capitalism but certain types of science, historiography, art, architecture, and bureaucracy (see 1958a:13–17). On these grounds, then, it seems fair to say that *The Protestant Ethic* takes as its subject matter the tradition-to-rational-legality evolutionary transition mentioned above in all its aspects, not merely its economic aspects.

Briefly, the story of *The Protestant Ethic and the Spirit of Capitalism* is this: Three new ideas were injected into the tradition culture of the Western European Catholic religious institution by two charismatic prophets, namely, Martin Luther and John Calvin. The ideas were: The world is a creation of a supreme, universal, rational, omniscient, and omnipotent deity and should be treated as such—that is, it should be carefully tended, rather than scorned and rejected (as when one escapes the world by entering a monastery).[18] Additionally, the same deity has assigned to every individual a particular role in tending the world (a "calling"). And finally, the same deity has also assigned to every individual a particular role in the afterworld (a "predestination").

A priest-routinized version of these ideas (the Protestant ethic) then diffused from the religious to the economic institution (via the individual participants shared by both institutions—as parishioners in the former, and as entrepreneurs and workers in the latter), where it engendered the "spirit of capitalism" and helped breed "those self-confident saints whom we can rediscover in the hard Puritan merchants of the heroic age of capitalism" (Weber 1958a:112). Let us examine this story more closely.

The Priestly Routinization of Calvin's Prophetic Charisma

Weber argues that "the question, Am I among the elect? [i.e., Am I predestined to be favored by the deity in the afterworld?] must sooner or later have arisen for every [Calvinist] believer and have forced all other interests into the background." For the originating charismatic leader himself, of course, this was no problem; Calvin "felt himself to be a chosen agent of the Lord, and was certain of his own salvation (Weber 1958a:110).

However, it was very much a problem for the administrative staff (the preacher-priests) of the movement as it pursued its "practical pastoral work," because that staff "had immediately to deal with all the suffering caused by the doctrine [of predestination]" (1958a:111). How was this suffering routinely dealt with? Pointing out that "Calvin's theology must be distinguished from Calvinism, the theological system from the needs of religious practice" (1958a:229; see also 1978a:1199), Weber argues that

> insofar as predestination was not reinterpreted, toned down, or fundamentally abandoned, two principal, mutually connected, types of pastoral advice appear. On the one hand it is held to be an absolute duty to consider oneself chosen, and to combat all doubts as temptations of the devil, since

> lack of self-confidence is the result of insufficient faith, hence of imperfect grace. . . . On the other hand, in order to attain that self-confidence intense worldly activity is recommended as the most suitable means. (1958a:111–12)

Weber is aware, however, that inasmuch as a very large number of different pastoral advices could have been invented as routinizations of Calvin's charisma, the question arises, Why were these advices, and not some other conceivable advices, adopted? He answers, implicitly, that the advices actually adopted were the ones the laypersons to whom they were addressed (namely, the business entrepreneurs mentioned above, and their employees) found most consonant with their own already established orientations.

Thus, in Weber's view, the advices in question were as much the results of what the advisees wanted to hear as of what the advisors wanted to say—and what the advisees wanted to hear was governed chiefly by their innately self-interested *Zweckrationalität* (see chapter 2)—for "all the religious movements which have affected large masses have started from the question, 'How can *I* become certain of *my* salvation?'" (Weber 1958a:229, italics added). Calvin's charisma (and that of his ideas), then, became routinized—in a tacit negotiation between preacher-priests and laypersons within the Protestant church—into a set of means-comparing and means-choosing rules shared by both sides, namely, the *Wertrationalität* of "ethical rationalism" (Weber 1951b:227).

These rules enjoined the laity to be (1) unquestioningly self-confident of their divinely ordained personal salvation in the afterworld, (2) unremittingly active in their divinely ordained personal vocation in this world, and (3) unflaggingly faithful that the activity in question constituted divine warrant for the self-confidence in question. It followed that "the individual could only be sure of his state of grace if he felt reason to believe that, by adhering to a principle of methodical conduct, he pursued the sole correct path in all his action—that he worked for God's glory. Methodical conduct, the rational form of asceticism, is thus carried from the monastery into the world" (Weber 1978a:1200), and "proof through ascetic conduct was necessary . . . particularly in vocational life, as the subjective guarantee of *certitudo salutis*. It is . . . one of the most important manifestations of an individual's predestination for salvation" (Weber 1978c:1115).[19]

Let us now consider how Weber claims this now rationally routinized Calvinist charisma—originating in the religious institution—affected the economic institution.

Two Spirits of Capitalism

Weber does not explicitly call our attention to it, and I do not think it has been noted before, but *The Protestant Ethic and the Spirit of Capitalism* argues that not one but two quite different (and complementary) "spirits" of capitalism were generated by the Protestant ethic. Thus, although Coleman is right when he says "some sort of combined or joint or aggregate effect of the economic behavior of many individuals in bringing about capitalistic development [should be] proposed," he errs when he adds that "it is here . . . that Weber's analysis is almost totally silent" (1990:9). Mannheim comes much closer to the argument I shall make: "It is the merit of Max Weber to have clearly shown . . . how often the same religion is variously experienced by peasants, artisans, merchants, nobles, and intellectuals" (1955:7; see the discussion of equi-initiality in appendix A)—though, in *The Protestant Ethic*, Weber differentiates only two varieties of such experience. The two varieties he chooses, however—namely, that of entrepreneurs, and that of workers—are crucial in generating the role-complementarity that is most characteristic of capitalism.

Weber identifies his view of this role-complementarity when he says that for the Protestant entrepreneur, "everything is done in terms of balances: at the beginning of the enterprise an initial balance, before every individual decision a calculation to ascertain its probable profitableness, and at the end a final balance to ascertain how much profit has been made" (1958a: 18). But for the Protestant worker, "not only is a developed sense of responsibility absolutely indispensable, but in general also an attitude which, at least during working hours, is freed from continual calculations of how the customary wage may be earned with a maximum of comfort and a minimum of exertion. Labour must . . . be performed as if it were an absolute end in itself, a calling" (1958a:61–62; compare 63). Protestant entrepreneurs in a capitalistic economic institution, then, constantly compare and select among alternative means on the basis of the profitability of these means to the entrepreneur—and that seems clearly the efficiency criterion attributed to *Zweckrationalität*— whereas Protestant workers in the same sort of economic institution apply the duty-bound, self-sacrificing, effectiveness criterion attributed to *Wertrationalität* (see chapter 2).

How did they get that way? Of the entrepreneur's efficiency-seeking spirit of capitalism, Weber says, "What the great religious epoch of the seventeenth century bequeathed . . . was above all an amazingly good, we may even say pharisaically good, conscience in the acquisition of money, so long as it took place legally. . . . With the consciousness of standing in the fullness of God's grace and being visibly blest by Him, the bourgeois business man . . . could follow his pecuniary interests as he would and feel that he was fulfilling a duty in doing so" (1958a:176–77; see also 1978c:1124). The businessman was, moreover, freed from any sense of guilt that might result from seeing the depressed circumstances to which his exploitation of them reduced his employees: "The development of the [idea of] calling quickly gave to the modern entrepreneur a fabulously clear conscience [by giving] to his employees as the wages of their . . . cooperation in his ruthless exploitation of them through capitalism the prospect of eternal salvation" (1950:367).

And of the Protestant ethic's contribution to the workers' willing cooperation in their own exploitation, Weber argues that "naturally the whole ascetic literature of almost all denominations is saturated with the idea that faithful labour, even at low wages, on the part of those whom life offers no other opportunities, is highly pleasing to God" (1958a:178; see also 1978c:1124).

Two Psychological Origins

These two spirits of capitalism, however, depend on quite different psychological raw materials. Thus (in accord with the definition of *Zweckrationalität* discussed in chapter 2), Weber regards the propensity toward *acquisition* as phylogenetically innate, and so refers to "the acquisitive instinct" (1958a:60) and claims "the impulse to acquisition, pursuit of gain, of money, of the greatest possible amount of money. . . . has been common to all sorts and conditions of men at all times and in all countries of the earth" (1958a:17). Weber does not, however, regard the propensity to *work* as innate: "Wherever modern capitalism has begun [to increase] the productivity of human labour by increasing its intensity, it has encountered the immensely stubborn resistance of . . . pre-capitalistic labour" (1958a: 60).[20] Thus the psychological raw materials for the entrepreneur's spirit of capitalism were already present in the human genetic endowment and needed only to be liberated, but those for the worker's spirit had to be inculcated.

Consequently, "worldly Protestant asceticism. . . . had the psychological effect of *freeing* the acquisition of goods from the inhibitions of traditionalistic ethics . . . in that it not only legalized it, but . . . looked upon it as directly willed by God" (Weber 1958a: 170–71, italics added), but the performance of labor "as if it were an absolute end in itself. . . . cannot be evoked by low wages or high ones alone, but can only be the product of a long and arduous process of *education*" (Weber 1958a:62, italics added; see also 1978a:129).

Different Economic Class Sites among the Laity

Now let us ask, In which category of Protestant lay individuals was the "freeing" of biologically innate tendencies most likely, and in which category was the "education" of socially learned tendencies most likely? Here it is important to recall that "the impulse to acquisition. . . . has been common wherever the objective possibility of it is or has been given" (see above), for this qualification suggests that Weber sees the early Western capitalist entrepreneurs as combining the objective opportunity ("possibility") to exercise their innate acquisitiveness with subjective belief in the divine rightness of doing so.[21]

The latter becomes an important point when Çe note that Weber treats capitalist workers as further divisible into two categories— those who have opportunities to exercise their acquisitiveness, and those who do not have such opportunities. For those in the first category, "a change of calling is by no means regarded as objectionable, if it is not thoughtless and is made for the purpose of pursuing a calling more pleasing to God. . . . Hence the faithful Christian must

A WEBERIAN THEORY

follow the call by taking advantage of the opportunity" (Weber
1958a:162). Not surprisingly, then, "with great regularity we find the
most genuine adherents of Puritanism among the classes which were
rising from a lowly status" (Weber 1958a:174, italics added) and,
accordingly, *changing* their callings. It is only to the second category
of workers, then—those in situations having no mobility
opportunities—that the Protestant ethic teaches that "labour must
. . . be performed as if it were an absolute end in itself, a calling," for
"faithful labour . . . *on the part of those whom life offers no other opportunities* is highly pleasing to God" (see above).[22]

Thus (and rearranging Weber's words somewhat but not his
meaning), it was "the emphasis on the ascetic importance of a *fixed*
calling" that "provided an ethical justification" of labor when the
"objective possibility" of upward mobility was absent, but emphasis
on the possibility of a *"change* of calling" when such possibility was
present that explained the "self-made man" and his rise "from a
lowly status" (1958a:163, italics added).

Everything depended, then, on the Protestant lay individual being
able accurately to size up, and then seize, the situation (and thus,
somewhat paradoxically, it depended on objective, scientific,
rationality—see chapter 2), for " 'if God show you a way in which
you may lawfully get more than in another way (without wrong to
your soul or to any other) if you refuse this . . . you cross one of the
ends of your calling, and you refuse to be God's steward' " (Weber
1958a:162).

It seems fair to conclude that in Weber's view, when the Protestant
ethic spread to the economic institution, it *liberated* innate self-
interest rationality in those lay individuals who, using objective rationality, saw they were in a situation of opportunity. It did this by
supplementing that rationality with *Wertrationalität* of a sort which
enjoined dutiful obedience to a divinely ordained calling to become
as rich as possible. Such obedience, in turn, encouraged the continual
efficiency calculations mentioned above.

By contrast, however, the very same Protestant ethic *suppressed*
innate self-interest rationality in those individuals who either did not
use scientific rationality or, using it, concluded they were not in a
situation of opportunity. It did this by restraining that rationality
with a *Wertrationalität* of a different content—namely, one demand-

ing obedience to a divinely ordained calling in which one simply worked as hard as possible—and this encouraged calculation of *effectiveness* only. (It does not seem accurate to say such work was "freed from [*all*] continuous calculation" [see above], for the question, Am I working flat out as hard as I possibly can? also entails a calculation.) The net result, then, was to designate both "labour as a calling," and "the employer's business activity as a calling" (Weber 1958a:178). With this conferral of divine honor (blessing) on both houses of the Western capitalistic economic institution, an especially powerful class role-complementarity came into existence: to the "indispensable ethical qualities of the modern capitalist entrepreneur. . . . [was] added the pious worker's special will for work" (Weber 1951:247).

So far, I have been discussing *Zweckrationalität* as though a person's self-interest were necessarily limited to his/her biological life. The enormous power of the religious institution, however, can be said to rest on the proposition that once a spiritual afterlife is believed to exist, *Zweckrationalität* (defined as in chapter 2) automatically extends to it as well. Thus, not only may religion-supported role differences in the economic institution generate differences in expectations regarding this-life, but the same role differences in the economic institution may also generate differences in expectations regarding an afterlife. Accordingly, Weber says, entrepreneurs typically became oriented to this-life, whereas workers typically became oriented to the afterlife:

> Strata with high social and economic privilege. . . . assign to religion the primary function of legitimizing their own life pattern and situation in the world. . . . What the privileged classes require of religion, if anything at all, is this legitimation. . . . Correspondingly different is the situation of the disprivileged. Their particular need is for release from suffering. . . . [The] hope for and expectation of just compensation, a fairly calculating attitude, is, next to magic (indeed, not unconnected with it), the most widely diffused form of mass religion all over the world. (1978a:491–92, italics removed; Joe Hill had the same idea)

Weber's dynamic of the routinization of the Protestant ethic in the religious institution and its diffusion to the two spirits of capitalism in the economic institution is summarized in figure 16.[23]

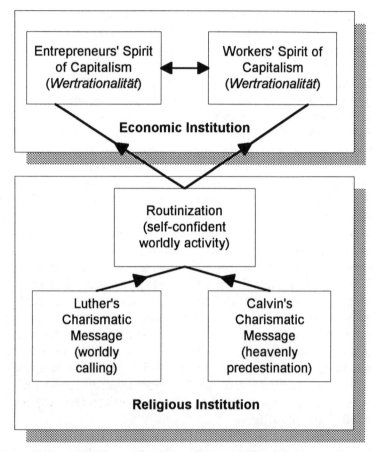

Figure 16. The Protestant Ethic and the Spirit of Capitalism

Summary

This chapter has concentrated on developing an image of some of the intra-institutional dynamics of human society, supplementing the inter-institutional picture presented in chapters 3, 4, and 5 as follows. Regarding long-term intra-institutional evolution so far, the economic institution evolved from the "instinctively reactive search for food" to "capitalistic monopolies"; the scientific institution evolved from hit-or-miss invention of useful objects to the "controlled experiment" aimed at developing general laws and theory—which then exerted increasingly firm guidance over further technological invention; the political institution evolved from violence "not bound by norms" to a normatively binding "political coercive apparatus. . . . [that] monopolizes the legitimate application of violence"; and the religious institution evolved from "belief in spirits" and the high status of "magicians" to belief in "divine rational legal authority" and the high status of "priests."

Regarding processes that cycle within the political institution, (1) decision makers come into, and leave, power as a result of a probabilistic dynamic involving classes, status groups, and parties; (2) decision making takes place in a process involving citizens, political parties, political leaders, and government administrators; and (3) decision-administration occurs through a process involving complementary role behaviors on the parts of superordinate and subordinate bureaucratic officials, and subjects/clients of the bureaucracy. Within the religious institution, the decision maker, decision making, and decision-administration processes come together in relations among prophets, priests, and laypersons. Weber's most famous work is devoted to an examination of a prophet-priest-layperson dynamic that occurred in the sixteenth- and seventeenth-century Western European Protestant church and its interaction primarily with the economic institution of that time and place.

7

SUMMARY AND SPECULATIONS

THIS CHAPTER BEGINS by briefly summarizing the theory set forth in the preceding chapters. It then extrapolates from that theory some broad speculations about what the future may hold for human society.

The Structure of the Individual

The theory rests chiefly on postulates (summarized in figures 3 and 4) about the phylogenetically given behavioral structure of the human individual.[1] This structure acts as one set of more or less fixed constraints on human society (the other set of constraints is the structure of the ecosystem—ultimately, the cosmic environment—in which that society exists). Every human individual, then, is postulated here as the possessor of both rational and nonrational psychological (neuroendocrine) behavior capabilities, each in two varieties, as well as certain capabilities for physiological (skeletalmuscular and visceral) behavior. Although the theory looks upon evolutionary change in these behavior capabilities as having been negligible so far, it allows for and recognizes an indefinitely large amount of evolution in their actual manifestations.

Undoubtedly the most important and most evident of these evolutions so far has been the typically slow, halting, uneven, sometimes retrogressive, but nonetheless massive, net increase in individual choice. The evolution seems "important" because maximizing our range of choice among possible adaptations to the changing exigencies of environment constitutes one of the two most powerful survival weapons of any species (the other is finding and adapting to an environment in which such exigencies are relatively unchanging and the range of choice can therefore approach zero). The evolution seems "evident" insofar as although not a single paleolithic individual could choose (or even imagine) an urban industrial life, nowadays tens of thousands of city folk can and do freely choose an approximately paleolithic life when they hit the trail and transform themselves into no-electricity and no-running-water summer campers.

The increasing choice to which I refer has two varieties: we have (1) discovered, invented, and employed more and more alternative means of reaching any given end, and we have also (2) imagined and formulated an increasing number of alternative ends toward which any given means may be directed. If we define freedom as the ability to choose among alternatives, then it seems beyond doubt that human freedom has greatly increased during our species' earthly tenure so far—although, as mentioned above, not evenly across individuals and societies.[2]

Having differentiated two kinds of choices (among alternative ends, and among alternative means), the theory then differentiates between two classes of each. Some ends (specifically, the personal self-preservation ends of *Zweckrationalität*) are not yet to any large degree subject to our choice. They are simply given—chosen for us, so to speak—as outcomes of natural selection passed down in our phylogenetic heritage. Other ends (i.e., those of *Wertrationalität*), however, are part of our sociocultural heritage—chosen by us and passed down from one generation to the next via socialization and learning. The same phylogenetic-versus-sociocultural distinction applies to the means whereby we pursue any given end: some means are chiefly phylogenetic in origin (hands, arms, legs, brains, eyes, ears, larynxes), and others are chiefly sociocultural in origin (skills, tools, domesticated plants and animals, machines).

Next, and of obvious importance to a theory of human society, I have noted the powerful enhancement of the human ability to choose among alternatives that results whenever two or more individuals begin to think and act as a sustained collectivity. Here, the theory holds that the choices made by lone individuals become rational, according to the definition offered in chapter 2, whenever such individuals consciously apply a rule (any rule) in their comparing and choosing among alternatives. These choices, however, cannot be *reliable* rational choices—insofar as reliability is defined in terms of intersubjective confirmation between two or more individuals. For the same reason, lone individuals cannot make reliable rational evaluations of the effectiveness or efficiency with which a given outcome is produced by employing given means in pursuit of given ends. Only sustained collectivities of individuals can achieve both reliable rational choices of means and reliable rational evaluations of results. Moreover, only such collectivities can provide the massed physiological power, and the organized physiological dexterity, required to accomplish the large and complex manipulations of the environment entailed by the pursuit of ends such as, say, building the pyramids of Gizeh or the PCs of Apple. Finally, and no less important, only sustained collectivities can formulate, propagate, and enforce particular choices among all the myriad possible ends to which individuals could conceivably devote their lives.

All these advantages of sustained collectivities—in particular, the self-sustaining collectivities we call "societies"—have shown themselves to be powerful weapons in the so far successful struggle of our species to survive and, more than that, to dominate (without wrecking) this planet's ecosystem.

Now all societies, regardless of the species of organism in which they are found, seem to incorporate three basic sets of institutions—one for taking-in new participants, another for organizing the activities of these participants while they last, and a third for letting out (or putting out) participants when they become regarded as in some way unfit or unwilling to participate further. The most clearly distinguishing characteristic of societies formed by humans lies in our extraordinarily robust development of the middle, participant-organizing, set of institutions.

The Structure of Society

The theory identifies four interacting institutions in the participant-organizing set (see figure 5), and each member of a given society is regarded as participating in all four of them—in various roles and statuses. The economic and scientific institutions (specialized producers of wealth, and empirical knowledge, respectively) guide members' comparisons and choices among alternative means toward given ends. The political and religious institutions (specialized producers of decision-making power, and honor, respectively), however, guide the same members' comparisons and choices among alternative ends as well as means.

In brief, then, just as every human individual is here regarded as encompassing an invariant roster of psychological and physiological behavioral capabilities that may express themselves in many relationships to each other and in many stages of development, so every human society is regarded as encompassing an invariant roster of participant-organizing institutions (economic, scientific, political, and religious) that may exist in many relationships to each other and in many stages of development. It is especially through these institutions that human society does things for the human individual that the individual cannot do alone—thereby contributing materially as well as intellectually to the survival success of the human species.

Describing the Evolution of Society

Figure 6 describes the evolution of human society (and also of localized societies—albeit at widely different rates of speed) as having developed in four directions more or less simultaneously: (1) toward an increasingly (but never exclusively) rational culture, which has enhanced the amount of choice available to individuals and to societies; (2) toward greater institutional differentiation, which has raised the level of specialized collective human effort available for identifying and focusing on any given problem in which such choice is involved; (3) toward greater organizational scale, which has increased the total amount of such effort that can be mobilized; and (4) toward greater spatial extension and consolidation, which has increased the amount and variety of ecosystem and population resources on which such effort may draw. To this, figure 6 adds the proposition that societal change along each of these paths has been discontinuous (stepwise) as well as continuous (rampwise)—and occasionally retrogressive, although predominantly progressive.

Explaining the Evolution of Society

Figure 7 schematizes the Weberian hypothesis that it is cultural evolution which has piloted evolution in the three other dimensions—in both their ramp phases and their step phases. Rampwise evolution is hypothesized as driven by learned nonself-interest rationality culture (*Wertrationalität*) and also by "tradition" nonrationality culture. Stepwise evolution, however, is driven by "affectual" nonrationality culture as manifested in intensely emotional responses to cognitive attributions of exceptionality—that is, charisma—plus innate self-interest rationality culture (*Zweckrationalität*) as manifested in the routinization of that charisma.

To these hypotheses regarding overall societal evolution, the theory adds several more detailed hypotheses (see figures 8, 9, 10, 14, and 15) concerning the evolution, so far, of each participant-organizing institution. In brief, the economic institution is claimed to have evolved toward capitalistic monopolies; the scientific institution, toward empirically based general theory; the political institution, toward monopolizing the use of physical force and violence; and the religious institution, toward belief in the existence of divine rational legal authority. In addition, recurrent processes that produce political decision makers, decision making, and decision-administration are hypothesized—along with largely parallel processes in the religious institution that involve interactions among prophets, priests, and laypersons. Finally, the theory hypothesizes interactions between the early Protestant church (a part of the religious institution in Western European societies) and the contemporaneous economic institution, such that two complementary "spirits" of capitalism were engendered—one motivating business entrepreneurs, and the other motivating wage workers.

The theory presented here, then, takes a set of postulates about the invariant nature of human individuals as foundation on which to build hypotheses about the institutional structure of the societies such individuals construct, and hypotheses about how this structure—and consequently human society as a whole—has evolved over time.

With that, let us turn, as promised, to some speculations the theory might lead us to make about the future of human individuals, human society, and the human species as a whole.

Speculations

First, however, let us consider whether this book should bother itself with any such speculations. Comte answers this question in a way most to my liking when he connects explanation to prediction, and prediction to action: "It is only by knowing the laws of phenomena, and thus being able to foresee them, that we can, in active life, set them to modify one another for our advantage. . . . From science comes prevision; from prevision comes action" (1975:88).

Not surprisingly, Weber agrees with this idea. "One does science," we recall his saying, "first, for purely practical . . . purposes: in order to be able to orient our practical activities to the expectations that scientific experience places at our disposal" (1946:138). Following these two leaders (who are not often aligned in this way, but see appendix A), I regard the formulation of theory-based predictions— or, as some prefer to call them, forecasts—as an indispensable component of science from which sociologists should not shrink (after all, everybody else makes predictions about human society and usually with worse theory and data than we have). We should make such predictions even when, being unable to attach reliable probabilities and confidence limits to them, we have to call them, as I do here, merely speculations.

With every prediction or speculation, however, we should keep in mind that (1) for any number of reasons we can make mistakes, and (2) the world we study is itself ineluctably probabilistic, perpetually full of surprises, ready at any time to upset our apple carts no matter how few mistakes we make. In all our predictions and speculations, in short, we must be prepared to be wrong.

Some, however, advise us to avoid the risk. Moderates say we should stick to explaining phenomena that have already occurred, and extremists go so far as to claim science itself has no place in the study of human social phenomena. But suppose, pigheaded and in spite of everything, those of us who keep faith in sociology as a science wanted to improve our predictions—on the clear ground that predictions are indispensable, in every science, both for testing the validity of human knowledge of the world and for exercising and evaluating deliberate, goal-oriented, human influence over the world (see Wallace 1988:24–28; compare Gibbs 1972:63–70). In that case, far from giving up on predicting, we should derive and critically evaluate *more and more* predictions from our theories, because only practice and instructive failure can improve them.

However, in addition to those who believe human social phenomena cannot be predicted there are those who believe such phenomena can, but *should* not, be predicted. "There are many by whom behavioral science is hated and feared as making possible the manipulation of man, adding to the rule of force the new dimensions of brainwashing and engineered consent" (Kaplan 1964:410). Now it certainly seems true that by strengthening and refining our knowledge and know-how—what Weber calls "the expectations that scientific experience places at our disposal"—we sociologists would make such manipulations more feasible. But that likelihood seems a poor reason for concluding that ignorance would make the world free (momentarily happy, perhaps—behold the clam). The same knowledge and know-how seems usable by actors on different sides of any given issue, if it is made available to them all—and that, admittedly, is a big "if." By the same token, however, if a given item of knowledge or know-how does not even exist, neither the good guys nor the bad guys can use it, and that can leave the species as a whole more vulnerable to disaster than otherwise.

If we must (and now that we know the choice is there, we must) choose between seeking and not seeking the predictive accuracy that brings enhanced knowledge and know-how, then I side firmly with Kaplan who warns that "if we turn our backs on knowledge, forgo the opportunity [in order to] ward off the danger, we are as if dead already" (1964:410). In order to win any brass rings on this merry-go-round, in my judgment, we simply must reach for them—and risk falling off (and then get up to reach again).

What might these brass rings be? In a word, they are the continued survival success of the human species—continued, that is, not for merely another century or two but for hundreds of millions, perhaps billions, of years to come in a cosmic environment where life—any life at all—seems a rare and perpetually endangered phenomenon.

Of course, we ourselves are responsible for much of the endangerment we face at this moment in our history—including wars and genocides; runaway population growth; grossly unequal distribution of wealth, power, honor, and knowledge; nationalism, ethnocentrism, racism, sexism; ecosystem pollution; and so on. To survive these self-generated threats without plunging ourselves into still-worse fixes, our greatest need is for reliable predictions of the likely consequences of alternative social actions. Only through such predictions can we try to look before we leap; without them, we might as well toss coins to decide what we do and don't do.

In addition to the threats we bring on ourselves, however, we face other threats, far more implacable and ultimately more decisive, from the cosmic environment that improbably gave rise to our species in the first place. In this category we must include the very high probability, in the fullness of time, of repeated collision courses between Earth and world-wasting asteroids and comets, the evolution of more uncontrollably virulent microorganisms than we have experienced so far, the possibility of too-near supernovas or an unexpectedly destabilized Sun, and so on and on (for discussions of many such threats, see Asimov 1979; Erickson 1991; Matthews 1992; Browne 1993a: Flam 1993b). Again, our best defense against such threats rests on making good predictions—not only of what the cosmos may dish up to us, but of different ways we can cope. As Asimov puts it, "It may well be that there is no catastrophe that is . . . unavoidable. And certainly the chances of avoiding one increase, if we stare the catastrophe boldly in the face and estimate its dangers" (1979:14)—and both the "staring" and the "estimating" here are made possible only by predictions, predictions, predictions.

Indeed, it seems that by far the most powerful survival weapon our species possesses, the one from which all others derive (or to which they contribute), is our ability to predict likely future events, predict their likely effects on us, predict the feasibility and likely impact of alternative human responses to those events, and then to activate some chosen combination of those responses (see chapter 2 and appendix B). If we wish our species to last, we should try our best to enhance that complex ability in all fields.

So it seems altogether proper that Weber should offer speculations about the human future—but unfortunately they are all warnings of catastrophe. "Everywhere," Weber says, "the casing of the new serfdom is ready. Its final completion awaits only the stage at which the slowing-down of technological and economic 'progress' and the victory of loan interest over commercial profit, in conjunction with the exhaustion of the remaining 'free' land and 'free' markets, make the masses 'docile.' . . . all too much care has been taken to make sure that the trees of democratic individualism do not grow to the skies" (1978b:281, 282, italics removed; see also 1958a:181 182). Even mass political democracy, he tells us, curtails individual freedom. It does this not only through what is normal to it, namely, the suppression of minorities by the majority (majority rule—see Spencer 1961:156), but through its reliance on bureaucracy. Thus, because "democratic mass parties are bureaucratically organized, . . . every advance of simple election techniques based on numbers alone as, for instance, the system of proportional representation, means a strict and inter-local bureaucratic organization of the parties and therewith an increasing domination of party bureaucracy and discipline" (Weber 1978a:984).

"Given the basic fact of the irresistible advance of bureaucratization," Weber almost cries out, "how can one possibly save any remnants of 'individualist' freedom in any sense?" (1978a:1403; see also Beetham 1985:46, 47; Bologh 1990:120).[3] Democracy and freedom, he claims, are possible "only where, over a period of time, they are supported by the resolute will of a nation not to allow itself to be led like a flock of sheep." And at present, he argues, that will is weak indeed: "We 'individualists' and supporters of 'democratic' institutions are swimming 'against the stream' of material developments" (Weber 1978b:282, italics removed)—a swim still further weakened, one presumes, by "the intellectual's characteristic flight from the world" (Weber 1978a:506).[4]

And when we ask what can engender and sustain a nation's (or any other collectivity's) will not to allow itself to be led like a flock of sheep; what can individualists and supporters of democratic institutions do to keep swimming against the stream; Weber turns sharply and uncharacteristically deterministic: "The historical origins of modern freedom presupposed a certain conjunction of unique and unrepeatable conditions," and therefore "anyone who wishes to be the weather-vane of [such future] 'developmental trends' might as well abandon these outdated ideals as quickly as possible" (1978b:282).

So much for Weber's warnings against future threats to human freedom. It must be emphasized, however, that despite the deterministic expression cited above, all his (and anyone else's, in any field) predictions remain probabilistic—and of course he was very well aware of that (see appendix A). So it is entirely conceivable that Weber was driven by hope, not despair, in issuing his warnings because the usual intention of a warning is not merely to bemoan some threat but to stimulate ways to avert it.

Nevertheless, a warning falls on deaf ears if the warned cannot imagine any possible and feasible alternatives to the threat in question. Indeed, we slip insensibly into subjective determinism whenever we can think of no alternatives to a given course of events—thereby surrendering the freedom of choice among alternatives that probabilism objectively permits.[5] If human freedom can be identified with the ability to choose among alternatives, then it is only to the extent that such alternatives objectively exist and, most important, we are subjectively aware of them, that we can choose among them. To paraphrase D. S. and W. I. Thomas, an objectively open door believed to be closed is closed in its consequences. And here one especially notes Weber's insistence that freedom depends on a culture of rationality (which, as chapter 2 has indicated, always involves consciously regulated comparing and choosing among alternatives): "The error in the assumption that any freedom of the will . . . is identical with the 'irrationality' of action, or that the latter is conditioned by the former, is quite obvious," for, Weber says, "the characteristic of 'incalculability' . . . is the privilege of—the insane"—who, one imagines he would add, either perceive no alternatives to a given compulsory act, or, perceiving alternatives, have no systematic way of comparing and choosing among them. "On the other hand," Weber continues, "we associate the highest measure of an empirical 'feeling of freedom' with those actions which we are conscious of performing rationally . . . in which we pursue a clearly perceived end by 'means' which are the most adequate in accordance with the extent of our knowledge" (1949:124–25).[6]

What I propose to do below, then, is to sketch a more optimistic alternative to Weber's "new-serfdom" speculation, thereby facilitating rational choice between speculations—and to this extent, between the futures they portray. Grounding myself on the theory set forth in the preceding chapters, my focus will center on possible and feasible freedom-enhancing developments in the scientific, economic, political, and religious institutions, respectively.[7] I shall also try to show that all these developments, if and when they are realized, will be extensions (not simple or easy ones, however) of developments already well under way. That is to say, I shall try not to pull any rabbits out of a hat.

From the Scientific Institution

In order to maximize human freedom and maximize the evenness of its distribution across the entire human population, we have first to produce the objective potential for such changes. No amount of actualization effort can succeed if the potential is objectively absent— and, for reasons discussed in chapter 3 and appendix B, the scientific institution's (applied) knowledge product is here proposed as the key potentiator because it brings the predictions developed by pure science to bear on humanly desired outcomes (see Wallace 1983:423–34).

In my judgment, the future enhancement and universal distribution of individual freedom depends, above all, on the production of the following four scientific inventions. First is the invention of ways permanently to eliminate war and control the production and distribution of arms. Second is the invention of ways to control world population growth and the growth of ecosystem pollution. Third is the invention of ways to access and transmit to all parts of the world massive amounts of essentially inexhaustible, cheap, safe, clean, energy. And fourth is the full globalization of the scientific institution itself. Though invented by the scientific institution, it should go without saying that these steps can only be implemented by collaboration with the political, economic, and religious institutions.

Ending War

To give it its due (as chapter 4 has emphasized), war, in the long past
and even up through aspects of the Cold War technological competitions, has conferred major benefits on the evolution of human society
as a whole—although, needless to say, at great cost to many of its
individual participants. However, it is by now a commonplace to
note that the predictable costs of war have recently risen far above
the level of any predictable benefit (see Sivard 1991:13–17). With the
scientific invention and political, economic, and religious implementation of nuclear, chemical, and biological weapons, war has finally
gained the power to crash our entire species.[8] These watershed physical science inventions have made it clear that some new social science inventions (and their political, economic, and religious
implementations) are required to guard against further use of the
former—or else we are dead by our own hand.

War, in short, must be quickly phased out everywhere in the
world—to at least the same degree that it has already been phased
out between, say, Massachusetts and Mississippi, and more recently,
France and Germany, Japan and the United States, the former Soviet
Union and the United States, and, one hopes, among the nations of
the Near East. These successes, admittedly local but nevertheless
dramatic against the background of the devastating wars that preceded them, assure us that the global phasing out of war is indeed
possible and becoming increasingly feasible.

I shall not attempt to sketch the outlines of more alternatives for
ending war than the one I happen to favor (but see Hollins, Powers,
and Sommer 1989; and Mearsheimer 1990, for several of these). For
the most part, my discussion is only intended to document the extent
to which a permanent end to war as a way of international life is now
regarded as having come at last, however precariously, within our
grasp.

Thus, Deutsch, referring to "the gradual atrophy of war," observes
that "even limited war is under long-time pressure toward lower
levels, toward more stringent limits. . . . [although] these long-term
pressures run in exactly the opposite direction of the short-term
pressures with which we are all familiar" (1969:173). Wriston says,
"One of the fundamental prerogatives assumed by all sovereign gov-

ernments has been to pursue their national interests by waging war. Today this prerogative is being severely circumscribed by information technology. No one who lived through America's Vietnam experience could fail to understand the enormous impact that television had in frustrating the government's objective in Southeast Asia" (1992:13). And Hollins, Powers, and Sommer—who devote their monograph to the proposition that "the era of armaments [may be] drawing to a close" (1989:196)—add that "for the greater part of a century, a broad consensus has been building across national and social boundaries heretofore thought insurmountable that war as an institution has outlived its usefulness (if it ever had any)" (1989:1; see also Spencer 1898:vol. 3, 610).[9]

I do not mean to underestimate the presently large and complex obstacles to eliminating war—especially war that begins on a small scale, with "conventional" weapons, and between nations not yet counted among the world's Great Powers. What I do wish to emphasize, however, is that for the first time in human history the potential costs of war (because even the smallest and most modestly weaponed war can now escalate and widen to the level of a global cataclysm) objectively outweigh, and are more and more widely perceived to outweigh, its potential benefits. By itself, of course, such *zweckrational* cost-benefit analysis cannot guarantee the elimination of war because it does not address the powerful *wertrational*, and nonrational, motivations for war—for example, traditions that still require politicians to preside over massive sacrifices of human lives (including their own nationals) in order to validate their leadership status; the popular charisma of hatred and counterhatred, plot and counterplot, revenge and counterrevenge, killing and risking being killed; and above all, a political statism whose norms reward leaders of nations who seek "opportunities to take advantage of [other nations]" and who pursue "the narrower aim of maximizing [the] power advantages of [their own state] over potential adversaries" (Mearsheimer 1990:50).

Nevertheless, the radically changed cost-benefit analysis does seem to be a distinctly new foundation on which to shift charisma from war to peace, and move toward a worldwide psychical contagion of the charisma of peace, a contagion that can provide a new and radically different punctuation in the future course of human history. In addition, the changed analysis may help build a more globally universal, smarter, and stronger police force capable of arousing both self-interested avoidance of punishment among would-be warmakers, and duty-bound humanitarianism among peacekeepers.

In the end, however, our best hope for guaranteeing a permanent and universal end to war and genocide may well lie in nurturing a vast sociocultural change that is already under way. I have in mind a proliferation of worldwide voluntary associations that cater to the full range of peaceful human interests, skills, and ideologies, and whose membership boundaries cut across all ascriptive lines of nationality, ethnicity, race, and gender in so many changing ways that all such lines will eventually become lost to all but the historian's memory.[10] Simmel cites a localized but historically pivotal precedent of such a flowering:

> The period of the Renaissance demonstrated most clearly the power of intellectual and educational interests to bring together in a new community like-minded people from a large variety of different groups. Humanistic interests broke down the medieval isolation of social groups and of estates. They gave to people who represented the most diverse points of view and who often remained faithful to the most diverse occupations, a common interest. (1955:135–36; see also Mannheim 1955:5–13)

And Gleick reports on the new technologies that such voluntary associations have at their disposal:

> At any given moment, several dozen people in the United States, Britain, Taiwan, Hong Kong, Norway, Sweden, and a handful of other countries can be found . . . playing bridge with one another on [Internet, the global computer network]. . . . If we are telephone users, our communities are no longer the square mile around our homes. We are developing an ability to relocate ourselves within many more slices of the human universe. In the past, people with [certain] special interest[s]—medieval fabrics or military-strategy games or expressionist art—made their way to cities or universities, the only places that accumulated critical masses of like-minded people. Now the possibilities are richer. . . . We are learning . . . to maintain new forms of "virtual community" or "community without propinquity." (1993:62, 64)

It should be emphasized that the general category "voluntary associations" includes communities of scientists and their students—sharing any of a very large and evolving variety of substantive and methodological interests. Such communities, of course, have long depended on print-and-paper journals and books—and on face-to-face meetings. But interactions in these communities are now being very greatly speeded-up and globalized by Internet (see Pool 1993). The resulting "electronic communities" and "collaboratories" "in which the nation's [and the world's] researchers can perform their research without regard to physical location—interacting with colleagues, accessing instrumentation, sharing data and computational resources, [and] accessing information in digital libraries" (Wulf 1993:854) are already revolutionizing the way science is done (see also Holden's report on how computer networks are revolutionizing the way science is taught [1993]). None of these communities seems likely to be long confinable to sociocultural boundaries other than those of achievable interest and skill.

Another type of voluntary association—namely, the social movement (i.e., a voluntary association that deliberately promotes some social change or nonchange; see Lauer 1976:xiii; McAdam, McCarthy, and Zald 1988:695)—has proved a major instrument of attenuating and eventually terminating all ascribed sociocultural boundaries, both within and among nations. On this, Irwin asks us to "consider . . . how the repressive political climate of the McCarthy era began to change in the mid-1950s. Pacifists protested against nuclear testing. . . . Black Americans created the civil rights movement. . . . These events made principled dissent from Cold War attitudes, civil disobedience, and mass nonviolent resistance more familiar as ways to change government policies" (1989:11; see also Jackson 1976).[11] In short, it seems not unreasonable to believe that an abundance of globally inclusive, mutually overlapping, voluntary associations—organized around virtually limitless combinations of peaceful common interests and skills can act as powerful brakes on all the ascriptively defined group polarizations that have been so fundamental to war, genocide, and enslavement in the past.

Moreover, there seems a strong likelihood that these same global voluntary communities will directly enhance human individuality and individual freedom.[12] Regarding their impact on human individuality, Simmel formulates the key hypothesis here: "As the individual leaves his established position within *one* primary group, he comes to stand at a point at which *many* groups 'intersect,'" and "the larger the number of groups to which an individual belongs, the more improbable is it that other persons will exhibit the same combination of group-affiliations." Then, "because his pattern of participation is unique," the individual's personality becomes unique (see Simmel 1955:140–41; second italics added). Furthermore, "the individual may add affiliations with new groups. . . . [and this] is sufficient, quite apart from the nature of the groups involved, to give him a stronger awareness of individuality in general, and at least to counteract the tendency of taking his initial group affiliations for granted" (Simmel 1955:151).[13] Accordingly, it seems reasonable to expect that the breakdown of ascriptive group homogeneities brought about by a proliferation of globe-encircling voluntary associations will lead to a much richer heterogeneity of individual interest, skill, and ideology.

Regarding the impact of voluntary associations on individual freedom, one notes Weber's contrast of "a sand-pile of unrelated individuals" with "a maze of highly exclusive, yet absolutely voluntary sects, associations and clubs, which provide the center of the individual's social life" (1978a:1207). Weber clearly implies that individual freedom lies more in the maze than the sandpile when he argues that his model for the voluntary association—namely, the religious sect (see 1978a:1206)—"requires the free consensus of its members . . . [and] does not want to be an institution dispensing grace, like a church" (1978a:1204).[14] The sect, Weber says, is a powerful mechanism of individual freedom, for it "gives rise to an inalienable personal right of the governed as against any power, whether political, hierocratic or patriarchal. Such freedom of conscience . . . is the most basic Right of Man because it comprises all ethically conditioned action and guarantees freedom from compulsion" (Weber 1978a:1209). Moreover, Weber emphasizes the "measure of influence which . . . social circles [i.e., voluntary associations that include occupants of different statuses in the economic, political, scientific, and/ or religious institutions of society] are able to exert upon the content and the direction of administrative activities by means of 'public opinion'" (1978a:985), and it seems clear that that influence can be greatly facilitated by further contributions from the scientific institution to the means of generating, processing, storing, and communicating information of all kinds.

Controlling World Population Growth and Pollution

The second sorely needed scientific freedom-potentiation is the invention of rapid, effective, and safe ways of bringing the growth of the world's population—and of that population's ecosystem—under strict control. "In early 1992, the U.S. National Academy of Sciences and the Royal Society of London issued a report that began: 'If current predictions of population growth prove accurate and patterns of human activity on the planet remain unchanged, science and technology may not be able to prevent either irreversible degradation of the environment or continued poverty for much of the world'" (Brown 1993:3). And in 1993, more than 1,670 of the world's senior scientists (including a majority of the living recipients of the Nobel Prize in the sciences) issued a "Warning to Humanity" in which they noted that "pressures resulting from unrestrained population growth put demands on the natural world that can overwhelm any efforts to achieve a sustainable future. . . . A World Bank estimate indicates that world population will not stabilize at less than 12.4 billion, while the United Nations concludes that the eventual total could reach 14 billion, a near tripling of today's 5.4 billion" (World Scientists 1993).

However, although the scientists go on immediately to emphasize that "even at this moment, one person in five lives in absolute poverty without enough to eat, and one in ten suffers from serious malnutrition," it justifies the recommendation that "We must move away from fossil fuels to more benign, inexhaustible energy sources" only on the ground that it would "cut greenhouse gas emissions and the pollution of our air and water" (1993). That is to say, they do not cite the ability of such energy eventually to wipe out poverty and malnutrition everywhere, halt all and reverse some environmental degradation, and enable the Earth (with the aid of extraterrestrial colonies) to support even a twenty- or thirty-fold increase in its present population, as well. Let us turn, then, to the energy prospect.

Inexhaustible, Cheap, Safe, Clean Energy

This soon-to-be desperately needed potentiation from the scientific institution derives from the fact that the Earth's stocks of fossil fuels (petroleum, coal, and natural gas, combined) will soon be exhausted, with "petroleum . . . growing scarce by the mid-2000s" (*World Book* 1993:6, 281; see also Asimov 1979:314). Perutz points out that the present abundance of fossil fuels "marks no more than a moment in man's history. . . . If we want to preserve civilization for our descendants we have to find other energy sources" (1989:64, 67). And we have to find such sources soon, Perutz says, because there is a limited amount of fossil fuels to be found in the Earth and we are rapidly exhausting it. Even in the most unlikely event that global human society could be held to its present level of energy use, world reserves of fossil fuels can last only about another 275 years. And, as Asimov warns us, "We must ask ourselves whether . . . the supply of available energy, which has been rising steadily all through human history, will finally peak and begin to decline, and whether that will carry down with it human civilization" (1979:315).

It now seems certain that only enormous new energy resources can enable human society to avoid that collapse and sustain anything like its present population in a viable global climate, atmosphere, and biosphere beyond the next few hundred years—no matter what conservation and efficiency-enhancing steps we take (see Starr, Searl, and Alpert 1992). And it goes without saying that only on such a foundation can we even dream of individual freedom spreading to the limits of such a population.[15] Consequently, it seems clear that "the United States and the world may, in time [one should really say "must" and "soon"], come to rely largely on energy sources that are essentially inexhaustible, possibly including advanced nuclear fission reactors, [nuclear] fusion, and many diverse sources [including solar, wind, geothermal, water, and biomass] that are commonly lumped under the term 'renewable energy'" (United States Department of Energy 1987:198; see also World Scientists 1993).[16]

The virtually unassailable empirical claim behind the need for such a shift to "essentially inexhaustible" energy sources is most simply and directly expressed by White: "Culture evolves as the amount of energy harnessed per capita per year is increased, or as the efficiency of the instrumental means of putting energy to work is increased" (1969:368–69; see also Adams 1982:27, 25). The first factor, White claims, is "the primary and basic one" (1969:375) because no matter how efficient and recyclable the instrumental means may be, the total amount of energy harnessed per capita sets the absolute upper limit on their useable outputs. Harnessed energy is the potentiation; the means of application concretize and channel that potentiation.

Moreover, White argues, "increases in the amount of energy harnessed result in technological progress all along the line, in the invention of new tools and in the improvement of old ones" (1969:376). Indeed, the tool-invention-and-improvement consequences of the large-scale introduction of fossil fuels to produce steam to produce electricity have been, and are still, unfolding in what we know as the industrial, electrical, electronic, and information revolutions. These have already diminished or wiped out many differences among townships, provinces, states, cantons, prefectures, and so on, *within* countries. Accessing "inexhaustible energy sources" of the sort described can potentiate further levelling, at a uniformly high level, not only within but *among* countries, eventually removing entirely the now-vast economic differences between the developed and the developing countries of the world (see Falk 1992:21–29). Thus, Homer-Dixon et al., referring to both kinds of levelling, call attention to "significant causal links between scarcities of renewable resources and violence. To prevent such turmoil, nations should put greater emphasis on reducing such scarcities. This means that rich and poor countries alike must cooperate to restrain population growth, to implement a more equitable distribution of wealth within and among their societies, and to provide for sustainable development" (1993:45).[17] Similarly, Deutsch claims that "if the world's population could be brought up to $4800 per capita income yearly" (the figure may be outdated, but the basic idea of a high global minimum wage continues to be a powerful one), "we could expect that most of the world most of the time would no longer have an *economic* motive for fighting. . . . [and this would be] something unheard of to this day" (1969:185).[18] Almost needless to say, the same principle of equalization of incomes, at a very high level, applies to the economic motive for crime within countries (see Blau and Blau 1982).

Kennedy and Reich agree on a self-interested, *zweckrational*, motivation for being concerned about the causal links to which Homer-Dixon et al., and Deutsch, refer. Reich points to "the inability of [highly paid individuals] to protect themselves, their families, and their property from the depredations of a larger and ever more desperate population outside" (1992:303), and the consequent self-interest of such individuals in the welfare of that "population outside."[19] And Kennedy answers the question, "Why should rich societies care about the fate of far-off poor people?" as follows: "It is that economic activities in the developing world . . . are adding to the damage to the world's ecosystem. . . . the prospect that human economic activities are creating a dangerous greenhouse effect of global warming. . . . would inevitably concern Wisconsin and Jutland as well as Bombay and Amazonia" (1993:96, 105; see also Lenssen 1993:106).

Because of the powerful economic, political, and (perhaps less directly) scientific, and religious interests that have become vested in exploiting fossil fuels to the bitter end, it may not be wise to expect a major upturn in the charisma and resource allocation needed to access new energy sources much before we are flat up against the final exhaustion of all fossil fuel sources (see, however, Browne 1993b). Then the real work will begin, for Starr, Searl, and Alpert tell us that "the history of fuel transitions (wood-coal-oil) shows that in a peacetime commercial environment almost half a century is required to significantly shift fuel patterns" (1992:285; see also Dyson 1988:273). But once we do harness some essentially inexhaustible, cheap, safe, clean, easily transmissible energy, the resultant worldwide economic superabundance seems likely to transform human society in almost endless ways. This achievement, indeed, will inaugurate the next big step in the sociocultural maturation of our species.

Globalizing the Scientific Institution

Finally, as indicated above, participation in the modern scientific institution at all levels of knowledge and skill, including the highest, has to become fully globalized. Weinberg puts it this way:

The radical attack on science [may be] one symptom of a broader hostility
to Western civilization. . . . Modern science is an obvious target for this
hostility; great art and literature have sprung from many of the world's
civilizations, but ever since Galileo scientific research has been overwhelmingly dominated by the West. . . . In the end this issue will disap-
pear. Modern scientific methods and knowledge have rapidly diffused to
non-Western countries like Japan and India and indeed are spreading
throughout the world. We can look forward to the day when science can
no longer be identified with the West but is seen as the shared possession
of humankind. (1992:190)

The day Weinberg forecasts seems on its way, for recent reports tell
us that "nowhere is [the pursuit of scientific knowledge] being applied with more enthusiasm today than in the so-called Tigers of
Asia—South Korea, Taiwan, Hong Kong, and Singapore—and in
China, the region's emerging superpower" (Kinoshita 1993a:345);
and that "Asia's investment in science and technology has sky-
rocketed over the past decade. . . . Today, the Asian Tigers spend
close to $80,000 a year on each research scientist and engineer, about
two-thirds the amount in Japan and over half the amount in the
United States' (Kinoshita 1993b:348).

From the Economic Institution

Leontiades tells us, "One of the most important phenomena of the
twentieth century has been the international expansion of industry.
Today virtually all major firms have a significant and growing presence in business outside their country of origin" (1985:3; see also
Clarke 1985:1–16; Kotabe 1992:1; Sider 1992:237); Reich says that
"there is coming to be no such thing as an American corporation or
an American industry. The American economy is but a region of the
global economy" (1992:243; see also 6–9, 172; Kennedy 1993:54; Portes and Walton 1981:187). Of course, as Kennedy points out, this
globalization is heavily dependent on modern science: "without the
vast increase in the power of computers, computer software, satellites, fiber-optic cables, and high-speed electronic transfers, global
markets could not act as one, and economic and other information—
politics, ideas, culture, revolutions, consumer trends—could not be

delivered instantaneously to the more than 200,000 monitors connected to this global communications system" (1993:50–51).[20] Almost needless to add, economic globalization extends to the labor force as well: "Upward of 15 million migrants are now living in Western Europe, probably between 6 to 10 million in the USA. . . . Added together, the mass migrations of the mid-20th century amount to at least half as many people as emigrated from Europe to North America in the great migrations of the 19th and early 20th centuries" (Power 1979:1, 2. Zlotnik forthcoming estimates 100 million immigrants globally in 1985.).[21]

But speaking of the labor force, in addition to the increasingly free global migration of the human labor force that was just mentioned, one can also already see signs of the time Marx envisions—the time when the labor force will no longer consist of a class, occupation, and job division of labor among humans, but there will be a new division between all humans on one side and machines on the other. In the latter, Marx writes, the machine side will be carried out by "an automatic system of machinery . . . set in motion by an automaton, a moving power that moves itself; this automaton consisting of numerous mechanical and intellectual organs" (1973:692, italics removed). And on the human side, "the human being . . . [will] relate more as watchman and regulator to the production process itself. . . . He steps to the side of the production process instead of being its chief actor. . . . The free development of individualities . . . [based on] the general reduction of the necessary labour of society to a minimum, which then corresponds to the artistic, scientific etc. development of the individuals in the time set free, and with the means created, for all of them" (1973:705, 706; also see Kennedy 1993:82–94).

Whatever other, less-important and in many cases failed, predictions Marx may have made, this one seems increasingly well realized in these days of industrial robotization. A few centuries more and all basic economic production seems likely to be carried out not as it is now—by a host of humanly operated private enterprises—but by a single, highly differentiated, world-serving, array of robotically operated, fusion-powered, public utilities.

In addition to all this, one other contribution from the economic institution (with assistance from the other institutions as well) seems especially relevant to human freedom.

Mass Communication, Education, and Recreation

Where the organizational scale, spatial extension and consolidation, institutional specialization, cultural rationality, reliance on bureaucracy and machine technology of human society are all increasing (see chapter 4), every individual participant's firsthand knowledge of that society tends to be confined to a rapidly shrinking slice of the whole. A subdivision of the economic institution that is devoted to the mass, interactive, dissemination of information about all aspects of human society and of the universe at large, can increasingly counter this confinement, spread awareness of all manner of alternatives in human concerns, and thereby contribute greatly to individual choice and freedom.

Weber mentions mass communications as "a source of influence operating similarly on all the individuals, as by means of the press" (1978a:23), and claims that "the newspaper. . . . brought together in the first place political news and then mainly all sorts of curiosities from the world at large" (1950:295; see also 1946:97–98; see Spencer 1898:vol. 1, 533, 536). Carrying these ideas further, Schramm notes that "all the dams broke at once and loosed the torrent of communication. More people went to school. There they learned to read and became more deeply interested in their governments and in the world beyond the realm of their eyes and ears. The growth of popular governments required people to inform themselves and helped them to do so by providing schools and facilitating the distribution of newspapers" (1972:49–50). Swatos helps make the connection to individual freedom by arguing that as part of its universal dissemination of information, "the media can have a tremendously decharismatizing effect by providing 'instant analysis'—that is, criticism—of any figure or event. The extraordinary and the everyday are so merged here as to become indistinguishable, and of course, one may at any time turn the dial elsewhere or the tube off" (1984:206; see also Glassman 1984:231).[22] And insofar as decharismatizing special individuals is a prerequisite for charismatizing ordinary individuals equally, the result is that the shared charisma response we now call "the dignity of the individual, irrespective of the groups of which he is a part" (Merton 1976:190; see also Simmel [1950:282]) can become a major support of individual freedom.

To all this one must add that in no known society has the individual's daily life been without relief from the serious work that marks the participant-organizing institutions as discussed so far. Therefore, we should not forget the importance of play (an issue on which Weber is unfortunately silent) in future, as well as past and present, human society. "Play," Huizinga says, "presents itself to us in the first instance: as an intermezzo, an interlude in our daily lives. As a regularly recurring relaxation, however, it becomes the accompaniment, the complement, in fact an integral part of life in general" (1955:9, italics removed; see also Wilson 1988:1–2, 5).

Now although play has long been present in all human societies (indeed, in all primate and many large-brained nonprimate social groups), only in a few highly industrialized societies has it evolved into an identifiable service industry—i.e., as an emergent mass communication, education and *recreation* subdivision of the economic institution. Thus, Schramm (writing in 1957) notes that "Only fifty years ago there [was] no radio and no television; movies were represented by a few nickelodeons; newspapers were a combination of party papers and yellow press" but, he asks, "What would people have thought 50 years ago, if someone had told them that in the future most homes would contain a relatively inexpensive little box into which one could look and see and hear the Metropolitan Opera, the New York Music Hall stage, the Olympic games in Melbourne, the meetings of the United Nations, the fighting in a distant part of the world, and the candidates for national office?" (1972:53, 54).

And what may people two or three hundred years, a thousand years, a million, a thousand million years from now have at their disposal for mass communication, education, and recreation? What instantaneous, user-friendly, unobtrusively portable, individualized, and sensitively interactive access to all the transcribed and imaged information ever collected or projected by humankind, to all the play and recreation of the world and of AI-generated virtual worlds, and to participation in an almost limitless variety of worldwide voluntary associations?[23]

From the Political Institution

It seems clear that a more intense and more widespread attribution of charisma to the individual political participant (i.e., egalitarianism and democracy) is a contribution from the political institution which is already moving ahead rapidly—though, of course, not universally and not without setbacks. McColm observes that whereas there were only 12 countries counted as democratic in 1942, a mere fifty years later there were "91 democracies and another 35 countries in some form of democratic transition—a staggering 126 out of the 183 nations evaluated—compared to forty-four democracies in 1972 and 56 in 1980." Indeed, McColm tells us, the year 1991 "was the first year in which both the number of Free countries and their populations outnumbered the Not Free countries and their populations," and

> the past three years have seen the greatest expansion of freedom in history. One-third of the nations on earth, encompassing nearly 30 percent of the earth's population, have consciously decided to radically alter their political systems for more open and democratic forms of government. . . . The world population has increased by 1.36 billion people since 1977, while people living in Not Free societies have actually declined in real terms by 56.4 million. . . . the population of Free societies has increased by 570 million . . . and Partly Free societies have increased by 847.9 million over this same period. (1992:47, 51)

But by itself, democracy in separate societies is no guarantee that wars and genocides between such societies will end. Different ethnic, racial, and nationality groups typically attribute strong positive charisma to their own individual members but negative charisma to the members of other groups. Under the sway of such stereotypes and prejudice, each group can find it easy to vote, democratically, for war against one or more other groups.[24]

Indeed, it would seem that the principal military function of the nation-state in advanced industrial democracies today is coming to be defense of its borders and interests against incursions from the industrially underdeveloped societies (just as one function of the economy in those same advanced democracies remains selling arms to the underdeveloped societies—see Sivard 1991:17). It has been argued that

> Were all humanity a single nation-state, the present North-South divide [between developed and developing nations] would make it an unviable, semi-feudal entity, split by internal conflicts. Its small part is advanced, prosperous, powerful; its much bigger part is underdeveloped, poor, powerless. A nation so divided within itself would be recognized as unstable. A world so divided should likewise be regarded as inherently unstable. (Report of the South Commission 1990:2)

To this, I would add that the instability in question is now most effectively served by the military and police forces of the industrially advanced democracies. Such forces are now charged, above all, with defending the physical segregation of the world's highest levels of living from dilution by the world's lowest levels of living—a gap represented by the fact that the richest fifth of the world's population disposes of fifty-one times as much GNP per capita as does the poorest fifth (see Falk 1992:26). (And, of course, the segregators, for all their democracy and belief in human freedom and equality, take segregation to be their inalienable right, whereas the segregated regard it as unspeakably inhumane and duplicitous.) One is not surprised, then, to read Makhijani's conclusion that "the structure of the world economy is in its most essential ways like that of apartheid in South Africa"—a structure he calls "global apartheid" (quoted in Falk 1992:3).

On the grounds that the termination of apartheid at the global, as well as local and regional, levels best serves the survival of the human species (and is, moreover, coming to pass whether we like it or not), the most needed accompaniment to global democratization seems clearly to be global political consolidation—in which we shall witness, as Tilly so neatly puts it, "obituaries for the state" (1975b:683)—a consolidation that seems nascent in the now "worldwide system of states" (Tilly 1975a:81; see also 1975b:636–38). In other words, we should look forward to an eventual democratic world federation of which all persons, everywhere, will be citizens, owing their primary allegiance to a single world government, and in which all such citizens will be as free to come and go across all former national boundaries as Americans now come and go across the Mason-Dixon line.

But more than global political consolidation is needed. We need also global economic, religious, and scientific consolidations (already nascent in the now-worldwide systems of economic, religious, and scientific institutions)—in a word, a global *societal* consolidation. And if the documentation cited throughout this chapter can be believed, that consolidation is in fact rapidly emerging—although not across all societies at the same rate of speed, and no society has participated in its emergence without occasional stagnations and retrogressions into war-making nationalism.[25]

It must also be emphasized that globalization can no longer be achieved by military conquest and global empire (it probably never could, but formerly only for technological reasons having to do with difficulties of long-distance communication and transportation). The nearly universal value that, over the last two hundred years or so, has come to be placed on "self-determination" at all levels—from nations and ethnic groups right down to individual persons—puts such conquest out of the question in future history. This means globalization can proceed further only to the extent that it is perceived on all sides as *voluntary*. And that may often require the breaking of old social bonds perceived to be imposed, before the parties can come together again, voluntarily, in new concert. Carmichael and Hamilton put the point this way: "Before a group can enter the open society, it must first close ranks. . . . through the organization of its own institutions with which to represent its needs within the larger society. . . . 'Enroute to integration, [a group on whom a social bond has been imposed] needs to develop a greater independence— a chance to run its own affairs and not cave in whenever [the imposing group] barks'" (1967:44, 45; see also Fanon 1968:73–95).

One should, then, expect a period (indeed, we are living in it now) in which renegotiations of, and sometimes secessions from, social bonds that are regarded as intolerable encroachments on the self-determination of one or more of its members are common. Throughout this period, however, all the other forces discussed here may be expected to go on strengthening. Sooner or later, the voluntary global consolidation of human society seems very likely to be realized. And a very good thing, too, especially when one considers the alternative: "When I try to think of reasons why nuclear weapons won't inexorably combine with our genocidal tendencies to break the records we have already set for genocide in the first half of the twentieth century, our accelerating [intergroup] cultural homogenization is one of the chief grounds for hope that I can identify. Loss of [intergroup] cultural diversity may be the price that we have to pay for survival" (Diamond 1992:234).[26] It seems no accident that Alexander Hamilton made the same point as Diamond when arguing for a more localized consolidation some two hundred years ago, and his words are worth recalling:

> A man must be far gone in Utopian speculations who can seriously doubt that, if these States should either be wholly disunited, or only united in partial confederacies, the subdivisions into which they might be thrown would have frequent and violent contests with each other. . . . To look for a continuation of harmony between a number of independent, unconnected sovereignties in the same neighbourhood, would be to disregard the uniform course of human events, and to set at defiance the accumulated experience of ages. (1961:108–9)

From the Religious Institution

Any lowering of barriers to individuals freely choosing among different religious faiths should be regarded as a contribution to individual freedom—that is, the freedom to accept any existing faith or set of faiths, or to reject all faiths, or to construct one's own unique faith. Thus, when Dulles (commenting explicitly as a Catholic on the Second Vatican Council of 1962–65) predicts that "the coming decades . . . will witness the maturation of a broadly ecumenical theology in which adherents of different religions and ideologies can fruitfully collaborate" (1980:40), that collaboration would enhance individual freedom to choose among various combinations of collaborators. The same is true of Kung's (also a Catholic) radical syncretism: "As far as the future goes, only one thing is certain: At the end both of human life and the course of the world Buddhism and Hinduism will no longer be there, nor will Islam nor Judaism. Indeed, in the end Christianity will not be there either. In the end no religion will be left standing, but the one Inexpressible, to whom all religions are oriented" (1988:255).

Arguing along more or less the same general lines, and speaking as a Jew, Agus refers to an obligation "to render our specific historical tradition transparent to the comprehension of those raised in other traditions, especially within the Judeo-Christian family" (1980:110). Such transparency would enhance individual freedom—as would Nasr's (speaking as a Muslim) view that "the followers of one religion [are now able] to think about and comment on the theological perspectives of another religion, especially in a world such as ours where traditional barriers between various civilizations have been lifted" (1980:112). Speaking as a Hindu, Mitra says Hindu thinkers "are tolerant and careful listeners" to other theologies: "In Hinduism," he says, "anathema is itself an anathema" (1980:121), and this tolerance, too, would enhance individual freedom to choose, reject, or independently to construct. In addition, we should not forget Durkheim's claim that "a social life of a new sort is developing. It is this international life which has already resulted in universalizing religious beliefs" (1965:493), and Spencer's claim that there are two types of religion—"the religion of enmity and the religion of amity," the first type "is supreme at the beginning [of history]" and the second "will be supreme at the end" (1961:161), for they, too, forecast enhancement of the freedom in question. Finally, one notes Wuthnow's citing the impact of growing political globalization on religious globalization: "When individual and national authority are understood . . . in the context of social relations that affect all of humanity, then a broader, more encompassing, and even more transcendent sense of the sacred becomes necessary" (1991:36).

Science and Religion

Now, against this background, consider the even more drastically freedom-enhancing view of Lukas Vischer, then director of the Secretariat of the Commission on Faith and the Constitution of the World Council of Churches: "A strange new community [among different faiths] has come into being," he says, "a community of questioning and searching, a community of fundamental agreement and, in many respects, also of fundamental uncertainty" (1979:105).[27]

One might not be far wrong to imagine this "fundamental uncertainty" emerging not only from interactions within and among the various religious faiths themselves, but from interactions between them and twentieth-century natural science: "When the century began we knew little of the cosmos beyond our immediate stellar neighborhood. By the time it was three-quarters over we knew that galaxies exist, that stars are born and die, that the universe expands and was born in an eruption whose rumbling echoes we still can detect" (Ferris 1983:219). Further: "At one time, it was believed that there was only one universe—the one in which we live. To hypothesize about the possible existence of other universes was thought to be a [science fiction] speculation. . . . This is true no longer. Theories that evoke the existence of other universes have become commonplace, and some physicists have speculated that the number of universes might be infinite" (Morris 1987:xi; see also 161–64; Weinberg 1992:38, 174, 222; and Gribbin 1986:387–92, 1993:254–55).

In short, the scientific institution has persistently undermined the religious institution's typically anthropocentric view of the world. Weinberg calls this anti-anthropocentrism the *Copernican principle* (see also Gott 1993), and even goes so far as to claim that "no one has ever discovered any correlation between the importance of *anything* to [humans] and its importance in the laws of nature" (1992:254, his italics). Thus, a long succession of revolutionary scientific paradigms has displaced humans away from what we used to think of as our absolute uniqueness among life-forms on Earth; displaced the Earth away from what we used to think of as its centrality in the solar system; displaced the solar system away from the center of our galaxy (and, recently, away from uniqueness in that galaxy); displaced our galaxy away from the center of the observable universe; and displaced our era far, far away from both the beginning and the ending of that universe.[28] There are even two other crucial displacements now being energetically pursued. These are the displacements of natural intelligence, and of natural life-forms, from what we used to think of as their status as the only possible intelligence and the only possible life-forms. Regarding the prospects for artificial intelligence, one computer scientist is quoted as saying, "There's no question that machine vision will eventually exceed human capabilities" (Fox 1993:685), and the next section of this chapter will cite far more sweeping speculations. Regarding the prospects for artificial life, one of the leaders in this endeavor tells us that "by the middle of this century, mankind had acquired the power to extinguish life on Earth.

By the middle of the next century, he will be able to create it. . . . Artificial life is more than just a scientific or technical challenge, it is also a challenge to our most fundamental social, moral, philosophical, and religious beliefs. Like the Copernican model of the solar system, it will force us to re-examine our place in the universe and our role in nature" (Langton 1989:43, 44).

So we come to the following extrapolation from Weber's analysis of the influence of the Protestant religious institution of the sixteenth and seventeenth centuries in Western Europe on the economic institution of that time and place (see chapter 6): In the twentieth century, the scientific institutions of the world's industrialized societies have intensified their ongoing impact on the religious institutions of all societies. That impact may be expected to be felt more and more deeply in the centuries to come, bringing "fundamental uncertainty" in all religious institutions and thereby enhancing individual freedom to choose among, create, or reject, religious beliefs and practices—as all other beliefs and practices.[29]

In concluding this discussion of a many-sided alternative to Weber's forecast of a "new serfdom," two qualifications must be added. First, the freedom contributions projected above imply certain accommodative changes in the participant-intake, and the participant-outlet, institutions. The most important of these changes may occur in those participant-intake institutions having to do with childbearing and child rearing. Here one may speculate that, sometime in the next few hundred years, the biological conception of children will become almost completely decoupled from sexual intercourse— through the invention of easy, safe, inexpensive, and highly reliable contraceptive methods together with equally reliable *in vitro* conception, implantation, and, conceivably, gestation methods. Although sexual intercourse may in this way complete its long passage from strict societal control into the realm of socially unhampered individual freedom, contraception and pregnancy seem likely to come under strict social control for the sake of managing population growth (including licencing—with appropriate age and competency requirements), at least until we begin to expand the human habitat to permanent extraterrestrial environments. Along with this and other changes (especially including gender equalizations in all the institutions of society), in centuries to come both childbearing and child rearing may become specialized, highly skilled, professional occupations. Again, this seems a possible and feasible extension of developments already well underway, in industrialized societies, with the professionalization of obstetrics, pediatrics, and teaching.

Second, none of my speculations is meant to promise a free lunch to anybody—although at least two considerations should not be overlooked. First, the basic costs of our species' continued survival have already been paid, blindly and unknowingly, by all our ancestors all around the world and across the many millennia of human existence so far. Second, over the past couple of hundred years we have begun to *understand* what we have been doing, and, more importantly, what we are capable of doing. As a result, our survival now depends more and more on the extent to which we develop and publicly disseminate knowledge-based predictions of the costs and benefits to various parts of human society that may be entailed in pursuing a given line of social action (my own bet is on large-scale computer simulations—see Little 1993). But equipped with such predictions—gradually supplanting the more risky trial-and-error techniques of the past—we may stand a good chance of picking our way through the minefields that stretch before us.

Among the deadliest of these minefields (not counting the diseases, asteroids, and other more cosmic threats that were mentioned earlier) must be included the great likelihood that as the institutional contributions to human freedom projected here are brought within reach, there will be lags and unevennesses in their distributions across the world's population. These will undoubtedly generate new privileges and new deprivations (and further entrench some old ones) in the realms of wealth, power, knowledge, and honor. As Kennedy reminds us again and again, "History . . . [produces] winners and losers. Economic change and technological development . . . are usually not beneficial to all" (1993:15; see also 53, 71, 78, 80, 346)—and one must add that the same is true of political, scientific, and religious change. The consequences of such lags and unevennesses may prove extremely costly—namely, technologically sophisticated terror and violence aimed both ways across these privilege-deprivation lines.

It is essential to notice, however, that by "not beneficial to all"

Kennedy really means not immediately and equally beneficial to all, for he quickly adds that "technological progress can have a trickle-down effect, so that the standards of living of all members of society improve over time" (1993:15). An optimist seizes on this qualification because it means that despite his overwhelming pessimism, Kennedy, too, thinks we have a chance.[30] That is to say, if we can just make sure that the freedom contributions sketched in this chapter "trickle down" and globalize *fast* enough, we yet may make it safely through these last few centuries of *Homo sapiens sapiens'* sociocultural adolescence—a period which began with the invention of agriculture some ten thousand years ago—into the next, socioculturally adult, period. Not that that adulthood will have no problems; its problems, however, will be different—as different as the problems of our historic adolescence have been from those of our prehistoric childhood.

A Possible Long-Term Future

Society

It seems unanimous among all the concerned physical sciences that our 4.6 billion-year-old Sun is now approaching the middle of the journey of its life, with some 6 billion years to go before its death throes—first fire, then ice—render the Earth unfit for any living inhabitants (see Bartusiak 1986:33–34). Someone has said that if the distance from the tip of one's nose to the tip of one's outstretched middle finger were taken to represent the age of the Earth so far, then the first rasp of a nail file on the nail of that finger would erase all *past* human history and prehistory. But to that one must add that considerably more than the distance from fingertip to nose tip represents the potential span of *future* human history on Earth.

In this view, there should still be literally thousands of millions of years left in which to carry the evolution of human society's spatial extension beyond Earth, beyond our solar system, to the limits of our galaxy, and perhaps even beyond (see Darling 1993:141–58). So when, in chapter 2, I referred to a "first" pulse in the spatial extension of human society, I did so in order to imply that more such pulses may well lie ahead. Indeed, one may think of the full story of our species as a succession of habitat-expanding pulses: To start with, outward from the Great Rift Valley of eastern Africa to populate the entire Earth; then outward from Earth to populate the entire Solar System; then outward from the Solar System to populate the entire Galaxy.

The hypothetical explanation proposed earlier in this essay for the first dispersion may well hold for future dispersions as well. Not only do we have powerful drives to secure the physical resources of individual life, but we also appear to have a "manipulation or exploration drive" (Thorpe 1956:10) as another, independent, motivation for dispersion. In this connection, Bartusiak suggests that "direct imaging of more Earth- or Jupiter-like bodies outside our solar system could come with future generations of infrared telescopes launched into space in the 1990s and the 21st century. . . . [Such images] could be the bait that finally lures humankind itself out of the solar system" (1986:26).

But no matter what the motivational causes for these actual past and possible future dispersions may be, at least two crucial species-survival consequences seem to be associated with them all. First, they (like diversified investments of any kind) protect the species from being totalled by localized catastrophes. Second, they develop the species' adaptive capabilities in diverse ways, thereby providing it with a large repertoire of coping mechanisms to combine and choose from. Dyson (defending his claim that "the expansion of life over the universe is a beginning, not an end") says: "At the same time as life is extending its habitat quantitatively, it will also be changing and evolving qualitatively into new dimensions of mind and spirit. . . . The acquisition of new territory is important, not as an end in itself, but as a means to enable life to experiment with intelligence in a million different forms" (1979:237).

Note, once again, that no implications of deterministic certainty should be read into this probabilistic speculation of future dispersions of our species, for "one cannot claim 'manifest destiny' that we will become starfarers as a natural evolution of current trends. Success will depend on our choice of near-term investment strategies—

and in no small part on national and international will" (Brin 1985:43, italics removed). And that, it seems to me, is simply another way of saying human society's next outward pulses (like the first one) must be intensely charismatic, at least for some of us, or they will not occur at all (see Gott 1993:319).

But if such pulses are charismatic and if they do occur, then we may say, with Deutsch, that although "no one can tell today what men will bring back from the solar system. . . . we do know that whenever human beings have stepped into a larger and radically new environment they have not come back empty-handed" (1969:179). More important, however, we may also speculate, with Finney and Jones, that many of these human beings may decide not to come back at all but to colonize these new New Worlds—with the eventual result that "distances of many light years . . . will divide our spacefaring descendants into myriad independent entities." After this, Finney and Jones continue, "will inevitably come diversity, first cultural then biological. . . . [for if] our descendants spread far and wide through space, the forces of evolution now braked on Earth will be released once more" (1985:263, 23).

Individuals

Even without that far-future interstellar dispersion, however, it may become more and more inaccurate to go on calling human society simply "human" for at least two reasons—namely, genetic engineering and robotics.

On the first reason, Hart asks, "Will genetic engineering actually be employed to alter human beings?"; answers, "I think the answer to that question is definitely yes"; and then offers the following speculation: "The first applications of genetic engineering to human beings are likely to be obviously benign. A typical user might be a person who suffers from some hereditary disease or defect and who wishes his or her child to be spared the same handicap. . . . Major structural or biochemical changes will, of course, be much rarer, since social and governmental pressures are likely to oppose them" (Hart 1985:282–83). Hart believes such major changes will, nevertheless, eventually occur—so that "by the time our descendants succeed in colonizing the Milky Way Galaxy [a time Hart estimates to be 2 million years hence] they will have divided up into many different species (all derived from *Homo sapiens sapiens* but by genetic engineering rather than by natural evolution)" (1985:284; see also Valentine 1985).

On the second reason, it seems clear that our erstwhile human society has always pursued with great energy and ingenuity the transformation of its human participants into those fully "prosthetic God[s]" alluded to by Freud ("With every tool man is perfecting his own organs, whether motor or sensory, or is removing the limits to their functioning" [1961:43, 41; see also Stewart 1991:36–45]), and Marx ("Nature becomes one of the organs of [man's] activity, one that he annexes to his own bodily organs, adding stature to himself in spite of the Bible" [1967:vol. 1, 179]). Applying the principle of this transformation to a mode of species evolution that Darwin certainly never envisioned, Jastrow argues that "human beings are not the last word in the evolution of intelligence on the Earth, but only the root stock out of which a new and higher form of life will evolve" (1981a:91). Moravec, who declares himself "an author who cheerfully concludes the human race is in its last century" (he means its last hundred years) adds that "machines. . . . are visibly overtaking us. Sooner or later they will be able to manage their own design and construction, freeing them from the last vestiges of their biological scaffolding, the society of flesh and blood humans that gave them birth" (1989:167).

Moravec then adds the hope that "there may be ways for human minds to share in this emancipation" (1989:167, 168), and Jastrow muses that one such way may be the transferring of human minds into less delicately vulnerable forms of matter. At some future time, Jastrow says, "at last the human brain, ensconced in a computer, [will have] been liberated from the weaknesses of the mortal flesh. The union of mind and machine [will have] created a new form of intelligence. . . . [a form which] must be the mature form of intelligent life in the universe" (1981b:166; see also Moravec 1988:108–12).

From this far-out speculation (which seems only a long, complicated extrapolation from false teeth, eyeglasses, books, and hearing aids), it is but one small additional step to imagine communities of our phylogenetic-cum-technological descendants that are so widely separated from each other in interstellar space-time,[31] and composed of individuals so powerfully self-sufficient and so immensely long lived (see, for example, Hart 1985:284–89), that individual freedom can then reach a maximum. At that point, some presently unimagined *super*societal level of organizational complexity may emerge—for "as [the products of human society] become ever more elaborate and complex . . . so the possibility arises that a new threshold of complexity will be crossed, unleashing a still higher organizational level, with new qualities and laws of its own" (Davies 1988:196). In what strikes me as a related and especially interesting speculation, Hogan imagines that each individual participant in such a higher level of organizational complexity may come to

> perceive the universe through billions of sensory channels distributed all over the surface of the Earth and beyond. On top of that, its "senses" [could] cover the whole spectrum from high-power proton microscopes in research labs to the big orbiting astronomical telescopes . . . from galactic gravity-wave detectors to the infrared sensors lowered into the ocean trenches. . . . [Such] an intelligence, controlling robot extensions, [could move] pieces of itself around in millions of places at one time. (1979:65; see also Dyson 1988:112–13)[32]

I, for one whose lifetime occurs so near to the very first stirrings of intelligence on Earth (if, most improbably, nowhere else), cannot even vaguely imagine what conceptions of the good, the true, and the beautiful may be developed by intelligences equipped with such perceptions as Hogan describes, and such brains as Jastrow and Moravec describe—while communicating about them in ways as unimaginable to us as our ways are to, say, fish (see McCorduck 1979:345–46; Darling 1993:172–77).

Nevertheless, it is distinctly gratifying (as a Devonian coelacanth might have been gratified if it had imagined us, its human descendants) to think that even our still puny, half-witted, nearsighted, and narrowminded efforts to understand human society, and deliberately to improve its survival chances, may be signal moments in the grandest evolution one can now imagine—an evolution toward a universe that is *itself* intelligent.[33]

Postscript on Optimism and Pessimism

Some may regard the speculations laid out above as altogether too optimistic to be taken seriously when set against the bloody horrors reported in almost any day's news. Weber's "new serfdom" speculation may seem to fit them better. But if what we know about the history of life on Earth teaches any lesson at all, it is that every deluge so far has eventually come to an end—and that fact encourages us to ask every doomsayer, After the deluge, what?

And, indeed, it is easy to admit that, sooner or later, some sort of deluge will claim our entire species: "The belief and faith that civilization, won at such great cost in pain and labor, simply cannot go down in destruction because such an end would be too monstrous and senseless, is but a naive and anthropocentric whimper. The cosmos does little know nor will it long remember what man has done here on this tiny planet. The eventual extinction of the human race— for come it will sometime—will not be the first time that a species has died out" (White 1949:391). Gott, indeed, calculates (on certain assumptions that I regard as oversimple—see note 34) that "our species [has] a total longevity between 0.205 million and 8 million years" (1993:316).

But even after such a deluge, Margulis and Sagan argue, all need not be lost: "Even if all anthropoids—all humans, monkeys, and apes—become extinct, [organisms] would still abound in those assets (e.g., nervous systems, manipulative appendages) that were leveraged into intelligence and technology in the first place. Given time to evolve in the absence of people, the descendants of raccoons— clever, nocturnal mammals with good manual coordination—could start their own space program" (1986:236). "The most severe mass extinctions the world has ever known, at the Permotriassic boundary 245 million years ago," Margulis and Sagan go on to note, "were rapidly followed by the rise of mammals, with their sharp eyes and large receptive brains"—concluding that "with each crisis the biosphere seems to take one step backwards and two steps forward" (1986:237; see also Gould, Ferris, and Benton, all discussed in chapter 4).

The point can be pushed still further: If even the entire terrestrial biosphere should drown in one deluge or another, Sargent and Beckwith assure us that even *then* all need not be lost: "Ten years ago it was possible to argue that the solar system is unique. Today the evidence strongly suggests that planetary systems are abundant in the Galaxy. From statistical arguments alone, the likelihood is that many of them will have conditions favorable for life" (1993:29). Ferris spells out, and extends, the statistical argument to which Sargent and Beckwith refer: "Within the range of our telescopes lie perhaps one hundred billion galaxies, each home to a hundred billion or so stars. Astronomers estimate that at least half those stars have planets. . . . If intelligent life has arisen on but one planet in a billion, then fully ten thousand billion planets have given birth to an intelligent species" (1992:19; see also Gribbin 1993:255). Even Gott allows that "some intelligent life may last into the far future"—ruefully (and to my mind unjustifiably) adding that "it is just not likely to be us or our descendants" (1993:318).[34]

From the above arguments, it seems fair to draw the following conclusions: If one's perspective centers only on one's own precious self, pessimism makes more sense than optimism because we are all dead in the short run, and long dead in the long run. If it centers on one's ethnic group or race or nation, pessimism still makes good sense because the boundaries of all such groupings are already blurring and their sociocultural relevance will be entirely gone from the lives of foreseeable future generations. If it centers on the human species as a global whole, however, optimism immediately starts to make more sense. Then, if we transcend even anthropocentrism, and extend our horizon to all intelligent beings wherever and whenever they may exist, optimism (though it can never have the field to itself) makes far more sense than pessimism.

So the less parochial one's perspective, the more reasonably optimistic one's expectations. This may sound uselessly abstract, but it actually carries some very important practical implications: pessimism (no hope) has been found to induce passivity, while optimism (can do) engenders effort.[35]

APPENDIX A

PRECONCEPTIONS

THE PRECONCEPTIONS ON whose foundations I have put together the theory set forth in the main body of this book seem divisible into two categories. The first category specifies a general form that I believe any scientific analysis should follow. The second category specifies the substantive content that I believe distinguishes social scientific (especially sociological) analysis. This appendix is devoted to a brief explication of these two categories.

Analytical Form

The analytical form I have in mind is basically positivistic, but includes only its originally *Comtean* meaning (and before Comte, his teacher Saint-Simon [1760–1825], who wrote with less system and detail—see 1964:21–23), not the mostly behavioristic distortions the word has acquired since Comte (see Popper 1961:34–53)—especially in the "logical positivism" of the Vienna Circle (see Bergmann 1967). In my judgment, we should, at all costs, avoid throwing out the Comtean baby with its post-Comtean bath water.

Let us consider how two leading modern-day sociologists characterize positivism. Wiley tells us that " 'positivist' " is a term

> used today for anyone who is on the highly quantified or mathematical side of sociology. . . . [But more] technically, positivism often means (1)

scientism, or the dictum that sociology must use natural science models outlawing empathy/gestalt/teleology/verstehen/typification/elective affinity/dialectics/functionalism, and so on, except as a prescientific heuristic device. In addition, subjective states . . . are inadmissible as data except as they are externalized or objectified in questionnaire responses and the like. . . . Or it can mean (2) seeing the world of symbols in both culture and social structure as "external and constraining" in a Durkheimian sense. This version of positivism opposes the "reality construction" argument of symbolic interactionism and phenomenology. (1979:50)

Wiley's list comes close to what I mean by *Comtean positivism* in only one of its many items—but even here it is off the mark. The positivism that I adopt, rather than applying a model of so-called natural science to sociology, applies the *same* model (in appropriately modified ways) to *all* the sciences—including the physical, biological, and social sciences—on the ground that they are all natural sciences, sciences of natural phenomena. Admittedly, these two formulations come down to the same thing—namely, one basic model for all the sciences—but they differ sharply in their implications: Wiley's model implies subordination of the social sciences to the physical and biological sciences, whereas the model adopted here implies their equality under the general umbrella of natural science. Accordingly, the model I have in mind is not a fixed one whose relationship to a given science is simple application, but is an evolving model that interacts with the problems of each science and therefore both influences and is influenced by them.

Regarding the other items on Wiley's list, in my judgment, Comtean positivism does not include them—at least not in the form represented in the list. This positivism does not require quantification or mathematization; it does not outlaw gestalt, typification, elective affinity, dialectics, functionalism, or certain meanings of teleology—for example, homeostasis, and planful human action. Comtean positivism does not rule out the study of subjective states, no matter how they are externalized—and even when they are not externalized at all but are merely hypostatized as playing a role in some behavior that is externalized. Comtean positivism does not necessarily see the world of symbols as external and constraining but allows us also to see symbols as internal and liberating (i.e., in the latter view, it is the actor's subjective interpretation of the symbol, not the physical symbol itself which matters, and that interpretation may be voluntary). Finally, in the updated version discussed below, this positivism certainly does not oppose "reality construction" arguments.[1]

The second, and in some ways more complicated, characterization is Giddens's—when he argues that three tenets constitute what he calls "the 'positivistic attitude' in sociology." Let us consider the first two of these tenets together:

> 1. That the *methodological* procedures of natural science may be directly adapted to sociology. According to this standpoint, the phenomena of human subjectivity, of volition and will, do not offer any particular barriers to the treatment of social conduct on a par with objects in the natural world. . . .
> 2. That the. . . . *goal* of sociological analysis can and must be to formulate "laws" or "law-like" generalizations of the same kind as those which have been established in relation to natural reality. (1979:3-4, second italics added)

Of course, the same objection applies to the first tenet here as that lodged, above, against Wiley's reference to the "use of natural science models." But in Giddens's statement, the terms *"directly* adapted," *"particular* barrier," and "generalizations of the *same* kind" attract special attention. Are these intended to be substantively meaningful restrictions? Are they meant to excuse from "the positivistic attitude" adaptations that are not "direct" (whatever that may mean)? Are they meant to excuse standpoints claiming human subjectivity does offer a barrier but no more *particular* a barrier than other variables in natural science that are not now (or even not ever) directly observable (like, say, individual quarks, or the instinct that we think makes honeybees do the waggle-dance)? Are they meant to excuse generalizations of a *different* kind than those referring to "natural reality"? Or are all these qualifications of Giddens's merely obfuscations? The question is important, from my point of view, because appendix B will interpret Weber as proposing certain definite adaptations of what Giddens calls "natural science" methodological procedures—but I do not know whether Giddens would call them "direct" or not. That appendix will also acknowledge human subjectivity as a "particular" (but not unique) barrier to natural science. Should such an acknowledgement be regarded as part of "the 'positivistic attitude' in sociology" or not? I think so, by Comte's definition of positivism, but would Giddens think so by his definition?

Consider Giddens's third tenet of "the 'positivistic attitude in sociology":

> 3. That sociology has a *technical* character . . . in other words, that the findings of sociological research do not carry any logically given implications for practical policy or for the pursuit of values. Sociology, like natural science, is "neutral" in respect of values. (1979:4)

This, too, is a profoundly confusing assertion, because ordinarily, things are called "technical" because they *do,* or at least are thought to, carry implications for practical policy and the pursuit of values, so it is hard to see what Giddens means by using the term as though it had the opposite meaning. Of course, he may really want to complain about the idea that sociology, like every other science, is completely unable to *prescribe* values (although this is not what he says). If so, chapter 3 has dealt with that and appendix B will have more to say about it.

Finally, there is one vitally important feature of Wiley's and Giddens's views that they share with Weber (see appendix B)—namely, the line they draw between things "human" and "social," on the one hand, and things "natural," on the other. The positivism adopted here looks upon all human phenomena (including human sociality) as natural phenomena and calls for studying this naturalness rather than any extranaturalness they may or may not also possess. Not that extranaturalness is denied by this positivism (it is agnostic on the matter), and not that it would deny to other viewpoints the option of studying extranaturalness when they presume such a thing exists. It is simply that this positivism does not choose that option.

With that, let us set aside all views of what the term *positivism* may or may not presently denote in the social sciences, and consider Comte's original characterization.[2] In my judgment, this characterization is what clearly delineates the baby we dare not throw out with its bathwater.[3]

Auguste Comte (1798–1857) first laid down the three defining features of positivism: (1) "positive sociology. . . . [is] distinguished . . . by the steady subordination of the imagination to observation" (1975:219);[4] (2) "the positive philosophy . . . regards all phenomena as subjected to invariable natural laws" (1975:75, italics removed);[5] and (3) "all positive speculations owe their first origin to the occupations of practical life. . . . it is only by knowing the laws of phenomena, and thus being able to foresee them, that we can, in active life, set them to modify one another for our advantage" (1975:321, 332).[6] On the following evidence, it seems undeniable that Weber embraced all three of these defining features of Comtean positivism.

First, it was Max Weber who stressed that " 'empirical generalizations' [must be] used to verify 'interpretations' of human action," and that these "only appear to differ from the generalizations used to verify interpretations of concrete 'natural processes.' This appearance," Weber says, "is unimaginably superficial" (1975a:170).[7]

Second, it was Max Weber who, echoing Comte's stress on the search for natural laws of hunan social life, argued that "the forms of social action follow 'laws of their own'" (1978a:341); that "even the most perfect adequacy on the level of meaning has causal significance from a sociological point of view only insofar as there is some kind of proof for the existence of a probability that action in fact normally takes the course which has been held to be meaningful" (1978a:12); and that the distinction he drew between "cultural" and "natural" sciences "does not imply that the knowledge of universal propositions, the construction of abstract concepts, the knowledge of regularities and the attempt to formulate 'laws' have no justification in the cultural sciences. Quite the contrary . . . a valid interpretation of any individual effect without the application of . . . knowledge of recurrent causal sequences . . . would in general be impossible" (1949:79).[8]

Finally, it was Max Weber who, by way of adopting Comte's insistence that the findings of pure science should be applied to the practical problems of human life, reminded us that "our [social science] . . . first arose in connection with practical considerations"; that "in social sciences the stimulus to the posing of scientific problems is in actuality always given by practical questions'" (1949:51, 61, italics removed); that "one does [science] first, for purely practical, in the broader sense of the word, for technical, purposes: in order to be able to orient our practical activities to the expectations that scientific experience places at our disposal" (1946:138; see also 1949:18).[9]

Given these crucial convergences (ignored by all previous interpretations of Weber with which I am familiar), I believe it appropriate to think of Max Weber as a positivist in Comte's original sense. There are, however, at least three highly significant particulars on which Weber's—and my own—brand of positivism differs sharply from Comte's.

An Equifinal Positivism

Comte claims, deterministically, that only *one* path is possible for human history ("the progressive march of civilization follows a natural and unavoidable course"; "the succession of the three states [is something] through which the human mind has to pass"; "these three states succeed each other necessarily in an order prescribed by the nature of the human mind" [1975:39, 285, 41]).

Weber, by contrast, holds that *many* paths to the same end are possible: "The same result," Weber says, "may be reached from other starting-points" (1978a:454); "processes of action which seem to an observer to be the same or similar may fit into exceedingly various complexes of motive in the case of the actual actor" (Weber 1978a:10); "behavior that is identical in its external course and result can be based on the most varied constellations of motives, and the most plausible motive may not be the one that came into play" (Weber 1981:151); "the very 'need' to eat . . . may be essentially conditioned by various effective circumstances operating as 'stimuli'—for example, a physically empty stomach or . . . merely habituation to eating at particular hours of the day" (Weber 1975b:29, italics removed); and "similar ethical maxims may be correlated with very different dogmatic foundations" (Weber 1958a:97). The same holds for society and social relations: "Common customs may have diverse origins"; "the most diverse reasons can lead to a 'No' [in a plebiscite]"; "the subjective meaning need not necessarily be the same for all the parties who are mutually oriented in a given social relationship"; and "orientation to the situation in terms of the pure self-interest of the individual and of the others to whom he is related can bring about results comparable to those which imposed norms prescribe" (Weber 1978a:394, 1455, 27, 30).

In short, Weber adheres to the analytic principle variously called *equifinality, functional equivalence, structural substitutability* and, in biology, *convergent evolution.* All these terms—I shall use *equifinality*—refer to the idea that there is more than one way to skin a cat; more than one road leading to Rome; more than one alternative causal explanation for the same observed phenomenon (see also Durkheim 1982:123; Simmel 1955:27; Merton 1957:52; Heider 1958:101; Moore 1959:838; Quine 1960:8; Kaplan 1964:9; von Bertalanffy 1968:18; Wilson 1975:25, 392; Dawkins 1987:303, 304; Barrow 1991:66).[10] This principle implies its complement—here called the principle of equi-initiality for terminological symmetry (initial-final) with equifinality (compare Wallace 1983:410–13)—meaning that there may be more than one alternative effect of any given initial cause. For example, Weber says, "action that is 'identical' in its meaning relationship occasionally takes what is, in the final effect, a radically varying course" (1981:156); Durkheim says that "it is a proposition true in sociology as in biology, that the organ is independent of its function, i.e. while staying the same it can serve different ends" (1982:121); and chapter 6 quoted Mannheim as claiming that a central theme of *The Protestant Ethic and the Spirit of Capitalism* is how "the same religion is variously experienced" by people occupying different statuses.

Together, equifinality and equi-initiality imply probabilistic rather than deterministic assumptions about the world as humanly experienced.[11]

A Probabilistic Positivism

Comte gives no hint of having a variable probability in mind when he lays down his pivotal substantive definition: "The exercise of a general and combined activity is the essence of society" (1975:20). Indeed, Comte flatly denies probability can ever be central to sociology—charging that "the efforts of geometers to press the calculus of probabilities beyond its legitimate scope have only resulted in offering . . . some almost trivial propositions as to the theory of certainty" (1975:58).

By contrast, probability is the essence of all Weber's key definitions (and here Weber stands splendidly alone among classical sociological theorists): "The social relationship . . . consists entirely and
exclusively in the existence of a probability that there will be a meaningful course of action"; "if we take [the sociological] point of view,
we ask: What actually happens in a group owing to the probability
that persons engaged in social action . . . orient their own conduct
towards these norms?"; "'class situation' means the typical probability of (1) procuring goods, (2) gaining a position in life and (3)
finding inner satisfactions"; "'power' is the probability that one actor within a social relationship will be in a position to carry out his
own will despite resistance, regardless of the basis on which this
probability rests" (1978a:26–27; 311, italics removed; 302, italics removed; 53); and "a 'state' . . . ceases to exist in a sociologically relevant sense whenever there is no longer a probability that certain
kinds of meaningfully oriented social action will take place. This
probability may be very high or it may be negligibly low. But in any
case it is only in the sense and degree in which it does exist that the
corresponding social relationship exists" (1978a:27; see also Scaff
1989a:78 n. 15).[12]

Now although the claim is implicit in what has been said above, it
seems worth separate and special emphasis that the concept of an
objective fate, destiny, or inevitability, is absent from the theory set
forth here. This contrasts, for example, with Marx and Engels's many
inevitability assertions, such as that "the separation of society into an
exploiting and an exploited class, a ruling and an oppressed class,
was the necessary consequence of the deficient and restricted
development of production in former times," that "division into
classes. . . . will be swept away by the complete development of
modern productive forces" (1969:vol. 3, 147–48); that "the feudal
relations of property. . . . had to be burst asunder" (1969:vol. 1, 113);
that "the bourgeois period of history has to create the material basis
of the new world"; and that "consciousness is something that the
world must acquire, like it or not" (1978:663).[13] The theory of human
society proposed here rejects such determinism in favor of probabilism, and rejects the concept of historical inevitability in favor of a
value-added, conditional probability that is (1) subject to an unknown degree of modification through the development and inter-

vention of collective intelligence, and (2) characterized by sudden (quantum, qualitative, punctuational, revolutionary, or catastrophic) leaps and lapses, as well as gradual change.[14]

The idea of sudden leaps and lapses directs us to the third major particular on which Weber's (and my own) brand of positivism departs from Comte's.

A Punctuational Positivism

In accord with Weber's reliance on the concept of probability, and given his deliberate observation that a "probability may be very high or it may be negligibly low" (see above), the theory of human society set forth here mainly on Weber's inspiration takes cognizance not only of the role of high probability, ordinary, events but of the sometimes incomparably more important role of *low* probability, *extraordinary*, events. The contrast with Comte's judgment that "it is the *commonest* sort of facts that are most important" (1975:242, italics added) could hardly be greater.

Because he emphasizes "the commonest sort of facts" and neglects uncommon sorts of facts, Comte's image of the overall dynamic of human society is exclusively gradualistic: "The human understanding, slow in its advance, could not step at once from the theological into the positive philosophy. . . . an intermediate system of conceptions has been necessary to render the transition possible. . . . the metaphysical philosophy . . . spare[s] our dislike of abrupt change, and . . . afford[s] us a transition almost imperceptible" (1975:74, 292). The image of human societal evolution as advanced in chapter 4, however, includes *steps* as well as ramps. That is to say, it includes sudden discontinuities not as "noise" to be filtered out and ignored by the theory, but as essential features of the evolution itself.

Let us, then, sum up the first category of systematics that underlie this book. On the one hand, the book accepts Comte's original positivism for the primacy it gives to observation, the pursuit of natural laws, and the pursuit of practical (technical) usefulness. On the other hand, it rejects Comte's secondary emphases on unilinearity, determinism, and gradualism—stressing, instead, equifinality (and equi-initiality), probabilism, and punctuation. The analytical orientation of this book may thus be called *neo*-positivistic or *neo*-Comtean, but it remains fundamentally positivistic, in keeping with Comte's original criteria, nonetheless.

Substantive Referents

In the second category of preconceptions, the theory presented in this book is founded on a generic definition of social phenomena (including societies) as such, and it is essential to make that definition explicit—especially because Weber's definition of "social action" may seem to deviate from it in such a way as to question the appropriateness of calling the theory "Weberian."

Defining Social Phenomena

The definition that seems to me inclusive of all other definitions to be found in the social science literature goes as follows: To qualify as (generically) "social," a phenomenon must be described in terms of one or more observed or observable interorganismic behavior regularities (for details, see Wallace 1983; 1988).[15] According to this definition, at least two organisms must be involved in every phenomenon we can legitimately call "social," and at least one behavior of the first organism must be somehow regular in time and/or space with at least one behavior of the second organism.

In the present theory, the described organisms are human; the described shared behaviors are physiological (roughly speaking, people doing things together, customarily called *social structure*), and/or psychological (roughly speaking, people experiencing thoughts and/or emotions together, customarily called *cultural structure*, or simply, *culture*); and the described regularities occur in such dimensions as spatial extension and density, and temporal duration and tempo—which may vary continuously and/or discontinuously.[16]

Weber's Definition of "Social Action"

In what appears to be a sharp dissent from this definition, Weber tells us "interpretive sociology . . . treats the single individual and his action as the basic unit" (1981:158), and "action is 'social' insofar as its subjective meaning [to the single acting individual] takes account of the behavior of others and is thereby oriented in its course" (Weber 1978a:4).[17]

In other words, whereas the definition cited above requires us to describe the behavior of at least two individuals, Weber appears to permit a single individual's behavior to qualify as a social phenomenon. But let us look more closely.[18]

When Weber refers to "the single individual and his action as the basic unit," our first question is "basic unit" of what? This is a key question because it follows from the generic definition, and from the principle of equifinality discussed earlier in this appendix, that there are two quite different "basic units" in sociological analysis. There is a "basic unit" of *description* (i.e., an interorganismic behavior regularity), and there is a "basic unit" of *explanation* (i.e., each participating individual organism's behavior, taken separately).

Now in setting forth his "interpretive sociology" (see appendix B), Weber tells us that "the historian [and, by extension, the sociologist] deals with the explanation of events and personalities which are 'interpreted' and 'understood' by direct analogy with our own intellectual, spiritual, and psychological constitution" (Weber 1949:175). So when he claims "interpretive sociology . . . treats the single individual and his action as the basic unit," it seems clear he has in mind the basic unit of explanation, not the basic unit of description.[19]

In describing these to-be-explained "social relationships," however, it is equally clear that Weber sees them involving behavior regularities between two or more individuals, rather than within just one individual: "The term 'social relationship' will be used to denote the behavior of a plurality of actors," and "as a defining criterion, it is essential that there should be at least a minimum of mutual orientation of the action of each [actor] to that of the others" (1978a:26, 27; see also 14, and 322 for a parallel definition of "social class").

So it seems fair to conclude that once we separate descriptive units from explanatory units, what at first seemed to be a discrepancy between Weber's definition of "social action" and this book's generic definition of a social phenomenon disappears: both definitions refer to interindividual behavior regularity as the basic unit of description, and both definitions refer to the individual organism's behavior as the basic unit of explanation.

Unfortunately, however, there is another, much more vexing issue lodged in Weber's assertion that "action is 'social' insofar as its subjective meaning takes account of the behavior of others and is thereby oriented in its course" (see above). Weber here confounds what ought to be a purely descriptive issue with an explanatory issue when he says subjective meaning *orients* action. With this confounding, he biases anyone who accepts his *definition* of social action to accept the particular *explanation* of it that he happens to favor— namely, the actor's *subjective meaning*—and to accept that explanation before doing the empirical research necessary to find out the extent to which it does or does not hold in actual fact. Then, having established this biasing foothold, Weber presses on to the following subjectivist dogma: "The real empirical sociological investigation begins with the question: What *motives* determine and lead the individual members and participants in [a] community to behave in such a way that the community came into being in the first place and that it continues to exist?" (1978a:18, italics added).

I call this a *dogma* because it arbitrarily stamps "anathema" on every sociological investigation that dares proceed without investigating the actors' motives—looking, instead, to factors like ecosystem, technological artifacts, and the like (Braudel, for example, says, "Do not tell me that geography has nothing to answer for where France is concerned" [1988:65]), or factors of human physiology. In addition, of course, there is the extremely uncomfortable fact that when we define social action as "oriented in its course" by the actor's subjective meaning, we impose on ourselves the logically impossible requirement of having already explained the action in question. That is to say, we must already have identified the actor's social action and subjective meaning, and we must already have found that the latter orients (and thereby helps to explain) the former—before being able even to consider that social action as a potential object of such explanation in the first place.

This criticism of Weber should not be overstated, however, for he (as is so often the case), has seen this point before us and, backing away from the subjectivist explanatory dogma quoted above, he acknowledges that "sociology, it goes without saying, is by no means confined to the study of social action; this is only, at least for the kind of sociology being developed here, its central subject matter, that which may be said to be decisive for its status as a science. But this does not imply any judgment on the comparative importance of this and other factors" (1978a:24).

Seizing on the implications of this latter statement, the present book rejects all explanatory dogmas—whether the blinders they impose compel us to look only for subjective meaning, or only for some other kind of causal variable (for discussions of the full menu of such variables so far developed in sociology, see Wallace 1983 and 1988). At the same time, however, note that when we reject prejudicial explanatory dogmas, we in no way prevent them from being restated as testable explanatory hypotheses and examined empirically, in competition with rival hypotheses.

It seems fair to conclude that although the theory offered here remains strongly Weberian, it is so only with some significant clarification of Weber's own analytical and substantive preconceptions.

APPENDIX B

A WEBERIAN METHOD FOR STUDYING HUMAN SOCIETY

BUILDING ON THE neo-Comtean positivism set forth in appendix A, and supporting the integrative interpretation of Weber's (and others') substantive theory set forth in the main body of this essay, the present appendix proposes a general Weberian research method. The basic argument is schematized in figure 17, conveying the following claims that are intended both to systematize and to question and extend Weber's own. The following five assertions form the core of this scheme:

First, from the standpoint of the present book, Weber's dichotomization of the sciences (i.e., natural versus cultural) suffers from two principal weaknesses: The categories imply that human cultural phenomena are somehow not natural phenomena; and *sociocultural* seems preferable to *cultural* insofar as the sciences Weber seems to have in mind here (history, economics, political science, sociology, social psychology, anthropology, demography) include studies of what appendix A has called social structural, as well as cultural structural, phenomena. Thus, a more accurate labeling would be *sociocultural* versus *nonsociocultural*, but these are clumsy and unfamiliar terms—so I shall use Weber's *cultural* and *natural* terms here, with the indicated reservations.

Second, research in the natural sciences is "empirical" in that it relies on the inferences we call "observations"—made largely by

Processes

Subject Matter	Pure Science (Knowledge-Seeking)	Applied Science (Control-Seeking)
"Natural" Phenomena	Sensory Observations; Causal Inferences ———————— Standard Measures	Deductive Predictions ———————— General Theories
"Cultural" Phenomena	Empathic Understandings ———————— Ideal Types	Intuitive Predictions ———————— Ideologies

Figure 17. Methods of the "Natural" and "Cultural" Sciences

"the five senses"—to construct empirical descriptions and explanations. Research in the cultural sciences relies more on the inferences we call intuitions—made largely by what is popularly called a sixth sense—to construct empathic understandings of their subject matter (see also Freund 1978:168).

Third, in the natural sciences, different empirical descriptions and explanations are expressed in terms of measures that have become standardized in a given science (for example, meters, seconds, grams, volts) and thereby rendered comparable to each other—both across phenomena and across investigators. In the cultural sciences, however, standard measures of this kind are almost entirely lacking. Weber proposes to remedy this lack by offering "ideal types" as a language of standard measures that can render different empathic understandings comparable to one another—both across phenomena and across investigators.

Fourth, research in the natural sciences and in the cultural sciences consists of two interdependent phases conventionally called *pure* and *applied*—a distinction Weber clearly expresses when he contrasts "an increasing theoretical mastery of reality by means of increasingly precise and abstract concepts" with "the methodical attainment of a definitely given and practical end by means of an increasingly precise calculation of adequate means" (1946:293). The latter "calculation of adequate means" depends on predictions (e.g., If we do X rather than Z, then Y will result) generated by the former "theoretical mastery" and the "attainment of . . . end" (or failure to do so) feeds back to confirm or disconfirm "mastery" in the former—and so on (see Wallace 1983:358–360).

And finally, ordinarily, applied research in both kinds of science relies on predictions deduced not from single laws but from configurations of many laws—configurations tailored to address a particular problem and also to accord with whatever general theories (in the case of natural science) or ideologies (in the case of cultural science) happen to be held by the investigator.

Restating these claims more succinctly, the Weberian method to be set forth here proposes the following basic symmetries: (1) statements of primarily empathic understanding in the cultural sciences are like statements of primarily sensory observation and causal inference in the natural sciences;[1] (2) ideal types in the cultural sciences are like standard measures in the natural sciences; (3) pure and applied cultural sciences are like pure and applied natural sciences;[2] (4) intuitively configured predictions based on empathic understandings in applied cultural sciences are like deductively drawn predictions based on sensory observations and causal inferences in applied natural sciences; and (5) Ideologies in the cultural sciences are like general theories in the natural sciences.

Pure Science

In examining these symmetries in the light of Weber's work, it seems important to establish, before anything else, his claims of identity between key features of the subject matters of pure natural science and pure cultural science. To begin with, he argues, with considerable force, that predictability (called "calculability" here) is not necessarily lower in human cultural phenomena than in other phenomena:

> "experienced" concrete reality contains no trace at all of a species of "incalculability" peculiar to human conduct. Every military order, every criminal law, in fact, every remark that we make in conversation with others, "counts" on. . . . a calculability which is sufficient for the purposes which the command, the law, and the concrete utterance are intended to serve. . . . There is no logical difference between these cases and "natural processes." The "calculability" of "natural processes" in the domain of "weather forecasting," for example, is far from being as "certain" as the "calculation" of the conduct of a person with whom we are acquainted. (Weber 1975a:120–121, italics removed)

Moreover, says Weber, cultural phenomena are intrinsically no more complex than any other phenomena: "No matter how complex a course of human 'actions' may be, 'objectively' it is in principle impossible for it to include more 'elements' than could be identified in [any] single event in the physical world. . . . This is because the event, like every individual event, no matter how simple it may appear, includes an intensively infinite multiplicity of properties—if, that is, one chooses to conceive it in this way" (1975a:124, italics removed).

Despite these similarities in their subject matters, however, Weber claims there are two fundamental differences between the kind of knowledge that the natural sciences seek, and the kind sought by the cultural sciences. These differences may be summarized in the following two statements: First, empirical propositions in the natural sciences do not include motives, whereas propositions in the cultural sciences do include motives. That is to say, "In the social sciences we are concerned with psychological and intellectual phenomena the empathic understanding of which is naturally a problem of a specifically different type from those which the schemes of the exact natural sciences in general can or seek to solve" (Weber 1949:74).[3] Therefore the cultural sciences, Weber says, "can accomplish something which is never attainable in the natural sciences, namely the subjective understanding of the action of the component individuals" (1978a:15; see chapter 2).

Second, the natural sciences seek knowledge of all events that may be defined in some simple, unidimensional way (i.e., uniformities), whereas the cultural sciences seek knowledge of one multidimensional, complex, event at a time (i.e., uniquenesses). Thus, Weber claims the natural sciences pursue their explanations by relying on "propositions of causal necessity. . . . [that] are invariably concerned only with single, isolated components of processes . . . which are abstracted from an infinitude of other components," whereas in "the domain of historically relevant human conduct . . . a change is produced by the complex interrelations of many participating individuals" (1975a:124; see also 1978a:15).

Empathic Understanding

Now insofar as "motives" are mental configurations (of individual actor's meanings), and "complex interrelations" are also mental configurations (of motives of the many actors participating in a given social relationship), what is most obviously needed in the cultural sciences, Weber holds, is a method for reliably inferring the nature of these mental configurations. This method is called "empathic understanding" (*Verstehen*) because it "can form concrete components of 'mental' reality and their relations into a conceptual construct" (Weber 1975a:139, italics removed). Empathic understanding requires the investigator to cultivate the "capacity to 'feel himself' empathically into a mode of thought which deviates from his own" (Weber 1949:41; see also 1975a:126, 129; and Ricoeur 1981:162),[4] and in so doing to accomplish a succession of three inferences—as follows. First, the method is used to infer the configurations of means and ends that constitute each of the many *meanings* that each actor assigns to the many things in his/her environment and imagination. Second, the method is used to infer the particular configuration of such meanings that constitute each actor's *motive* (Weber sometimes uses *meaning* for *motive*). Motive, Weber claims, explains each actor's action toward his/her environment—including his/her participation in the social relationship being studied. Finally, the method is used to infer a particular configuration of motives (Weber refers to this configuration as an *average* or *ideal* motive) that incorporates and summarizes the motives of all the actors in the social relationship. This latter configuration explains the social relationship as a whole. Having reached that point of understanding, the investigator's work is done.

Weber himself does not offer any such explicit summary of the investigative uses of empathic understanding, but its principal bases are as follows.

Chapter 2 quotes Weber to the effect that the "meaning" of a thing is "its relation to human action in the role either of means or of end; a relation of which the actor or actors can be said to have been aware" (1978a:7). But insofar as there are ordinarily many individual things in an actor's environment, and each thing stimulates an indefinitely large number and variety of psychological responses from the actor, there are ordinarily many individual meanings in his/her mind. The first task of empathic understanding is to grasp how the actor configures these many responses into meanings that are salient for him/her. The second use of empathic understanding is to grasp how the actor configures these meanings into a motive—for "a motive is a complex of subjective meanings" (Weber 1978a:11).[5] The method of empathic understanding culminates in configuring a single, complex, typical, motive across all actors in a given social relationship (for "the 'meaning' relevant in this context is always a case of the meaning imputed to the parties in a given concrete case, on the average, or in a theoretically formulated pure type" [Weber 1978a:27]). This ends the investigation.

Throughout this hierarchically cumulative configuration-inferring process, however, Weber is repeatedly confronted with the same key problem: What happens if different empathic understandings of the same actor's meanings and motives (and therefore different understandings of the same social relationship) are put forward by different investigators? How are we to choose between them? (And note that to the extent to which such empathic statements depend on "sympathetic *self-analysis*" [Weber 1978:5, italics added; see also Abel 1948:216], differences of this kind are almost bound to occur.)

Ideal Types: Standards for Comparing Empathic Understandings

Weber's solution to this problem is to say that the comparison of different sixth-sense empathic understandings should proceed basically in the same way as the comparison of different five-sense observations: "All interpretation of meaning," Weber says, "like all scientific observations, strives for clarity and verifiable accuracy of insight and comprehension" (1978:5)[6]—and this call for *"verifiable accuracy"* clearly implies at least two "interpretations of meaning": an initial one and a verifying one, made by different investigators of the same phenomenon. Weber thereby commits himself to proposing some inter-investigator, discipline-wide, standard for comparing the two interpretations.[7] Without such a standard there can be no "verifiable accuracy" and there can be no cultural science based on such accuracy—just as without such agreed-upon standards as the second, meter, gram, and volt there can be no natural science based on verifiably accurate measurements of time, space, mass, or energy (see Popper 1961:44; Kaplan 1964:128; Merton 1976:44–45). Weber elaborates on this point as follows: "The attainment of a level of explicit awareness of the viewpoint from which the events [being analyzed] get their significance remains highly accidental. . . . [as long as] 'each [investigator] sees what is in his own heart.' Valid judgments always presuppose the logical analysis [i.e., analysis according to procedures accepted by all investigators] of what is concretely and immediately perceived, i.e. the use of concepts [that are shared by all investigators] (1949:107, italics removed), and "only through ideal-typical concept-construction do the viewpoints with which we are concerned in individual cases become explicit" (Weber 1949:110)—and become, therefore, comparable across both cases and investigators.[8]

At this point, it may be useful to consider the physicist Barrow's remark that "many of the 'soft' sciences . . . fail to produce a significant body of sure knowledge because their subject matters do not provide obvious and fruitful idealizations. . . . It is not easy to see how one can model an 'approximate society.'" Fortunately, however, Barrow adds that "in practice, this may be a failing of our minds to find the right way to go about the search for idealizations or it may be the consequence of some intrinsic incompressibility associated with the phenomena in question," and then goes on to ask the crucial question: "Can we be sure that there are any examples in this [latter] category at all?" (1991:281–282). On the presumption that we *cannot*, ever, be sure that human social phenomena (or any other phenomena, for that matter) fall in the category of "intrinsic incompressibility," Weber—and, the present book in its entirety—may be understood as pursuing just such "fruitful idealizations" (including a model of an "approximate society" in chapters 3 through 7) as Barrow mentions.

In his pursuit of these goals, Weber argues that only with the discipline-wide measurement standards represented by ideal types can social scientists agree on the exact respects in which different investigators' empathic understandings of a given actor's (and a given set of actors') meanings and motives agree and disagree— hence, whether one investigator should be understood as verifying or falsifying, or as being irrelevant to, another investigator's insight about that actor and consequently about the social relationship in which s/he participates.[9] In Weber's words, "Only through ideal-typical concept-construction do the [different analytical] viewpoints with which we are concerned in individual cases become explicit" (1949:110), and "an idealtypical concept . . . is developed to facilitate empirically valid [i.e., interinvestigator agreed-upon] interpretation in the following eay: the given facts [i.e., the observed physical behavior] are compared with a possible interpretation—an interpretive scheme [i.e., an ideal type that is agreed-upon beforehand as a common standard]" (Weber 1975a:189, italics removed).[10]

Note that the aim of empathic understanding is not only to put together configurations, but to put together configurations that are *unique.* That is to say, the configurations are meant to estimate particular social actors' particular motivations for manifesting their particular actions in a particular social relationship. But in emphasizing this point, we should not lose sight of the very substantial degree of interdependence that Weber sees between the search for uniformities and the search for uniquenesses. Thus: "A valid interpretation of any individual effect without the application of . . . knowledge of recurrent causal sequences . . . would in general be impossible. Whether a single individual component of a relationship is, in a concrete case, to be assigned causal responsibility for an effect . . . can in doubtful

cases be determined only by estimating the effects which we generally expect from it" (Weber 1949:79, italics removed).[11] "When we are
engaged in 'interpreting' human action, we often omit the explicit
formulation of the content of our experience into 'generalizations'. . . . [although] we use these generalizations 'implicitly'" (Weber 1975a:170–171, italics removed).[12] Conversely, in underscoring
the dependence of studies of uniformities on prior knowledge of
uniquenesses, he says "'laws' . . . [are perceived] in the infinitely
manifold stream of [unique] events," and "an ideal type is formed by
. . . the synthesis of a great many . . . concrete individual phenomena" (Weber 1949:72, 90, italics removed).

What Weber seems to be claiming, then, is that both the natural
and the cultural sciences require statements of uniquenesses *and*
statements of uniformities; the two differ only on which is typically
the means and which is typically the end of their investigations (see
above). But why should this difference exist? Why should explaining
unique phenomena be the goal of the cultural sciences? Why should
these sciences not be satisfied with explaining uniform phenomena?

Applied Science

Unfortunately, Weber does not give an explicit answer to this
question—so I shall try to paste one together. Popper's view seems
an especially helpful starting-point: "Pure and applied generalizing
sciences are respectively interested in testing universal hypotheses,
and in predicting specific events. . . . if we are interested in specific
events and their explanation, we take for granted all the many universal laws which we need" (1950:447–448). Consider, for example,
how the medical practitioner prescribes a course of medication for a
patient. The practitioner mentally constructs a more or less unique
configuration of presumably universal physiological and phar-
macological propositions—a configuration that takes into account
the patient's unique medical history and symptoms, and the unique
properties attributed to given dosages of given medications and their
interactions. The core of this and similar applied science examples
would seem to be precisely the *intuitive* quality of the analysis—a

quality expressed when we refer to such practical fields as being arts as well as sciences.

Seen in this light, Weber's repeated insistences that "one does [science] first, for purely practical purposes" (1946:138); that "our [social science] . . . first arose in connection with practical considerations. . . . It was a 'technique' in the same sense as, for instance, the clinical disciplines in the medical sciences are" (1949:51; see also 61);[13] strongly suggest a connection between his view of the cultural sciences as concerned with uniquenesses, on the one hand, and his emphasis on the primacy of the "practical" side of these sciences, on the other.[14]

Indeed, the connection seems very nearly explicit in Weber's description of the gap between the yield of the pure science laboratory or field experiment (where physical and/or statistical isolation of one cause at a time and/or one effect at a time is the aim), and the needs of practice in "the real world": "For pedagogical purposes, the results of experimental psychology are extremely meager. From a pedagogical point of view, 'common sense' and 'practical experience' are much more significant. . . . pedagogy views the concrete student or the collection of concrete students as individuals. . . . From the standpoint of the 'nomological' sciences, every individual student represents a concrete constellation of an infinitude of individual series of causes" (Weber 1975a:138–139, italics removed). Thus, when he says that "the social-scientific interest has its point of departure, of course, in the real, i.e., concrete, individually-structured configuration of our cultural life" (1949:74, italics removed), Weber is thinking of the cultural sciences as primarily (but of course not exclusively) applied sciences. *That*, I think, is why he claims that in such sciences, "the knowledge of the universal or general is never valuable in itself. . . . Our aim is the understanding of the characteristic uniqueness of the reality in which we move" (see above).

General Theories and Ideologies

Up to this point, we have examined all the elements in the two Pure Science cells of figure 17, and the elements called "Deductive Conclusions," and "Intuitive Configurations," in the Applied Science cells. In order to consider the remaining elements ("General Theories," and "Ideologies") in the latter cells, we have to introduce another aspect of Weber's view of social science method—namely, the role of values.

The Inevitability of Values in All Sciences

Weber expresses a position, part of which the present book emphatically rejects, when he tells us:

> The "points of view," which are oriented towards "values," from which we consider cultural objects . . . change. Because, as long as they do, new "facts" will always be becoming historically "important". . . . This way of becoming conditioned by "subjective values" is, however, entirely alien in any case to those natural sciences which take mechanics as a model, and it constitutes, indeed, the distinctive contrast between the historical and the natural sciences. (1949:159–160, italics removed; see also 77)

The idea that scientific knowledge of so-called natural phenomena can be pursued without being predicated on "subjective values" (see also Mannheim 1955:49, 79; but compare 305, 306) is what must be rejected here. Indeed, Weber himself seems to reject it when he says, "No science [Weber does not qualify the term here, so we may assume he has in mind all the sciences] is absolutely free from presuppositions, and no science can prove its fundamental value to the man who rejects these presuppositions"; and "science presupposes that what is yielded by scientific work is important in the sense that it is worth being known" (1946:153, 143).

In line with these latter opinions, Whitehead draws no distinction whatever among the sciences when he says "feeling is the agent which reduces the universe to its perspective for fact" (1938:13). Nagel, too, says that "there is no difference between any of the sciences with respect to the fact that the interests of the scientist determine what he selects for investigation" (1961:486); and Lynd says that "in the world of science there is no such thing as 'pure' curiosity. . . . Research without an actively selective point of view becomes the ditty bag of an idiot" (1946:183).

But if values in general play unavoidably major roles in both kinds of science, values in the cultural sciences may still have their own special content. What value content does Weber think is presupposed—or should be presupposed—by these sciences? He answers: "We require from the historian and social research worker . . . that they must understand how to relate the events of the real world consciously or unconsciously to universal 'cultural values' and to select out those relationships which are significant for us" (Weber 1949:81–82; see also 169–70). This answer instantly creates a logical impasse, however, for how is it possible for the historian or social researcher to know what the "universal 'cultural values'" are without researching them; and how can they be researched if they must already be known beforehand?[15]

Faced with this impossibility, Weber silently (perhaps embarrassedly) abandons the "universal 'cultural values'" requirement, permitting, instead, "the choice of the object of investigation . . . [to be] determined by the evaluative ideas which dominate the investigator and his age"—and even retreating so far as to allow "the direction of [the investigator's own] personal belief, the refraction of values in the prism of his mind, [to give] direction to his work" (1949:84, 82).

With this final relaxation of institutional constraint over the individual scientific investigator, however, Weber's argument plunges toward the opposite and no less deadly pitfall—namely, solipsism and the consequent denial of the interinvestigator communication, competition, and consensus on which every science, whether cultural or natural, is founded.

What "saves" Weber's argument here is what "saves" science as a whole—namely, simply *letting go* of the investigator's values and seizing upon the investigator's observations (see also Oakes 1988:146)—for, as chapter 3 has argued, science can neither make nor defend any particular choice among values. No science can say its practitioners must hold some particular value; one need not even accept the value of science itself. Every science, however, does require (through its disciplinewide standard methods and techniques) its practitioners to observe the same thing when claiming to investigate a given named phenomenon.

Underlying this position, of course, is the assumption that when the observation process is constrained strictly enough, the observer's values can have only a vanishingly small effect on what different observers observe. Weber puts it this way:

> It has been and remains true that a systematically correct scientific proof in the social sciences, if it is to achieve its purpose, must be acknowledged as correct even by a Chinese—or—more precisely stated—it must constantly strive to attain that goal. . . . our Chinese can lack a 'sense' for our ethical imperative and he can and certainly often will deny the ideal itself and the concrete value-judgments derived from it. Neither of these two latter attitudes can affect the scientific value of the analysis in any way. (1949:58–59, italics removed)

But how does Weber think this can be done? If the social scientist must depend on values to lend significance to reality and thereby determine his/her selection and ordering of phenomena to be studied (see above), how is it possible to construct a social science proof which is independent of values?

The answer is that it is not possible, and Weber knows it. The solution, he therefore says, lies in every social scientist depending on *some* values, but these values need not be his/her *own* values. That is to say, the investigator must, by employing different ideal types founded on different values, be able to *take the values of others* and, in this sense, become not value *free* but value *variable* (compare Parsons 1971:33).[16] Thus: "For the purpose of characterizing a specific type of attitude, the investigator may construct either an ideal-type which is identical with his own personal ethical norms . . . or one which ethically is thoroughly in conflict with his own normative attitudes; and he may then compare the behavior of the people being investigated with it. Or else he may construct an ideal-typical attitude of which he has neither positive nor negative evaluations" (Weber 1949:43, see also 11, 61; compare Abel 1948:218).[17] The important thing, Weber says, is that "the maker of a judgment [should] clarify for others and for himself the nature of the ultimate subjective core of his judgments, to make clear the ideals on the basis of which he proceeds to judge the events he is observing" (Weber 1989b:200, italics removed), not that s/he should (or ever could) divest him/herself of such ideals (see Marianne Weber 1975:317).

Now just as Weber can imagine "an infinite number of possible value scales" (1978a:86, see chapter 3), he can also imagine an infinite number of possible ideal types referring to the same social phenomenon: "It must be accepted as certain that numerous, indeed a very great many [ideal types] can be worked out, of which none is like another, and none of which can be observed in empirical reality . . . but each of which . . . claims that it is a representation of the 'idea' of [the same phenomenon]" (Weber 1949:91, italics removed). The implications of this statement are worth spelling-out: (1) Whenever "a very great many" ideal types referring to the same phenomenon exist, their proponents may be expected to compete for dominance within the science studying that phenomenon; and (2) insofar as "at the very heart of [the historical sciences] lies not only the transiency of all ideal types but also at the same time the inevitability of new ones" (Weber 1949:104, italics removed), the consequence will be an endless succession of such competitions, and an endless succession of winners and losers in them.[18] One hears in this implication not only an echo of Weber's remark that " 'history' continues inexorably to bring forth new 'aristocracies' " (see chapter 7, note 3), but an echo of his remark, quoted in chapter 3 as exemplifying his value agnosticism, that "different gods struggle with one another, now and for all time to come." It seems we must conclude that not only was Weber a value agnostic and a religion agnostic but, ultimately, a science agnostic as well. Not only do "we know of no scientifically ascertainable ideals" (also quoted in chapter 3); we also know of no scientifically ascertainable, final, or ultimate knowledge.

Values and the Applied Sciences

So much for Weber's argument that value-orientations are required for gaining pure science knowledge of cultural phenomena (and others' similar arguments regarding pure science knowledge of natural phenomena). Applied science know-how regarding cultural phenomena carries a similar requirement, according to Weber: "The distinctive characteristic of a problem of social policy is indeed the fact that it cannot be resolved merely on the basis of purely technical considerations. . . . Normative standards of value can and must be the objects of dispute in a discussion of a problem of social policy" (1949:56, italics removed).

Here too, then, Weber simply *lets go* of the investigator's values—allowing them to vary unconstrained by the scientific institution, but not, as chapter 3 has shown, unconstrained by the political and religious institutions, where they are objects of "dispute." By short extension, ideologies—which, in addition to configurations of empirical propositions about how the world works, also contain "normative standards of value"—remain objects of such dispute as well.[19] Similarly, general theories in natural science—while containing sets of empirical propositions regarding the world and how knowledge of that world may be achieved—rest on disputable "normative standards of value" asserting the human worth of such knowledge.[20]

Now, as a setting for briefly summarizing this appendix, we have Parsons's claim that "what Weber did was to take an enormous step in the direction of bridging the gap between the two types of science [i.e., the sciences of human behaviour and the natural sciences] and to make possible the treatment of social material in a systematic scientific manner rather than as an art" (1947:10–11). This appendix has argued that this "enormous step" actually consists of four smaller steps which remain only vaguely, incompletely, and unsystematically differentiated and integrated in Weber's own writings. The first step bridges the gap between the pure phases of the cultural and the natural sciences; the second step bridges the gap between their applied phases; and the third and fourth steps bridge the gaps between the pure, and the applied, phases of each.

NOTES

Chapter 1. Introduction

1. By specifying human society, not just society, I mean to acknowledge and welcome (1) Weber's recognition of nonhuman animal social phenomena: "There are . . . various forms of social organization among animals: monogamous and polygamous 'families,' herds, flocks, and finally 'states,' with a functional division of labor" (Comte, too, tells us, "It is a very irrational disdain that makes us object to all comparison between human society and the social state of the lower animals" [1975:245]); and (2) Weber's recognition that "it would be theoretically possible to formulate a sociology of the relations of men to animals, both domestic and wild" (1978a:15; see also 1978b:389). See Wallace 1983, for exploration of an integrated sociology of both human and nonhuman organisms. See also note 11 of this chapter.

2. For some other, equally laudatory, assessments, see Hennis 1988:21; Schluchter 1989:3; Turner 1981:30; Fine 1990:141; Bologh 1990:1; Bendix 1960:17; Schneider, in Weber 1975b:24; Wuthnow 1987:18; and Scaff (who is so carried away as to dream that "whoever controls the interpretation of Weber can entertain hopes of also governing scientific activity" [1989a:34]). Compare Tribe 1989:1, 12. Since Weber's death, and especially over the past three decades or so, the literature on his work (and on him, personally) has grown almost explosively: "During the first half of the 1970s about one hundred publications a year dealt with Weber, articles as well as chapters and sections in books, not counting major monographs and . . . textbook summaries or ritual references" (Roth and Schluchter 1979:1). "The specialist [in Weber's work] has had to read about five new books a year over the past half-decade, in addition to whatever articles came to hand. Already by the mid-1970s over 2,400 items of Weberiana had been listed by two German bibliographers" (Sica 1988:xi).

3. In contrast with these views, Schroeder asserts that "there is an underlying unity in Weber's social thought," but he confines that unity to "the relation between culture and social life. . . . How, to put it differently, beliefs translate into social reality" (1992:2). The present book will argue for a broader, and a more detailed, perspective on Weber's work. Giddens, too, argues that "however diverse their substantive content, [Weber's] works do have an intrinsic unity" (1972:9). The unity

Giddens proposes, however, depends on a reconstruction of Weber's time and place; the unity to be proposed here depends on the work itself, without regard to any such reconstruction. Similarly, Dahrendorf says, "There is a nucleus of power that holds [Weber's work] together, gives it strength and meaning," but the nucleus Dahrendorf identifies is "Max Weber the person. . . . It is in the achievement and aspirations, battles and frustrations of his life that the strands of his writings come together" (1987:580). The "nucleus of power" identified in the present book lies, again, within the work itself—which, of course, is not to deny that other factors may also hold it together.

4. There are at least three major difficulties here, however. Firet, the English-language quotations from Weber to be found in this book may have been mistranslated from the German language published editions—indeed, I shall point out more than one such instance. Second, Weber's "unbelievably bad handwriting" (Scaff 1989:xi) may have been misread in preparing the German-language published editions. Summing up these first two difficulties, Scaff says, "The condition of [Weber's] writings, especially in translation, is . . . worse than for any other major thinker of the last century" (1989:9). My response to these difficulties is to encourage the reader's awareness of them and to look forward to an improved Weber archive in the future. In the meantime, however, I accept Andreski's view of a proper division of intellectual labor: "Given that so much time and effort has been invested . . . by the specialists, it is unlikely that somebody who can only dabble with primary sources would come up with new facts. . . . Since he does not need to spend so much time burrowing in primary sources, a comparatist of today ought to pay more attention to the logical structure of the argument" (1984:145). Therefore, I have relied (with appropriate misgivings) principally on the standard English translations of Weber's published German-language works—referring to the latter only when my own interpretation seemed to require it, as cited in the text—and I have not tried to examine Weber's handwritten manuscripts at all. The third difficulty, of course, is that every quotation cited here is a sample lifted out of context (true, by definition, of any quotation) and either in or out of context, it may be unrepresentative in some way that has escaped me. I shall welcome whatever corrections in this regard may be forthcoming from readers of this book.

5. Marianne Weber also says that for Weber, "the great limitation of [discourse] was that it did not permit the simultaneous expression of several correlative lines of thought" (1975:309)—implying, in the idea of "correlative" lines of thought, that although Weber may have cared little about the systematic presentation of his thought, the thought itself was systematic.

6. Kaplan says, "Scientists and philosophers use a logic—they have a cognitive style which is more or less logical. . . . [This] logic-in-use is embedded in a matrix of an a-logic-in-use, even an il-logic-in-use" (1964:8, 10; see also Popper 1961:31–32).

7. The frequently expressed claim that "there is little hope for a proper understanding of Weber without an adequate conception of the problem situation as he perceived it" (Burger 1987:xiv; see also Dahrendorf 1987:580; Giddens 1972:8; Schluchter 1989:xiv; and Albrow 1990:13) is rejected here, unless by "Weber" is meant the man, not the work, and by "proper understanding" is meant a specifically biographical understanding—and neither restriction seems adopted by those who make this claim. At any rate, the present book is concerned only with Weber's work and with the applicability of that work to our own social science problem situation as we

perceive it. For this purpose, knowing how Max Weber perceived *his* problem situation seems no more necessary for interpreting and applying what he wrote to *our* problem situation than knowing what Alexander Graham Bell was thinking is necessary for our using a telephone. I find Albert's opinion much more congenial: "Sociology is not so much concerned with Weber's biography as with the question of a serviceable methodological [and theoretical] conception" (1971:56), and Shils's opinion that "classics of the sort in which Weber's works are comprised should be read freely and not just exegetically. . . . what is below the surface of his texts contains possibilities for understanding the world as it is which are richer than what is on the surface of the text" (1987:571). It will come out in chapter 5, however, that I do not always agree with Shils regarding just what is below the surface of Weber's texts.

8. This, of course, is why every science is an intrinsically sociocultural endeavor, relying on what people other than the theorist know and do—and therefore on that centuries-long conversation of quotations called "citations," "confirmations," and "refutations." Therefore, Kuhn tells us, "the solutions that satisfy [the scientist] may not be merely personal but must instead be accepted as solutions by many" (1962:167); why Popper says that "the objectivity of scientific statements lies in the fact that they can be inter-subjectively tested" (1961:44, italics removed); why Kaplan says that "the intersubjective becomes the mark of objectivity" (1964:128); and why Merton says that "science is a social world, not an aggregate of solipsistic worlds" (1976:44–45). Also see Schutz 1953:9. In addition, note that analyses of the "language" of science turn, either explicitly or implicitly, on "usage," that is, publicly communicable, interinvestigator, conventions about the referents of given linguistic terms (see Quine 1963:24–27 and passim). But compare all this with Braithwaite's contrary opinion that "the publicity of its data [should not be used] (as many writers would wish to use it) as the hall-mark of a science . . . it is [the] hypothetico-deductive method applied to empirical material which is the essential feature of a science" (1960:8–9) and Sztompka's opinion that "scientific results are objective if and only if they are true" (1979:220–21). One wonders, however, how it is possible to know what the "hypothetico-deductive method" is, or to recognize "empirical materials," or to know that an investigator is "applying" the former to the latter, or, especially, to validate the "truth" of results, without some public, interinvestigator, consensus concerning all these matters—as expressed in the common "language" and conversation of science. Without reliance on the always tentative, sometimes tenuous, and ideally (but of course never really) egalitarian consensus produced by our conversation of quotations, no scientist could ever claim s/he "knows" anything.

9. If my hope turns out false and I have not seen further, at least it is not because I have not chosen giants' shoulders to stand on (see Merton 1965:270, for an alternative explanation).

10. Weinberg rightly says, "At any one moment there are so many things that might be done . . . that without some guidance from our preconceptions one could do nothing at all" (1992:167).

11. "Mainly," because Cusack reports that "48 million dogs and . . . 27 million cats" (1988:15) share in American society alone, and Wilson reports that certain species of ant keep aphids and similar insects in their societies (see 1975:356–58).

12. This usage of "structure," which draws on the term's commonly accepted identification with the absence of change (see Lipset 1975:172; Bottomore 1975:159; Laumann and Pappi 1976:6; Parsons 1961:36; Homans 1975:53, 54) to imply a cross-

sectional perspective, is conveniently brief for a title, but it is admittedly misleading. I do not mean to imply that evolution (the presence of change) is random—although there certainly seems to be some randomness built into it (see appendix A). Indeed, the structure (i.e., the nonrandom aspects—see Wallace 1983:29, 39–49, 156) of human societal evolution is exactly one of the things this book will try to elucidate (see chapter 4).

13. I say all these things happen in the "typical" human society to allow for the fact that at least one atypical human society (the Shakers) depended entirely on conversions (immigrants) to maintain itself, and in 1965 it stopped accepting even converts (see *World Book* 1993:vol. 17, 341).

Chapter 2. Structure of the Individual

1. Comte's very similar view is that "social phenomena must always be founded on the necessary inevitableness of the human organism, the characteristics of which, physical, intellectual, and moral, are always found to be essentially the same, and related in the same manner, at every degree of the social scale. . . . No sociological view can therefore be admitted . . . that is contradictory to the known laws of human nature" (1975:255). Marx and Engels agree: "The first premise of all human history is, of course, the existence of living human individuals. . . . The social structure and the State are continually evolving out of the life-process of definite individuals" (1947:7, 13).

2. Some of the material in this chapter first appeared in Wallace 1990. Compare the image of the Weberian human individual presented here with Schroeder's (see 1992:14). Most of the differences are too complex even to outline here, but it may be noted that of "rationality," a central component of the image to be presented below, Schroeder says only that "an abstract typology of 'rationality' in [Weber's] writings is impossible" (1992:36), and of "irrationality" (discussed below as nonrationality) Schroeder says it should be identified entirely with "'other-worldly'" and "non-everyday or transcendent ends" (1992:35). The present chapter will argue against these views.

3. Compare Marx and Engels's claims of early historical primacy for material interests, and future primacy for ideal interests (see 1947:19; 1978:15; 1969:vol. 3, 149).

4. Note that material interests may be served by psychological means as well as by physiological means, and ideal interests may be served by physiological means as well as by psychological means.

5. See also Popper 1950:461. By contrast, Mead regards meaning as a quality of the external world, "out-there," existing independently of our mental labeling: "The meanings of things or objects are actual inherent properties or qualities of them; the locus of any given meaning is in the thing which, as we say, 'has it'" (1962:122 n. 29; see also 76). For Mead, our mental labeling of the world has only sociological import; for Weber it has ontological import as well. Thus, when Weber agrees with Tolstoy that "death for [civilized man] is a meaningless occurrence," he means that modern agnostics like himself, who have been taught to regard everything as "provisional and not definitive" (1946:140), do not label death as either means or end but only as a "stimulus, [a] favoring or hindering circumstance" (compare Sayer 1991:152–53).

6. Sayer says, "Science, in its very rationality, undermines exactly those standpoints from which value is capable of being derived: above all religious ethics" (1991:150). Bologh, too, claims "the dilemma of modern life arises from the decline of (religious) ethics" (1990:127). But as chapter 3 will argue, Weber does not regard religion as the sole, or necessarily the main, source of value, or ethics, in society—nor does he believe science can ever undermine values or ethics as such.

7. For some views of Weber's conceptualization of "rationality" with which this statement is at odds in one way or another, see Parsons 1937:58 and 1947:14, 16, 80; Bendix 1960:89–90; Marcuse 1971:135; Giddens 1972:42, 44; Andreski 1984:59; Sayer 1991:114; Burger 1987:215; Albrow 1990:124, 154; Bologh 1990:122; Brubaker 1984:2; Segady 1987:89, 135; Kalberg 1980:1150; Levine 1981:10, 15; Ritzer 1992:96, 97, 99; Hennis 1983:157; Orum 1988:397; Swidler 1973:36, 39; Schluchter 1979a:14–15; Martindale and Riedel 1958:xviii; Tominaga 1989:129; Weiss 1985:128; Tenbruck 1980:321, 326, 343; Wrong 1970:26; Wuthnow 1987:203 1988:489; Beetham 1985:68–69; Wiley 1987:13. 14; Kellner 1985:94, 106; Mommsen 1985:252 and 1987:40; Kalberg 1985:57; Parkin 1982:36; Turner et al. 1989:196–97; Huff 1984:68; Hindess 1987:139, 142; Sica 1988:171 194; Alexander 1983:26–28, 152; Collins 1986b:42–44, 62–79; Schroeder 1992:34–42.

8. For a general description of the mental process implied by this definition, see Bell, Keeney, and Raiffa 1977:2–4. Definitions of the term *rationality* seem to fall into two classes. One of these requires only that the actor's *method* of arriving at a given action or belief be consciously rule guided and comparative—regardless of whether that action or belief be deemed substantively sound or not. The other class of definition requires, in addition to this method, that the *substance* of the action or belief in question be deemed sound (i.e., objectively effective, efficient, or true; morally good; or esthetically beautiful—on the latter see Weinberg 1992:132–65). For treatments of one or both classes of definition, see Hempel 1965:463, Lukes 1971:207–13, Hacking 1982:52, Hollis and Lukes 1982:12ff, Benn and Mortimore 1976:4, Levi et al. 1990:3–4. The generic definition of rationality offered in this book is of the method-centered type, and so it permits variability and change in what may be deemed substantively sound. Indeed, a method-centered definition is presupposed by all substance-centered definitions in which—as is typically the case in the sciences, and in political democracies—the ultimate test of a substantively sound action or belief is whether some publicly designated rule-guided method of comparing and choosing among competing alternatives was employed in producing it. It is this substance-validating method of comparison and choice (often called simply and very broadly "criticism"—see Popper 1961:44) that Habermas seems unwittingly to be glossing as substantive "knowledge," "the objective world," "facts," and "objective judgment" when he asserts that "an expression satisfies the precondition for rationality if and insofar as it embodies fallible knowledge and therewith has a relation to the objective world (that is, a relation to the facts) and is open to objective judgment" (1984:9). In addition, the method-centered definition of rationality here called *generic* is meant to subsume all other method-centered definitions. For a leading example, March and Simon say, "When we first encounter [classical 'economic man' or 'the rational man of modern statistical decision theory'] in the decision-making situation, he already has laid out before him the whole set of alternatives from which he will choose his action. . . . To each alternative is attached a set of consequences—the events that will ensue if that particular alternative is chosen. . . . the decision maker has a 'utility

function' . . . that ranks all sets of consequences. . . . [and he] selects the alternative leading to the preferred set of consequences" (1958:137). This statement, and others similar to it, seem easily reducible to "rule-guided comparison and choice among alternative means to a given end."

Nozick's discussion helps clarify the meaning of the method-centered versus substance-centered classification of rationality set forth above. Nozick tells us, "Two themes permeate the philosophical literature. First that rationality is a matter of reasons. A belief's rationality depends upon the reasons for holding that belief. These will be reasons for thinking the belief is true (or perhaps for thinking it has some other desirable cognitive virtue, such as explanatory power). Second, that rationality is a matter of reliability. Does the process or procedure that produces (and maintains) the belief lead to a high percentage of true beliefs? A rational belief is one that arises through some process that reliably produces beliefs that are true (or have some other desirable cognitive virtue)" (1993:64). Now the references to "process or procedure" in Nozick's second theme may make it seem that his distinction is a substance-centered versus method-centered one. But when one notices that the rationality determinant in *both* themes is what is presumed to be objectively "true" (i.e., the reasons for thinking the belief must be "true," and the process or procedure that leads to it must reliably lead to "true" beliefs), it becomes clear that both themes are substance-centered. A possible allusion to the method-centered type of definition is discernible, however, when Nozick indicates that rationality calls for making comparisons—and leaves open (by saying nothing about) whether the outcomes of those comparisons must be deemed substantively sound or not: "Rationality involves not simply doing something because of the reasons *in favor of* it but also taking into account (some) of the reasons *against* it" (1993:71–72). Nozick's more comprehensive image of "a neural network model of reasons for and against" in which each reason is assigned a distinctive relative weight in influencing the final choice (see 1993:73) is also method-centered—so long as no restrictions are placed on the substance of those reasons, the choice, or its outcome.

9. Slater says, "Where we speak of substituting conscious for unconscious bonds we may also speak of substituting cultural for instinctual connection" (1966:202), but I would also include learned habit (tradition) as part of unconscious rule-bound comparison and choice.

10. In this connection, one notes that Denny (unfortunately, equating rationality and logicality) cites Evans-Pritchard's study of "statements from Nuer religious thought, such as *a cucumber is an ox,* that were taken by earlier scholars as examples of prelogical or magical thinking" as showing that such statements "are made in relation to a third term not mentioned in them but understood. . . . A cucumber is equivalent to an ox in respect to God who accepts it in place of an ox [as a sacrifice]" (Denny 1991:75; see also Evans-Pritchard 1967). Applying the generic definition of rationality set forth in this chapter, one would say the outcome of comparing the sacrifice of a cucumber to the sacrifice of an ox, under Nuer rules, is that they are regarded as equivalent (i.e., equifinal—see Appendix A) means to the same end, namely, pleasing God.

11. When Parsons claims that "in [this] case one must not only be concerned with the choice of means to a particular end . . . but also with the weighing of values, i.e., ultimate ends, against each other" (1937:643–44) and lets it go at that, he overlooks

the problem of the criterion to be used for the weighing of values. One should ask: In what *respect* can one say a given ultimate end "outweighs" another?

12. On this basis, it seems fair to see a close connection between *Zweckrationalität* and what Weber refers to as "practical rationalism"—which he defines as "see[ing] and judg[ing] the world consciously in terms of the worldly interests of the individual ego" (1958a:77).

13. Indeed, Weber goes so far as to contradict his own clearly expressed subjectivism ("what matters is not the objective necessity of making economic provision, but the belief that it is necessary" [1978a:64]) when he declares that "economic laws. . . . cannot be deduced from a psychological analysis of the individual but rather from . . . the competitive price mechanism of the *objective situation* as stipulated by the theory" (1975a:202, italics in original; see also 1978a:84).

14. Weber rejects the view that such "convictions" and "causes" are instinctual in members of the group holding them (see his rejection of the idea that the "'Volk' are bearers of homogeneous 'instinctual forces' [which are] the ontological ground of the individual cultural phenomena" [1975a:204]). By arguing that *Wertrationalität* manifests a "clearly self-conscious formulation of the ultimate values governing the action and [a] consistently planned orientation of its detailed course to these values" (1978a:25), Weber highlights its call for a consciously regulated comparison and choice among alternative means—thereby indicating exactly why he names it, too, a "rationality." Insofar as the "values" to which Weber refers may certainly be idealistic and moral, Weber clearly rejects Alexander's claim that the "dichotomy [between action that is rational and action that is not rational] refers to whether people are selfish (rational) or idealistic (nonrational), whether they are normative and moral (nonrational) or instrumental and strategic (rational)" (1988:84).

15. Note that allowing end-effect to vary independently of end-object, as in this figure, seems fully in accord with Weber's own thought when he claims (as mentioned earlier here) that "the 'masses' as such, at least in their subjective conception and in the extreme case, have nothing concrete to lose but their lives. The valuation and effect of this danger strongly fluctuates in their own minds. On the whole, it can easily be reduced to zero through emotional influence" (1978a:921). And conceivably, it is this same independence that leads Weber to contrast the terms *Zweck*, literally "purpose" or "goal" (in the sense of a target to be aimed at), with *Wert*, literally "value" (in the sense of some preferred quality or effect to be brought about in the target).

16. Weber does not discuss combinations (b) and (c). However, the former seems exemplified by the phenomenon called "acquired taste," and Wilson discusses a variety of phenomena among nonhuman animals that appear to fall in cell (c). These include innate "altruism" (defined as an individual's acting so as to increase the survival fitness of another at the expense of his/her own fitness) as well as "spite" (defined as an individual's acting so as to diminish another's fitness at the expense of his/her own) and "selfishness" (defined as an individual's acting so as to raise his/her own fitness at the expense of another's)—and he could well have discussed innate cooperativeness (definable as an individual's acting so as to increase both his/her own, and another's, survival fitness). See Wilson 1975:121, 122, 123, 125, 128. Note also Simon's claim that "the existence of heritable docility, and the consequent possibility for a society to cultivate and exploit altruism, has very strong implications for

social theory, including economic, and the theories of political institutions and other organizations," and that "altruism . . . is wholly compatible with natural selection and is an important determinant of human behavior" (1990:1668). In sharp contrast with both Wilson and Simon, however, Coleman altogether inexplicably insists on "the *unnatural* character of the relation [when an] actor . . . acts so as to maximize the realization of interests of another actor, not himself" (1990:145, italics added).

17. On the near universality of sociality among nonhuman life forms, see, among others, Allee 1958:10; Wilson 1975; and Wilson 1978:16, 18−19. In offering a general explanation for such universality, Dawkins says that "the basic rationale is that, if a design is good enough [i.e., if it shows enough species-survival advantages] to evolve once, the same design principle is good enough to evolve twice, from different starting points in different parts of the animal kingdom" (1987:95, italics removed)— when the conditions for that survival are similar, as they are likely to be on this single planet of ours.

18. Weber gives an example of this distinction when he claims "the 'poor white trash,' i.e., the propertyless and, in the absence of job opportunities, very often destitute white inhabitants of the southern states of the United States of America in the period of slavery were the actual bearers of racial antipathy. . . . because the social honor of the 'poor whites' was dependent upon the social *déclassement* of the Negroes" (1978a:391).

19. Nozick devotes but a single sentence to Weber's work, referring summarily to "Weberian rationality" (1993:180) but giving no hint of what that rationality comprises, and no hint of how it might inform Nozickian rationality (and vice-versa). I would suggest, however, that the latter is directly derivable from the former—that is to say, from Weber's conceptualizations of *Zweckrationalität, Wertrationalität,* and affectual and traditional nonrationality (discussed later in this chapter). Nozick appears to reinvent *Wertrationalität*—under his own rubrics of "principles" and "symbolic utility"—and (rightly, in my judgment) to press for its integration into modern decision theory alongside what he refers to as "the familiar [or "standard"] kind of utility" (1993:48; see 34−35), which, presumably, Nozick would claim already incorporates *Zweckrationalität.* "A broader decision theory is needed," Nozick says (and certainly Weber would agree), for "by incorporating an action's symbolic meaning, its symbolic utility, into (normative) decision theory, we might link theories of rational choice more closely to anthropology's concerns" [1993:32]). Consider, then, how Nozick conceptualizes principles and symbolic utility—and how closely he parallels Weber's ideas. Principled people, Nozick says, do not "simply act on whim or the passion of the moment" (whimsical or passionate action would come under Weber's affectual nonrationality), and they do not "maximize [their] own self-interest and recommend that others do the same" (1993:3) (maximization of self-interest would conform to Weber's *Zweckrationalität;* see below for Nozick's contrast of rational behavior with traditional behavior). Instead, principled persons voluntarily "bind [themselves] to act as the principles mandate" (Nozick 1993:10). And although Nozick gives some New Year's resolution-type examples of principles ("never eat snacks between meals"; "Never smoke another cigarette"), by adding that "one might think of principles as deeper and less mechanical than [such] rules . . . but for present purposes I do not make any distinction between them" (1993:17) Nozick clearly opens his concept "principles" to all the *Wertrationalität* examples Weber

cites—namely "duty, honor, the pursuit of beauty, a religious call, 'personal loyalty,' or the importance of some 'cause' no matter in what it consists"—and also to include what Weber calls the "ethics" of ultimate ends, and of responsibility (discussed later in this chapter). Indeed, at one point Nozick tells us that "in some Prisoner's Dilemma situations, performing the . . . 'cooperative action' may have a symbolic value for the person. It may stand for his being a cooperative person" (1993:56)—exactly as Weber would say doing one's duty, or defending one's honor, or acting responsibly, etc., may stand for being a dutiful, or honorable, or responsible, etc. person.

Nozick's discussion of "symbolic utility" also closely follows Weber's *Wertrationalität*: "When utility is imputed to an action or outcome in accordance with its symbolic meaning. . . . [it] will look strange to someone outside that network of meanings. Recall the dire consequences some people bear in order to avoid 'losing face' or the deaths people risked and sometimes met in duels to 'maintain honor' or in exploits to 'prove manhood'" (1993:28–29). And Nozick's contrast between symbolic utility and "the familiar kind of utility" seems an unmistakable echo of Weber's contrast between *Wertrationalität* and *Zweckrationalität*: "A large part of the richness of our lives," Nozick says, "consists in symbolic meanings and their expression, the symbolic meanings our culture attributes to things or the ones we ourselves bestow. It is unclear, in any case, what it would be like to live without any symbolic meanings. . . . what would we then desire? Simply material comfort, physical security, and sensual pleasure?. . . . Simply wealth and power?. . . . Simply the innate, unconditioned reinforcers evolution has instilled and installed in us?" (1993:30). Paradoxically, however, Nozick assures us that "symbolic utility is not a different kind of utility. . . . Rather, symbolic utility is a different kind of *connection*—symbolic—to the familiar kind of utility. . . . The symbolic utility of an action *A* is determined by *A*'s having symbolic connection to outcomes (and perhaps to other actions) that themselves have the standard kind of utility" (1993:48; see also 55). (This chapter has already noted that Weber posits both ideal, and material, human interests—which is to say, two *different* but equally important, interdependent, and phylogenetically coeval utilities.) In a similar paradox (one that contrasts traditional behavior and rational behavior, as mentioned above), Nozick tells us, on the one hand, that "the stereotype of behavior in traditional societies is that people act a certain way because things have always been done that way. In contrast, rational behavior is aimed at achieving the goals, desires, and ends that people have." On the other hand, however, Nozick claims that "sometimes it will be rational to accept something because others in your society do" (1993:64, 129). Weber would say traditional nonrationality can be effective, efficient, and/or cognitively valid, but he certainly would not say it can be rational (despite his claim that traditional behavior "may shade over into" *Wertrationalität* [1978a:25]), chiefly because he employs a method-centered definition of rationality whereas Nozick employs a substance-centered definition (see note 8 above). That is to say, when Nozick says "accepting something because others in your society do" (i.e., following tradition) can be rational, he means rational in a substance-centered sense, not a method-centered sense—as follows: "We are all fallible," he says, "so the consensus of many other fallible people is likely to be more [!?] *accurate* than my own particular view when it concerns a matter to which we all have equal access" (Nozick 1993:129, italics added; compare Wallace 1983:371).

20. Note that this way of defining an ethic (Weber offers no explicit definition of his own) views it as a kind of rationality—namely, a rationality that is culturally

approved. We thus have the possibility of ordering rationalities according to the degree to which they are so approved (or disapproved) in a given society or societal subgroup.

21. Compare Wrong 1970:60; Aron 1971:97; and compare Habermas' linking "efficiency" to what he calls "instrumental" action and "efficacy" to "strategic" action (see 1984:285).

22. Note that the effectiveness and efficiency strategies merge when costs are thought to be negligibly small compared to benefits (or when benefits are thought to be negligibly small compared to costs), and also when cost and benefit are analytically combined into the single variable "utility." Weber seems to acknowledge this merging when he claims "an ethic of responsibility . . . [may eventually force one into an ethic of ultimate ends, at which point one must finally say] 'Here I stand; I can do no other'" (1946:127).

23. Thus, when Weber argues that "if . . . an 'ethos' . . . takes hold of the masses on some individual question, its postulates of *substantive* justice, oriented toward some concrete instance and person, will unavoidably collide with the formalism and the rule-guided and cool 'matter of factness' of bureaucratic administration" (1978a:980, see also 1978b:82), I do not think he means that substantive rationality and formal rationality collide, but that particularistic mercy as the ultimate value implicit in the "ethos" in question collides with universalistic detachment as the ultimate value implicit in "matter of factness." And when he says, "The propertyless masses especially are not served by the formal 'equality before the law' and the 'calculable' adjudication and administration demanded by bourgeois interests. . . . [because in these masses'] eyes justice and administration should serve to equalize their economic and social life-opportunities in the face of the propertied classes" (Weber 1978a:980), I think he means equality of *achievement* as the ultimate value implicit in the masses' interpretation of "justice" collides with equality of *opportunity* as the ultimate value implicit in "equality before the law." For a closely related discussion of the logical incompatibility of freedom and equality, assuming innate and ineluctable differences in ability, see Simmel 1950:65–67, 73–84, 275–76.

24. These remarks by Weber, and those cited below, seem very clearly to rule out Albrow's conclusion that "for [Weber] rational method and science were identical with each other" (1990:154).

25. Regarding the empiricality of science, Weber says that "the [explanatory] situation is absolutely identical in such fields of knowledge as mathematics and the natural sciences . . . they all begin as hypotheses, flashes of imaginative 'intuition,' and are then 'verified' against the facts. . . . The same is true in history" (1978b:121; see Popper's reinvention of this point [1961:31–32]). Regarding the intersubjectivity of science, Weber says, "Even the knowledge of the most certain propositions of our theoretical sciences—e.g., the exact natural sciences or mathematics, is, like the cultivation and refinement of the conscience, a product of *culture*" (1949:55, italics added; again see Popper 1961:44–48).

26. Therefore, when he also says that "the highest degree of rational understanding is attained in cases involving the meanings of logically or mathematically related propositions" (Weber 1978a:5), I think he means *formally* rational understanding. For a comparison of Simmel and Weber on this point, see Atoji 1984:68–75.

27. The nominal scale neither contains a natural origin nor any distances between scale points—only differences (compare Torgerson 1958:15–21).

28. For a partly similar analysis, see Parsons 1937:35–36.

29. A Weberian picture of what I have referred to as the "theoretical" side of the rationalities would have the same four phases, except "psychological thought" would be substituted for "physiological act" throughout—such that the rational individual plans and evaluates his/her thoughts (silently thinking, That's something I will have to think through later, and I have to stop letting my mind wander) as well as his/her physiological acts.

30. Although Weber does not say so, the availability of means can assist in selecting an ultimate end to which those means should be devoted by enabling the individual to ask, Which end can these means most effectively, or most efficiently, serve? This, however, leaves unanswered the question of how the "ends" that may be compared and chosen according to this criterion come to be conceived of as ends. Chapter 3 addresses these latter questions.

31. Weber prefers the term *irrational*, but he applies it only to affectual orientation, not to traditional orientation (see 1975a:125, 159; 1978a:6, 9), which he simply calls *traditional*. In the absence of a term used by Weber to subsume them both, and that would reflect his emphasis on their shared noncalculative (rather than miscalculative) nature, I employ *nonrational*. Similarly, Benn and Mortimore argue that "to describe an act as 'non-rational' . . . is to say, as of an act done under deep hypnosis, that in the circumstances in which it was done, the subject either could not have had a reason for doing it, or that to assess it in terms of reasons is somehow out of place" (1976:3).

32. Andreski seems mistakenly critical of Weber when he says, "If by 'emotional' action we mean actions accompanied by emotion, then this attribute neither presupposes nor excludes rationality" (1984:36), for clearly Weber means more than "accompanied by"; he means *motivated* by. Similarly, Andreski says, "Assuming that the most important goal is to survive, sticking to the old and proven ways may be the most rational course in primeval conditions" (1984:36). But clearly Weber means a course of action is nonrational (traditional) if it is taken *merely* because it is old. Habermas (wrongly, in my judgment) relegates "traditional action" to a "residual category" (1984:281).

33. In contrast with this inclusion of nonrationalities in the human individual's psychological makeup, we have Coleman's remarkable effort to exclude them: "The theoretical aim of social science," Coleman says, "must be to conceive of . . . action in such a way that makes it *rational* from the point of view of the actor" (1990:18, italics added). Now Coleman also says he uses a "conception [of rationality that] is based on the notion of different actions . . . having a particular utility for the actor and . . . the actor chooses the action which will maximize utility" (1990:14). Therefore, the claim that social science must "conceive of . . . action in such a way that makes it rational from the point of view of the actor" seems a theory-impoverishing distortion insofar as from the actor's point of view, it is at least possible for a given action to be purely the result of tradition-ingrained habit (conditioned reflex) or innate predisposition (unconditioned reflex)—therefore not inclusive of alternative utilities, not choiceful, and therefore not rational. Coleman also claims that "the success of a social theory based on rationality lies in successively diminishing that domain of social activity that cannot be accounted for by the theory" (1990:18, italics added). Against this view, I would argue that a theory based on rationality does not have to drive out all other explanatory factors in order to be successful—any more than a theory employing,

NOTES TO PAGES 39–42

say, human locomotion as one factor accounting for social activity has to diminish the domain of a theory of human cognition in order to be successful. In short, I see no justification for insisting that the theory game must be zero-sum with respect to all the explanatory factors involved in it. In a larger symmetry, many types of factors complement each other; to portray them otherwise, in my judgment, only serves to incite disciplinary self-destruction.

34. Habermas, however, holds that "the ends themselves can be more or less rational, i.e., chosen correctly in an objective sense, in view of given values, means, and boundary conditions" and then adds that "the rationality of values underlying action preferences is . . . measured . . . by whether they are so fundamental that they can ground a mode of life based on principles" (1984:170, 171, italics removed; see also 172, 281). Habermas thus overlooks (1) that any value whatsoever can ground such a life if the actors living the life so decide, and (2) that choosing "correctly in an objective sense" is inevitably a matter of shared (and changeable) subjective opinion.

Nozick, too, argues that goals can be rational (see 1993:134), and proposes a set of twenty-three "conditions" for ensuring that rationality. Although it is not feasible to review them all here, the tenth is both revealing and relatively easy to address. This condition states that "the [goal-rational] person does not have desires she knows are impossible to fulfill." Then Nozick continues: "Perhaps it is all right to prefer to fly unaided, but it is not rational for a person to *desire* this. (It might be rational, though, to wish it were possible.)" (1993:144). The grindingly heavy twists and turns of this statement, especially its unexplicated distinctions between preferring, desiring, and wishing for, may be enough to sink it. But one may also wonder what Nozick would say about those "unaided" near-zero gravity, and moon-gravity, flying maneuvers so many of us have watched on television and desired to emulate. More generally, it is an altogether familiar fact that one person's, or one generation's, or one culture's, "known" impossibility can be another's "known" possibility. The difference may lie solely in information rather than rationality. Indeed, Nozick himself offers the opinion (shocking, after his "known impossibility" theorem) that "the boldness of rationality consists in its willingness to formulate what before was not even within the purview of thought and to countenance a belief previously dismissed as outrageous," although he immediately qualifies: "Provided that when all the reasons are considered, it *is* indeed more credible than any competitor" (1993:175; see also 173). But of course *all* the reasons are never, and can never, be considered; we can only consider reasons as we discover or invent them. This ongoing emergence of reasons is exactly what denies the fixity Nozick seems to think inheres in "knowing" what is possible and what is impossible. Bologh's view of the whole matter of rational goals is much more in accord with my own (and Weber's): "There is no rational method for determining values as there is for choosing among alternative means" (1984:176; see also Giddens 1972:42; and Dahrendorf 1987:577). Chapter 3 explores this point further.

35. For example, Simmel says the meaning an actor attaches to a process becomes irrelevant "in the case of direct physical violation" (1950:182). That is to say, in that case (physical imprisonment, manacles, torture, maiming, drugging, etc.) the actor is compelled, we say, "against his/her will." A short extension of this view leads to the conclusion that *no* act can be completely explained by the actor's subjective meaning alone; the Earth's gravity, for just one example, has played an indispensable but meaning-independent part in all but the few extraterrestrial human acts so far.

36. Actually, eighteen—assuming that each cell is partitioned into the innate and learned components mentioned above.

Chapter 3. Structure of Society

1. Boulding regards all "open" systems as characterized by "throughput" (see 1956:15). The term is used here, however, to acknowledge that some open systems display an ongoing input-output flow of energy, but with very little throughput (turnover) in their constituent parts—as is the case with many parts of most living organisms after they reach maturity. Societies, however, are not only open, but throughput open, systems. Spencer is a classical originator of the image of human society as such a system ("Integrity of the whole [society] as of each large division [of that society] is perennially maintained, notwithstanding the death of component citizens" [1898,I:456]), but Spencer only briefly and indirectly gives thought to the institutionalized provisions a society makes for recruiting, and for discharging, these "component citizens" (see 1898:vol. 1, 153–26, 470). Parsons, too, notes that "a social system is always 'open,' engaged in processes of interchange with environing systems" (1961:30), but Parsons does not consider systematically the social system's institutional arrangements for recruiting and discharging its participants. In fact, although there is some discussion of certain institutions surrounding death in Parsons's analysis of the social system (1951), neither birth, immigration, nor emigration institutions are discussed there; no mention of birth or death (or birth rates and death rates), emigration, or immigration (or migration in general) is to be found in Parsons and Smelser's analysis of the economy and society (1956); no mention of death, emigration, or immigration in Parsons's "Outline of the Social System" (1961); and no mention of birth, death, or migration in Parsons' cross-sectional and longitudinal analyses of human societies (1971b and 1966). Parsons and Bales (1955), however, do address certain institutional (specifically, familial) aspects of participant-recruitment and socialization.

2. The problem of cohort-flow is located at the juncture between the participant-intake and participant-organizing institutions (see Waring 1976).

3. With undue narrowness, however, Weber adds that such relationships can engender social action "only by becoming the normal, though not the only, bases of a specific economic organization: the household" (1978a:358).

4. The outstanding exceptions to the indicated ethical agnosticism on Weber's part are his commitments to (1) the ultimate value of science ("Science . . . presupposes that what is yielded by scientific work is important in the sense that it is 'worth being known'. . . . To affirm the value of science is a presuppositon for teaching [in the lecture-room]. I personally by my very work answer in the affirmative " [1946:143, 152]) and (2) the ultimate value of nations—especially the German nation ("Our successors will . . . [hold us responsible] for the amount of elbow-room we conquer for them in the world" [1989b:198]—see chapter 4).

5. See Weber 1951a:588.

6. Durkheim agrees: "In fact, only society can pass a collective opinion on the value of human life; for this the individual is incompetent" (1951:213). See also Albrow 1990:224–25.

7. Simmel says a given individual "may belong, aside from his occupational position, to a scientific association, he may sit on a board of directors of a corporation, and occupy an honorific position in the city government" (1955:150), but he does not claim that any complement of such memberships is obligatory with every individual participant in every society. Similarly, Merton says, "Status-sets plainly provide one basic form of interdependence between the institutions and subsystems of society. This stems from the familiar fact that the same persons are engaged in distinct social systems [I think he means distinct institutions and subsystems of the same society]" (1957:381). Merton, however, does not identify these "social systems," nor does he explicitly claim that engagement in them all is obligatory with each participant.

8. See also Wrong 1970:53; Burger 1985:12, 35; Schluchter 1989:xv.

9. It seems remarkable, however, that there should be no entry at all for "science" or "scientific" in the index of *Economy and Society* (Weber 1978a)—inasmuch as there are several index entries and textual mentions of *"Wissenschaft"* in *Wirtschaft und Gesellschaft* (Weber 1956).

10. Compare Gieryn's astonishing but apparently serious view that "science is neither an institution, a profession, a structure, nor anything else that endures with constant meaning through space and time. Rather, science is nothing more—and nothing less—than what Richard Feynman or *The New York Times* and their readers say it is" (Cozzens and Gieryn 1990:11).

11. Weber says, "If I were asked seriously how high I estimate the importance of [the methodical inclusion of natural science in the service of the economy], my answer, after repeated careful examination, is *very* high" (1978c:1129).

12. Contrast this with Mayrl's unsupported claim that "Max Weber's commitment to human liberty through rational self-determinism presented a potential conflict with his equally strong commitment to scientific explanation" (1985:124) and with Burger's even more incredible (but no better supported) claim that in Weber's view "empirical science ought to be separated from practical discussion. . . . for the solution of practical tasks, historical and systematic empirical knowledge cannot provide any conclusive or valid guidance" (1977:174).

13. Comte puts this point better than Weber: "The craving of our understanding to know the laws of phenomena. . . . [is an] original tendency that acts as a preservative . . . against the narrowness and incompleteness that the practical habits of our age are apt to produce" (1975:89).

14. Note how similar to this view are those of Popper (1961:31–32) and Kaplan (1964:10–11), although neither mentions Weber.

15. The empiricality of science means that it describes, explains, and predicts phenomena "without those supernatural interventions, which an empirical explanation has to eliminate as causal factors" (Weber 1946:147).

16. In his own restatements of this limitation, Popper says that "the laws we find are always hypotheses; which means they may always be superceded. . . . *We do not know: We can only guess*. . . . every scientific statement must remain *tentative for ever*" (1961:247, 278, 280).

17. Hempel shares this view of Weber (see 1965:86), and restates the limitation itself by claiming that even if we possessed "all the information that an ideal science might provide," we still "would not have resolved our moral problem, for this requires a decision as to which [alternative course of action] is the best; which of them we ought to bring about. . . . [The] burden of this decision would still fall upon our

shoulders: it is we who would have to commit ourselves to an unconditional judgment of value. . . . Even [an] ideal science . . . cannot relieve us of this responsibility" (1965:88–89). See also Turner and Factor (1984:38), and Bologh (1990:123).

18. So much for the egregious misperception that "Weber's sociological work was, as regards its final intentions, so designed as to. . . . enable people to choose rationally between different sets of values in any given situation" (Mommsen 1974:110).

19. A near-complementarity between Marx and Weber, regarding the future of machinery, seems noteworthy. Marx, alone among classical theorists in sociology, foresaw the robot: "An automatic system of machinery . . . set in motion by an automaton, a moving power that moves itself; this automaton consisting of numerous mechanical and intellectual organs" (1973:692, italics removed). Fittingly (given his emphasis on the causal primacy of mentality), Weber *almost* foresaw artificial intelligence: "The fully developed bureaucratic apparatus compares with other forms of organization exactly as does the machine with the non-mechanical modes of production. . . . An inanimate machine is mind objectified. . . . [just as is] that animated machine, the bureaucratic organization" (1978a:973, 1502; see Inbar 1979, for a more explicit prediction, and advocacy, of "computerized bureaucracies").

20. Weber distinguishes "two types of economic action: (1) The first is the satisfaction of one's own wants, which may be of any conceivable kind, ranging from food to religious edification, if there is a scarcity of goods in relation to demand. . . . (2) The second . . . concerns profit-making by controlling and disposing of scarce goods" (1978a:339, 340).

21. Also see Dobbin for discussion of "the effects of institutionalized cultural meanings on how problems and their solutions are conceptualised in the first place, [and how choices are made] from among policy alternatives that are narrowly constrained by past [institutional] experience" (1993:142).

22. Pareto agrees: "All governments use force," adding, "and all assert that they are founded on reason" (1935:1526). Weber explains just why "the tasks of politics can only be solved by violence" when he notes that "the distinction between an order derived from voluntary agreement and one which has been imposed is only relative. For so far as the agreement underlying the order is not unanimous . . . the order is actually imposed upon the minority" and that imposition depends on "fear or . . . motives of expediency" (1978a:37)—that is, the expediency of pain-avoidance. (Freud says, "The power of [the] community is set up as 'right' in opposition to the power of the individual, which is condemned as 'brute force.' This . . . constitutes the decisive step of civilization" [1961:42]; Weber specifies "the power of the community" as residing in the political institution of the community.) Weber claims there are "diabolic forces lurking in all violence" (1946:125–26). He does not specify what these forces might be, but because of them, "he who seeks the salvation of the soul, of his own and of others, should not seek it along the avenue of politics, for the quite different tasks of politics can only be solved by violence" (Weber 1946:126). Weber realizes, however, that at some point staff members' willingness to administer violence when their chief commands them to do so must depend not on that chief's personal application of violence to them (for although the chief may be "stronger than any individual member, [s/he] is weaker than the members taken together"), but on the psychical "solidarity of interests, both on the ideal and material levels, of the members of the administrative staff with their chief." Such solidarity "is max-

NOTES TO PAGES 67-68

imized at the point where both the legitimacy of the status of the members [of the staff] and the provision for their economic needs is dependent on the chief retaining his position" (1978a:264; see also Wrong 1970:36ff). Finally, then, stability of the political institution depends on the economic institution (for meeting the staff's "economic needs") and on the religious and scientific institutions (for conferring prestige on the staff's status and lending expertise to their roles, and for providing the technology of violent force). This dependence is reciprocated as follows: The thing a political institution enforces is an "order" (see above); that order is prescribed by socially constructed behavioral rules called "law"; and that law is of two kinds—one that prescribes the behavior of individuals in their political institutional statuses, and one that prescribes their behavior in all other institutional statuses, as follows: "Sociologically," Weber says, "one might define public law as the total body of those norms which regulate state-oriented action, that is, those activities which serve the maintenance, development, and the direct pursuit of the objectives, of the state. . . . Correspondingly, private law would be defined as the totality of those norms which, while issuing from the state, regulate conduct other than state-oriented conduct" (1978a:641, 642). (Weber also notes that "from a legal point of view, the public rights of [an individual] are but those spheres of activity in which he acts as an agent of the state for specifically delimited purposes," and "a 'right,' in the context of the 'state,' is guaranteed by the coercive power of the political authorities" [1978a:642, 315]). It is in the realm of private law, then, that the dependence of the economic, religious, and scientific institutions on the political institution reciprocates its dependence on them. (Compare this relegation of Weber's analysis of law to a position secondary to his analyses of politics, economics, religion, and science with Parsons's exactly opposite conclusion that "the core of Weber's substantive sociology lies neither in his treatment of economic and political problems nor in his sociology of religion, but in his sociology of law" [1971b:40; see also 45].)

23. Weber defines "power" as "the probability that one actor within a social relationship will be in a position to carry out his own will despite resistance, regardless of the basis on which this probability rests" (1978a:53; see also 926, 942), and note that, contrary to Bologh's view (see 1990:176, 187), Weber seems sure to regard a struggle for liberation from the domination of another's power as a struggle for one's own power—which is to say, as a struggle to "carry out [one's] own will."

24. This scheme may be compared with that of Parsons and Smelser. In the latter, we find wealth claimed as the product of the adaptive subsystem (economy), power the product of the goal-attainment subsystem (polity), solidarity the product of the integrative subsystem, and prestige the product of the pattern maintenance subsystem (see Parsons and Smelser 1956:46-51). There are certain similarities between the schemes (wealth and power as products of economic and political institutions, and prestige as product of a third institution), but the most important dissimilarity (apart from the absence of any subsuming dimensions in Parsons and Smelser's scheme—but see Parsons 1960) is the absence of any subsystem in Parsons and Smelser's scheme that is specialized for the production of empirical knowledge. Similarly, Eisenstadt claims that "people [are] placed in structurally different positions, that is, in different cultural, political, family, or economic positions. . . . [which entail having certain] resources . . . at their disposal—for instance manpower, money, political support, or religious identification. . . . These resources serve as means for the implementation of various individual goals, and they may in them-

selves become goals or objects of individual endeavors" (1968:xxxviii). Eisenstadt, too, overlooks empirical knowledge as a resource, just as he overlooks science as a principal institution of society. Wuthnow proposes a "three sector" model of society (state, market, and voluntary) in which religion, and scientific academies, are regarded as among the components of the voluntary sector (see 1993a:19, 20).

25. Wuthnow notes that "most religious organizations orchestrate rituals in such a way as to prevent the full benefits of the organization [presumably including salvation] from being distributed to persons who are not actively contributing members" (1987:172); see also Turner 1981:112.

Chapter 4. Evolution of Society: Descriptive Model

1. I would argue, first, that the reason Weber claims these types cannot be placed in "simple" line is mainly because he holds charismatic domination can occur at any point in the line (see chapter 5), but he may also want to allow for retrogressions in the line. Second, by "diverse combinations" Weber is not likely to mean such combinations are totally without any leading features which would justify characterizing one combination as, say, more traditional or more rational than another.

2. By contrast, although Parsons rightly (though ambiguously) asserts the independence of description from explanation as set forth in chapter 1 ("One need not develop a truly advanced general analysis of the main *processes* [explanation] of social change in order to make general claims about the *structural patterning* [description] of evolutionary development" [1966:111, his italics]), he relies on this independence in order to excuse himself from trying to explain societal evolution: "The problems of [explanatory] historical causation concerning the genesis of [certain societal] systems lie outside the scope of the present discussion. . . . It is not necessary for our purposes to analyze the processes which generated [their] breakthroughs" (Parsons 1966:69, 70).

3. Parsons goes so far as to say that "the primary, over-all principle is that of differentiation in relation to functional exigency; this is the master concept for the analysis of social structure" (1961:44; see also 1966:22–25) and, with similar emphasis, Douglas says that "primitive means undifferentiated; modern means differentiated" (1966:77; see also Burger 1987:213; Albrow 1990:282). The present theory argues that the three other principles discussed in this chapter (i.e., cultural rationality, organizational scale, and spatial extension and consolidation) are no less "master" concepts for the analysis of societal evolution.

4. Schroeder, too, argues for the differentiation of "spheres of life" as an element in Weber's work, but Schroeder discusses only the differentiations between "the intellectual sphere—dominated by science—and the sphere of politics," the "conflict . . . between the brotherly ethic of the Christian religions and the unbrotherliness of modern economics," and "the way in which the sphere of science became separated from the other spheres of life, particularly the sphere of religion" (1992:23, 24, 123).

5. Thus, "The god of the Middle East was fashioned on the model of the king. . . . [and in] the Middle East the old centralized bureaucratic administration undoubtedly promoted the concept of the supreme deity as a King of Heaven" (Weber 1951b:21). In addition, "Except for the world politics of the great powers which threatened their homeland and constituted the message of their most impressive oracles, the [Jewish]

prophets could not have emerged. . . . [And without] the promises of prophecy an increasingly 'civic' religious community [like the Jews] would never voluntarily have taken to . . . a pariah situation and gained proselytes for sharing it" (Weber 1952:268, 364; see also 1951b:23).

6. Indeed, Weber attributes the decline and fall of the Roman Empire to rigid dominance of the economy by the polity: "To have a true image of the Later Roman Empire in modern terms, one must imagine a society in which the state owns or controls and regulates the iron, coal, and mining industries . . . [etc.] In addition the state would have enormous domains, would run workshops to produce military supplies as well as goods for bureaucrats, would own all ships and railways, and would conclude state treaties to regulate wool imports" (1976:365).

7. The city is the arena wherein relations between the economic and political institutions were worked out because the city is "in the first place the seat of commerce and industry," but it is also "regularly the seat of government, both political and ecclesiastical" (Weber 1950:317, 318; see also 1978a:1224).

8. Weber notes, however, that "the profitableness of imperialism as compared with the capitalist interests of pacifist orientation. . . . [combined] with the extent to which economic needs are satisfied by a private or a public economy. . . . is highly important for the nature of expansive economic activities backed up by political communities. . . . Therefore, imperialist capitalism has always existed wherever to any relevant degree the polity per se, or its subdivisions (municipalities), satisfied its wants through a public economy. The stronger such an economy has been, the more important imperialist capitalism has been" (1978a:918).

9. To Tilly's concept of the "stateness" of government, "as measured by formal autonomy, differentiation from nongovernmental organizations, centralization, and internal coordination" (1975a:34), then, one should add parallel concepts, measured in parallel ways, pertaining to the religious, economic, and scientific institutions. In contrast with the institutional comprehensiveness of the latter view of societal modernization, Habermass claims that "like Marx, Weber conceives the modernization of society as the differentiation of the capitalist economy and the modern state" (1984:158, italics removed), thereby omitting the five other differentiations discussed by Weber. Speaking of Marx, it may also be said that to those several micro-level "alienations" and "estrangements" of social individuals from each other on which Marx focuses (see 1977:61–74), the present Weberian theory adds a similar claim at the meso-level (namely, the "estrangement" of social institutions from each other).

10. It is to the indicated prehistoric societal symmetry—albeit one dominated by the religious institution—that modern religious fundamentalisms seem eager to return all human societies. Mendelsohn says, "Fundamentalists believe that the 'decoupling' of science and religion . . . has removed normal restraints against the often destructive forces of modern technology. Designed by God to be harmonious partners in the subordination of nature, science and religion instead enter into an inappropriate competition brought on by the secularizing trends of the early modern period and the Enlightenment. Fundamentalists have made claims to be the restorers of the lost harmony" (1993:24); and the same could be said about fundamentalist beliefs concerning the "decoupling" of all the other participant-organizing institutions from the religious one (see Marty and Appleby 1993a:esp. 11).

11. Reich observes a presently emergent nonbureaucratic way of systematizing rights and responsibilities: "In fact, the high-value enterprise cannot be organized

[bureaucractically]. The three groups that give the new enterprise most of its value—problem-solvers, problem-identifiers, and strategic brokers—need to be in direct contact with one another to continuously discover new opportunities. . . . This is no place for bureaucracy" (1992:87, italics removed). To the extent that this observation is valid, and to the extent that it holds not only in the economic institution of society but also in the political, scientific, and religious institutions (a possibility Reich does not discuss), then it seems fair to say that in the indicated "high value enterprises" of all these institutions, problem solving, problem identifying, and brokering "symbolic analysts" (see Reich 1992:108–9, 177) represent a new machine-assisted status system that also helps hold the participant-organizing institutions together.

12. Durkheim says *any* "synthesis . . . of particular consciousnesses. . . . has the effect of disengaging a whole world of sentiments, ideas and images which, once born, obey laws all their own" (1965:471).

13. Compare Schroeder's claim that "Weber's writings contain a developmental framework by means of which the role of belief-systems in social life can be distinguished in three stages: magic, religion, and science. . . . [This schema] can thus be seen to dominate Weber's analysis of cultural life" (1992:11, 13). Although Schroeder leaves rationality undefined generically (see 1992:36), he argues that "in Weber's view, magic has a rational aim which is pursued by irrational means, whereas religion is characterized by an increasingly irrational aim and increasingly rational means to salvation" (1992:34)—and one presumes Schroeder wants to say science has both rational aims and rational means. Of course, chapter 2 has argued that neither aims nor means can be rational, that only a procedure for selecting means can be rational, and that no procedure for selecting aims can be rational. But set all that aside. Consider the claim, above, that science can replace religion (also see Schroeder 1992:113) because "science, like religion, aims at being an all-encompassing system of thought" (Schroeder 1992:13). Without batting an eye, however, Schroeder also tells us Weber held that "science . . . does not add to our understanding of how people should live or help us decide whether certain values are better than others" (1992:128). With this, Schroeder admits that in Weber's view science does not, and cannot, after all, aim at being an "all-encompassing system of thought," and its replacement of religion (or politics) in deciding social values is, therefore, not to be expected. That religion (and politics) may change radically in the future, however, is a matter touched on in "Summary and Speculations."

14. For other comments on Weber's nationalism, see Aron 1971:91ff; Habermas 1971:66; Mommsen 1970:190, 1971:109–16, and 1974; Albrow 1990:284; Giddens 1972:16ff; Beetham 1985:36–59; Turner and Factor 1984:59–69; Bologh 1990:75–80; and compare Baumgarten 1971:122–27; and Murvar 1984). Of course, Weber shared his belief in "the deadly seriousness of the population problem" with Malthus (see 1966), Comte (see 1975:282–83), Durkheim (see 1984:201, 208), Marx and Engels (see 1947:8, 20), Spencer (see 1898:vol. 1, 471, 494–97), and Simmel (see 1950:96, 135, 145–69), but the intensely nationalistic conclusions Weber draws from it are unique in this company.

15. "Almost certainly, hominids separated from apes in tropical or subtropical Africa during the late Miocene, sometime between 10 million years ago (mya) and 6 mya. Africa is indicated partly by its possession of humanity's closest living relatives, the chimpanzee and the gorilla, and, much more directly, by its unique human fossil record. This shows not only that people existed in Africa at least 2.5 million years

earlier than in Eurasia, the continent with the second oldest record; it also suggests an African origin for the first Eurasians" (Klein 1989:399; see also Fagan 1990:15, 20).

16. In the currently dominant hypothesis (called *rapid replacement, Noah's Ark,* or *Garden of Eden,* an early human species, *Homo erectus,* migrated first (about 1.8 million years ago) into Eurasia, but was later (about 150,000 years ago) replaced by the most recently evolved human species, *Homo sapiens,* when it, too, migrated out of Africa: "At the moment the bulk of the genetic and fossil evidence . . . strongly favors the [hypothesis] that modern *Homo sapiens* originated in Africa and subsequently dispersed to other parts of the globe, largely or entirely supplanting local nonmodern populations" (Klein 1989:356; see also Fagan 1990:15–62). The second hypothesis (called *multiregional* or *candelabra*) rejects a single point of origin for *Homo sapiens,* arguing either that *Homo erectus* "diversified into morphologically distinct regional populations, each of which then evolved progressively toward modern *H. sapiens*" (Klein 1989:255) or that what we now think of as the species *Homo erectus* was really nothing more than an archaic subspecies of *Homo sapiens* (see Wolpoff et al. 1984:464– 67).

17. Leakey and Lewin note that "some five thousand languages [have been] documented in recent historical times. . . . each rooted through complex evolutionary relationship to an original mother tongue" (1992:274–75).

18. See Dawkins 1987:237–39, and Diamond 1992:120–21 for the essentially Darwinian—that is, natural selection plus sexual selection—argument implied here, and Molnar 1992:227–34 for discussion of natural selection and skin color, in particular. Note also that most paleoanthropologists recognize only two subspecies of the species *Homo sapiens.* These are *Homo sapiens neanderthalensis* and *Homo sapiens sapiens* (sometimes called "modern man"), and since the former became extinct about thirty-five thousand years ago, "All living human beings belong to the subspecies *Homo sapiens sapiens*" (Swedlund, 1992:vol. 16, 53; see also Klein 1989:348, 416–17). (Confusingly, however, races are also sometimes referred to as subspecies of *Homo sapiens,* thereby either ignoring the *H. s. neanderthalensis* versus *H. s. sapiens* subspecies distinction [for an example of this, see Molnar 1992:25, 186] or treating the latter as a species distinction or even as a merely ethnic distinction [for the latter two treatments, see Leakey and Lewin 1992:231, 270].) Species differentiation among different subpopulations of *Homo sapiens sapiens* had neither time enough to occur, nor was geographical isolation complete enough, nor human phenotypic plasticity narrow enough, nor sociocultural and technological inventiveness small enough (see Smith and Layton 1987). Indeed, the Neolithic flowering of sociocultural and technological inventiveness (discussed below) put an end to further biogenetic differentiation among human subpopulations by initiating widespread interethnic, and interracial contacts, including gene exchanges, among them.

19. Note that the socioculturally, ethnically, and racially differentiated groups that emerged following the first human dispersion out of eastern Africa are not the same as those we see around us today, some 100–200,000, or even 1.8 million, years later. Those earlier groups have long since given way (each through its own evolution, and through contact with other groups). The present groups are only their very distant, and very mixed, descendants (see, for example, Diamond's sketch of the history, starting about 5000 B.C., of the so-called Indo-European languages, 1992:249– 75).

20. Diamond takes the radically negative view that "the adoption of agriculture

. . . was in many ways a catastrophe from which we have never recovered. With agriculture came the gross social and sexual inequality, the disease and despotism, that curse our existence" (1987:64). Fortunately, however, Diamond has tempered this view by claiming "the introduction of agriculture [was] a mixed *blessing*"— rather than an unmitigated, or even mixed, "catastrophe"—and "agriculture inextricably combines causes of our *rise* and *fall*"—rather than only, or even mainly, our fall (1992:138, 139, both italics added; see also 180–91). The point I would emphasize, however, is not that agriculture necessarily brought a better life for *individuals* (although it seems clear that it did so—for a larger absolute number of individuals, even when it did not do so for a larger proportion of the world's population) than did the hunting and gathering economies that preceded it. It did, however, bring a better life for the *human species as a whole*—a better chance for species survival. Agriculture clearly brought a more populous life, for it is estimated that although the total world population during the 2 million years of hunter-gatherer Paleolithic times did not at any time exceed 5 million, it rose to 200 million during the roughly 5,000 years of the agricultural Neolithic times (see Campbell 1985:397; Desmond 1975:21–23; Diamond 1992:237; Molnar 1992:295–99). Moreover, of the estimated 70 billion human beings born in the last 200,000 years, about 8 percent of these were born within the last .05 percent (100 years) of that time (see Gott 1993:316). Agriculture also brought an occupationally more complex life, a technically more competent life, and a territorially more widespread life for human society as a whole.

21. Here, one recalls Spencer's claim regarding the overriding importance of conquest in strengthening the consolidation of human society as a whole: "By force alone were small nomadic hordes welded into large tribes; by force alone were large tribes welded into small nations; by force alone have small nations been welded into large nations" (1961:176). Carneiro offers a partial explanation: "As population density increases, and arable land comes into short supply, fighting over land ensues. Villages vanquished in war, having nowhere to flee, are forced to remain in place and to be subjugated by the victors" (1981:64). A similar idea underlies Braudel's reference to "the slowly-constructed unity of a France which reveals its strength . . . along the boundaries of its territory. Did not provinces acquired on the periphery have to be domesticated, subjugated and brought to heel during a long training period? And did not the long ribbon of the frontiers have to be constantly defended, watched and pushed forward?" (1988:373). Note, however, Spencer's claim that "war . . . after a certain stage of progress . . . becomes a cause of retrogression. . . . the direct effect of war on industrial progress is repressive. . . . [and] perpetual warlike activities . . . cultivate aggressiveness to the extent of making it a pleasure to inflict injury" (1961:178, 179). Chapter 7 returns to this point.

22. Barth adopts Weber's emphasis here on "subjective belief" and on "presumed identity" as the sole criterion of ethnicity when he gives "primary emphasis to the fact that ethnic groups are categories of ascription and identification by the actors themselves" (1981:199; see also 15). Contrast this with van den Berghe's primary criterion of objective—that is, biogenetic—relatedness. Van den Berghe says, "Ethnicity is common descent, either real or putative," but he goes on to add that "when putative, the myth has to be validated by several generations of common historical experience" (1987:16; see also 27)—implying that when it is biogenetically "real," the relationship does not need to be so validated and is somehow automatically self-validating. Therefore, when van den Berghe claims "the biological golden rule is 'give unto

others as they are related unto you" (1987:20, see also 7), he does so without considering the distinctively sociological question of how "others" come to be defined as
being "related unto you" and, of course, how "related" is itself defined. To answer
van den Berghe's questions—"Why should parents sacrifice themselves for their
children? Why do uncles employ nephews rather than strangers in their businesses?"
(1987:19)—requires that we answer a prior question: How do parents and uncles
identify certain people, and not others, as being their children and their nephews?
Van den Berghe does not address this question, but simply takes for granted that
somehow they do make these identifications, and accurately, too: "It is very difficult
and quite exceptional . . . for an [ethnic group] to form if the core of the group is not
made up of people who know themselves to be related to each other" [1987:23–24]).
But the validity of such "knowledge" varies widely with the mechanism that is used
to establish it—widely enough to prevent almost any sociological analyst from taking
that validity for granted (compare van den Berghe 1987:27). Indeed, every such
mechanism, among nonhuman as well as human species (including imprinting, phe-
romones, colony odor, display of intercourse-evidence, birth witnessing, etc.) can
yield objectively false "knowledge." When that is the yield, the evidence seems clear
that the falsity often goes undiscovered and objective "kin" are treated the same as
objective "nonkin," and vice-versa (see Lorenz 1970; Wilson 1971:esp. 272–77).

23. Weber says, "The belief in ethnic affinity has at all times been affected by
outward differences in clothes, in the style of housing, food and eating habits, the
division of labor between the sexes and between the free and the unfree" (1978a:391).

24. See Stuckert 1976; Griffin 1977. This distinction is what Weber is seeking to
draw when, on the one hand, he refers to "race identity" as constituted by "common
inherited and inheritable traits that actually derive from common descent" (this is
objective race), but then adds that "of course, race creates a 'group' only when it is
subjectively perceived as a common trait" (1978:385). See also Molnar's distinction
between "biological [and] social definitions of race" (1992:290; see also 291).

25. Weber attributes the special power of ethnicity in uniting large numbers of
individuals to its egalitarian applicability: "The idea of a chosen people derives its
popularity from the fact that it can be claimed to an equal degree by any and every
member of the [group]" (1978a:391).

26. "The monopolistic closure . . . of political, status or other groups and . . . the
monopolization of marriage opportunities . . . restricted the *connubium* to the offspring from a permanent sexual union within the given religious, economic and
status group" (Weber 1978:386).

27. Basically, Simmel anticipates my whole argument here (except that he does
not allude, in this passage, to politics): "The very universality of the processes which
belong to human society, whether looked at from the point of view of religion or
trading or logical thinking, at least opens the door to a universal society; and, in fact,
these tendencies all express themselves where the social development has gone far
enough to make it possible" (1950:284).

28. Adams, too, notes the "prevailing ability [of early Mesopotamian civilization]
to dissolve the ethnic identifications of immigrants and to foster urban loyalties
instead" (1966:174). Mead suggests a sequence in the manner in which one group
may manifest its dominance over another group: First, there is "the conflict of one
tribe with another which undertakes to wipe out the other"; then there is the "overcoming of the other and holding the other in subjection"; finally, there "came the

administrative attitude which was more . . . functional superiority. . . . The passage [in the case of the Roman Empire] is from a sense of political superiority and prestige expressed in a power to crush, over into a power to direct a social undertaking in which there is a larger co-operative activity." Mead concludes by saying, "Conceivably, there may appear a larger international community than the empire, organized in terms of function rather than force" (1962:284, 285–86).

29. Adams uses the phrase "ethnic amalgam" (1966:133). Tilly says that "the Europe of 1500 had a kind of cultural homogeneity only rivaled, at such a geographical scale, by that of China [as a result of the] earlier unification of the Roman Empire"—although he adds that "well-defined vernaculars . . . already divided Europeans into linguistic groups incapable of mutual communication" (1975a:18, 19).

30. If common present language may be taken as prima facie evidence of past common ethnicity, Deutsch's observations illustrate the power of nationalism to cut across such ethnicities: "As for language, members of the British people may speak English or Welsh; Canadians, English or French; South Africans, English or Afrikaans; Irishmen, English or Gaelic; Belgians, Flemish or French; and the Swiss, German, French, Italian, and Romansch" (1966:18).

31. Note that in addition to such convictions, Weber recognizes other cultural affinities, too: "As a rule . . . the pretension to be considered a special 'nation' is associated with a common language as a culture value of the masses. . . . [and/or] with differences in the other great culture value of the masses, namely, a religious creed" (1978a:922–23).

32. Weber says the concept " 'nation' directs us to political power. . . . to a specific kind of pathos which is linked to the idea of a powerful political community of people" (19768a:397–98).

33. The term *sacrifice*, often used in connection with war deaths, seems significant for its religious connotations, for with that sacrifice warriors are said to "hallow" and "consecrate" the fields of war and, by short extension, war and the warring nation itself.

34. Durkheim's view is more general than McNeill's: "It is the appearance of [a common outward sign] that informs individuals that they are in harmony and makes them conscious of their moral unity. It is by uttering the same cry, pronouncing the same word, or performing the same gesture in regard to the same object that they become and feel themselves to be in unison. . . . It is the homogeneity of . . . movements that gives the group consciousness of itself and consequently makes it exist" (1965:262, 263).

35. Note that from the standpoint being put forward here, every modern and future effort to set up or maintain "ethnically pure" or "racially pure" nations—or enclaves within nations—is, by definition, retrogressive with respect to consolidation.

36. Wuthnow says, "The trajectory of modern [Western] culture needs to be understood in terms of relatively abrupt periods of cultural upheaval, not as the gradual accumulation of minor incremental changes," and goes on to claim that "Weber . . . reveals a persistent ambiguity on this score" (1989:530–31). I am claiming that the trajectory in question needs to be understood in terms of both abrupt and incremental changes, and that the espousal of such duality is not the same as ambiguity.

37. Gould, for example, says, "The Cambrian explosion was the first filling of the ecological barrel for multicellular life. . . . Life was radiating into empty space and

could proliferate at logarithmic rates" (1989:228)—thereby implying an intrinsically biological tendency to radiate and proliferate rather than to withdraw and dwindle, or merely to hold the line. Even after the biggest crunches of species extinctions that we know of, life has bounced back: "The history of life is . . . a record punctuated by brief, sometimes geologically instantaneous, episodes of mass extinction and subsequent diversification" (Gould 1989:54).

38. Schluchter expresses a view similar to my own when he says that "Weber advocated a theory of alternatives based on the fundamental conviction that no religion, no cultural formation was capable of exhausting humanity's historical possibilities" (1989:204)—although Schluchter does not regard such a theory as evolutionary, and I do. Verba describes the model I have in mind (which he calls "the branching tree" model) as conceiving of "a sequence of choice points (not necessarily points of conscious decision, but points where developments can go one way or the other). At any point in a sequence of development, there may be alternative next stages. But which one is chosen closes the options for others" (1971:308; see also Krasner 1984:240–44). Verba goes on to say, "Closely related to this is the notion of irreversibilities—choices of one branch which once chosen does not allow backtracking" (1971:308; I am indebted to my colleague Frank Dobbin for calling Verba's argument to my attention). Weber, in contrast, does allow backtracking—as when he says "the routinization of charisma. . . . [may result in] traditionalization or . . . legalization" (quoted above). Similarly, Stanley says biological evolution "does not move inexorably in one direction," and "reversals of evolution are not only possible, they are clearly indicated [in the fossil record]" (1981:155).

39. Note that the notion of continuous-discontinuous evolution includes what Marx and Engels refer to as dialectical change, except the latter not only implies a description of change (as being continuous and discontinuous) but also an explanatory causal model of that change (as depending on a bilateral class struggle, or, more generally, conflictful interaction between thesis and antithesis—see Wallace 1983:340–42; 1988:56–57). A somewhat different, but compatible, explanation will be offered in chapter 5. Note also that flat but cyclical change would be represented by a society oscillating—that is, moving first progressively and then retrogressively—between, say, the natural norms and tradition stages, or between the latter and the rational-legal stage, of culture (see Sorokin's discussion of oscillation between "sensate" and "ideational" cultures [1937–41]).

40. Ferris explains the role of sudden punctuations in biological evolution as follows: "Our planet offers only so many ways for a creature to make a living. Given a reasonable amount of time in a fairly stable environment, various species will arise and adapt until they have filled every ecological niche. . . . the chance is small that a new species will appear that can do the job better than the existing species do and thus find an opening in a saturated ecologic market. . . . [For example,] in the age of the dinosaurs, no mammal grew larger than a house cat. Then came catastrophe—a comet intruder, we presume—and the beautifully adapted dinosaurs. . . . died out, but the several small mammals that made it through found themselves in vastly improved circumstances" (1992:166, 167). Ferris then quotes physicist Richard Muller: "Had it not been for the large comet that hit 65 million years ago, mammals might never have wrested the Earth from the dinosaurs" (1992:168; see Benton 1993:769–70 for discussion of the same claims regarding the beginning of dinosaur evolution).

41. Note that both gradual (ramp) and punctuational (step) changes are scale dependent: what appears, on a macro scale, to be a ramp may be revealed as a series of steps on a micro scale. See also Dawkins 1987:248.

42. In addition, of course, the "environmental catastrophes" (including the "impacts of extraterrestrial bodies") to which Gould refers in the quotation above as "unpredictable" become less and less so (of course, never reaching perfect predictability—see Barrow 1991:155–84) to the extent that the catastrophes hold off long enough to permit the scientific institutions of the technologically most advanced societies to go on cumulating empirical knowledge of the world.

Chapter 5. Evolution of Society: Explanatory Model

1. Kuhn argues for a difference between "normal science" (ramp) and "extraordinary science" (step): "Normal science consists in . . . extending the knowledge of those facts that the paradigm displays as particularly revealing, by increasing the extent of the match between those facts and the paradigm's predictions, and by further articulation of the paradigm itself" (1970:24). Then, along comes an anomalous finding—one large enough and widely recognized enough to precipitate a "crisis": "All crises begin with the blurring of a paradigm and the consequent loosening of the rules for normal research. . . . And all crises close with the emergence of a new candidate for paradigm and with the subsequent battle over its acceptance (1970:84). In "extraordinary science. . . . [the scientist will] often seem a man searching at random, trying experiments just to see what will happen, looking for an effect whose nature he cannot quite guess" (1970:86–87). Anticipating Kuhn (originally 1962), Watson had written (originally 1938) that "generally speaking, we proceed in science like the mechanic who is continually adding gadgets to deal with this or the other defect in his machine. Sooner or later the gadgets weaken the whole structure, and he is well advised to make a new engine. . . . In science the process that corresponds to the designing of a new machine is the invention of a new method of representation" (1960:239). Adopting a form of argument similar to both Watson and Kuhn, the paleontologist Gould claims that "the reasons for differential survival [during times of mass extinctions of biological species] are qualitatively different from the causes of success in normal times" (1989:306) and suggests the latter reasons involve more continuous and systematic adaptive advantage and natural selection. The former reasons, however, are more discontinuous and more random: "Along comes a mass extinction, with its 'different rules' for survival. Under the new regulations, the very best of your traits, the source of your previous flourishing, may now be your death knell. A trait with no previous significance . . . may now hold the key to your survival" (Gould 1989:307).

2. In support of this claim, Weber first asserts that the strongest support of tradition culture is "the effect of . . . magical grounds, the deep repugnance to undertaking any change in the established conduct of life because supernatural evils are feared" (1950:355), and then credits the charismatic prophets of Biblical Israel with overcoming the traditional primacy of magic (although "it has not been possible even today to overcome it entirely" [Weber 1950:363]) with the more rational primacy of miracle ("the miracle is more rational than magic charm" because the former "springs from meaningful, understandable intentions and reactions of the godhead" [Weber

1952:222–23]). Similarly, "Since Judaism made Christianity possible and gave it the character of a religion essentially free from magic, it rendered an important service from the point of view of economic history," and "prophecies have released the world from magic and in doing so have created the basis for our modern science and technology, and for capitalism" (Weber 1950:361, 362).

3. Given these seemingly unambiguous words, it is astonishing to find that some of Weber's interpreters claim he believed "charisma is temporally bound—a social form that is limited to premodern stages of social evolution and development," and "for Weber, then, pure charisma . . . can occur only under preindustrial social conditions" (Bradley 1987:40); that "according to Weber's own projection, charisma could hardly flourish in a 'disenchanted' world" (Glassman and Murvar 1984:4); and that "in a rationalized world charismatic revolution is impossible" (Swatos 1984:205).

4. Kuhn makes a strikingly close approach to Weber's hypothesis of the key role of charisma in evolutionary discontinuities. Kuhn says: "Observation and experience . . . cannot alone determine a particular body of [scientific] belief. An apparently arbitrary element, compounded of personal and historical accident, is always a formative ingredient of the beliefs espoused by a given scientific community at a given time" (1970:4). See also Tilly's interpretation of Black's answer to the question of "under what conditions do national states become dominant organizations in an area?" as emphasizing the role of "modernizing leaders" (1975b:606).

5. With an apparently similar idea in mind, Ibn Khaldun says, "One cannot expect [prophets] to be able to work the wonder of achieving superiority without group feeling. . . . If someone who is on the right path were to attempt (religious reforms) in this way, his isolation would keep him from (gaining the support of) group feeling, and he would perish" (1969:127–28). Comte also sees very clearly the distinction between the roles of cognition and affect in social innovation: "In order to establish a new social system, just conceptions will not suffice. It is necessary that the mass of society should feel attracted by it. This condition. . . . is needed above all for the satisfaction of the moral craving for enthusiasm inherent in man when he enters upon a new career. Without such enthusiasm he could neither overcome his natural inertness nor shake off the powerful yoke of ancient habits" (1975:50, italics added). Mannheim agrees: " 'Ideas' did not drive [the peasants] to revolutionary deeds. Their actual outburst was conditioned by ecstatic-orgiastic energies" (1955:213).

6. Very similarly, Durkheim argues (1) that insofar as a command "excludes all idea of deliberation or calculation, it gets its efficacy from the intensity of the mental state in which it is placed. It is this intensity which creates what is called a moral ascendancy," and (2) that a collective representation manifests a "simple radiation of the mental energy which it contains. It has an efficacy coming solely from its psychical properties, and it is by just this sign that moral authority is recognized" (1965:238). Dahrendorf, too, refers only to "the unusual, the unexpected, the unique" (1987:577) as objects of charisma, without mentioning transcendence.

7. And, of course, "charisma might . . . be manufactured; rationality might . . . 'create' irrationality" (Swatos 1984:205, italics removed).

8. Durkheim elaborates: "Feeling himself dominated and carried away by some sort of an external power which makes him think and act differently than in normal times, [a man] naturally has the impression of being himself no longer. . . . So it is in the midst of these effervescent social environments and out of this effervescence itself that the religious idea seems to be born" (1965:249, 250—see also Durkheim's refer-

ence to "moral contagion" 1984:311). Marx, too, seems clearly to have psychic contagion in mind when he says "social contact begets in most industries an emulation
and a stimulation of the animal spirits that heighten the efficiency of each individual
workman" (1967:vol. 1, 326).

9. Perhaps this is what Dostoievsky means when he says, "If everything on Earth
were rational, nothing would happen" (see Barrow 1991:202).

10. Shils says, "Attenuated and dispersed charisma . . . exists in *all* societies. . . .
[It] enters into obedience to law and respect for corporate authority" (1968:390, italics
added). And Eisenstadt says "charismatic activities and orientations . . . are inherent,
even if in varying degrees, in all social relations and organizations" (1968:xxii), and
Geertz, too, says that "charisma does not appear only in extravagant forms and
fleeting moments but is an abiding, if combustible, aspect of social life that occasionally bursts into an open flame" (1983:123).

11. A somewhat higher intensity of charisma seems implied by Weber's notion of
the "charisma of office" (see above), and the notion that "modern bureaucracy . . . has
developed a high sense of status honor; without this sense the danger of an awful
corruption and a vulgar Philistinism threatens fatally" (1946:88).

12. One might suggest that the arts are devoted to promulgating ways of perceiving whereby literally *everything* becomes charismatic. As Blake puts it: "To see a
world in a grain of sand, / And heaven in a wild flower, / Hold infinity in the palm of
your hand / And eternity in an hour."

13. Nowhere is the raising of this banner more explicit than in the anthem
"Deutschland Über Alles."

14. Note, however, that despite his (and Marx's) emphasis on struggle in the
economic institution, Engels argues that the proletariat's know-how must come in
large part from the scientific institution: "To impart to the now oppressed proletarian
class a full knowledge of the conditions and of the meaning of the momentous act it is
called upon to accomplish, this is the task of the theoretical expression of the proletarian movement, scientific socialism" (Marx and Engels 1969–70:vol. 3, 151).

15. Thomas Mann, however, makes the relationship between esthetic charisma
and erotic charisma the central theme of *Death in Venice* (with secondary attention to
the more general conflict of charisma's turbulence with rationality's regularity), and
concludes that "we poets cannot walk the way of beauty without Eros as our compa-
nion and guide" (1955:72).

16. It is this application, moreover, that provides a crucial supplement to the
"rationality" of modern civilization: "What gives the situation of the 'civilized' . . . its
specific rational quality in contrast to the situation of the 'primitive' is . . . (1) the
generally established belief that the conditions of civilized everyday life, be they
streetcar or lift or money or court of law or military or medicine, are in principle
rational, that is, are human artifacts accessible to rational knowledge, creation, and
control . . . (2) the confidence that these conditions function rationally, that is, according to known rules, and not irrationally as do the powers the primitive seeks to
influence through his sorcerer" (Weber 1981:179; see also 1946:139). What Weber is
pointing to here is the historical shift of the typical charisma attribution and response
from one set of technological artifacts to another—not to any absolute decline in the
power of charisma attribution and response in general.

17. Of course, if we decide later that the artifact in question is really ordinary, its
charisma (our awe) fades and we say we have acquired "taste" and become "sophisti-

cated." The reverse can also happen: we may attribute charisma to phenomena once thought to be ordinary by discovering their extraordinariness.

18. The distinction between *unpredicted* and *unpredictable* is important here. What is essential to the theory is that charisma be unpredicted—in order for it to be genuinely shocking to those who do not predict it—but any given instance of charisma may (or may not) be predictable in principle. Barrow argues strongly for the existence of a purely random element in the universe, but, he says, "we do not . . . know where to draw the dividing line between those aspects of the Universe which are attributable to law and those which issue from the revolving doors of chance" (1991:183; see also Weinberg 1992:37–38).

19. Weber also notes that "the emerging innovation is most likely to produce consensus and ultimately law, when it derives from a strong inspiration or an intense identification. In such cases a convention will result or, under certain circumstances, even consensual coercive action against deviants" (Weber 1978a:322). Kuhn's distinction between the (perceived) "anomaly" that generates "crisis" (and Weber would insist that that anomaly must be "charismatic" in order to do this) and the "new paradigm" that resolves such a crisis (see 1970:52–91) strikingly reproduces Weber's distinction between charisma and its routinization.

20. Note that when Weber speaks of the "routinization of charisma" he has in mind only personal charisma, and mainly in the religious and political institutions. The concept, however, seems no less applicable to charisma responses that may be directed to all the other kinds of possible objects discussed in this chapter. That is to say, the charisma of a new technological artifact may be routinized into ordinary (rational and traditional) use—which, Rybczynski says, often inhibits susceptibility to the charisma of a still newer artifact: "When the typewriter first became popular, it was still considered ill-mannered to use it for personal letters—they had to be written by hand. Today, the word processor is replacing the typewriter, but efficient, automated dot-matrix printers are not used for business letters because the result does not look as if it had been typewritten" (1985:225–26). The charisma of the natural environment becomes routinized into domesticated plants and animals (including cut flowers and caged pets), zoos, museums, holy places, and roadside look-outs. The charisma of sexual love becomes routinized into cohabitation, and the charisma of esthetic pleasure becomes routinized into various arts, styles, movements—and criticism. The charisma of the dead becomes routinized into funerals, elegies, anniversaries, tombstones with flower-holders. The charisma of the individual becomes routinized into the "dignity" and "rights" of "man" (see Madden 1973:vol. 1, 437–38).

21. Marx and Engels share Weber's turning-point image when arguing that class struggles "each time ended, either in a revolutionary reconstitution of society at large, or in the common ruin of the contending classes" (1969:vol. 1, 109). Note the similar form of Kuhn's view of the outcomes of paradigm crisis in science: "All crises close in one of three ways. Sometimes normal science ultimately proves able to handle the crisis-provoking problem. . . . On other occasions, . . . [the] problem is labelled and set aside for a future generation with more developed tools. Or, finally . . . a crisis may end with the emergence of a new candidate for paradigm and with the ensuing battle over its acceptance" (1970:84; compare 1962:84).

22. Weber says, "Calvin's theology must be distinguished from Calvinism, the theological system from the needs of religious practice" (1958a:229)—thereby stressing the distinction between charisma and its routinization—and says that routinized

"practical pastoral work" comprised two "types of pastoral advice. . . . On the one hand it is held to be an absolute duty to consider oneself chosen. . . . On the other hand, in order to attain that self-confidence intense worldly activity is recommended as the most suitable means" (1958a:111–12; see also 1978a: 464–67).

23. One finds in the published German original from which the above translated word "expediency" derives, not literally "expediency"—that is, *Angemessenheit, Fuglichkeit, Ratsamkeit,* or *Zweckmassigkeit*—but *zweckrationalen Motiven, zweckrational motivierten Orientierung,* and simply *zweckrational* (1956:16, 125). This, as chapter 2 has argued, is the same term to which Weber repeatedly links innate self-interest. "Expediency," then, is indeed an accurate translation of *zweckrational Motivien* (etc.) if one understands by it Webster's definition of "expediency" as "cultivation of or adherence to means and methods that are opportune or temporarily advantageous as distinguished from those that are right or just; specif: self-interest" (italics removed).

24. One finds an interesting parallel to this image of the dialectic that drives human societal evolution in Weber's image of the dialectic between nonrational melody and rational chordal structure in music: "Without the tensions motivated by the irrationality of melody, no modern music could exist. They are among its most effective means of expression. . . . chordal rationalization lives only in continuous tension with melodicism which it can never completely devour" (1958c:10).

Chapter 6. Institutional Evolutions and Processes

1. Clearly, this section will take issue with Turner et al., who claim Weber "believed economic development does not occur in evolutionary stages since unpredictable events, such as wars, ecological changes, charismatic leaders, and myriads of other phenomena, alter the course of history" (1989:180)—and note that chapters 4 and 5 have already argued that evolution in no way excludes (indeed, it partly depends on) events that are unpredicted in the practice of the time and place, though not necessarily unpredictable in principle.

2. Again, Weber's view is paralleled to an extraordinary degree by Kuhn's view of the overall evolution of physical science—that is, the unanticipated cognitive identification of anomaly, followed by crisis, and then the response to crisis (see Kuhn 1961:10–22).

3. Kuhn refers to a very similar preparation for a new paradigm, after a crisis, in the physical sciences as "the recourse to philosophy and to debate over fundamentals" (1961:90).

4. Note Weber's emphasis on the role of technological artifacts in the political institution: "To maintain a dominion by force, certain material goods are required, just as with an economic organization" (Weber 1958a:81); "the technique of chariot warfare emerged . . . providing the opportunity and incentive to great conquest expeditions into distant regions" (1952:6; see also 1946:255; 1952:100; 1958b:71; 1978a:1150, 1222); "war in our time is a war of machines"; "by contrast [with the Orient], all . . . city unions of the Occident . . . were coalitions of *armed* strata of the cities. This was the decisive difference"; and "a certain development of the means of communication . . . is one of the most important prerequisites for the possibility of bureaucratic administration" (Weber 1978a:981, 1262, 973).

5. On the general relation between war and the political institution, Weber concurs with Spencer, who says: "Everywhere the wars between societies originate governmental structures," and "so long as the [political] subordination is established by internal conflict . . . it remains unstable; but it tends toward stability in proportion as the regulating agents . . . are habituated to combined action against external enemies" (1898:vol. 1, 520, 527).

6. The latter quotation reads, "In contrast to classes, status groups are normally groups" (Weber 1978a:932). Note the difference in the translated terminology: " 'Classes' are not *communities*" and "status groups are normally *groups*." The German edition, however, has Weber using the same term, *Gemeinschaften*, in both cases (see Weber 1956:531, 534), and the translators' failure to adhere to Weber's own consistency is therefore confusing. A consistent translation as "community" would seem preferable to "group," because it links the entire argument here to Weber's discussion (see 1978a:40–43) of "communal" and "associative" (in the German edition, *Gesellschaften*) types of social relationships.

7. Marx, as well as Weber, emphasizes that status groups are pivotal (Marx refers to the "class for itself" [1955:150]), but neither Marx nor Weber recognize that status groups are way stations on two-way streets.

8. Noting the possibility of a specifically religious party among other status group parties, Weber says that in a democracy, "hierocracy has no choice but to establish a party organization and to use demogogic means, just like all other parties" (1978a:1195). However, he does not include the possibility of a scientific party because he holds that the scientist, as scientist, is fundamentally unrecruitable to any political (or religious) cause whatever: "I do not know how one might wish to decide 'scientifically' the value of French and German culture" (Weber 1946:148).

9. Note the implication here of stepwise (see chapter 5), change in decision makers such that the individual members of "parties" often come into, and leave, positions of power together. This schema may be compared with Pareto's interest in the less formally organized collectivities (or categories) he calls the "governing elite" and the "non-governing elite" (see 1935:1421–32), and the more continuous flow of individuals through them: "The governing class is restored not only in numbers, but—and that is the more important thing—in quality, by families rising from the lower classes and bringing with them the vigour and the proportions of residues necessary for keeping themselves in power" (1935:1430).

10. "A bureaucratic organization may be limited and indeed must be by agencies which act on their own authority alongside the bureaucratic hierarchy. . . . Such limiting agencies have the following principal functions: (a) supervision of adherence to the rules . . . (b) a monopoly of creation of the rules . . . (c) above all a monopoly of the granting of the means which are necessary for the administrative function" (Weber 1978a:271–72).

11. "Plebiscitary democracy . . . is a variant of charismatic authority, which hides behind a legitimacy that is formally derived from the will of the governed. The leader (demagogue) rules by virtue of the devotion and trust which his political followers have in him personally" (Weber 1978a:268).

12. "It is only this school of intensive work in the realities of administration . . . that equips an assembly to be a selecting ground, not for mere demagogues, but for effective politicians with a grasp of reality. . . . Only this kind of relationship between officials and professional politicians guarantees the continuous control of the admin-

istration, and through this the political education of both leaders and led" (Weber, quoted in Beetham 1985:100).

13. I am unaware of where "Weber . . . observed that [bureaucracy] is oriented to the creation and enforcement of rules in the public interest" (Turner et al. 1989:218). Rather, Weber seems to claim bureaucracy is oriented to serve the interest of "the [political] parties which. . . . create the norms which govern the administrative process," otherwise, they "overthrow it by withdrawal of confidence" (1978a:294)—presumably, in their own interest, not the public interest.

14. Note that, according to Weber, behind every such role-differentiated (right-and-obligation) cultural structure, there stands physical or psychical coercion, but behind that coercion there stands a further, role-undifferentiated, consensual, cultural structure (legitimacy) that supports that coercion. Thus, "Sociologically, the statement that someone has a right by virtue of the legal order of the state . . . normally means the following: He has a chance, factually guaranteed to him be the consensually accepted interpretation of a legal norms, of invoking in favor of his ideal or material interests the aid of a 'coercive apparatus' which is in special readiness for this purpose. . . . A 'right,' in the context of the 'state,' is guaranteed by the coercive power of the political authorities" (Weber 1978a:315). The question of whether a further coercion stands behind that "consensually accepted interpretation"—and the infinite regress of coercion and consensus that is thereby implied—is left open by Weber.

15. Freud makes a similar comment: "The domestication of animals and the introduction of cattle-breeding seems everywhere to have brought to an end the strict and unadulterated totemism of primaeval days" (1950:136–37). Weber also notes that "rationalization [of music] has been partly the effect of instruments and has been fixed or supported in its fixing by them. Indeed, it is only with the aid of instrumental illustration can the idea be maintained that the overwhelming quantity of intervals is rational. The idea appears . . . even in systems which are not acquainted with the octave but which have forms of instrumental accompaniment" (1958c:38, see also 42, 83, 84, 88, 89, 94).

16. Weber says the ancient Jews looked upon Yahweh as a god "who despite his passionate wrath in the last analysis acted rationally and according to plan" (1952:223).

17. Some of the material in the following discussion first appeared in Wallace 1989.

18. Schroeder says, "Among the features of Protestant dogma that Weber emphasizes in the *Protestant Ethic* is that it radically devalues the world"; and "only when the purely religious goal of Protestantism was aimed in a non-religious, practical direction—did the believer exhibit the type of conduct that contributed to economic activity suited to capitalist social relations" (1992:15, 16). The second comment may be a tautology, but barring that, it seems to me Weber emphasizes that Protestantism radically revalued (not "devalued") the world, raising economic activity to the level of a religious (not "non-religious") activity (i.e., a divine calling).

19. To this influence of the individual's own internal thinking on his/her conduct, Weber adds the no-less-important external influence of his/her peer group: "In Catholicism, as in Lutheranism, it is in the last analysis only the representative of the 'office' who must determine with the individual communicant if the latter is qualified for communion. In Calvinism. . . . the responsibility for preventing its desecration by

the participation in communion of a bearer of obvious signs of damnation belongs to every individual member of the congregation" (Weber 1978c:1116).

20. The sentence immediately preceding this reads: "A man does not 'by nature' wish to earn more and more money, but simply to live as he is accustomed to live and to earn as much as is necessary for that purpose" (Weber 1958a:60). But for consistency with his reference, on the same page, to "the acquisitive instinct" (see also 1958a:17), it seems reasonable to interpret Weber as intending to claim that "a man does not 'by nature' wish to earn more and more money" *if it requires more and more work.*

21. Weber, however, does allow that where there's a will there's a way: "Where it [the spirit of capitalism] appears and is able to work itself out, it produces its own capital and monetary supplies as the means to its ends, but the reverse is not true" (1958a:68–69).

22. Marx and Engels's theory depends primarily on this category of workers to "abolish . . . labour" by "overthrow[ing] the State" because among them, an individual "has no chance of arriving at the conditions which would place him in the other class" (1947:78).

23. Note Weber's important qualifying remarks that "the religious determination of life-conduct [is] one—note this—only one, of the determinants of the economic ethic" (1946:268), and that "in the last resort the factor which produced capitalism is the rational permanent enterprise, rational accounting, rational technology and rational law, but again not these alone. Necessary complementary factors were the rational spirit, the rationalization of the conduct of life in general, and a rationalitic economic ethic" (1950:354; see also 1978c:1128–29).

Chapter 7. Summary and Speculations

1. These are postulates for the social sciences, but of course they are testable hypotheses for psychology, physiology, and genetics. Almost needless to add, this hypothesis-postulate relation is one way that all the natural sciences are connected.

2. Clearly, then, I reject Freud's conclusion that "the liberty of the individual is no gift of civilization. It was greatest before there was any civilization" (1961:42).

3. Focusing on the other side of the coin identified by his contemporary Pareto ("History is a graveyard of aristocracies" [1935:1430]), Weber tells us that " 'history' continues inexorably to bring forth new 'aristocracies' " (1978b:282). In view of the latter inexorability, Weber says, "It is utterly ridiculous to suppose that it is an 'inevitable' feature of our economic development under present-day advanced capitalism . . . that it should have an elective affinity with 'democracy' or indeed with 'freedom' (in *any* sense of that word)" (1978b:282, his italics). Similarly, Pareto says, "Whether universal suffrage prevails or not, it is always an oligarchy that governs" [1935:1526], and Michels formulates the "iron law of oligarchy" as an epigram: "Who says organization says oligarchy" (1958:418; see also Merton 1973:439–59).

4. Weber's pessimism, however, can easily be exaggerated. It is true, as Sayer says (1991:151), that Weber claims "not summer's bloom lies ahead of us, but rather a polar night of icy darkness and hardness," but Sayer does not tell us this only sets the stage for the much less pessimistic set of queries and conclusion that follow immediately: "*When this night shall have slowly receded.* . . . what will have become of all of

you by then? Will you be bitter or banausic? Will you simply and dully accept world and occupation? Or will [you choose] . . . mystic flight from reality? In every one of such cases, I shall draw the conclusion that they have not. . . . experienced the vocation for politics in its deepest meaning. . . . Only he has the calling for politics who is sure that he shall not crumble when the world from his point of view is too stupid or too base for what he wants to offer" (Weber 1946:128, italics added).

5. Simmel says, "Even in the most oppressive and cruel cases of subordination, there is still a considerable measure of personal freedom. We merely do not become aware of it because its manifestation would entail sacrifices which we usually never think of taking upon ourselves" (1950:182)—thereby clearly implying that becoming aware of alternatives is a necessary prerequisite to exercising freedom, and that freedom is neither a breakfast food nor a free lunch.

6. Gerth and Mills erroneously (as this quotation conclusively shows) claim that "for Weber . . . the quest for freedom is identified with irrational sentiment and privacy" (1946:73). Bologh, however, seems exactly right that Weber "identified . . . freedom with rationality. Traditional and emotional modes of action . . . are not free because they are not the outcome of conscious deliberation and choice" (1990:122; see also Loewith (1950:110, 112).

7. Gerth and Mills seem correct when they say "Weber's liberal heritage and urge prevented him from taking a determinist position. He felt that freedom consists not in realizing alleged historical necessities but rather in making deliberate choices between alternatives. The future is a field for strategy rather than a mere repetition or unfolding of the past. Yet the possibilities of the future are not infinite, nor are they clay in the hands of the wilful man" (1946:70). In general agreement with this view, Eisenstadt argues that "the foci of [Weber's basic philosophical orientations and concerns] were the problems and predicaments of human freedom, creativity, and personal responsibility in social life in general and in modern society in particular" (1968:xv; see also Honigsheim 1968:81). (Note that Eisenstadt properly cautions that "while deeply concerned with analyzing the condition of freedom, [Weber] did not . . . construct . . . schemes which assumed, as it were, the ultimate victory of freedom" [1968:xv]—which is to say that Weber's theory is probabilistic rather than deterministic—see appendix A.) Mommsen concurs: "Weber always maintained that every social order should be so designed as to give maximum opportunity to individuals to act on their own free initiative" (1974:96; see also 1970:187, 188), as does Roth: "It was the essence of Weber's scholarship and partisanship to help human beings gain greater control over their destinies and make them less dependent on unperceived forces" (1979c:193, italics removed; see also Albrow 1990:282). Other commentators, however, take a very different view: Glassman and Murvar say, "Max Weber left us with a set of pessimistic predictions about the emergent structure of modern society—predictions which haunt us today. . . . Weber offered little hope to optimistic dreamers" (1984:3). Cohen says, "While Marx overstates the logic of democratic demands, Weber exaggerates the forces which impede them" (1985:284). Hennis says, "Weber lacks any sense of historical-philosophical hope and all kind of revolutionary promise" (1988:99). Mommsen says, "Max Weber's theory of democratic domination emphasizes onesidely the process of policy formation from the top downwards and the significance of the leading politician, while the great majority of citizens as such tend to recede into the background" (1989:18).

8. Spencer anticipated this reversal, but for different reasons (see 1961:178–80).

War's present danger to our species, however, is by no means limited to the threat of nuclear holocaust and nuclear winter. "It has been estimated that world military expenditures now amount to over $900 billion a year. . . . and world expenditure on weapons research is greater than the combined spending for developing new energy technologies, improving human health, increasing agricultural production, and controlling pollution" (Glossup 1987:3-4; see also Sivard 1991:11-12; World Scientists 1993). The case of Costa Rica seems instructive: "Costa Rica . . . abolished its army in 1949. . . . As a result of this bold move, [it] was able to spend more on education, health, and family planning. . . . [Now] life expectancy there is 77 years, two years more than the United States" (Brown 1992:182).

9. Markusen and Yudken, who focus on the post–Cold War United States, rightly warn that that consensus will not easily come into full control, given the huge momentum that our (and the former Soviet Union's) defense industries have built up during the past half-century: "Forty-plus years of cold war have cultivated a set of business institutions and practices that are rigid, if sophisticated, and tailor-made for serving the unique Pentagon client. Changing basic business cultures and converting military-dedicated labs and engineers to new frontiers will not happen overnight" (1992:240).

10. Wuthnow argues that "the voluntary sector symbolizes personal freedom, individualism, and the capacity to choose and to make a difference as an individual, despite the growing role of large-scale institutions" (1993b:302).

11. Indeed, to Great Individual (e.g., Moses, Jesus, Muhammad, Buddha, Genghis Khan, Newton, Newcomen) theories of history, Great Institution (e.g., those regarding one or more of the participant-organizing, participant-intake, or participant-outlet institutions as the main engine of history) theories of history, and Great Society (e.g., The Rise of the West, The Renaissance in Italy, The American Century, etc.) theories of history, one should add Great Voluntary Association theories of history. First in this latter category one finds theories that look upon social movements—especially those fostering social revolutions—as central (see Skocpol 1979:3-4; McAdam, McCarthy, and Zald 1988:727-28). In this connection, Hollins, Powers, and Sommer claim that "a big-step approach may ultimately prove a more practical route to peace than the cautious and ineffective strategies that have been pursued for the past generation. With the mobilization of a broad-based movement linking principles with pragmatism, the transition to a world beyond the threat of cataclysmic war could be under way by the turn of the century" (1989:194).

12. See Coleman 1957:esp. 21–25, for analysis of the role of voluntary associations (and mass communications media) in mitigating polarization of groups in communities; and see Blau 1977:107–12 for a related analysis.

13. Simmel admits that "external and internal conflicts arise through the multiplicity of group affiliations, which threaten the individual with psychological tensions or even a schizophrenic break. But it is also true," he says, that "multiple group-affiliations can strengthen the individual and reenforce the integration of his personality. . . . The ego can become more clearly conscious of [its inner] unity, the more he is confronted with the task of reconciling within himself a diversity of groups interests" (1955:141–42).

14. The "church," however, is a "compulsory" organization (Weber 1978a:54).

15. Reich (1992) pays no attention at all to the need to open new energy sources, and Kennedy (1993) pays all but no attention to it, saying only that during the

Industrial Revolution, "coal [was] needed to fuel [the] machines," but in the next century "developing countries have to be assisted . . . in adopting a 'noncarbon' path toward industrialization" (1993:7–8, 116). And although Kennedy also says "the greatest test for human society as it confronts the twenty-first century is how to use 'the power of technology' to meet the demands thrown up by 'the power of population'" (1993:12), he does not recognize the pivotal distinction—discussed immediately below—between the power of energy supply technology and the power of energy application technology.

16. See also Flavin and Young 1993:188. For discussion of the prospects for fusion power, including the report that "the United States, the European Community, Japan and Russia [have] agreed to a $1.2 billion, six-year effort to design the International Thermonuclear Experimental Reactor, under the direction of the International Atomic Energy Agency, headquartered in Vienna, Austria," see Anonymous 1993:62. Sooner or later, however, we will probably have to switch over to some method of collecting in outer space, and then transmitting to Earth, much larger amounts of direct solar power than Earth now intercepts, because, as Dyson puts it (exaggeratedly, to be sure): "For a society with the same complexity as the present human society on Earth, starting from the present time and continuing forever [sic] the total reserve of energy required is about equal to the energy now radiated by the Sun in eight hours. The total energy reserve contained in the Sun would be sufficient to support forever [sic] a society with a complexity 10 trillion times greater than our own" (1988:115; see also Criswell 1985:52, 60–75; Jones and Finney 1985:91; Dyson 1979:212; Asimov 1979:328–29).

17. Flavin and Young emphasize that although "the size of the world economy has quintupled since 1950, bringing unprecedented though unevenly distributed prosperity to many nations. . . . destruction and degradation of natural assets—air, land, water, forests, plant and animal species—has subsidized [this growth]" (1993:180). But even in the midst of this overall growth, the "have" versus "have-not" gap between countries has widened as per capita GNP fell in 49 countries containing 846 million people during the eighties (see Brown 1993:5).

18. Hartmann, writing of the huge amounts of energy and raw materials to be found in outer space, says, "If new raw materials and energy can be poured into the world economy from space, resource differences between nations could be reduced as a factor in world instability" (1985:38–39). Kennedy, however—because he overlooks the need and likelihood of the kind of new energy source, and its leveling potential, emphasized here—seems to look upon "the geographical disjunction between where the population pressures are and where the technological resources are" (1993:12; see also 14, 22, 34, 91–92, 331) as permanent.

19. Reich adds a humanitarian *wertrational* motivation: "There is also the possibility that symbolic analysts will decide they have a [moral] responsibility to improve the well-being of their compatriots, regardless of any personal gain" (1992:303), and I would call attention to the same possibility on a global scale—as does Deutsch (see 1969:188–89).

20. We may go further: Not only do technological artifacts and know-how seem to be major factors in bringing different human groups together into the same society, they are also powerful equalizers among groups that are already in the same society. Duberman says, "Now that machines have largely eliminated the need for muscles, contraception relieves women of frequent childbearing, and social mores encourage

smaller families, it is no longer necessary to assign jobs to people because they are of one sex or the other. Men and women can now develop as individuals" (1975:20–21). Moreover, says Duberman, "the development and distribution of effective, easily administered contraceptive devices. . . . means that society can lessen its interest in the sexual behavior of its members because such behavior no longer need result in the birth of children" (1974:51)—a lessening that seems sure to be contributing to the growing social equalization of heterosexuals and homosexuals.

21. It has been claimed that these most recent migrations have a large "trans-migration" component: "Immigrants are understood to be transmigrants when they develop and maintain multiple relations—familial, economic, social, organizational, religious, and political—that span [national] borders" (Schiller et al. 1992:ix; see also Said 1993:317, 332).

22. Wriston adds: "The current attack on the power of sovereigns is the prolifera-tion of knowledge that used to be confined to small groups of leaders but is now popping up on screens all over the world. When a monopoly of information is broken, the power structure is in danger" (1992:136). Simmel, too, argues that insofar as life in the "metropolis" entails "the intensification of nervous stimulation which results from the swift and uninterrupted change of outer and inner stimuli" (i.e., greatly enhanced information, both qualitatively and quantitatively), "it grants to the individual a kind and an amount of personal freedom which has no analogy what-soever under other conditions" (1950:410, 416).

23. "Imagine schoolchildren entering cyberspace to orbit a virtual sun. . . . Or why not scamper through the underbrush of a Mesozoic swamp to watch virtual dinosaurs behave the way scholars believe they did? 'You could have a body that's in human form, but why limit yourself?'. . . . 'Why not be a pterodactyl?'" (Stewart 1991:39; for a discussion much closer to home, both in time and in subject matter, see Jones 1990:1–3).

24. As noted in chapter 4, Freud tells us, "It is always possible to bind together a considerable number of people in love, so long as there are other people left over to receive the manifestations of their aggressiveness" (1961:68).

25. "Even the tribe of Israel," Dyson notes, "which . . . maintain[ed] its separate existence without an army and without war for two thousand years, has in modern times chosen national sovereignty as a preferable alternative, accepting the attendant burdens of intermittent warfare" (1988:202).

26. I have interjected "intergroup" twice in this quotation to make clear that I do not think Diamond's claim is meant to apply to interindividual heterogeneity. The eventual globalization of human society is by no means a new idea: Simmel says that "the very universality of the processes which belong to human society, whether looked at from the point of view of religion or trading or logical thinking, at least opens the door to a universal society; and, in fact, these tendencies all express them-selves where the social development has gone far enough to make it possible" (1950:284). Durkheim claims that a "social life of a new sort is developing. It is this international life which has already resulted in universalizing religious beliefs. As it extends, the collective horizon enlarges; the society ceases to appear as the only whole, to become a part of a much vaster one, with undetermined frontiers, which is susceptible of advancing indefinitely" (1965:493). Freud, too: "Civilization is a pro-cess . . . whose purpose is to combine single human individuals, and after that families, then races, peoples and nations, into one great unity, the unity of mankind"

(1961:77); and Mead looks forward to "a universal society that includes the whole human race, and into which all can so far enter into relationship with others through the medium of communication. They can recognize others as members, and as brothers" (1962:282). More recently, Hannerz says, "There is now a world culture. . . . the world has become one network of social relationships, and between different regions there is a flow of meanings as well as of people and goods" (1990:237). Robertson shares my view that "much of world history can be fruitfully considered as sequences in 'miniglobalization,' in the sense that, for example, historic [e.e., ancient] empire formation involved the unification of previously sequestered territories and social entities" (1990:21) and, referring specifically to modern empire formation, Said claims that "partly because of empire, all cultures are involved in one another. . . . Imperialism consolidated the mixture of cultures and identities on a global scale. . . . [and] there seems no reason except fear and prejudice to keep insisting on their separation and distinctiveness, as if that was all human life was about" (1993:xxv, 336). As a result, Said says, "exile . . . becomes something closer to a norm, an experience of crossing boundaries and charting new territories" (1993:317; see Mannheim 1955:154–64, for the classic conceptualization of the intellectual as boundary-crossing exile).

For views that are in various ways negative regarding the eventuality of a single global society, see Featherstone 1990:1; Smith 1990:188; Walzer 1982:6; Alexander 1980:5–7; Alba 1990:302, 318. Reich offers a complicated, mainly negative, argument that poses a sharply illuminating contrast with the position being set forth here. In explicating what he calls "impassive cosmopolitanism," Reich claims that "without strong attachments and loyalties extending beyond family and friends, [cosmopolitans with a global perspective] may never develop the habits and attitudes of social responsibility. They will be world citizens, but without accepting or even acknowledging any of the obligations that citizenship in a polity normally implies. . . . Without a real political community in which to learn, refine, and practice the ideals of justice and fairness, they may find these ideals to be meaningless abstractions" (Reich 1992:309).

But what, one wonders, makes a national political community necessarily more "real" in this respect than a global one? Reich's answer is that "we learn to feel responsible for others because we share with them a common history, we participate with them in a common culture, we face with them a common fate. . . . 'We think of ourselves not as human beings first, but as sons, and daughters . . . tribesmen, and neighbors.'" (1992:310). But this answer—surely a subtly threatening one to those of our nation's population who are native American, Hispanic American, Asian American, African American, or recently immigrated to this country from anywhere—stirs other questions: Do we not all share a common human history, a common human culture, a common human fate? If we do, *why should we not think of ourselves as human beings first,* sons and daughters of the same prehistoric parents, tribesmen and neighbors on the same Earth?

By contrast with Reich, Kennedy repeatedly implies (although he does not say explicitly) that a global nation may well lie in our future. Thus: "The key autonomous actor in political and international affairs for the past few centuries [i.e., the nation-state] appears not just to be losing its control and integrity, but also to be the wrong sort of unit to handle the newer circumstances"; "various trends from global warming to twenty-four-hour-a-day trading are transnational . . . reminding us that the earth, for all its divisions, is a single unit. [These trends] are largely out of the control of the authorities of the traditional nation-state"; "trends in technology and communications loosen state controls, erode all borders, and question our traditional concern with national or regional identities as opposed to membership in the entire human race" (1993:131, italics removed, 129, italics removed, 285; see also 286).

27. One is reminded of Mannheim's discussion of the emergence of a culture of ideological skepticism in post-feudal societies: "It is primarily the intensification of social mobility. . . . [that shakes] the belief in the general and eternal validity of one's own thought-forms. . . . [It] is the decisive factor in making persons uncertain and sceptical of their traditional views of the world" (1955:7, see also 281–82). The uncertainty of which Vischer speaks may be generated not only by social mobility in Mannheim's sense, but also by vicarious mobility—via the media of mass communication.

28. In expressing his own uncertainty, the astronomer Jeans asks, "Do [the] colossal uncomprehending masses [of what is now estimated to be 100 billion observable galaxies, and the perhaps ten-fold greater mass of dark matter] come nearer to representing the main ultimate reality, or do we? . . . . Are they perchance only a dream, while we are brain-cells in the mind of the dreamer? (quoted in Ferris 1983:243; see Morris 1987:127–28; Weinberg 1992:221–23; Flam 1993a; Borges 1964:45–50).

29. I do not mean to belittle the role of religious fundamentalism, which embodies a certainty of belief that seems so largely a rebound from the developing uncertainty emphasized here (see Marty and Appleby 1993b:1; Marty and Appleby 1993c:620]). Marty and Appleby argue, however, that "in polities in which some form of church-state separation has been adopted, fundamentalism seems less likely to dictate the course of national self-definition," and "as a general rule fundamentalists in democratic or quasi-democratic societies could hope only for a piece of the pie. . . . When they ventured into the larger, vibrantly plural world of political competition, fundamentalists found it necessary to compromise" (1993c:640, 641; see also 1993b:1; 1993c:620). Consequently, if the theory and speculations offered in this book prove valid, religious fundamentalism will become still more limited in the future.

30. Similarly, Reich says, "Everyone on the planet benefits from smaller and more powerful semiconductor chips. . . . [although] the nation whose workers first gain the insights are likely to benefit disproportionately. This advantage may cause other nations' citizens to feel relatively poorer, notwithstanding their absolute gain" (1992:308, italics removed).

31. Hart quotes Clarke to the effect that "all the star-borne colonies of the future will be independent. . . . Their liberty will be inviolably protected by time as well as space" (1985:281). Regarding the logical (and increasingly foreseeable) extreme of *individuals* who are widely separated from each other, House, et al., arguing that "social isolation is a major risk factor for mortality from widely varying causes," and "social relationships have a predictive, arguably causal, association with health," regret that "just as we discover the importance of social relationships for health, and see an increasing need for them, their prevalence and availability may be declining" (1988:544, 540, 544). Conceivably, however, the social relationships required for the health of our very distant descendants may be less hands-on, less spatiotemporally proximal, and more media-mediated, than at present.

32. One notes, in this connection, Marshall's prediction that "shortly after the turn

of the century, an array of satellites will be observing earth, gathering data on every-thing from ocean color and ozone concentration to ice flows and vegetation" (1993:846; see also Holden 1993; Darling 1993:140–41), and sooner or later these and many other data may be available on Internet to its worldwide millions of individual and group users. Of course, one can also imagine some individuals and groups withdrawing—either avocationally or in increasingly serious vocation—from the "real" world into the virtual worlds of multi-sensory computer simulations where it will be "'possible to reach out and feel objects with your skin that don't exist in the physical world' . . . [where] virtual friendships are common, creativity thrives and life resembles an open-ended video game." Stewart continues: "As it happens, a group at Carnegie Mellon University is already exploring ways to automate dramatic action. The Oz Project hopes to use interactive fiction and other techniques to give 'deep structure' to virtual reality, with computer-generated characters and content that adapts to the actions of real-life participants in a story's plot" (Stewart 1991:44–45).

33. Darling offers a similar speculation, but attaches to it certain other claims (e.g., "there never was a Big Bang. . . . All the universe, past, present, and future, exists at once, as a closed, self-sustaining, self-creating cycle" [1993:185]) that I do not.

34. Here one is compelled to note that Gott's statistical prediction ("The odds are against our colonizing the galaxy and surviving to the far future . . . because living things usually do not live up to their maximum potential" [1993:319]—a view that contains much of the oversimplification to which I have already referred) overlooks his own admission that the odds are also against the existence of any intelligent life at all: "There must be of the order of 1 improbable event required for the formation of intelligent life" (1993:316). Two points seem relevant here: (1) in a large enough and durable enough universe, events with very small probabilities will occur; and (2) it is the nature of intelligence, once improbable events have led to its formation, to discover conditions under which certain desired events—no matter how small their probabilities—can be realized. (Contrast this with Gott's view: "We should not as-sume that our intelligence is likely to increase our longevity vastly above that of other species" [1993:316].)

35. See Scheier and Carver 1992. Despite his odds-based predictions (see note 34), Gott concludes with this acknowledgment of the possibility of success against the odds: "We should know that to succeed the way we would like, we will have to do something truly remarkable" (1993:319).

Appendix A

1. Indeed, history left Comte, who died in 1857, no choice but to take for granted the deterministic and observer-independent Newtonian model of the world. What seems to be the leading 20th century model is both probabilistic and observer-dependent (see Pagels 1982:47–48, 74, 118–22; Morris 1987:218; Barrow 1988:152–57; Ferris 1992:106–9; Darling 1993:102–16, 180–81), and this is the model adopted by Weber when he consistently stresses probability in all his definitions, descriptions, and explanations (see below), and when he speaks of "the meaningless infinity of the world process," remarking that it is only *"human beings* [that] confer meaning and

significance" on that process (1949:81). It seems noteworthy, especially for those who would draw a great divide between Weber and Durkheim, that the latter goes even further on observer-dependence when he says that "the universe does not exist except in so far as it is thought of" (1965:490).

2. Note that the substantive claims of Comte's theory (e.g., his "law of three stages") is not at issue here.

3. Some of the more influential rejections of applying the term *positivistic* to Weber's work may be cited: Parsons claims "Weber's whole position is definitely and fundamentally a voluntaristic theory of action, and neither a positivistic nor idealistic theory" (1937:683). Alexander claims that "Weber never shared the slightest whiff of Durkheim's positivism" (1983:152; see also 1982:17)—only seeming to leave open the possibility that Weber may have shared a whiff of Comte's (see Giddens 1978:243–45, for discussion of Comte's impact on Durkheim) positivism. Mayrl says, "The differences which underlie the similarities between Weber and the positivists are . . . profound" (1985:113). Hennis claims Weber "was neither scientist nor positivist" (1988:61). Even Collins, who declares himself "sympathetic to [the] positivist effort to build an explanatory [social] science," claims Weber argues "against the encroachments of positivist causal generalizations," and pushes himself to the obviously untenable extreme of claiming Weber opposed "*any* deductive system of general principles" (1986a:3–4; italics added). Schroeder is more difficult to quote succinctly. In my judgment, he is correct to attribute the view that "social reality consists both of the values or beliefs of persons . . . and of material or other social forces which are separate from these" to Weber, but he then goes on to assert that this "dualistic" view "is irreconcilable with positivism, which stipulates that there is only one—so to speak continuous—social reality" (Schroeder 1992:8–9). Ignoring the phrase "so to speak" here, however, both these assertions seem refuted by Comte's statement that "human life under every aspect, social as well as individual. . . . embraces . . . three kinds of phenomena of which our life consists—thoughts, feelings, and actions" (1975:320; see also 321, 329, and especially 403–4 regarding "material" forces).

4. It should be emphasized that this statement does not imply the prohibition of imagination—indeed, Comte says that "positivism is eminently calculated to call the imaginative faculties into exercise" (1975:319). What is intended is precisely the "subordination" of imagination to observation. That is to say, wherever the two conflict, the positivism Comte (and I) advocate awards the victory to observation: "Consider the law: 'When iron is heated, it expands.' Another law says 'When iron is heated, it contracts.' . . . The first law is accepted, rather than the second, only because it describes a regularity *observed in nature*" (Carnap 1966:199; see Wallace 1983:371–72, 389–94, for my own justification of this choice). But obviously the two need not conflict; they may very well complement one another—and this is a situation every Comtean positivist strives for in interpreting past observations and predicting future observations. Thus, lest anyone think Comte himself argues that to observe things "positivistically" means observing them "without any need for interpretation" (Wuthnow 1987:12), or by "utilizing a theory-free observation language" (Hekman 1983:3, see also 28), we have his own words directly opposing such a view: "No real observation of any kind of phenomenon is possible, except insofar as it is first directed, and finally interpreted, by some theory" (Comte 1975:241). Popper expresses the same idea: "The naive empiricist [note that Popper does not say 'the positivist'] . . . thinks that we begin by collecting and arranging our experiences, and

so ascend the ladder of science. But if I am ordered: 'Record what you are now experiencing' I shall hardly know how to obey this ambiguous order. Am I to report that I am writing; that I hear a bell ringing; a newsboy shouting; a loudspeaker droning; or am I to report, perhaps, that these noises irritate me?. . . . A science needs points of view, and theoretical problems" (1961:106). Comte's claim that positivism "supposes a continuous progress of speculation subject to the gradual improvement of observation, *without the precise reality being ever fully disclosed*" (1975:221, italics added) seems of profoundly agnostic import in this context, insofar as it implies the impossibility of any final, complete, knowledge of anything (including everything—compare Weinberg 1992). Note also, in direct opposition to Wiley's claim that positivism declares "subjective states [of actors] inadmissable as data," Comte's unambiguous assertion that positivism "embraces . . . the three kinds of phenomena of which our life consists—thoughts, feelings, and actions. . . . These three orders of phenomena react upon each other so intimately that any system which does not include all of them must inevitably be unreal and inadequate" (1975:320, 321). Incidentally, Durkheim—cited as a positivist by Wiley—also includes "manners of acting, thinking and feeling" in his definition of "social facts" (1982:52). Almost needless to add, if the comments cited above are any indication, Comte would categorically reject Alexander's opinion that "the two postulates central to the positivist persuasion are, first, that a radical break exists between empirical observations and nonempirical statements, and, second, that . . . more general intellectual issues—which are called 'philosophical' or 'metaphysical'—have no fundamental significance for the practice of an empirically oriented discipline" (1982:5; see also Alexander and Colomy 1990:4).

5. Comte adds that "the phenomena of the inorganic world are, for the most part, simple enough to be calculable; those of the organic world are too complex for our management. But this has nothing to do with any difference in their nature" (1975:176–77). Expressing a similar faith in sociology's ability eventually to discover laws of social phenomena, Durkheim says, "The human mind would suffer a grievous setback if this segment of reality [namely, human social phenomena] . . . should escape it even temporarily. There is nothing necessarily discouraging in the incompleteness of the results thus far obtained. They should arouse new efforts, not surrender" (1951:36).

6. In light of this third feature, Burger's reference to "the positivistic conception of a merely contemplative, theoretical knowledge" (1977:166) is remarkable. Burger's misconception, however, calls attention to the fact that Comtean positivism includes not only empiricism, of which observation and the pursuit of natural laws are indispensable elements, but practical application, as well. Comtean positivism, then, combines empiricism with praxis (see Wallace 1983:355–88).

7. Kaplan agrees (without citing Weber): "I do not believe that the role of theory in behavioral science is any different from what it is in physical or biological science. . . . everywhere, so it seems to me, theory works in essentially the same way" (1964:303).

8. Contrast this with the baffling claim made by Turner et al. that "the [broad] scope of Weber's empirical concerns suggests that he was not primarily interested in development of abstract laws of human behavior and organization" (1989:172). One would have thought a broad scope of empirical concerns is precisely what generates an interest in abstract laws. Turner et al. also claim that "Weber rejected the search for general laws in favor of historical theories," and that he "knew that an emphasis on

the development of general theories would not allow for the examination of such issues [as why capitalism originated in the West rather than somewhere else]" (1989:191, 192). This, too, seems negated by the above direct quotations from Weber.

9. Weber identifies himself as a scientist: "To affirm the value of science is a presupposition for teaching. . . . I personally by my very work answer in the affirmative" (1946:152).

10. Dawkins says, "Sometimes there are two, or more, alternative [biochemical] pathways to the same useful end. . . . Either of the two alternative pathways will do the job, and it doesn't matter which one is used" (1987:171). Robertson relies on the principle of equifinality (regarding a point discussed in chapter 7) when he says, "The world-as-a-whole could, in theory, have become the [single, global] reality which it now is in ways and along trajectories other than those which have actually obtained. . . . [including] the imperial hegemony of a single nation or a 'grand alliance' between two or more dynasties or nations; the victory of 'the universal proletariat'; the global triumph of a particular form of organized religion; the crystallization of 'the world spirit' [etc.]" (1990:21). Pareto also expresses equifinality when he says "identical facts may be explained by an infinite number of theories—all equally true, for all reproduce the facts in their explanation" (1966:144–45; see also Mannheim 1955:282). In two recent expressions of the principle of equifinality, Leakey and Lewin emphasize that "similar anatomy [i.e., outcome] does not always imply close evolutionary [i.e., causal] relationship. . . . [for] identical anatomy may appear in two [genetically] unrelated groups when they adapt to identical pressures of natural selection" (1992:79); and Weinberg says, "A symmetry principle [in physics] is simply a statement that something looks the same from certain different points of view" (1992:136; see also 155, 194–95ff). Chomsky uses the term *transformational grammar* to signify the systematic limits placed on equifinality in linguistic phrase structure ("many pairs of sentences are assigned similar or identical representations on some level" [1957:107, see also 85–86, 90, 93]). This makes it essential to add that whether there is more than one way to skin a cat depends on how broadly or narrowly one identifies the skinned-cat condition. Thus, although Dawkins describes many cases of equifinal "convergent [biological] evolution" (for example, eyes in octopi and humans), he also notes that "when we look *in detail* we find . . . that the convergence is not total. The different lines of evolution betray their independent origins in numerous points of detail" (1987:94, italics added). And Barrow says, "Biochemists believe that, whereas we can envisage different forms of life, based upon chemistries other than carbon or even based upon something non-chemical, only carbon-based life can evolve spontaneously" (1991:195). Equifinality, then, does not require us to think of any two causes (or causal chains) as producing *absolutely* identical effects; we only need think of these effects as identical in the sense that they are undiscriminated by whatever conceptualization or other measurement procedure is employed for the purposes at hand. Note that adherence to the principle of equifinality should not be mistaken for analytical indecisiveness. Sica makes this mistake when he quotes Weber as saying that "for sociology, not every course of action which is progressing in an 'objectively correct rational' manner was conditioned by subjectively rational purpose" and then interprets this invocation of equifinality as an "admission of indecision and defeat" (1988:191; see also 10; compare Albrow 1990:162). Finally, note that equifinal causation is not multiple causation (Weber relies on the latter, too). In multiple causation, a given effect is produced only as the sum of many contributing

causes, none of which would be sufficient to produce the effect by itself. Here, the causes are *supplements* to each other. In equifinal causation, however, each cause is separately sufficient to produce the effect. Here the causes are *substitutes* for each other (although they may operate simultaneously—in which case, we say the effect is overdetermined). When Freund claims "the essence of [Weber's] critique is aimed at the difficulty, often the impossibility, of finding a single antecedent cause for a social phenomenon, as causal monism would have it" (1978:170), he is referring to Weber's reliance on multiple causation. But Weber attacks more than causal monism; he also attacks causal determinism—and although multiple causation is indeed his weapon in the first case, equifinal causation is his weapon in the second.

11. Feigl defines determinism as "ideally complete and precise predictability, given the momentary conditions, the pertinent laws, and the required mathematical techniques" (see also Hempel's discussion of "Laplace's demon" [1965:88]), and contrasts it with "statistical . . . predictability on the basis of stable frequency-ratios or according to strict laws governing frequency ratios" (1953:411, italics removed; 409). The metaphysical assumption that only statistical predictability is possible is here called 'probabilism.' Einstein's belief that God does not play dice with the world is deterministic; the belief that "it is dice that are playing God with the universe" expresses probabilism (see Bartusiak: 1986:259–60).

12. Marianne Weber also calls attention to Weber's probabilism (see 1975:680), as does Deutsch (see 1971:119–20). Passing from probabilistic definitions and descriptions to probabilistic explanations and predictions (and although the methodological implications cannot be followed up here), note Weber's clear uniting of the physical and "historical" sciences: "the . . . case of favorable chance or 'objective probability,' determined from general empirical propositions or from empirical frequencies, has its analogues in the sphere of *all* concrete causality, including the historical" (1949:183, italics in the original). The notion of "objective probability" would seem to reject Tilly's claim that analysts "must choose between probabilistic and deterministic modes of explanation" (1975a:15; see also 16), on the ground that explanation, in any field, can only be probabilistic—whether the analyst thinks so or not. See note 13.

13. Weber may seem to argue for determinism and inevitability when he claims causal explanation should be conceptualized as follows: "The totality of all the conditions back to which the causal chain from the 'effect' leads had to 'act jointly' in a certain way and in no other for the concrete effect to be realized. In other words, the appearance of the result is, for every causally working empirical science, determined not just from a certain moment but 'from eternity'" (1949:187, italics removed). This statement, however, should be read in the context in which Weber himself places it— namely, that of a defense of probabilism in the social sciences (see Weber 1949:180–87)—and therefore as a statement of the limiting cases of probabilism (where probability = 1, or 0). Probabilism, of course, is opposed to determinism only with respect to the latter's exclusivity, for probabilism, in principle, includes the two limiting cases to which determinism restricts itself.

14. It is worth emphasizing that probabilism has achieved near universality in the natural sciences during the twentieth century. For example, Hempel says, "Contemporary physical theory has cast considerable doubt on the classical conception of the universe as a strictly deterministic system: the fundamental laws are now assumed to have a statistical or probabilistic rather than a strictly universal, deterministic, character" (1965:89). More recently, Davies confirms this assumption, saying "strict deter-

minism no longer has any place in science" (1988:143; see also 114); and Feynman is even more categorical: "There is probability all the way back . . . in the fundamental laws of physics there are odds. . . . It is not our ignorance of the internal gears, of the internal complications, that makes nature appear to have probability in it. It seems to be somehow intrinsic" (1967:145, 147).

15. Note that the definition of social phenomena as "interorganismic behavior regularities" is fully congruent with the general natural science formula for defining any phenomenon as some more or less complex "inter-entity behavior regularity." For example, a biological organism may be defined as an intercellular behavior regularity; a cell as an interprotoplasmic (e.g., cytoplasm, organelles, nucleus, chromosomes, etc.) behavior regularity; any component of protoplasm as an inter-molecular behavior regularity; a molecule as an interatomic behavior regularity . . . and so on.

16. For fuller discussions of the distinction and relationship between social structure and cultural structure, see Wallace 1969:5–11; 1983:29–49; 1986; 1988:34–37; see also Namenwirth and Weber 1987:19. Also note that, in contrast with Turner's claim that "associated with [a] concentration on cultural factors is a tendency to [concentrate on] characteristics of individuals rather than . . . social structures" (1981:236), the above definition regards both cultural and social structural phenomena as equally interindividual (only the type of behavior—psychological in the first case, and physiological in the second—differs). In neither case, therefore, is there any descriptive tendency to concentrate on the characteristics of individuals, although, for reasons indicated in the text below, there is a strong explanatory requirement that we do so. In this latter connection, consider Gilbert's claim that human (and perhaps also nonhuman—see 1989:444) collectivities are "plural subjects. . . . formed when each of a set of individual agents expresses willingness to constitute, with the others, the (plural) subject of a goal, belief, principle of action, or other such thing in conditions of common knowledge" (1991:236). For a large number of reasons (as Gilbert herself reluctantly admits—see 1991:238–39; and 1989:441), this claim cannot be admitted as a generic definition of social phenomena. However, it (along with many others) seems clearly subsumable under the generic "interorganismic behavior regularity" definition when the indicated (and presumably regular) interpersonal expressions of willingness are regarded as constituting the collectivity in question.

17. Gibbs says that "one is hard pressed to think of kinds of behavior that [could] not qualify as action, especially on recognition that one may attach a subjective meaning to a putative reflex"—and concludes that "the distinction between action and behavior is inconsequential" (1989:73). But when one recognizes that Weber's definition of social action stipulates that the subjective meaning in question *orients* physical behavior, and therefore must *influence* that behavior, the distinction between action and behavior becomes consequential indeed. That is, whenever subjective meaning does not influence the physical behavior in question (as one assumes would be the case when it is merely attached to a "putative reflex"), the combination remains only "behavior" and does not qualify as "action" in Weber's sense. However, Weber's definition of action as including a causally orienting subjective meaning leads to other problems—discussed below.

18. This appearance may be what leads Bologh to assert (erroneously, in my opinion) that "the very formulation of rational action . . . presupposes a separate, autonomous, independent individual, an individual who has no compelling ties to a

community of other human beings" (1990:122). The idea that Weber was centrally concerned with the individual is also emphasized in Hennis' claim that the *"sole object* [of Weber's sociology] is *Lebensfuhrung"*—which he defines as "a style of regulating life, a 'habitus,' a particular form of conducting one's [individual] life" (1988:44, 31). (Inexplicably, Hennis seems to contradict this view when he says, "I can find nowhere in Weber . . . a specifically 'humanitarian' interest in the fates of individual men, for man 'as such.' His interest was in the fate of individual collectivities, 'humankinds,' which were represented in major solitary 'types' and not various individuals" [1988:173; see also 69].) Albrow, too, thinks Weber's focus on the individual's action meant he was "erecting a scientific discipline around the question, 'Why do [individual] people do things—anything or everything?'" Albrow concludes that "sociology then arose out of rationality and became the discipline which examined the nature and limits of rationality in the world," and that "Weber found no clear dividing line between psychology and sociology" (1990:138, 139, 146; see also 200–1). In my judgment, however, Weber (and all other sociologists as well) have built our discipline around the question, Why do people do things, and think/feel things, *together*—whether in unison, cooperation, competition, conflict, consensus, complementarity, and/or dissensus with each other?' The principle of equifinality then compels us to ask why each *individual* participant in that collective behavior is doing (and thinking/feeling) what s/he is doing—including, among other possible explanations, both rational and nonrational motivations for those things.

19. It would be a mistake to think Durkheim opposes Weber on this count when he says, "If . . . we begin by studying [the] members separately, we will understand nothing about what is taking place in the group" (1982:129) for two reasons. First, Durkheim refers here to *what* is taking place, not *why* it is taking place—thereby indicating that description rather than explanation it at issue. Second, Durkheim's emphasis falls on the word "separately"—as becomes clear when we read "by aggregating together, by interpenetrating, by fusing together, individuals give birth to a being . . . which constitutes a psychical individuality of a new kind" (1982:129) and "individual consciousnesses result from the nature of the organic and psychical being taken in isolation, collective consciousnesses from a plurality of beings of this kind" (1982:145). Thus, Durkheim, too, identifies interorganismic behavior regularity as the unit of description. However, he clearly points to the individual participant in such regularities as the unit of explanation when, after asserting that "constraint [is] the characteristic of every social fact," he tells us this (sociologically explanatory) constraint is "due to the fact that the individual finds himself in the presence of a force which dominates him and to which he must bow" (1982:143)—namely, the force of the social collectivity.

Appendix B

1. On this, Weber says, "The role of 'intuition,' at least as regards its *essential* features, is the same in every domain of knowledge. Differences lie only in the *degree* to which an approximation to conceptual precision in discursive thought is possible and desirable" (1975a:170).

2. Whitehead says, "Science is a river with two sources, the practical source and the theoretical source. The practical source is the desire to direct our actions to

achieve predetermined ends. . . . The theoretical source is the desire to understand. . . . I most emphatically state that I do not consider one source as in any sense nobler than the other, or intrinsically more interesting" (1974:106). Sharing Whitehead's view, I dissent from Gibbs's: "What is the most promising candidate for [sociology's] central notion? The question is answered here with one word—control" (1989:18, italics removed). In my judgment, every natural science must answer that question with not one but two words: understanding and control.

3. This assertion that the cultural sciences are concerned with "psychological" phenomena should be juxtaposed with Weber's statement that it is "erroneous to regard any kind of psychology as the ultimate foundation of the sociological interpretation of action" (1978a:19, italics removed). In order to make sense of this juxtaposition, it seems useful to begin by distinguishing between psychology as a certain kind of phenomena and psychology as a discipline that studies those phenomena. With this distinction, Weber's position may be summed up as follows: First, he believes the discipline of psychology seeks causally to account for psychological phenomena by referring to nonpsychological (including external physical, and physiological) phenomena as stimuli, whereas the cultural science disciplines pursue almost the reverse goal—namely, that of causally accounting for (shared) physiological phenomena by referring to (shared) psychological phenomena as stimuli. Thus, Weber says, "While [psychology] instructs us how an external stimulus evokes psychic conditions ('sensations'), economics [one of the cultural, or social, sciences], rather is concerned with the fact that in virtue of such 'psychic' conditions a specifically oriented external behavior (action) is evoked" (1975b:28, italics removed). Second, where the discipline of psychology, therefore, seeks to discover the precise rules that govern the " 'psychic' conditions" in question, the cultural science disciplines are not concerned with discovering these rules; it concentrates, instead, on discovering the rules that govern (shared) physiological behavior. Thus: "The 'psychologist' [sees, in the concept of a 'need' to eat, for example,] an entire series of the most difficult principles in point of the inquiries that interest *him*—[but] economic 'theory' wholly fails to look into these things, and with the easiest scientific conscience at that! . . . For its purposes, indeed, [economic theory] operates with the explicitly stated assurance that all this sort of thing is simply a matter of indifference" (Weber 1975b:29, 30, italics removed). (Weber does not mean to imply that the cultural sciences—specifically in this case, economics—can be isolated from psychology and other disciplines: "At every step and on countless particular points of interest to our discipline, we economists are and must be involved in fruitful interchange of findings and viewpoints with workers in other fields. . . . But the matter of just how this interchange is to take place . . . in the sphere of *our* concerns—this depends unequivocally on the questions *we* pose" [1975b:31; see also 1978a:19; see also Honigsheim 1968:29, 67].) Finally—and as a consequence of the preceding two points—Weber concludes that the methods used by the discipline of psychology in investigating psychological phenomena are wholly inappropriate for the cultural science disciplines: "Think of 'purposive action,' 'expediency,' 'prior calculation,' " he says, "think of these and similar concepts as 'foundations' of a [cultural science] discipline! And [there can be] no recasting of these concepts to make them susceptible to the psychologist's usual work with revolving drums and other laboratory apparatus" (Weber 1975b:30). Instead of relying on such apparatuses, Weber says, "in the social sciences we are concerned with psychological and intellectual phenomena the *empathic understanding* of which is naturally a prob-

lem of a specifically different type from those which the schemes of the exact natural sciences in general can or seek to solve" (1949:74, italics added). In summary, then, Weber argues that neither the nature of cultural scientists' concern with psychological phenomena nor the particular type of such phenomena with which we are concerned is the same as in the discipline of psychology. As a consequence, Weber claims, we are prevented from using the methodology that psychologists use and are compelled to devise our own methodology—namely, that of empathic understanding.

4. Note also Weber's acknowledgment that empathic understanding performs an explanatory as well as a descriptive function in his method (see the discussion of Weber's conflation of these analytical tasks in appendix A): "Understanding may be of two kinds: the first is the direct observational understanding of the subjective meaning of a given act as such. . . . Understanding may, however, be of another sort, namely explanatory understanding. Thus we understand in terms of motive . . . what makes [a person] do this at precisely this moment and in these circumstances" (1978a:8).

5. Note also that the principle of equifinality (see appendix A) compels the investigator to infer each actor's motive separately, because "the subjective meaning need not necessarily be the same for all parties who are mutually oriented in a given social relationship" (Weber 1978a:27).

6. So when Hoy asks, "Is Hermeneutics ethnocentric?" (clearly implying the more extreme question—namely, Is hermeneutics solipsistic?), and when his answer is no, it is not, unless "we expect every other self-understanding to converge with ours. . . . [for that] does seem oppressive, Whiggish, and colonialistic" (1991:175; see also 156), Gadamer counters him: Yes, of course each communicant expects (or at least desires) every other self-understanding to converge with his/her own, for "the goal of all communication and all understanding," Gadamer says, "is agreement in the matter at hand" (1988:69)—and that agreement need not be ethnocentric in itself.

7. Hempel refers to "science as an intersubjective enterprise," and says this requires that "different observers must be able to perform 'the same operation' with reasonable agreement in their results" (1965:127, 123–24).

8. Durkheim argues the same point: "Conceptions with some objective foundation are not restricted to the personality of their author. They have an impersonal quality which others may take up and pursue; they are transmissible. This makes possible some continuity in scientific labor—continuity upon which progress depends" (1951:36).

9. It does not seem to be true, then, that "Weber wants to rid the 'interpretive' method of its 'intuitionist' character"—although it does seem true that "he wants to create an intersubjectively verifiable method, with the aid of which the social relations of people and groups . . . can be both 'understood' and 'explained'" (Käsler 1988:179–80). It would seem to be because of the same interest in intersubjective verifiability that Habermas emphasizes "the dialogue-constitutive universals" of language as generating "the form of intersubjectivity which makes mutuality of understanding possible" (1970a:369), Gadamer emphasizes that "hermeneutics . . . is not a mysterious communication of souls, but rather a participation in shared meaning" (1988:69), and that Ricoeur emphasizes that "whereas language is only the condition for communication . . . it is in discourse that all messages are exchanged. . . . Only discourse, not language, is addressed to someone" (1981:198, 202). It is also this reliance on a method for seeking intersubjective verification of the

validity of empirical statements, centering on the ideal type, that justifies Dahrendorf's conclusion that "the approach called *Verstehen* is . . . not an excuse for arbitrariness, indistinctness and imprecision; it is, on the contrary . . . governed by strict criteria of truth and falsehood" (1987:579).

10. Segady, therefore, seems correct when he says "Weber's intent lay in establishing a mode of Verstehen that did not so much supplant positivism, but attempted to augment it" (1987:103, see also 79)—although Segady does not say exactly what would be augmented in positivism. Burger, however, seems right to describe the significance of Weber's proposal for such standardized measurement as representing a denial of "the absolute incommensurability of the historical phenomena described in their terms" (1987:220–21). There is, however, an unresolved circularity in the way Weber treats the ideal type and its use: How can different investigators communicate and understand each other's images of a given *ideal* actor—say, an "ideal commander-in-chief" (Weber 1949:42)—without having already collected (directly, or vicariously) some information about, and arrived at some generalized understanding of, *real* actors of this sort (Weber himself says an ideal type is "arrived at by the analytical accentuation of certain elements of reality" [1949:90])? And how can that understanding be arrived at if one must already have an image of the ideal actor as an "interpretive scheme" against which to compare information about real ones? This problem has been called the *hermeneutic circle*, and Lubbe claims it is "resolved by repetition; the attempt to comprehend the object is repeated in that the attempt is conditioned by the understanding that has been gained during a previous attempt" (1978:96 n. 19).

11. Gould offers a relatively clear statement of a view that, in most modern sociological theory at least, is currently (and in my opinion, unfortunately) fashionable: "Historical explanations are distinct from conventional experimental results [as in physics] in many different ways. The issue of verification by repetition does not arise [in historical explanations] because we are trying to account for uniqueness of detail that cannot, both by laws of probability and time's arrow of irreversibility, occur together again. We do not attempt to interpret the complex events of narrative by reducing them to simple consequences of natural law; historical events do not, of course, violate any general principles of matter and motion, but their occurrence lies in a realm of contingent detail" and, says Gould, "the issue of prediction . . . does not enter into a historical narrative. . . . experiment, prediction, and subsumption under invariant laws of nature do not represent [the] usual working methods [of historical science]" (1989:278, 279). Weber would clearly demur. As we have just seen, he would argue that "a valid interpretation of an individual effect without the application of . . . knowledge of recurrent causal sequences . . . would in general be impossible." On this view, the issues of "verification by repetition" and of "prediction" do indeed arise in historical explanations of all kinds—both paleontological and sociological. And in fact, Gould tacitly admits this point when he acknowledges that "the firm requirement for all science . . . lies in secure testability, not direct observation. . . . History's richness drives us to different methods of testing, but testability is our criterion as well. . . . We search for repeated pattern" (1989:282). The admission becomes apparent as soon as one asks How can one ever find "pattern" without "verification by repetition," and how can one ever test without comparing an actual observation against some standard prediction of what that observation would (or would not) be? Indeed, Gould's own assertion of what he calls "the central principle of all history—

contingency" (1989:283), namely, that "any replay [of history], altered by an apparently insignificant jot or tittle at the outset, would have yielded an equally sensible and resolvable outcome of entirely different form" (1989:289) is itself a prediction—and, ironically, a far more deterministic one than Weber (or I) could be comfortable with. However, Gould's drastic modification of the centrality of "contingency" is worth noting: "Am I really arguing that nothing about life's history could be predicted, or might follow directly from general laws of nature? Of course not. . . . We do not live amidst a chaos of historical circumstances unaffected by anything accessible to the 'scientific method' as traditionally conceived" (1989:289). In my judgment, Gould's principle of "contingency" is a positive claim founded on negative evidence—that is, it claims that because laws have not yet been found that govern "life's history" and, indeed, such laws may never be found by us, they must not exist (see Gould's tacit admissions of this at 1989:236, 238, and 239). I prefer part of Weinberg's view: "Not only is it possible that what we now regard as arbitrary initial conditions may ultimately be deduced from universal laws—it is also conversely possible that principles that we now regard as universal laws will eventually turn out to represent historical accidents" (1992:38). The other part of Weinberg's view (which contradicts the first part, and which I do not accept) claims that "there is a final theory, and we are capable of discovering it" (1992:235). Note also that realization of this claim would negate the "sane world" that Weinberg himself seems to desire, insofar as he believes that "it is not the certainty of scientific knowledge that fits it for [the role of preserving a sane world] but its *uncertainty*" (1992:259, his italics). See chapter 3, note 16.

12. Contrast these two quotations, drawn directly from Weber's own work, with Segady's remarkable conclusion that in Weber's view, "the social sciences, unlike the natural sciences, set as their goal for research a form of explanation of social conduct in which, ultimately, nomological laws play *no part*" (1978:52, italics added). Contrast, too, Turner's equally remarkable reference to "Weber's *rejection* of objective, general, causal laws in sociological explanations" (1981:5, italics added).

13. Whitehead says, "The first great steps in the organisation of thought were due exclusively to the practical source of scientific activity, without any admixture of theoretical impulse" (1974:111).

14. Habermas says, therefore, "Max Weber took up a position which unmistakably allots to the social sciences the task of producing knowledge capable of being utilized technically" (1971:59), and see 1973:19–20, 254–55 for Habermas's view of the "circular" relationship between pure and applied science.

15. Habermas proposes to get around this impasse not through research on shared culture but through each investigator's private "self-reflection"—on the (I think highly questionable) argument that "the standards of self-reflection are exempted from the singular state of suspension in which those of all other cognitive processes require critical evaluation. They possess theoretical certainty"; and that "the human interest in autonomy and responsibility . . . can be apprehended a priori" (1971:314). At the same time, however, it is clear that Habermas does not really trust different individuals, each reflecting privately and exempt from critical evaluation, to apprehend the same "human interests." He therefore tells us "the solution demands [an] unrestricted communication about the goals of life activity and conduct" (Habermas 1970b:120). For further comment on this strategy, see Wallace 1983:474ff.

16. I use the expression "take the values of others" here, intending to call to mind Mead's "taking the role of others"—viewed by Mead, like Weber, as a process "which

one develops . . . into a more or less definite technique" (1962:153). See also Mannheim's similarly value-taking claim that "although [the intelligentsia is] situated between classes it does not form a middle class. Not, of course, that it is suspended in a vacuum into which social interests do not penetrate; on the contrary, it subsumes in itself all those interests with which social life is permeated" (1955:157).

17. I believe Weber's remark that "an 'ideal type' in our sense . . . has no connection at all with value-judgments" (1949:98, italics removed) is somewhat misleading. I think he means there *is* a connection insofar as the latter is one source of the former, but once an ideal type has been produced from this source, that genetic connection is severed and all investigators are then permitted to use the ideal type in question irrespective of their own personal value-orientations (Weber 1949:98).

18. Here one notices a strong consonance between Weber's portrayal of "ideal types" in the cultural sciences and Kuhn's portrayal of "paradigms" in the natural sciences. Kuhn, too, mentions the likelihood of many "competing articulations" and many "competitors for an existing paradigm," saying that "the proponents of competing paradigms will often disagree about the list of problems that any candidate for paradigm must resolve" (1962:90, 146, 147). And when we realize how closely Kuhn's claim that "paradigms. . . . provide models from which spring particular coherent traditions of scientific research" (1962:10) parallels Weber's claim that the ideal type "offers guidance to the construction of hypotheses" (1949:90), the two visions— Weber's referring to the cultural sciences and Kuhn's referring to the natural sciences—merge into *one* vision of *both* types of sciences.

19. Rule says, "What we mean by a political doctrine or philosophy [or ideology]. . . . is not simply a set of value affirmations . . . [but also] a series of empirical propositions on how societies work" (1978:73), and Feynman says, "A philosophy . . . is simply a way that a person holds [natural] laws in his mind in order to guess quickly at consequences" (1967:169). Note, therefore, that I reject Beetham's view of ideology as being necessarily "false or misleading" (1985:261, see also 263).

20. Ricoeur correctly says that "the fundamental reason why social theory cannot entirely free itself from the ideological condition [is because] it can neither carry out a total reflection, nor rise to a point of view capable of expressing the totality, and hence cannot abstract itself from the ideological mediation to which the other members of the social group are subsumed" (1981:239). Regrettably, however, Ricoeur omits the crucial point that the same impossibility applies to theories of all other, nonsocial, phenomena as well. The impossibility to which he refers seems an inescapable part of human finiteness (see Barrow 1991).

WORKS CITED

Abel, Theodore. 1948. "The Operation Called *Verstehen.*" *American Journal of Sociology* 54 (November): 211–18.

Adams, Richard N. 1982. *Paradoxical Harvest.* Cambridge: Cambridge University Press.

Adams, Robert McC. 1966. *The Evolution of Urban Society.* Chicago: Aldine.

Agus, Jacob B. 1980. "Six Jewish Thoughts." In *Consensus in Theology?* Edited by Leonard Swidler, 110–11. Philadelphia: Westminster.

Albert, Hans. 1971. "Discussion." In *Max Weber and Sociology Today.* Edited by Otto Stammer, 55–59. New York: Harper & Row.

Albrow, Martin. 1990. *Max Weber's Construction of Social Theory.* London: Macmillan.

Alexander, Jeffrey C. 1980. "Core Solidarity, Ethnic Outgroup, and Social Differentiation: A Multidimensional Model of Inclusion in Modern Societies." In *National and Ethnic Movements.* Edited by Jacques Dofny and Akinsola Akiwowo, 5–24. Newbury Park, Calif.: Sage.

———. 1982. *Positivism, Presuppositions, and Current Controversies.* Berkeley and Los Angeles: University of California Press.

———. 1983. *The Classical Attempt at Theoretical Synthesis: Max Weber.* Berkeley and Los Angeles: University of California Press.

———. 1988. "The New Theoretical Movement." In *Handbook of Sociology.* Edited by Neil J. Smelser, 77–101. Newbury Park, Calif.: Sage.

Alexander, Jeffrey C., and Paul Colomy. 1990. "The Structure and Dynamics of Traditions: Toward a Postpositivist Model of Knowledge Cumulation and Decline in the Social Sciences." Paper presented at the annual meetings of the American Sociological Association, Washington, D.C., 11–15 August.

Allee, W. C. 1958. *The Social Life of Animals.* Boston: Beacon.

Andreski, Stanislav. 1984. *Max Weber's Insights and Errors.* London: Routledge & Kegan Paul.

Anonymous. 1993. "Nuclear Fusion." *CQ Researcher* 3 (January 22): 49–72.

Aron, Raymond. 1971. "Max Weber and Power Politics." In *Max Weber and Sociology Today.* Edited by Otto Stammer, 83–100. New York: Harper & Row.

Asimov, Isaac. 1979. *A Choice of Catastrophes.* New York: Fawcett Columbine.

Atoji, Yoshio. 1984. *Sociology at the Turn of the Century.* Tokyo: Dobunkan.

Barber, Bernard. 1952. *Science and the Social Order.* Glencoe, Ill.: Free Press.

Barrow, John D. 1988. *The World Within the World.* New York: Oxford University Press.

———. 1991. *Theories of Everything.* New York: Fawcett Columbine.

Barth, Fredrik. 1981. *Process and Form in Social Life: Selected Essays.* Boston: Routledge & Kegan Paul.

Bartusiak, Marcia. 1986. *Thursday's Universe.* New York: Times Books.

Baumgarten, Eduard. 1971. "Discussion." In *Max Weber and Sociology Today.* Edited by Otto Stammer, 122–27. New York: Harper & Row.

Bayley, David H. 1975. "The Police and Political Development in Europe." In *The Formation of National States in Western Europe.* Edited by Charles Tilly, 328–79. Princeton, N.J.: Princeton University Press.

Beetham, David. 1985. *Max Weber and the Theory of Modern Politics.* Cambridge, England: Polity.

Bell, David E., Ralph L Keeney, and Howard Raiffa. 1977. "Introduction and Overview." In *Conflicting Objectives in Decisions.* Edited by David E. Bell, Ralph L. Keeney, and Howard Raiffa, 1–14. New York: Wiley.

Bendix, Reinhard. 1960. *Max Weber: An Intellectual Portrait.* Garden City, N.Y.: Doubleday.

Benn, S. I., and G. W. Mortimore. 1976. "Introduction." In *Rationality in the Social Sciences.* Edited by S. I. Benn and G. W. Mortimore. London: Routledge and Kegan Paul.

Benton, Michael J. 1993. "Late Triassic Extinctions and the Origin of the Dinosaurs." *Science* 260 (7 May):769–70.

Berger, Peter L., and Thomas Luckmann. 1967. *The Social Construction of Reality.* New York: Doubleday.

Bergmann, Gustav. 1966. *The Metaphysics of Logical Positivism.* Madison: University of Wisconsin Press.

Bernal, J. D. 1939. *The Social Function of Science.* London: George Routledge & Sons.

Blau, Judith R., and Peter M. Blau. 1982. "The Cost of Inequality: Metropolitan Structure and Violent Crime." *American Sociological Review* 47 (February): 114–29.

Blau, Peter M. 1977. *Inequality and Heterogeneity.* New York: Free Press.

Bologh, Roslyn Wallach. 1984. "Max Weber and the Dilemma of Rationality." In *Max Weber's Political Sociology.* Edited by Ronald M. Glassman and Vatro Murvar, 175–84. Westport, Conn.: Greenwood.

———. 1990. *Love or Greatness.* London: Unwin Hyman.

Borges, Jorge Luis. 1964. *Labyrinths.* New York: New Directions.

Bottomore, Tom. 1975. "Structure and History." In *Approaches to the Study of Social Structure.* Edited by Peter M. Blau, 159–71. New York: Free Press.

Boulding, Kenneth. 1956. "General Systems Theory—The Skeleton of Science." *General Systems Yearbook.* Vol. 1, 11–17.

Bradley, Raymond Trevor. 1987. *Charisma and Social Structure.* New York: Paragon.

Braithwaite, Richard Bevan. 1960. *Scientific Explanation.* New York: Harper.

Braudel, Fernand. 1988. *The Identity of France.* Vol. 1. London: Collins.

Brin, G. D. 1985. "Rocs' Eggs and Spider Webs: The First Hard Step Toward Building Starships." In *Interstellar Migration and the Human Experience.* Edited by Ben R. Finney and Eric M. Jones, 42–49. Berkeley and Los Angeles: University of California Press.

Broom, Leonard. 1959. "Social Differentiation and Stratification." In *Sociology Today*. Edited by Robert K. Merton, Leonard Broom, and Leonard S. Cottrell, Jr., 429–41. New York: Basic Books.

Brown, Lester R. 1993. "A New Era Unfolds." In *State of the World 1993*, 3–21. New York: Norton.

Browne, Malcolm W. 1993a. "An Asteroid Belt Near Earth's Path." *New York Times*, 24 June, p. A21.

——. 1993b. "Scientists at Princeton Produce World's Largest Fusion Reaction." *New York Times*. 10 December, p. A1.

Brubaker, Rogers. 1984. *The Limits of Rationality: an Essay on the Social and Moral Thought of Max Weber*. London: Allen & Unwin.

Burger, Thomas. 1977. "Max Weber, Interpretive Sociology, and the Sense of Historical Science: A Positivistic Conception of Verstehen." *Sociological Quarterly* 18 (Spring): 165–75.

——. 1985. "Power and Stratification: Max Weber and Beyond." In *Theory of Liberty, Legitimacy and Power*. Edited by Vatro Murvar. Boston: Routledge & Kegan Paul.

——. 1987. *Max Weber's Theory of Concept Formation*. Expanded ed. Durham, N.C.: Duke University Press.

Burns, Gene. 1990. "The Politics of Ideology: The Papal Struggle with Liberalism." *American Journal of Sociology* 95, no. 5 (March): 1123–52.

Campbell, Bernard. 1985. *Human Evolution*. 3d ed. New York: Aldine.

Carmichael, Stokely, and Charles V. Hamilton. 1967. *Black Power*. New York: Vintage.

Carnap, Rudolf. 1966. *Philosophical Foundations of Physics*. New York: Basic Books.

Carneiro, Robert L. 1981. "The Chiefdom: Precursor of the State." In *The Transition to Statehood in the New World*. Edited by Grant D. Jones and Robert R. Kautz. Cambridge: Cambridge University Press.

Childe, V. Gordon. 1942. *What Happened in History*. Harmondsworth, England: Penguin.

Chomsky, Noam. 1957. *Syntactic Structures*. 'S-Gravenhage: Mouton.

Clarke, Ian M. 1985. *The Spatial Organisation of Multinational Corporations*. New York: St. Martin's Press.

Cohen, Ira J. 1985. "The Underemphasis on Democracy in Marx and Weber." In *A Marx-Weber Dialogue*. Edited by Robert J. Antonio and Ronald M. Glassman, 274–99. Lawrence: University of Kansas Press.

Coleman, James S. 1957. *Community Conflict*. Glencoe, Ill.: Free Press.

——. 1990. *Foundations of Social Theory*. Cambridge: Harvard University Press, Belknap Press.

Collins, Randall. 1986a. *Weberian Sociological Theory*. Cambridge: Cambridge University Press.

——. 1986b. *Max Weber: A Skeleton Key*. Beverly Hills, Calif.: Sage.

——. 1988. *Theoretical Sociology*. San Diego: Harcourt Brace Jovanovich.

——. 1990. "Conflict Theory and the Advance of Macro-Historical Sociology." In *Frontiers of Social Theory*. Edited by George Ritzer, 68–87. New York: Columbia University Press.

Comte, Auguste. 1975. *Auguste Comte and Positivism*. New York: Harper & Row.

Criswell, David R. 1985. "Solar System Industrialization: Implications for Interstellar

Migrations." In *Interstellar Migration and the Human Experience.* Edited by Ben R. Finney and Eric M. Jones, 50–87. Berkeley and Los Angeles: University of California Press.

Cusack, Odean. 1988. *Pets and Mental Health.* New York: Haworth.

Dahrendorf, Ralf. 1987. "Max Weber and Modern Social Science." In *Max Weber and His Contemporaries.* Edited by Wolfgang J. Mommsen and Jurgen Osterhammel, 574–80. London: Allen & Unwin.

Daniels, Roger. 1990. *Coming to America.* New York: Harper.

Darling, David. 1993. *Equations of Eternity.* New York: Hyperion.

Davies, Paul. 1988. *The Cosmic Blueprint.* Simon & Schuster.

Davis, James A. 1990. "Comment on 'The Essential Wisdom of Sociology.'" *Teaching Sociology* 18 (October):531–32.

Dawkins, Richard. 1987. *The Blind Watchmaker.* New York: Norton.

Denny, J. Peter. 1991. "Rational Thought in Oral Culture and Literate Decontextualization." In *Literacy and Orality.* Edited by David R. Olson and Nancy Torrance, 66–89. Cambridge: Cambridge University Press.

Desmond, Annabelle. 1975. "How Many People Have Ever Lived on Earth?" In *Population Studies: Selected Essays and Research.* Edited by Kenneth C. W. Kammeyer, 18–32. Chicago: Rand McNally.

Deutsch, Karl W. 1966. *Nationalism and Social Communication.* Cambridge: MIT Press.

———. 1969. *Nationalism and Its Alternatives.* New York: Knopf.

———. 1971. "Discussion." In *Max Weber and Sociology Today.* Edited by Otto Stammer, 116–22. New York: Harper & Row.

Diamond, Jared. 1987. "The Worst Mistake in the History of the Human Race." *Discover* 8 (May): 64–66.

———. 1992. *The Third Chimpanzee.* New York: HarperCollins.

Dobbin, Frank. 1993. "Vive la différence!" In *High Speed Trains: Fast Tracks to the Future.* Edited by John Whitelegg, Staffan Hulten, and Torbjorn Flink, 124–44. North Yorkshire, England: Leading Edge.

Douglas, Mary. 1966. *Purity and Danger.* New York: Praeger.

Duberman, Lucille. 1974. *Marriage and Its Alternatives.* New York: Praeger.

———. 1975. *Gender and Sex in Society.* New York: Praeger.

Dulles, Avery. 1980. "Ecumenicalism and Theological Method" In *Consensus in Theology?* Edited by Leonard Swidler, 40–48. Philadelphia: Westminster.

Durkheim, Emile. 1951. *Suicide.* Glencoe, Ill.: Free Press.

———. 1965. *The Elementary Forms of the Religious Life.* Glencoe, Ill.: Free Press.

———. 1982. *The Rules of Sociological Method.* New York: Free Press.

———. 1984. *The Division of Labor in Society.* New York: Free Press.

———. 1986. *Les règles de la méthode sociologique.* Paris: Quadrige/PUF.

Dyson, Freeman. 1979. *Disturbing the Universe.* New York: Basic.

———. 1988. *Infinite in All Directions.* New York: Harper & Row.

Eisenstadt, S. N. 1968. "Introduction." In *Max Weber on Charisma and Institution Building.* Edited by S. N. Eisenstadt, ix–lvi. Chicago: University of Chicago Press.

Eldridge, Niles, and Stephen J. Gould. 1972. "Punctuated Equilibria: An Alternative to Phylogenetic Gradualism." In *Models in Paleobiology.* Edited by Thomas J. Schopf, 83–15. San Francisco: Freeman, Cooper.

Engels, Frederick. 1939. *Herr Eugen Dühring's Revolution in Science.* New York: International.

Enloe, Cynthia. 1981. "The Growth of the State and Ethnic Mobilization." *Ethnic and Racial Studies* 4 (April): 123–36.

Erickson, Jon. 1991. *Target Earth! Asteroid Collisions Past and Future.* Blue Ridge Summit, Pa.: TAB.

Fagan, Brian M. 1990. *The Journey From Eden.* London: Thames and Hudson.

Falk, Richard. 1992. *Economic Aspects of Global Civilization.* Princeton, N.J.: Princeton University Press.

Fanon, Frantz. 1968. *The Wretched of the Earth.* New York: Grove.

Featherstone, Mike. 1990. "Global Culture: An Introduction." *Theory, Culture & Society* 7 (June): 1–14.

Feigl, Herbert. 1953. "Notes on Causality." In *Readings in the Philosophy of Science.* Edited by Herbert Feigl and May Brodbeck, 408–18. New York: Appleton-Century-Crofts.

Ferris, Timothy. 1983. *The Red Limit.* New York: Quill.

———. 1988. *Coming of Age in the Milky Way.* New York: Morrow.

———. 1992. *The Mind's Sky.* New York: Bantam.

Feynman, Richard P. 1967. *The Character of Physical Law.* Cambridge: MIT Press.

———. 1985. *QED: The Strange Theory of Light and Matter.* Princeton, N.J.: Princeton University Press.

Fine, Gary Alan. 1990. "Symbolic Interactionism in the Post-Blumerian Age." In *Frontiers of Social Theory.* Edited by George Ritzer, 117–57. New York: Columbia University Press.

Finer, Samuel E. 1975. "State- and Nation-Building in Europe: The Role of the Military." In *The Formation of National States in Western Europe.* Edited by Charles Tilly, 84–163. Princeton, N.J.: Princeton University Press.

Finney, Ben R., and Eric M. Jones. 1985. "The Exploring Animal." In *Interstellar Migration and the Human Experience.* Edited by Ben R. Finney and Eric M. Jones, 15–25. Berkeley and Los Angeles: University of California Press.

Flam, Faye. 1993a. "Spinning in the Dark." *Science* 260 (11 June): 1593.

———. 1993b. "A Stellar Blast from the Past." *Science* 262 (26 November):1372.

Flavin, Christopher, and John E. Young. 1993. "Shaping the Next Industrial Revolution." In *State of the World,* 180–99. New York: Norton.

Fox, Karen. 1993. "Indoor Robots Start Flying Blind." *Science* 261 (6 August): 685.

Freud, Sigmund. 1950. *Totem and Taboo.* New York: Norton.

———. 1961. *Civilization and Its Discontents.* New York: Norton.

Freund, Julien. 1978. "German Sociology in the Time of Max Weber." In *A History of Sociological Analysis.* Edited by Tom Bottomore and Robert Nisbet, 149–86. New York: Basic.

Gadamer, Hans-Georg. 1988. "On the Circle of Understanding." In *Hermeneutics Versus Science?* Edited by H.-G. Gadamer, E. K. Specht, and W. Stegmuller, 68–78. Notre Dame, Ind.: University of Notre Dame Press.

Geertz, Clifford. 1983. *Local Knowledge.* New York: Basic Books.

Gellner, Ernest. 1983. *Nations and Nationalism.* Ithaca, N.Y.: Cornell University Press.

Gerth, H. H., and C. Wright Mills. 1946. "Introduction." In *Essays from Max Weber.* Edited by H. H. Gerth and C. Wright Mills, 3–75. New York: Oxford.

Gibbs, Jack P. 1972. *Sociological Theory Construction.* Hinsdale, Ill.: Dryden.

———. 1989. *Control: Sociology's Central Notion.* Urbana: University of Illinois Press.

Giddens, Anthony. 1972. *Politics and Sociology in the Thought of Max Weber*. London: Macmillan.

———. 1978. "Positivism and Its Critics." In *A History of Sociological Analysis*. Edited by Tom Bottomore and Robert Nisbet, 237–86. New York: Basic.

———. 1979. "Introduction." In *Positivism and Sociology*. Edited by Anthony Giddens, 1–22. London: Heinemann.

Gilbert, Margaret. 1989. *On Social Facts*. New York: Routledge.

———. 1991. "The Author Responds: More on Social Facts." *Social Epistemology* 5, 233–44.

Glassman, Ronald M. 1984. "Manufactured Charisma and Legitimacy." In *Max Weber's Political Sociology*. Edited by Ronald M. Glassman and Vatro Murvar, 217–35. Westport, Conn.: Greenwood.

Glassman, Ronald M., and Vatro Murvar. 1984. "Introduction." In *Max Weber's Political Sociology*. Edited by Ronald M. Glassman and Vatro Murvar, 3–11. Westport, Conn.: Greenwood.

Gleick, James. 1987. *Chaos: Making a New Science*. New York: Viking.

———. 1993. "The Telephone Transformed—Into Almost Everything." *New York Times Magazine*, 16 May 1993, 26–29, 50, 53–56, 62, 64.

Goode, William J. 1959. "The Theoretical Importance of Love." *American Sociological Review* 24 (February): 38–47.

Goody, Jack. 1977. *The Domestication of the Savage Mind*. Cambridge: Cambridge University Press.

Gordon, Anne. 1984. *Death Is for the Living*. Edinburgh: Paul Harris.

Gott, J. Richard III. 1993. "Implications of the Copernican Principle for Our Future Prospects." *Nature* 363 (27 May): 315–19.

Gould, Stephen Jay. 1989. *Wonderful Life: The Burgess Shale and the Nature of History*. New York: Norton.

Gouldner, Alvin W. 1976. *The Dialectic of Ideology and Technology*. New York: Seabury.

Green, Martin. 1974. *The von Richtofen Sisters*. New York: Basic.

Gribbin, John. 1986. *In Search of the Big Bang: Quantum Physics and Cosmology*. New York: Bantam.

———. 1993. *In the Beginning: After COBE and before the Big Bang*. Boston: Little, Brown.

Griffin, John Howard. 1977. *Black Like Me*. 2d ed. Boston: Houghton Mifflin.

Gross, David. 1988. "Weber in Context: The Dilemmas of Modernity." *Telos* 78 (Winter): 109–17.

Habenstein, Robert W., and William M. Lamers. 1955. *The History of American Funeral Directing*. Milwaukee: Bulfin.

Habermas, Jurgen. 1970a. *Toward a Rational Society*. Boston: Beacon.

———. 1970b. "Towards a Theory of Communicative Competence." *Inquiry* 13 (Winter): 360–75.

———. 1971. "Discussion." In *Max Weber and Sociology Today*. Edited by Otto Stammer, 59–66. New York: Harper & Row.

———. 1973. *Theory and Practice*. Boston: Beacon.

———. 1979. "History and Evolution." *Telos* 39, 5–44.

———. 1984. *The Theory of Communicative Action*. Vol. 1. Boston: Beacon Press.

Hacking, Ian. 1982. "Language, Truth and Reason." In *Rationality and Relativism*. Edited by Martin Hollis and Steven Lukes, 48–66. Oxford: Basil Blackwell.

Hamilton, Alexander, James Madison, and John Hay. 1961. *The Federalist*. Cambridge: Harvard University Press.

Hannerz, Ulf. 1990. "Cosmopolitans and Locals in World Culture." *Theory, Culture & Society* 7 (June): 237–51.

Hart, Michael H. 1985. "Interstellar Migration, the Biological Revolution, and the Future of the Galaxy." In *Interstellar Migration and the Human Experience*. Edited by Ben R. Finney and Eric M. Jones, 278–91. Berkeley and Los Angeles: University of California.

Hartmann, William K. 1985. "The Resource Base in Our Solar System." In *Interstellar Migration and the Human Experience*. Edited by Ben R. Finney and Eric M. Jones, 26–41. Berkeley and Los Angeles: University of California Press.

Heider, Fritz. 1958. *The Psychology of Interpersonal Relations*. New York: Wiley.

Hekman, Susan J. 1983. *Max Weber and Contemporary Social Theory*. Oxford: Martin Robertson.

Hempel, Carl G. 1965. *Aspects of Scientific Explanation*. New York: Free Press.

Hennis, Wilhelm. 1983. "Max Weber's 'Central Question.'" *Economy and Society* 12, no. 2, 135–80.

———. 1988. *Max Weber: Essays in Reconstruction*. Boston: Allen & Unwin.

Hindess, Barry. 1987. "Rationality and the Characterization of Modern Society." In *Max Weber, Rationality and Modernity*. Edited by Sam Whimster and Scott Lash, 137–53. London: Allen & Unwin.

Hogan, James P. 1979. *The Two Faces of Tomorrow*. New York: Ballantine.

Holden, Constance. 1993. "Computer Networks Bring 'Real Science' to the Schools." *Science* 261 (20 August): 980–81.

Hollins, Harry B., Averill L. Powers, and Mark Sommer. 1989. *The Conquest of War: Alternative Strategies for Global Security*. Boulder, Colo.: Westview.

Hollis, Martin, and Steven Lukes. 1982. "Introduction." In *Rationality and Relativism*. Edited by Martin Hollis and Steven Lukes, 1–20. Oxford: Basil Blackwell.

Homans, George Caspar. 1975. "What Do We Mean by Social 'Structure'?" In *Approaches to the Study of Social Structure*. Edited by Peter M. Blau, 53–65. New York: Free Press.

Homer-Dixon, Thomas F., Jeffrey H. Boutwell, and George W. Rathjens. 1993. "Environmental Change and Violent Conflict." *Scientific American*, February, 38–45.

Honigsheim, Paul. 1968. *On Max Weber*. New York: Free Press.

House, James S., Karl R. Landis, and Debra Umberson. 1988. "Social Relationships and Health." *Science* 241 (29 July): 540–44.

Hoy, David Couzens. 1991. "Is Hermeneutics Ethnocentric?" In *The Interpretive Turn*. Edited by David R. Hiley, James F. Bowman, and Richard Shusterman, 155–75. Ithaca, N.Y.: Cornell University Press.

Huff, Toby E. 1984. *Max Weber and the Methodology of the Social Sciences*. New Brunswick, N.J.: Transaction Books.

———. 1989. "On Weber, Law and Universalism: Some Preliminary Considerations." *Comparative Civilizations Review* 21 (Fall): 47–79.

Huizinga, J. 1955. *Homo Ludens: A Study of the Play Element in Culture*. Boston: Beacon.

Ibn Khaldun. 1969. *The Muqaddimah*. Princeton, N.J.: Princeton University Press, Bollingen.

Inbar, Michael. 1979. *The Future of Bureaucracy*. Beverly Hills, Calif.: Sage.

Irwin, Robert A. 1989. *Building a Peace System*. Washington, D.C.: ExPo.

Jackson, Maurice. 1976. "The Civil Rights Movement and Social Change." In *Social Movements and Social Change*. Edited by Robert H. Lauer. Carbondale: Southern Illinois University Press.

Jastrow, Robert. 1981a. "The Post-Human World." *Science Digest* 89 (January–February): 89–91, 144.

———. 1981b. *The Enchanted Loom*. New York: Simon and Schuster.

Jones, Eric M., and Ben R. Finney. 1985. "Fastships and Nomads: Two Roads to the Stars." In *Interstellar Migration and the Human Experience*. Edited by Ben R. Finney and Eric M. Jones, 88–103. Berkeley and Los Angeles: University of California Press.

Jones, Robert Alun. 1990. "Using Hypermedia to Teach the History of Social Thought." *Perspectives* 13 (July): 1–3.

Kalberg, Stephen. 1980. "Max Weber's Types of Rationality: Cornerstones for the Analysis of Rationalization Processes in History." *American Journal of Sociology* 85, no. 5, 1145–79.

———. 1985. "The Role of Ideal Interests in Max Weber's Comparative Historical Sociology." In *A Marx-Weber Dialogue*. Edited by Robert J. Antonio and Ronald M. Glassman. Lawrence: University Press of Kansas.

———. 1990. "The Rationalization of Action in Max Weber's Sociology of Religion." *Sociological Theory* 8 (Spring): 58–84.

Kaplan, Abraham. 1964. *The Conduct of Inquiry*. San Francisco: Chandler.

Käsler, Dirk. 1988. *Max Weber: An Introduction to His Life and Work*. Cambridge, England: Polity

Kellner, Douglas. 1985. "Critical Theory, Max Weber, and the Dialectics of Domination." In *A Marx-Weber Dialogue*. Edited by Robert J. Antonio and Ronald M. Glassman, 89–116. Lawrence: University Press of Kansas.

Kennedy, Paul. 1993. *Preparing for the Twenty-First Century*. New York: Random House.

Kerr, Richard A. 1992. "When Climate Twitches, Evolution Takes Great Leaps." *Science* 257 (18 September): 1622–24.

Kinoshita, June. 1993. "Counting on Science to Compete." *Science* 262 (15 October: 348–50.

Klein, Richard G. 1989. *The Human Career*. Chicago: University of Chicago Press.

Kotabe, Masaaki. 1992. *Global Sourcing Strategy*. New York: Quorum.

Krasner, Stephen D. 1984. "Review Article: Approaches to the State." *Comparative Politics* 16, no. 2 (January): 223–46.

Kuhn, Thomas S. 1962. *The Structure of Scientific Revolutions*. Chicago: University of Chicago Press.

———. 1970. *The Structure of Scientific Revolutions*. 2d ed. Chicago: University of Chicago Press.

Kung, Hans. 1988. *Theology for the Third Millennium: An Ecumenical View*. New York: Doubleday.

Lachmann, L. M. 1971. *The Legacy of Max Weber*. Berkeley, Calif.: Glendessary.

Langton, Christopher G. 1989. "Artificial Life." In *Artificial Life*. Edited by Christopher G. Langton, 1–47. Redwood City, Calif.: Addison-Wesley.

Lauer, Robert H. 1976. "Introduction. Social Movements and Social Change: The

Interrelationships." In *Social Movements and Social Change*. Edited by Robert H. Lauer, xi–xxviii. Carbondale: Southern Illinois University Press.

Laumann, Edward O., and Franz U. Pappi. 1976. *Networks of Collective Action*. New York: Academic.

Leakey, Richard, and Roger Lewin. 1992. *Origins Reconsidered*. New York: Doubleday.

Lenssen, Nicholas. 1993. "Providing Energy in Developing Countries." In *State of the World 1993*, 101–19. New York: Norton.

Leontiades, James C. 1985. *Multinational Corporate Strategy*. Lexington, Mass.: Lexington Books.

Levi, Margaret, Karen S. Cook, Jodi A. O'Brien, and Howard Faye. 1990. "Introduction: The Limits of Rationality." In *The Limits of Rationality*. Edited by Karen Schweers Cook and Margaret Levi, 1–18. Chicago: University of Chicago Press.

Levine, Donald N. 1981. "Rationality and Freedom: Weber and Beyond." *Sociological Inquiry* 51, no. 1, 5–25.

Lieberson, Stanley, and Mary C. Waters. 1990. *From Many Strands*. New York: Russell Sage Foundation.

Lindholm, Charles. 1990. *Charisma*. Cambridge, Mass: Basil Blackwell.

Lipset, Seymour Martin. 1975. "Social Structure and Social Change." In *Approaches to the Study of Social Structure*. Edited by Peter M. Blau, 172–209. New York: Free Press.

Little, Linda. 1993. "Computational Platforms: Setting the Stage for Simulation." *Bulletin of the Santa Fe Institute* 8 (Fall): 13–17.

Loewith, Karl. 1970. "Weber's Interpretation of the Bourgeois-Capitalistic World in Terms of the Guiding Principle of 'Rationalization.'" In *Max Weber*. Edited by Dennis Wrong, 101–22. Englewood Cliffs, N.J.: Prentice-Hall.

Lorenz, Konrad. 1970. *Studies in Animal and Human Behaviour*. 2 vols. Cambridge: Harvard University Press.

Lubbe, Hermann. 1978. "Positivism and Phenomenology: Mach and Husserl." In *Phenomenology and Sociology: Selected Readings*. Edited by Thomas Luckmann. New York: Penguin.

Lukes, Steven. 1971. "Some Problems About Rationality." In *Rationality*. Edited by Bryan R. Wilson, 194–213. New York: Harper.

Lynd, Robert S. 1946. *Knowledge For What?* Princeton, N.J.: Princeton University Press.

Lyman, Sanford. 1984. "The Science of History and the Theory of Social Change." In *Max Weber's Political Sociology*. Edited by Ronald M. Glassman and Vatro Murvar, 189–99. Westport, Conn.: Greenwood.

McAdam, Doug, John D. McCarthy, and Mayer N. Zald. 1988. "Social Movements." In *Handbook of Sociology*. Edited by Neil J. Smelser, 695–737. Newbury Park, Calif.: Sage.

McColm, R. Bruce. 1992. "The Comparative Survey of Freedom 1991–92: Between Two Worlds." In *Freedom in the World: Political Rights and Civil Liberties*. Edited by R. Bruce McColm (survey coordinator), 47–52. New York: Freedom House.

McConnell, Virginia F. 1971. "Problems in the Teaching of the History of Chemistry." In *Teaching the History of Chemistry: A Symposium*. Edited by George B. Kauffman. Budapest: Publishing House of the Hungarian Academy of Sciences.

McCorduck, Pamela. 1979. *Machines Who Think*. San Francisco: Freeman.

McLuhan, Marshall. 1964. *Understanding Media*. New York: Signet.

McNeill, William H. 1963. *The Rise of the West*. Chicago: University of Chicago Press.

———. 1985. *Polyethnicity and National Unity in World History*. Toronto: University of Toronto Press.

Madden, Edward H. 1973. "Civil Disobedience." In *Dictionary of the History of Ideas*. 5 vols. Edited by Philip P. Wiener. New York: Scribner's.

Mann, Michael. 1986. *The Sources of Social Power*. Vol. 1. Cambridge: Cambridge University Press.

Mann, Thomas. 1955. "Death in Venice." In *Death in Venice*, 3–75. New York: Vintage.

Mannheim, Karl. 1955. *Ideology and Utopia*. New York: Harvest Books.

March, James G., and Herbert A. Simon. 1958. *Organizations*. New York: Wiley.

Marcuse, Herbert. 1971. "Industrialization and Capitalism." In *Max Weber and Sociology Today*. Edited by Otto Stammer, 133–51. New York: Harper & Row.

Margulis, Lynn, and Dorion Sagan. 1986. *Microcosmos*. New York: Summit.

Markusen, Ann, and Joel Yudken. 1992. *Dismantling the Cold War Economy*. New York: Basic.

Marshall, Eliot. 1990. "Clovis Counterrevolution." *Science* 249 (17 August): 738–41.

———. 1993. "Fitting Planet Earth into a User-Friendly Database." *Science* 261 (13 August): 846, 848.

Martindale, Don, and Johannes Riedel. 1958. "Max Weber's Sociology of Music." In *The Rational and Social Foundations of Music*. By Max Weber. Carbondale: Southern Illinois Press.

Marty, Martin E., and R. Scott Appleby. 1993a. "Introduction: A Sacred Cosmos, Scandalous Code, Defiant Society." In *Fundamentalisms and Society*. Edited by Martin E. Marty and R. Scott Appleby, 1–22. Chicago: University of Chicago Press.

———. 1993b. "Introduction." In *Fundamentalisms and the State*. Edited by Martin E. Marty and R. Scott Appleby, 1–9. Chicago: University of Chicago Press.

———. 1993c. "Conclusion: Remaking the State: the Limits of the Fundamentalist Imagination." In *Fundamentalisms and the State*. Edited by Martin E. Marty and R. Scott Appleby, 620–44. Chicago: University of Chicago.

Marx, Karl. 1955. *The Poverty of Philosophy*. Moscow: Progress.

———. 1967. *Capital*. 3 vols. New York: International.

———. 1973. *Grundrisse*. New York: Vintage Books.

———. 1977. *Economic and Philosophic Manuscripts of 1844*. Moscow: Progress.

Marx, Karl, and Frederick Engels. 1947. *The German Ideology*. New York: International.

———. 1969. *Selected Works*. 3 vols. Moscow: Progress.

———. 1978. *The Marx-Engels Reader*. 2d ed. Edited by Robert C. Tucker. New York: Norton.

Matthews, Robert. 1992. "A Rocky Watch for Earthbound Asteroids." *Science* 255 (6 March): 1204–5.

Mayrl, William W. 1985. "Max Weber and the Causality of Freedom." In *Theory of Liberty, Legitimacy, and Power*. Edited by Vatro Murvar, 108–24. Boston: Routledge & Kegan Paul.

Mead, George Herbert. 1962. *Mind, Self, and Society*. Chicago: University of Chicago Press.

Mearsheimer, John J. 1990. "Why We Will Soon Miss the Cold War." *Atlantic Monthly,* August, 35–50.

Mendelsohn, Everett. 1993. "Religious Fundamentalism and the Sciences." In *Fundamentalisms and Society.* Edited by Martin E. Marty and R. Scott Appleby, 23–41. Chicago: University of Chicago Press.

Merton, Robert K. 1957. *Social Theory and Social Structure.* Revised and enlarged. Glencoe, Ill.: Free Press.

———. 1965. *On the Shoulders of Giants.* New York: Free Press.

———. 1973. *The Sociology of Science.* Chicago: University of Chicago Press.

———. 1976. *Sociological Ambivalence.* New York: Free Press.

Michels, Robert. 1958. *Political Parties.* Glencoe, Ill.: Free Press.

Miller, George A., Eugene Galanter, and Karl H. Pribam. 1960. *Plans and the Structure of Behavior.* New York: Holt, Rinehart, and Winston.

Mitra, Kana. 1980. "A Hindu Self-Reflection" In *Consensus in Theology?* Edited by Leonard Swidler, 121–24. Philadelphia: Westminster.

Molnar, Stephen. 1992. *Human Variation.* Englewood Cliffs, N.J.: Prentice-Hall.

Mommsen, Wolfgang J. 1970. "Max Weber's Political Sociology and His Philosophy of World History." In *Max Weber.* Edited by Dennis Wrong. Englewood Cliffs, N.J.: Prentice-Hall.

———. 1971. "Discussion." In *Max Weber and Sociology Today.* Edited by Otto Stammer, 109–16. New York: Harper & Row.

———. 1974. *The Age of Bureaucracy: Perspectives on the Political Sociology of Max Weber.* Oxford: Basil Blackwell.

———. 1984. *Max Weber and German Politics 1890–1920.* Chicago: University of Chicago Press.

———. 1985. "Capitalism and Socialism: Weber's Dialogue with Marx." In *A Marx-Weber Dialogue.* Edited by Robert J. Antonio and Ronald M. Glassman. Lawrence: University Press of Kansas.

———. 1987. "Personal Conduct and Societal Change." In *Max Weber, Rationality and Modernity.* Edited by Sam Whimster and Scott Lash, 35–51. London: Allen & Unwin.

———. 1989. *The Political and Social Theory of Max Weber.* London: Polity.

Moore, Wilbert E. 1959. "Sociology and Demography." In *The Study of Population.* Edited by Philip Hauser and Otis Dudley Duncan. Chicago: University of Chicago Press.

Moravec, Hans. 1988. *Mind Children.* Cambridge: Harvard University Press.

———. 1989. "Human Culture: A Genetic Takeover Underway." In *Artificial Life.* Edited by Christopher Langton. New York: Addison-Wesley.

Morris, Richard. 1987. *The Nature of Reality.* New York: McGraw-Hill.

Murvar, Vatro. 1984. "Max Weber and the Two Nonrevolutionary Events in Russia 1917: Scientific Achievements or Prophetic Failures?" In *Max Weber's Political Sociology.* Edited by Ronald M. Glassman and Vatro Murvar, 237–72. Westport, Conn.: Greenwood.

———. 1985. "Preface" and "Introduction." In *Theory of Liberty, Legitimacy and Power.* Edited by Vatro Murvar. Boston: Routledge & Kegan Paul.

Nagel, Ernst. 1961. *The Structure of Science.* New York: Harcourt, Brace & World.

Namenwirth, J. Zvi, and Robert Philip Weber. 1987. *Dynamics of Culture.* Boston: Allen & Unwin.

Nasr, Seyyed Hossein. 1980. "A Muslim Reflection on Religion and Theology." In *Consensus in Theology?* Edited by Leonard Swidler, 112–20. Philadelphia: Westminster.

Neugebauer, O. 1952. *The Exact Sciences in Antiquity.* Princeton, N.J.: Princeton University Press.

Nozick, Robert. 1993. *The Nature of Rationality.* Princeton, N.J.: Princeton University Press.

Oakes, Guy. 1988. *Weber and Rickert.* Cambridge, Mass: MIT Press.

Orum, Anthony M. 1988. "Political Sociology." In *Handbook of Sociology.* Edited by Neil J. Smelser. Berkeley, Calif.: Sage.

Pagels, Heinz. 1982. *The Cosmic Code.* New York: Bantam.

Palter, Robert M. 1961. "Preface." In *Toward Modern Science: Studies in Ancient and Medieval Science.* Edited by Robert M. Palter. New York: Noonday Press.

Pareto, Vilfredo. 1935. *The Mind and Society.* (Four Volumes.) New York: Harcourt Brace.

———. 1966. *Vilfredo Pareto: Sociological Writings.* Edited by S.E. Finer. London: Pall Mall.

Parkin, Frank. 1982. *Max Weber.* Chichester, England: Ellis Horwood.

Parsons, Talcott. 1937. *The Structure of Social Action.* Glencoe, Ill.: Free Press.

———. 1947. "Introduction." In *The Theory of Social and Economic Organization.* By Max Weber. Glencoe, Ill.: Free Press.

———. 1951. *The Social System.* Glencoe, Ill.: Free Press.

———. 1960. "Pattern Variables Revisited: A Response to Robert Dubin." *American Sociological Review* 25, no. 4 (August): 467–83.

———. 1961. "An Outline of the Social System." In *Theories of Society.* Edited by Talcott Parsons, Edward Shils, Kaspar D. Naegele, and Jesse R. Pitts, 30–79. New York: Free Press.

———. 1966. *Societies: Evolutionary and Comparative Perspectives.* Englewood Cliffs, N.J.: Prentice-Hall.

———. 1967a. "An Approach to the Sociology of Knowledge." In *Sociological Theory and Modern Society.* By Talcott Parsons. New York: Free Press, 139–65.

———. 1967b. "On the Concept of Political Power." In *Sociological Theory and Modern Society.* By Talcott Parsons. New York: Free Press, 297–354.

———. 1971a. *The System of Modern Societies.* Englewood Cliffs, N.J.: Prentice-Hall.

———. 1971b. "Value-freedom and Objectivity." In *Max Weber in Sociology Today.* Edited by Otto Stammer, 27–50. New York: Harper & Row.

Parsons, Talcott, and Robert F. Bales. 1955. *Family, Socialization and Interaction Process.* Glencoe, Ill.: Free Press.

Parsons, Talcott, and Neil J. Smelser. 1956. *Economy and Society.* Glencoe, Ill.: Free Press.

Partridge, Eric. 1959. *Origins.* New York: Macmillan.

Perutz, Max F. 1989. *Is Science Necessary?* New York: Dutton.

Phillips, David P. 1979. "Suicide, Motor Vehicle Fatalities, and the Mass Media: Evidence toward a Theory of Suggestion." *American Journal of Sociology* 84, no. 5, 1150–74.

Pool, Robert. 1993. "Beyond Databases and E-Mail." *Science* 261 (13 August): 841, 843.

Popper, Karl R. 1950. *The Open Society and Its Enemies.* Princeton, N.J.: Princeton University Press.

———. 1961. *The Logic of Scientific Discovery*. New York: Science Editions.

Portes, Alejandro and John Walton. 1981. *Labor, Class, and the International System*. New York: Academic.

Power, Jonathan. 1979. *Migrant Workers in Western Europe and the United States*. New York: Pergamon.

Quine, Willard Van Orman. 1960. *Word and Object*. Cambridge: MIT.

———. 1963. *From a Logical Point of View*. New York: Harper Torchbooks.

Reich, Robert B. 1992. *The Work of Nations: Preparing Ourselves for 21st-Century Capitalism*. New York: Vintage.

Ricoeur, Paul. 1981. *Hermeneutics and the Social Sciences*. Cambridge: Cambridge University Press.

Ritzer, George. 1992. *Metatheorizing in Sociology*. Lexington, Mass.: Lexington.

Roberts, Neil. 1984. "Pleistocene Environments in Time and Space." In *Hominid Evolution and Community Ecology*. Edited by Robert Foley, 25–54. New York: Academic.

Robertson, Roland. 1990. "Mapping the Global Condition: Globalization as the Central Concept." *Theory, Culture & Society* 7 (June): 15–30.

Rostow, W. W. 1960. *The Stages of Economic Growth*. Cambridge: Cambridge University Press.

Roth, Guenther. 1978. "Introduction." In *Economy and Society*. By Max Weber, xxxiii–cx. Berkeley and Los Angeles: University of California Press.

———. 1979a. "Charisma and the Counterculture." In *Max Weber's Vision of History*. Edited by Guenther Roth and Wolfgang Schluchter, 119–43. Berkeley and Los Angeles: University of California Press.

———. 1979b. "Religion and Revolutionary Beliefs." In *Max Weber's Vision of History*. Edited by Guenther Roth and Wolfgang Schluchter, 144–165. Berkeley and Los Angeles: University of California Press.

———. 1979c. "Duration and Rationalization: Fernand Braudel and Max Weber." In *Max Weber's Vision of History*. Edited by Guenther Roth and Wolfgang Schluchter, 166–93. Berkeley and Los Angeles: University of California Press.

———. 1979d. "Weber's Vision of History." In *Max Weber's Vision of History*. Edited by Guenther Roth and Wolfgang Schluchter, 195–206. Berkeley and Los Angeles: University of California Press.

Roth, Guenther, and Wolfgang Schluchter. 1979. "Introduction." In *Max Weber's Vision of History*. Edited by Guenther Roth and Wolfgang Schluchter, 1–7. Berkeley and Los Angeles: University of California Press.

Rule, James B. 1978. *Insight and Social Betterment*. New York: Oxford.

Rybczynski, Witold. 1985. *Taming the Tiger: The Struggle to Control Technology*. New York: Penguin.

Ryder, Norman B. 1964. "Notes on the Concept of a Population." *American Journal of Sociology* 69 (March): 447–63.

Said, Edward W. 1993. *Culture and Imperialism*. New York: Knopf.

Saint-Simon, Henri de. 1964. *Social Organization, the Science of Man, and Other Writings*. Edited by Felix Markham. New York: Harper & Row.

Sargent, Anneila I. and Steven V. W. Beckwith. 1993. "The Search for Forming Planetary Systems." *Physics Today* 46, no. 4 (April): 22–29.

Sarton, George. 1962. *Sarton on the History of Science*. Cambridge: Harvard University Press.

Sayer, Derek. 1991. *Capitalism and Modernity: An Excursus on Mark and Weber*. London: Routledge.

Scaff, Lawrence A. 1989a. *Fleeing the Iron Cage*. Berkeley and Los Angeles: University of California Press.

———. 1989. "Weber Before Weberian Sociology." In *Reading Weber*. Edited by Keith Tribe, 15–43. London: Routledge.

Scheier, Michael F., and Charles S. Carver. 1992. "Effects of Optimism on Psychological and Physical Well-Being: Theoretical Overview and Empirical Update." *Cognitive Therapy and Research* 16, no. 2 (April): 201–28.

Schiller, Nina Glick, Linda Basch, and Cristina Blanc-Szanton. 1992. "Towards a Definition of Transnationalism." In *Towards a Transnational Perspective on Migration*. Edited by Nina Glick Schiller, Linda Basch, and Cristina Blanc-Szanton, ix–xiv. New York: New York: Academy of Sciences.

Schluchter, Wolfgang. 1979a. "The Paradox of Rationalization: On the Relation of Ethics and World." In *Max Weber's Vision of History*. Edited by Guenther Roth and Wolfgang Schluchter, 11–64. Berkeley and Los Angeles: University of California Press.

———. 1979b. "Value-Neutrality and the Ethic of Responsibility." In *Max Weber's Vision of History*. Edited by Guenther Roth and Wolfgang Schluchter, 65–116. Berkeley and Los Angeles: University of California Press.

———. 1981. *The Rise of Western Rationalism*. Berkeley and Los Angeles: University of California Press.

———. 1989. *Rationalism, Religion, and Domination: A Weberian Perspective*. Berkeley and Los Angeles: University of California Press.

Schramm, Wilbur. 1972. "Its Development." In *Mass Media and Communication*. Edited by Charles S. Steinberg, 44–55. New York: Hastings House.

Schroeder, Ralph. 1992. *Max Weber and the Sociology of Culture*. Hawthorne, N.Y.: Aldine.

Schutz, Alfred. 1953. "Common-Sense and Scientific Interpretations of Human Action." *Philosophy and Phenomenological Research* 14, no. 1 (September): 1–37.

Schwartz, Douglas W. 1985. "The Colonizing Experience: A Cross-Cultural Perspective." In *Interstellar Migration and the Human Experience*. Edited by Ben R. Finney and Eric M. Jones, 234–46. Berkeley and Los Angeles: University of California Press.

Segady, Thomas W. 1987. *Value, Neo-Kantianism and the Development of Weberian Methodology*. New York: Peter Lang.

Sherif, Muzafer, and Carolyn W. Sherif. 1953. *Groups in Harmony and Tension*. New York: Harper.

Shils, Edward. 1965. "Charisma, Order and Status." *American Sociological Review* 30, no. 2 (April): 199–213.

———. 1968. "Charisma." In *Encyclopedia of the Social Sciences*. Vol. 2. Edited by David L. Sills, 386–90. New York: Macmillan; Free Press.

———. 1987. "Max Weber and the World Since 1920." In *Max Weber and His Contemporaries*. Edited by Wolfgang J. Mommsen and Jurgen Osterhammel, 547–73. London: Allen & Unwin.

Sica, Alan. 1985. "Reasonable Science, Unreasonable Life: The Happy Fictions of Marx, Weber, and Social Theory." In *A Marx-Weber Dialogue*. Edited by Robert J. Antonio and Ronald M. Glassman. Lawrence: University Press of Kansas.

———. 1988. *Weber, Irrationality, and Social Order.* Berkeley and Los Angeles: University of California Press.

Sider, Gerald. 1992. "The Contradictions of Transnational Migration: A Discussion." In *Towards a Transnational Perspective on Migration.* Edited by Nina Glick Schiller, Linda Basch, and Cristina Blanc-Szanton, 231–40. New York: New York Academy of Sciences.

Simmel, Georg. 1950. *The Sociology of Georg Simmel.* Glencoe, Ill.: Free Press.

———. 1955. *Conflict and the Web of Group Affiliations.* Glencoe, Ill.: Free Press.

Simon, Herbert A. 1965. "The Architecture of Complexity." In *General Systems Yearbook.* Vol. 10. Edited by Ludwig von Bertalanffy and Anatol Rapoport, 63–76.

———. 1990. "A Mechanism for Social Selection and Successful Altruism." *Science* 250, 1665–68.

Sivard, Ruth Leger. 1991. *World Military and Social Expenditures 1991.* 14th ed. Washington, D.C.: World Priorities.

Skocpol, Theda. 1979. *States and Social Revolutions.* Cambridge: Cambridge University Press.

Slater, Philip E. 1966. *Microcosm.* New York: Wiley.

Smelser, Neil J. and R. Stephen Warner. 1976. *Sociological Theory: Historical and Formal.* Morristown, N.J.: General Learning.

Smith, Anthony D. 1990. "Towards a Global Culture?" *Theory, Culture & Society* 7 (June): 171–91.

Smith, Malcolm and Robert Layton. 1987. "Why Haven't We Speciated?" *New Community* 13, no. 3 (Spring): 367–72.

Sorokin, Pitirim. 1937–41. *Social and Cultural Dynamics.* Four volumes. New York: American Book.

South Commission. 1990. *The Challenge to the South.* Oxford: Oxford University Press.

Spencer, Herbert. 1898. *The Principles of Sociology.* 3 vols. New York: Appleton.

———. 1961. *The Study of Sociology.* Ann Arbor: University of Michigan Press.

Stanley, Steven M. 1981. *The New Evolutionary Timetable.* New York: Basic.

Starr, Chauncey, Milton Searl, and Sy Alpert. 1992. "Energy Sources: A Realistic Outlook." *Science* 256 (15 May): 981–87.

Steinberg, Stephen. 1989. *The Ethnic Myth.* Expanded ed. Boston: Beacon.

Stevens, S. S. 1946. "On the Theory of Scales of Measurement." *Science* 103, no. 2684, 677–80.

Stewart, Doug. 1991. "Through the Looking Glass Into an Artificial World—Via Computer." *Smithsonian* 21 (January): 36–45.

Stuckert, Robert P. 1976. "'Race' Mixture: The Black Ancestry of White Americans." In *Physical Anthropology and Archaeology.* Edited by Peter B. Hammond, 135–39. New York: Macmillan.

Swatos, William H., Jr. 1984. "Revolution and Charisma in a Rationalized World: Weber Revisited and Extended." In *Max Weber's Political Sociology.* Edited by Ronald M. Glassman and Vatro Murvar, 201–15. Westport, Conn.: Greenwood.

Swedlund, Alan. 1992. "Human Races." *World Book* 16, 52–60.

Swidler, Ann. 1973. "The Concept of Rationality in the Work of Max Weber." *Sociological Inquiry* 43, no. 1, 35–42.

Sztompka, Piotr. 1979. *Sociological Dilemmas.* New York: Academic.

Tanner, Nancy Makepeace. 1985. "Interstellar Migrations: The Beginnings of a Familiar Process in a New Context." In *Interstellar Migration and the Human Experi-*

ence. Edited by Ben R. Finney and Eric M. Jones, 220–33. Berkeley and Los Angeles: University of California Press.

Taylor, Peter J. 1993. *Political Geography.* 3d ed. New York: Wiley.

Tenbruck, Friedrich H. 1980. "The Problem of Thematic Unity in the Works of Max Weber." *British Journal of Sociology* 31 (September): 316–51.

Thomas, William Isaac, and Dorothy Swaine Thomas. 1928. *The Child in America.* New York: Knopf.

Thorpe, W. H. 1956. *Learning and Instinct in Animals.* Cambridge: Harvard University Press.

Tilly, Charles. 1975a. "Reflections on the History of European State-Making." In *The Formation of National States in Western Europe.* Edited by Charles Tilly, 3–83. Princeton, N.J.: Princeton University Press.

———. 1975b. "Western State-Making and Theories of Political Transformation." In *The Formation of National States in Western Europe.* Edited by Charles Tilly, 601–38. Princeton, N.J.: Princeton University Press.

Tominaga, Ken'ichi. 1989. "Max Weber and the Modernization of China and Japan." In *Cross-National Research in Sociology.* Edited by Melvin L. Kohn, 125–46. London: Sage.

Topitsch, Ernst. 1971. "Max Weber and Sociology Today." In *Max Weber and Sociology Today.* Edited by Otto Stammer, 8–25. New York: Harper & Row.

Torgerson, Warren S. 1958. *Theory and Methods of Scaling.* New York: Wiley.

Trefil, James S. 1983. *The Moment of Creation.* New York: Macmillan.

Tribe, Keith. 1989. "Introduction." In *Reading Weber.* Edited by Keith Tribe, 1–14. London: Routledge.

Turner, Bryan S. 1981. *For Weber: Essays on the Sociology of Fate.* Boston: Routledge & Kegan Paul.

Turner, Jonathan H. 1986. "Series Editor's Introduction." In *Max Weber: A Skeleton Key.* Edited by Randall Collins. Beverly Hills, Calif.: Sage.

Turner, Jonathan H., Leonard Beeghley, and Charles H. Powers. 1989. *The Emergence of Sociological Theory.* 2d ed. Chicago: Dorsey.

Turner, Stephen P., and Regis A. Factor. 1984. *Max Weber and the Dispute Over Reason and Value: A Study in Philosophy, Ethics, and Politics.* London: Routledge & Kegan Paul.

United Nations. 1991. *Demographic Yearbook: 1989.* New York: United Nations.

United States Department of Energy. 1987. *Energy Security: A Report to the President of the United States.* Washington, D.C.: Government Printing Office.

van den Berghe, Pierre L. 1987. *The Ethnic Phenomenon.* New York: Praeger.

Valentine, James W. 1985. "The Origins of Evolutionary Novelty and Galactic Colonization." In *Interstellar Migration and the Human experience.* Edited by Ben R. Finney and Eric M. Jones, 266–76. Berkeley and Los Angeles: University of California Press.

Verba, Sidney. 1971. "Sequences and Development." In *Crises and Sequences in Political Development.* Edited by Leonard Binder. Princeton, N.J.: Princeton University Press.

Vischer, Lukas. 1979. "An Ecumenical Creed?" In *An Ecumenical Confession of Faith?* Edited by Hans Kung and Jurgen Moltmann, 103–17. New York: Seabury.

von Bertalanffy, Ludwig. 1968. "General System Theory—A Critical Review." In *Modern Systems Research for the Behavioral Scientist*. Edited by Walter Buckley, 11–30. Chicago: Aldine.

Wallace, Walter L. 1969. "Overview of Contemporary Sociological Theory." In *Sociological Theory: An Introduction*. Edited by Walter L. Wallace, 1–59. Chicago: Aldine.

———. 1983. *Principles of Scientific Sociology*. Hawthorne, N.Y.: Aldine.

———. 1986. "Social Structural and Cultural Structural Variables in Sociology." *Sociological Focus* 19 (April): 125–38.

———. 1988. "Toward a Disciplinary Matrix in Sociology." In *Handbook of Sociology*. Edited by Neil J. Smelser, 23–76. Newbury Park, Calif.: Sage.

———. 1989. "Max Weber's Two Spirits of Capitalism." *Telos* 81 (Fall): 86–90.

———. 1990. "Rationality, Human Nature, and Society in Weber's Theory." *Theory and Society* 19, 199–223.

Walzer, Michael. 1982. "Pluralism in Political Perspective." In *The Politics of Ethnicity*. Edited by Michael Walzer, Edward T. Kantowicz, John Higham, and Mona Harrington, 1–28. Cambridge: Harvard University Press.

Waring, Joan M. 1976. "Social Replenishment and Social Change." In *Age in Society*. Edited by Anne Foner. Beverly Hills, Calif.: Sage.

Watkins, Susan Cotts. 1991. *From Provinces into Nations*. Princeton, N.J.: Princeton University Press.

Watson, W. H. 1960. "On Methods of Representation." In *Philosophy of Science*. Edited by Arthur Danto and Sidney Morgenbesser, 226–44. New York: World.

Weber, Marianne. 1975. *Max Weber: A Biography*. New York: Wiley

Weber, Max. 1946. *From Max Weber: Essays in Sociology*. New York: Oxford University Press.

———. 1947. *Gesammelte Aufsätze zur Religionssoziologie*. Tubingen: J. C. B. Mohr (Paul Siebeck).

———. 1949. *The Methodology of the Social Sciences*. Glencoe, Ill.: Free Press.

———. 1950. *General Economic History*. Glencoe, Ill.: Free Press.

———. 1951a. *Gesammelte Aufsätze zur Wissenschaftslehre*. Tubingen: J. C. B. Mohr (Paul Siebeck).

———. 1951b. *The Religion of China*. New York: Free Press.

———. 1952. *Ancient Judaism*. New York: Free Press.

———. 1956. *Wirtschaft und Gesellschaft*. Tubingen: J.C.B. Mohr (Paul Siebeck).

———. 1958a. *The Protestant Ethic and the Spirit of Capitalism*. New York: Scribner's.

———. 1958b. *The Religion of India*. Glencoe, Ill.: Free Press.

———. 1958c. *The Rational and Social Foundations of Music*. Carbondale: Southern Illinois Press.

———. 1975a. *Roscher and Knies*. New York: Free Press.

———. 1975b. "Marginal Utility Theory and 'The Fundamental Law of Psychophysics.'" Translated, and with an introduction, by Louis Schneider. *Social Science Quarterly* 56 (June):21–36.

———. 1976. *The Agrarian Sociology of Ancient Civilizations*. London: NLB.

———. 1977. *Critique of Stammler*. New York: Free Press.

———. 1978a. *Economy and Society*. 2 vols. Berkeley and Los Angeles: University of California Press.

————. 1978b. *Max Weber: Selections in Translation.* Edited by W. G. Runciman. Cambridge: Cambridge University Press.

————. 1978c. "Anticritical Last Word on *The Spirit of Capitalism.*" Translated, with an introduction by, Wallace M. Davis. *American Journal of Sociology* 83 (March): 1105–31.

————. 1981. "Some Categories of Interpretive Sociology." *Sociological Quarterly* 22 (Spring): 151–80.

————. 1989a. "Developmental Tendencies in the Situation of East Elbian Rural Labourers." In *Reading Weber.* Edited by Keith Tribe, 157–87. London: Routledge.

————. 1989b. "The National State and National Economic Policy." In *Reading Weber.* Edited by Keith Tribe, 188–209. London: Routledge.

————. 1989c. "Germany as an Industrial State." In *Reading Weber.* Edited by Keith Tribe, 210–20. London: Routledge.

Weinberg, Steven. 1984. *The First Three Minutes.* Rev. ed. New York: Bantam.

————. 1992. *Dreams of a Final Theory.* New York: Knopf.

Weiss, Johannes. 1985. "On the Marxist Reception and Critique of Max Weber in Eastern Europe." In *A Marx-Weber Dialogue.* Edited by Robert J. Antonio and Ronald M. Glassman. Lawrence: University Press of Kansas.

White, Leslie A. 1969. *The Science of Culture.* 2d ed. New York: Farrar, Straus and Giroux.

Whitehead, Alfred North. 1938. *Modes of Thought.* New York: Capricorn.

————. 1974. *The Organization of Thought.* Westport, Conn.: Greenwood.

Wiley, Norbert. 1979. "The Rise and Fall of Dominating Theories in American Sociology." In *Contemporary Issues in Theory and Research.* Edited by William E. Snizek, Ellsworth R. Fuhrman, and Michael K. Miller, 47–80. Westport, Conn.: Greenwood Press.

————. 1987. "Introduction." In *The Marx-Weber Debate.* Edited by Norbert Wiley, 7–27. Newbury Park, Calif.: Sage.

Wilson, Edward O. 1971. *The Insect Societies.* Cambridge: Harvard University Press, Belknap Press.

————. 1975. *Sociobiology.* Cambridge: Harvard University Press, Belknap Press.

————. 1978. *On Human Nature.* Cambridge: Harvard University Press.

Wilson, John. 1988. *Politics and Leisure.* Boston: Unwin Hyman.

Wolpoff, Milford H., Wu Xin Zhi, and Alan G. Thorpe. 1984. "Modern *Homo sapiens* Origins: A General Theory of Hominid Evolution Involving the Fossil Evidence from East Africa." In *The Origins of Modern Humans: A World Survey of the Fossil Evidence.* Edited by Fred H. Smith and Frank Spencer, 411–83. New York: Alan R. Liss.

Woodcock, Alexander, and Monte Davis. 1978. *Catastrophe Theory.* New York: Dutton.

World Scientists. 1993. *World Scientists' Warning to Humanity.* Cambridge: Union of Concerned Scientists.

Wriston, Walter B. 1992. *The Twilight of Sovereignty.* New York: Scribner's.

Wrong, Dennis. 1970. "Introduction." In *Max Weber.* Edited by Dennis Wrong. Englewood Cliffs, N.J.: Prentice-Hall.

Wulf, Willam A. 1993. "The Collaboratory Opportunity." *Science* 261 (13 August): 854–55.

Wuthnow, Robert. 1987. *Meaning and Moral Order*. Berkeley and Los Angeles: University of California Press.

———. 1988. "Sociology of Religion." In *Handbook of Sociology*. Edited by Neil J. Smelser, 473–509. Newbury Park, Calif.: Sage.

———. 1991. "International Realities: Bringing the Global Picture into Focus." In *World Order and Religion*. Edited by Wade Clark, 19–37. Albany: State University of New York.

———. 1993a. "The Voluntary Sector: Legacy of the Past, Hope for the Future?" In *Between States and Markets*. Edited by Robert Wuthnow, 3–27. Princeton, N.J.: Princeton University Press.

———. 1993b. "Tocqueville's Question Reconsidered: Voluntarism and Public Discourse in Advanced Industrial Societies." In *Between States and Markets*. Edited by Robert Wuthnow, 288–305. Princeton, N.J.: Princeton University Press.

Zlotnik, Hania. Forthcoming. "Intentional Migration." In *A Reader on Population, Consumption, and the Environment*. Edited by Laurie Ann Mazur. Washington, D.C.: Island Press.

NAME INDEX

Hekman, Susan J., 284
Hempel, Carl G., 249, 258, 287, 291
Hennis, Wilhelm, 3, 5, 6, 50, 75, 245, 249, 277, 284, 289
Hindess, Barry, 249
Hogan, James P., 211
Holden, Constance, 189, 283
Hollins, Harry B., 186, 187, 278
Hollis, Martin, 249
Homans, George Caspar, 247
Homer-Dixon, Thomas F., 193, 194
Honigsheim, Paul, 5, 6, 277, 290
House, James S., 156, 268, 282
Hoy, David Couzens, 291
Huff, Toby E., 88, 118, 249
Huizinga, J., 198

Ibn Khaldun, 270
Inbar, Michael, 259
Irwin, Robert A., 189

Jackson, Maurice, 189
Jastrow, Robert, 210, 211
Jones, Eric M., 95, 279
Jones, Robert Alun, 280

Kalberg, Stephen, 249
Kaplan, Abraham, 8, 181, 221, 235, 246, 247, 258, 285
Keeney, Ralph L., 249
Kellner, Douglas, 249
Kennedy, Paul, 108, 194, 195, 196, 206, 207, 278, 279, 281
Kerr, Richard A., 112
Kinoshita, June, 195
Klein, Richard G., 1, 95, 132, 264
Kotabe, Masaaki, 195
Krasner, Stephen D., 112, 268
Kuhn, Thomas S., 112, 247, 269, 270, 272, 273, 294
Kung, Hans, 202

Lachmann, L. M., 55
Lamers, William M., 132
Langton, Christopher G., 205
Lauer, Robert H., 189
Laumann, Edward O., 247
Layton, Robert, 96, 264

Leakey, Richard, 95, 96, 97, 264, 286
Lenssen, Nicholas, 194
Leontiades, James C., 195
Levi, Margaret, 249
Levine, Donald N., 249
Lewin, Roger, 95, 96, 97, 264, 286
Lieberson, Stanley, 108
Lindholm, Charles, 123
Lipset, Seymour Martin, 247
Little, Linda, 206
Loewith, Karl, 52, 277
Lorenz, Konrad, 38, 266
Lubbe, Hermann, 292
Luckmann, Thomas, 86
Lukes, Steven, 249
Lyman, Sanford, 125, 126
Lynd, Robert S., 239

McAdam, Doug, 189, 278
McCarthy, John D., 189, 278
McColm, R. Bruce, 199
McConnell, Virginia F., 6
McCorduck, Pamela, 211
McLuhan, Marshall, 135
McNeill, William H., 96, 97, 101, 105, 108, 267
Madden, Edward H., 272
Mann, Michael, 98
Mann, Thomas, 271
Mannheim, Karl, 167, 188, 221, 239, 270, 281, 282, 286, 294
March, James G., 28, 220, 249
Marcuse, Herbert, 33, 122, 249
Margulis, Lynn, 212
Markusen, Ann, 278
Marshall, Eliot, 95, 282
Martindale, Don, 249
Marty, Martin E., 262, 282
Marx, Karl, 3, 14, 51, 77, 83, 108, 109, 117, 127, 134, 150, 196, 210, 222, 248, 259, 262, 263, 268, 271, 272, 274, 276, 277
Matthews, Robert, 182
Mayrl, William W., 258, 284
Mead, George Herbert, 248, 266, 267, 281, 293
Mearsheimer, John J., 106, 186, 187
Mendelsohn, Everett, 262

SUBJECT INDEX

ABOUT THE AUTHOR

Walter L. Wallace is a professor of sociology at Princeton University. He is the author of *Principles of Scientific Sociology, The Logic of Science in Sociology, Student Culture: Social Structure and Continuity in a Liberal Arts College*, and numerous journal articles and book chapters. He is also co-author of *Black Elected Officials*, and author-editor of *Sociological Theory: An Introduction*. He has been a Visiting Scholar and Staff Sociologist at Russell Sage Foundation, and a Fellow of the Center for Advanced Study in the Behavioral and Social Sciences. He is presently a member of the Sociological Research Association, the American Sociological Association (and past member of its Council), and the American Association for the Advancement of Science. He has been a member of the Executive Committee of the National Research Council's Assembly of Behavioral and Social Sciences, a Trustee and Council member of the Foundation for Child Development, a member of the Social Sciences Consultant Committee of *World Book*, and a member of the editorial boards of *Social Forces, The American Sociologist*, and *The Sociological Quarterly*.